ESTATE PLANNING:
What Anyone Who Owns Anything Must Know

Peter E. Lippett
Attorney at Law,
San Francisco

Reston Publishing Company, Inc.
A Prentice-Hall Company
Reston, Virginia

> For E.M.L., father, friend. He will surely recognize in these pages much of his wisdom about the subject most dear to his heart, the family.

Library of Congress Cataloging in Publication Data

Lippett, Peter E.
  Estate planning.
  1. Estate planning—United States.
  2. Inheritance and transfer tax—United States.
  I. Title.
  KF750.L54   343'.73'053   79-9959
  ISBN 0-8359-1778-9

© 1979 by Reston Publishing Company, Inc.
A Prentice-Hall Company
Reston, Virginia 22090

All rights reserved. No part of this book may be reproduced in any way, or by any means, without permission in writing from the publisher.

10 9 8 7 6 5 4 3 2

Printed in the United States of America

contents

Part One: The Fundamentals   1

1   What Is In This Book, And How It Will Help You   3

     Why This Book Will Benefit YOU, 3
     What This Book Does, 5
     Estate Planning Mistakes Are Everywhere, 6
     This Book Is Also For Non-Lawyer Professionals, 6
     What Is In This Book, 7
     Organization To Assist You, 8
     When Should You Use This Book? 10
     What Advisors Will You Need? 10
     A Few Messages From Me To You, 11

2   Forms of Property Ownership: Everything Flows From This   13

     Tenancy in Common, 14
     Joint Tenancy, 14
     Tenancy By The Entirety, 17
     Marital Property In The 42 Common Law States, 18
     Marital Property In The 8 Community Property States, 21
     Quasi-Community Property, 27
     Application, 28

3   Intestacy: If You Leave No Will   31

     Which State's Laws Will Govern Your Estate? 31
     General Patterns of State Intestacy Laws, 33
     Application, 38

4 All About Wills   **39**

    Types of Wills, 40
    Witnesses and Other Matters, 42
    Testamentary Capacity and Will Contests, 43
    Codicils and Revocation, 45
    What a Will Contains, 46
    Life Estates and Remainders, 49
    Creating a Trust By Will, 52
    Administrative Clauses, 52
    Appointment of Executors, Attorneys, and Guardians, 53
    Application, 56

5 Probate: That Hateful Thing Examined   **57**

    Why Probate Continues to Exist, 58
    Probate Expenses, 59
    Methods of Saving Probate Costs, 65
    Delay and Publicity, 66
    How To Avoid Probate, 67
    The Relationship of Avoiding Probate With Avoiding Taxes, 69
    Probate and Community Property, 70
    Timetable and Procedures of a Probate, 72
    The Advantages of Probate: Lowering Taxes, 79
    Should Probate Be Avoided? 83
    Application, 85

6 Trusts: Flexible Tools Of Many Uses   **87**

    Trustor, Trustee, Beneficiary: The Relationships, 88
    How a Trust is Created, 88
    Types of Trusts, 89
        Living Trusts and Testamentary Trusts, 89
        Court Trusts and Non-Court Trusts, 89
        Revocable and Irrevocable Trusts, 92
        The Pour-Over Trust, 92
        Life Insurance Trusts, 93
        Clifford Trusts, 94
        Other Types of Trusts, 94
    Selecting a Trustee, 95
    Powers and Duties of a Trustee, 99
    The Income of a Trust, 101
    Allocations Between Principal and Income, 105
    Invasions of Principal, 106
    A 1976 Tax Reform Act Change, 107
    Termination of Trusts, 108
    Application, 110

Part Two: Estate and Gift Taxes   113

7 Estate and Gift Taxes: Rates and Exemptions   **115**

    Estate and Gift Taxes Are Excise Taxes, 116
    The Federal Tax Is By Far The More Important, 116
    The Unitary Transfer Tax: Its Rates and Exemptions, 117
    The Orphan's Exclusion, 120
    Filing Estate Tax Returns, and Audit Odds, 121
    Gift Taxes, 122
    The Gift Tax Marital Deduction, 122
    The $3000 Annual Gift Tax Exclusion, 123
    Gift Tax Returns For Lifetime Transfers, 124
    State Death Taxes, 126
    Application, 127

| 8 | Property Subject to Estate Taxes | **129** |

Property In Which the Decedent Had An Interest, 129
Valuation, 131
Real Estate Used as a Farm or in a Business, 134
Marital Property, 135
Gifts In Contemplation Of Death, 136
Transfers With Retained Interests, 137
Annuities and Employee Benefit Plans, 140
Joint Tenancies and Tenancies by the Entirety, 141
Powers of Appointment, 143
Life Insurance, 146
Application, 148

| 9 | Estate Tax Deductions, Credits, and Payment Plans | **151** |

Deductions Reducing an Heir's Inheritance, 151
How To Avoid Estate Taxes (The Charitable Deduction), 154
The Marital Deduction, 156
A Note On Tax Law Complexity and on Future Reform, 160
Credits Against the Estate Tax, 160
Normal Payment Times and Extensions, 162
Flower Bonds, 164
Installment Payments for Closely Held Businesses, 165
Redemptions of Stock to Pay Estate Taxes (Sec. 303), 167
Application, 170

| 10 | Two Nasty Innovations of the 1976 Tax Reform Act | **173** |

1 Carryover Basis, 173
    Exclusion for Personal and Household Effects, 176
    The Fresh Start Adjustment: First Adjustment, 176
    Adjustment for Federal and State Death Taxes: Second Adjustment, 181
    $60,000 Minimum Basis: Third Adjustment, 181
    State Taxes Paid by Heir: Fourth Adjustment, 182
    Basis of Gifted Property, 182
    Unknown Basis, 183
    Computation and Information Requirements of Executors, 184
    Flower Bonds and 303 Redemptions, 184
    The Outcry Against Carryover Basis, and Possible Changes, 185
2 The Generation Skipping Transfer Tax, 186
    The Grandchildren Exemption, 191
    Effective Dates, 192
    Application, 192

Part Three: Estate Planning Techniques   **195**

| 11 | The Estate Planning Key: Saving The Second Tax | **197** |

An Overview of Estate Planning, 197
The Effects of Double Taxation, 201
Savings From Use of the Estate Planning Key, Table 11-5, 206
The By-Pass Trust, 207
Trust Income, 209
The "Perfect Tax Shelter", 210
Trust Principal, 211
Provisions for Remainder Beneficiaries, 214
Getting Around The Generation Skipping Tax, 220
When To Establish A By-Pass Trust, 223
Doesn't A By-Pass Trust Fail to Avoid Probate? 224
Saving State Death Taxes May Now Be More Important Than Ever, 225
A Short Speech About Attitudes and Values, 226
Application, 226

12 Planning The Surviving Spouse's Half: A-B Trusts — 229

Defining the Surviving Spouse's Half, 229
Marital Deduction Formula Clauses, 232
The Marital Deduction Trust, 236
The Estate Trust, 241
The Widow's Election, 242
Application, 251

13 Trust Planning: Living Trusts and Other Trusts — 253

Revocable Versus Irrevocable Trusts, 254
Funded and Unfunded Revocable Trusts, 257
Cost Analysis of Funded Revocable Living Trusts, 256
Other Reasons for Living Trusts, 258
How To Avoid Both Probate AND Double Death Taxes, 262
Life Insurance Trusts To Solve Common Insurance Mistakes, 263
Clifford (Ten-Year) Trusts, 267
Bank Account "Trusts", 270
Trusts For Minors With No Tax Savings In Mind, 271
Application, 274

14 Life Insurance: The Unique Estate Planning Asset — 277

Purpose: Estate Building, 277
Purpose: The Liquidity Crisis, 278
Carryover Basis Means More Cash Will Be Needed, 282
Insurance May Provide Cheap Dollars, 283
Removing Insurance Proceeds From the Gross Estate, 284
Gift Tax Consequences, 286
Transfers Within Three Years of Death, 288
Irrevocable Life Insurance Trusts, 288
Paying Premiums On Transferred Policies, 290
Special Community Property Problems, 292
Life Insurance In Business Planning, 296
Application, 299

15 Other Important Estate Planning Techniques — 301

The Private Annuity, 301
Estate Planning For Business Owners, 305
Remaining Advantages of Lifetime Giving, 312
Gifts To Minors, 317
Disadvantages of Gifts, 321
Planning With Charitable Gifts, 323
Planning For Carryover Basis, 326
How To Hold Title To Property, 331
Integrating All Property Into The Estate Plan, 338
Application, 339

16 Two Often Neglected Subjects: The Single Person and The Small Estate — 343

Estate Planning For The Single Person, 343
Planning For The Small Estate, 348
Application, 349

17 Some Thoughts By Way of Conclusion — 353

Glossary — 359

Index — 372

acknowledgements

I gratefully acknowledge the assistance and support of the following, although all responsibility for the contents of this book is mine alone:

Chuck Wells, for giving me the opportunity to start teaching the courses which directly led to this book. My students at the University of California Extension Division, Berkeley, for encouraging me to write. Charles G. Stephenson of the San Francisco Bar Association, and Roane T. Sias, for reading portions of the manuscript and providing valuable comments. IBM, for inventing the self-correcting typewriter, thus keeping me sane long enough to complete this book. Margaret Pugh, for her usual impeccable job in typing portions of the manuscript. Pookah, the only Alaskan Malamute who hides in the bathtub at the sound of her master typing; thanks for putting up with me, and you can come out now, it's over. And most especially, my wife, Joellen, for helping with the manuscript and galleys, and for being there.

part one
the fundamentals

1
what is in this book, and how it will help you

Why This Book Will Benefit YOU

Because you have an estate. Everyone does. The word estate has no magic meaning to it. It just stands for everything you own. Many people realize that they have an estate. But too many other people believe that they somehow don't qualify for having an estate because the value of their property has not reached a certain mysterious amount which has been decreed by someone or something to be an estate. But that is a myth. There is no minimum amount below which an estate doesn't exist. Some people's estates are valued at less than $10,000; other people's estates are worth millions. But they are all estates.

Since everyone has an estate, everyone can benefit from some planning for it. Planning will ensure that whatever you own will go to the persons you want to have it, and will suffer from the least possible amount of taxes and other expenses. Planning for the disposition of whatever you own is all the term estate planning means. There's nothing magic or mysterious about it.

WHAT IS IN THIS BOOK, AND HOW IT WILL HELP YOU

Why is estate planning connected in most people's minds with wealth? It's due to lack of information; it's due to never having been told that anyone can benefit from the proper planning of whatever they own. It's also due to a failure to realize that saving ten percent in needless taxes or expenses is vastly more crucial to the heirs of a small estate than saving ten percent of a gigantic estate. If a multi-millionaire wastes a couple of hundred thousand dollars, his heirs may not be too happy about it, but at least their standard of living is still secure. But saving, for instance, an extra $10,000 in a $100,000 estate may well be the difference between whether or not the heirs can make ends meet. And finally, there is a common misunderstanding that estate planning has primarily to do with saving taxes, and since only estates of a certain size are the ones faced with taxes, estate planning must be only for them. But that's just plain wrong. The truth is that in family and people terms, the non-tax benefits of estate planning far outweigh even the tax savings available. Non-tax benefits are available to, and crucial for, estates of any size, including those which aren't even faced with death taxes.

It is true that there is much in estate planning that will benefit wealthier persons. Some of the more sophisticated estate planning devices are only pertinent to estates of large size. But estate planning is by no means confined only to such estates, and this book will provide information to benefit owners of estates of any size.

After all, what is meant by words such as wealth, rich, large and small? Those words are completely incapable of a standard definition because they mean different things to different people. To a person on welfare, $10,000 may seem like extreme wealth. To a young couple just starting out, $100,000 may seem like wealth. To bankers, an estate under $250,000 or so may be classified, purely in their own minds, as small. And for some people, $100,000 is what they give for birthday presents.

It would be very helpful if each reader could, at least for the purposes of this book and while reading it, put out of mind all words such as large, small, wealth and rich. This book provides information for everyone, and as you are reading, you should simply decide for yourself whether or not a given subject interests you or is applicable to your estate. The amount you own is not the issue; the issue is only whether you think that something would be of benefit to you or to your heirs.

Most of the examples in this book are given in rather large amounts. The reasons for that are because it's more fun, because we want to demonstrate certain consequences where estates are clearly affected by a substantial amount of tax, and because we can keep the numbers in large round figures where it doesn't take too much mathematical ability to deal with them. But don't be fooled by those large figures, and try to apply whatever is being demonstrated to figures which approximate the size of your own estate.

What This Book Does

It provides information. Information which has been virtually unavailable to non-lawyers because so little is written in language designed for lay persons. There may be two general reasons for that lack of information. One may be that lawyers have delighted in throwing up a mystique about themselves and what they do, and have not wanted to let anyone else in on the secrets. That is one large reason why the legal profession isn't the most trusted and well respected of occupations. Some lawyers just want to keep their work mysterious, but others seem to believe that the lay public is incapable of understanding what lawyers do. Balderdash.

What this book is going to do is de-mystify. It's going to state the concepts which are involved in estate planning in language that is within the grasp of any interested reader. And then it's going to discuss some of the ways in which those concepts can be put to use, by you and for you.

A second reason why little is written for lay persons is because many estate planners don't think that the public wants information on subjects involved with law. But that is getting to be an outmoded viewpoint, and my experiences as a teacher, lecturer and practicing lawyer tell me exactly the opposite. We are now in the age of the consumer, and even the staid old law is going to have to recognize that. A basic principle of consumerism is a demand for the core information on which decisions are made. Consumers want to know why certain products might be beneficial or hazardous, and they want the information to refute any claims to the contrary. They are no longer willing to just take a statement on its face, such as, "My product is safe because I say it is." Consumers are even seeking good, basic information on medical matters.

The same is true of consumers of the law. Lawyers are just selling something, and you are consuming it. As a consumer, you have a perfect right to know the basic information about what you're purchasing and whether the product is sound. You don't have to sign an estate plan just because some high-priced degree holder puts it in front of you and tells you it's the best one for you. Not only do you have the right to more information than that, but in my opinion you should be demanding more information on a subject which is of such vital personal concern to you and your family. It is for such people that this information is provided.

How do I know that there are many lay persons who genuinely want to acquire this vital information? Because I hear their requests constantly; in fact, they are the ones who convinced me to write this book. People have asked me for years whether there is a good general book that will set it all out. In my opinion, the answer is no. Lectures are fine, but it is difficult to retain this information after having heard it just once. A permanent collection of all the vital information is what people want.

So, information is the key. That's what I have set out to provide for you. Let me tell you in a moment how the information will be brought together in ways which will relate it directly to your own estate.

Estate Planning Mistakes Are Everywhere

These mistakes provide another large reason for this book, aside from just supplying information. My experience, and that of almost every estate planner, is that people are making the most basic and disastrous mistakes, and they don't know it. What is worse, non-lawyers providing services to property owners are directly contributing to the mistakes by supplying wrong information. None of this is malicious; it is just that even those providing services have never been given even the most basic information. The odds are very strong that your own situation is riddled with mistakes; maybe not (I hope not), but I'll bet you're not aware of whether things are wrong or right, and if they're right, I'll bet you don't know why.

So a major reason why I wrote this book was to help you—by uncovering the mistakes, explaining what is wrong and why, and then giving you the information to correct them. There will be no lecturing or finger pointing, just clear explanations. You will be able to decide whether something is or is not a mistake for you.

This Book Is Also For Non-Lawyer Professionals

Many professionals other than lawyers affect the estate planning of their clients or customers. The pity is that such a large majority of those professionals have never been given the basic estate planning information which would enable them to best serve their clients. Probably a large number of such professionals aren't even aware that many of the things they do, or fail to do, can have disastrous effects on their clients' estate planning. If you are the client or customer, you may be totally unaware that what the professional is doing for you may have serious effects on your estate planning. And if you are the professional, you need to be given the information so that you can be aware of those effects.

Who are these non-lawyer professionals? Real estate brokers, title company or escrow company personnel, bankers, stock brokers, life insurance salesmen, investment advisors, financial planners and accountants are perhaps the major ones. How many bankers or stock brokers opening a new account, or real estate people helping a couple decide on the form of title for their new house, know the full story about whether or not title should be held in joint tenancy? My experience tells me that precious few have even the slightest notion on that subject.

In my opinion, this book ought to be on the desk of each of the professionals mentioned. Each of those professionals has an ethical responsibility to know basic facts concerning the estate planning effects of what is done for the client or customer.

This book is deliberately not loaded down with the kinds of footnotes, references and citations which lawyers need for their research. It's meant for the lay person and the non-lawyer professional. Any attempt to be either comprehensive or encyclopedic is not only impossible but would also just turn off the readers to whom this book is addressed. However, if any readers want to do further research, they can certainly do so with the assistance of law libraries or attorneys. This book will provide enough information to get you acquainted with subjects you can follow up if you choose.

What Is In This Book

Estate planning is a subject which involves law, and the reader for whom this book is written is not expected to be familiar with law. So I start by laying some foundations and discussing the tax law, and I then devote a major part of the book to estate planning techniques.

Unknown to most people, how you hold title to property is a key part of your estate plan and may literally determine what can and cannot be done for you. So I start by explaining some concepts concerning holding title to property. I will then cover what will happen if you die without a will, then discuss the subject of wills. Next is probate, that much despised post-death period which arouses intense emotions and must be thoroughly analyzed so that you have a good grasp of what is going on there. There may even be some surprises in that discussion. I finish laying the foundations by a thorough discussion of trusts, devices which play a very large part in estate planning.

The second part of the book is devoted to death taxes. It is a common fallacy that saving taxes is all that estate planning is about. Nothing could be further from the truth; in fact, estate planning is an intensely personal matter which concerns itself with unique people and unique situations. No two estate plans are, or should be, exactly alike, and no computer can just whip through the tax analysis and then spit out someone's estate plan. Estate plans are about living, breathing unique people, and only sympathetic considerations of what is best for particular people can make a successful estate plan. Still and all, the tax law and tax savings which might be possible are a large part of estate planning, and so the fundamental information will be presented for your knowledge and reference. If you are truly interested in acquiring full estate planning information, you will want to know about the tax laws.

The final part of the book has to do with estate planning techniques. I start with the "estate planning key" and discuss the tax savings which can be achieved. I then deal with proper planning for a surviving spouse. Next is a discussion which focuses on whether it is a good idea to set up a trust during your life, as opposed to doing so only at death. A chapter is then devoted to a unique estate planning asset, life insurance—don't skip that chapter, even if you don't have insurance or don't favor it, because there is some vital information contained in it. A wrap-up chapter on estate planning techniques deals with many other important plans and devices which do not conveniently fit into the other chapters and also collects many of the major points made throughout the book. Finally, I deal with two often neglected subjects, estate planning for the single person and for the smaller estate.

Organization To Assist You

I realize that estate planning involves law, and inevitably I am going to bring in some legal language. I've tried to avoid as much of the legal jargon as possible, but some terminology is impossible to avoid. What I've done is to assist you in dealing with it, first by giving you a comprehensive Glossary, which you will find at the end of the book, and then by listing at the beginning of each chapter the terms you will run into. It's my suggestion that before launching into any chapter, you refer to the Glossary for preliminary definitions of the listed words, which you will soon encounter.

Within each chapter I've tried to give you page references to the basic or original discussion of a subject whenever that subject crops up again. I realize that after just one quick reading, it's difficult to retain some of the concepts I'll deal with, and so I've tried to give you a quick road back to the basic discussion. There is no perfect order in which to present this material; I wish there were, but there isn't. So I've done the next best thing, which is to give you a road map to where the information will be found.

At the end of each chapter is a section entitled Application; this is where I have tried to tell you how to relate the material in the chapter to yourself and to your own personal situation. I will give you concrete suggestions on how to determine many matters for yourself, using the facts and values of your own situation. After you've finished the book, you might just skim back through, reading only the Application sections; I think you'll find them a pretty good guide to planning your estate and to applying the basic information to a real person—namely you.

I anticipate that you will have no difficulty in grasping the information contained in the book. I hope you share my assumption that you are entitled to this information, and that you are fully capable of understanding it. I want to assure you that in my many years of teaching, lecturing and lawyering, I have found interested lay persons more than capable of doing so. Sometimes there's a little hesitation at the beginning, wondering about the wisdom of getting into a bunch of legal junk. But it goes away quickly as you find the information fully understandable, and I just want to share that assurance with you. No one expects you to "learn" this information cold, as if you were studying for a law school exam, and of course there is some effort involved in grasping it all. You may have to stop and ponder a bit, but that's all to the good and is to be encouraged. And you're not expected to remember everything you've read after just meeting it once. That's why I've cross-referenced and given you a road map to the information, and done so again in the index. My intention is that this book be a permanent reference for you, a place where you can find the required information whenever you wish.

This book will often state, some may say to the point of nausea, that you and your advisors will have to discuss a given concept and make decisions about it. So we should have an understanding about that from the beginning. The material contained here is much too complex and much too voluminous to pretend that you will know everything by the time you are finished. In fact, the opposite is true. All this book can possibly do is scratch the surface and be an overview of a vast subject. I really want to insist that you realize that at the start. A separate fifteen volume work could easily be written on the subject of each chapter, and the precise point that is applicable to your estate may be buried somewhere in those encyclopedias. I have deliberately refrained from any temptation to get too comprehensive or encyclopedic in order to avoid boring you to tears, but for your part you must recognize that what this book contains is maybe one half of one percent of what could be said on any given subject.

You will have to rely on trained professionals to flesh out the material presented here and to apply all the various technical twists to your own individual situation. No reader of this book should be a do-it-yourselfer; there isn't enough material here to allow for that, and I would be dishonestly leading you astray if I left any impression that it were otherwise. Also, the laws of each state

WHAT IS IN THIS BOOK, AND HOW IT WILL HELP YOU

are so unique that you absolutely must take steps to find out how the generalities contained in this book apply under the particular law of your own state.

When Should You Use This Book?

You should use this book before you consult with your advisors to prepare yourself for your consultation and to get fresh in your mind the questions you want to ask and the subjects you want to discuss. You can also use it during and after those consultations to check up on the advice you have received and to refresh your memory as to why something was recommended for you. And you can use it in periodically reviewing your estate plan, a good habit to get into.

The book's information will enable you to initiate a discussion of any subject which interests you, either upon a first consultation or upon a review of an existing estate plan. You can lead instead of follow; you can be the informed consumer seeking greater information on matters you are already informed about. You can pursue what interests you, not just what interests your advisor. You will surely have a more rewarding and a more productive consultation as a result of being already informed. You may even have a less expensive consultation as well, because your advisor will not have to take the time to explain many basic concepts to you. And very importantly, you will have an understanding of the estate planning implications of services performed for you by the non-lawyer professionals mentioned earlier.

What Advisors Will You Need?

There is a common catch phrase in estate planning about the "estate planning team," which is said to contain an attorney, an accountant, a bank's trust officer, a life insurance person and often an investment planner. However, except in unusual circumstances characterized largely by the client's willingness to pay virtually unlimited fees, that "team" rarely has an actual meeting. In fact, you will have probably consulted with any or all of those persons at one time or another, and when estate planning is being done, some of them may confer and check with each other. But there is hardly ever a team huddle on the 50-yard line of your life.

It sounds pretty arrogant of me to pretend that laywers are the key to this whole business, but in many ways this is true. Lawyers are the only ones trained and licensed to draw up the actual documents which will implement most of your estate plan. As such, they're right in the center of everything that is going on relative to your estate plan. So a lawyer is probably your key advisor.

You can see how other professionals might be involved. An accountant can do the often sophisticated analysis necessary to inform both you and your attorney as to the magnitude of your estate and can also help the attorney in arriving at various tax analyses which may become necessary. The life insurance underwriter will, of course, advise both you and your attorney as to the insurance implications of your estate. The bank trust officer will be able to inform you as to how he would perform the function of being your executor or trustee and how a trust might actually operate in the context of your estate. He may also have some suggestions to make to your lawyer concerning the administrative clauses which a trust should contain, drawing on his experience of what does and doesn't work well in the real world of operating trusts. And an investment or financial planner can provide valuable information as to the nature of your current assets and proposals for what form your future investments might take.

So when you read in the following chapters about "your advisors," it can mean any or all of the above professionals. Very often it means your lawyer, particularly in those areas where you need to determine the local law of your state and how that law applies to generalized estate planning concepts.

A Few Messages From Me To You

One: Estate planning is an intensely personal matter. Only generalities can be stated in a book such as this. But your estate plan involves real and unique people with real and unique problems or advantages. Don't get trapped into thinking that something said in the book must be meant to apply to you; only you can make that decision.

Two: No recommendations. This book is not intended to make any recommendations to any reader about anything. This is due to many reasons, one being the one just stated: namely, that estate planning is a personal matter. There is no way I can or should make any inferences about what is right for you, without having ever even met you—to say nothing of analyzing your personal situation. Another reason is because the laws of each state differ so much that it would be dangerous for me to imply, or for you to assume, that something I state can be automatically applied in every state. A third reason is that the material contained in this book is just too much of an overview to allow you to rely entirely on what is said without exploring it further with your own advisors. So please, don't take anything written in this book as even an implied recommendation or piece of advice.

Three: I need your indulgence concerning masculine and feminine pronouns. I don't want to be forced to write "he or she" in every sentence. I wholeheartedly and happily acknowledge women's rights, but purely for author's convenience I am usually going to just say "he." In almost no instance does it make any difference whether it is a male or a female to which something applies; in the rare cases where it does make a difference, I will say so. When speaking of married couples, I will usually write that the husband has died and the wife survived, not only because there is a slight statistical edge for husbands dying before wives, but also again just for the convenience of language. So please indulge me on that score.

2
forms of property ownership: everything flows from this

Glossary For This Chapter

Commingling
Common law state
Community property
Curtesy
Dower
Joint tenancy
Management
Marital property
Partition
Quasi-community property
Right of survivorship
Severance
Tenancy by the entirety
Tenancy in common
Tracing
Undivided interest

It is necessary that the first subject for examination be property ownership, because everything else follows from it. If you leave no will, the determination of who inherits from you depends upon your ownership interests in various forms of property. Your will is only operative on certain forms of ownership and not on others. Probate only happens to specific forms of ownership and not to others. Tax effects also depend upon ownership rights. So this is where we must begin.

We are concerned only with property co-owned by two or more people and not with property owned by one person alone. In the latter situation, there is nothing to say; obviously, the property simply belonged to its owner and will pass to his heirs at his death. But where two or more people co-own property, whether they are married to each other or not, then differing consequences begin to occur. We shall first examine co-ownerships where the owners may or may not be married to each other; for the purposes of our dis-

FORMS OF PROPERTY OWNERSHIP: EVERYTHING FLOWS FROM THIS

cussion, it makes no difference one way or the other. There are two basic forms of such co-ownership, **tenancy in common** and **joint tenancy.**

Tenancy in Common

Two or more persons, up to an infinite number, may own property as tenants in common. Each tenant owns an **undivided interest**, which means his own specified percentage of the whole, often based upon his contribution to the purchase of the property. The percentage may be any that is agreed to by the co-tenants, including unequal portions and portions not reflecting investment percentages. The percentages can be large, such as 99%, or minute fractions, as in oil and gas deals or other major investments with many owners, such as .0003487.

The most important point is that this undivided interest is an asset of its owner, and this asset behaves precisely like all of his solely owned property. Thus, an undivided interest in a tenancy in common passes pursuant to the owner's will, or by the laws of intestacy if he leaves no will. It may be sold, leased, given away, or mortgaged to secure a loan and may also be levied upon by creditors or taken in bankruptcy.

Tenancy in common is the standard form of common ownership and is usually presumed if nothing else appears to contradict it. A deed saying only "John Jones and Sam Brown" is normally presumed a tenancy in common, although it leaves unresolved the matter of who owns what percentage (usually equal, if nothing is said). Because there are co-owners, a tenant in common should face the possibility of disputes over one thing or another. To deal with such possibilities in advance, a comprehensive agreement among co-owners is often advisable.

In the event of a dispute, if there is no voluntary settlement or contract which governs, the only solution may come by resort to an inherent feature of a tenancy in common: the right to go to court in what is known as a **partition** suit. A court would there determine the respective interests if they don't otherwise appear, would value the property, and if no physical split-up of the property is feasible, will order the property sold at public auction. The net proceeds will then be divided among the co-tenants according to their respective interests. Partition is a form of property divorce, and any party may resort to it unless in a prior agreement that right has been waived or made subject to a right of first refusal or other similar procedure.

Joint Tenancy

The other standard form of co-ownership among persons who may or may not be married to each other is **joint tenancy with right of**

survivorship. Every kind of property may be held in joint tenancy, and the title would say "George Jones and Sam Brown, as joint tenants." There may be two or more co-owners, but the interests of the co-owners are not broken down into percentages. The main feature of joint tenancy is the feature of survivorship. This means that when any joint tenant dies, his interest automatically, by legal definition and at the very instant of his death, belongs to the surviving joint tenant or tenants. Thus, if in the above example George Jones dies, then Sam Brown automatically becomes the outright owner of the entire property, free of any co-ownership. But if there are more than two joint tenants, upon the death of the first of them, nothing really happens; the ownership simply remains with the survivors who continue as joint tenants among themselves, and the decedent just drops out at that point. The last to survive will become the sole owner, free of any co-ownership, and for this reason joint tenancy is sometimes nicknamed "winner take all."

Its Survivorship Feature

It is apparent that a joint tenancy should not be entered into without some thought. The survivorship feature is like a will, in that a joint tenant must be content to have his co-owners automatically succeed to his interest upon his death, to the exclusion of any other heir. A joint tenancy should never be entered into except with a person or persons you are content to have "inherit" your interest. Due to the automatic survivorship feature, a will has no effect on joint tenancy property, and any attempt in a will to bequeath joint tenancy property will be entirely disregarded. But no one should fall victim to a frequency fallacy, which is that people with all their property in joint tenancy do not need wills. If there are only two joint tenants, the will of the first to die will indeed be unnecessary and without any effect. But thereafter the surviving joint tenant owns the entire property outright, and at his death the only way to pass the property to his chosen heir is via his will (unless he creates another joint tenancy with that heir). So joint tenants definitely need wills, because there is no way of knowing in advance which of them will need a will and which one won't.

Severance

Joint tenants have the same right to partition as do tenants in common. In fact, it is even more important in a joint tenancy, so that the co-owner is not locked into a bad situation should he no longer want his co-tenant to "inherit" from him. In other ways, a joint tenancy is more fragile than a tenancy in common. Because of its special nature and the special relationship among joint tenants, there are many things that an individual joint tenant may not do without causing unfair consequences to his co-owners. For instance, if a buyer desired to purchase George Jones's interest, it would not be fair to substitute the unknown buyer into the special heir-like relationship without the consent of Sam Brown. Most laws therefore provide that in such a sale, that act immediately **severs** the joint tenancy and turns it into a tenancy in common among the remaining tenants and the new owner. Other acts may or may not cause a severance, many too many to list here. Such acts are what make a joint tenancy such a potentially fragile thing.

How To Create A Joint Tenancy

Whereas a tenancy in common is usually the presumed form of co-ownership, a joint tenancy must be specifically created to avoid that presumption. This is done by the use of the words "as joint tenants" on the governing document of title. On stock certificates, you will often see the following rather unnecessary legend: "As joint tenants with right of survivorship, and not as tenants in common." Many people are confused about the difference between the following types of titling: "George Jones *and* Sam Brown" (no other words being present) versus "George Jones *or* Sam Brown." In most states there is no meaningful distinction between those two conjunctions, although many people wrongly assume that "or" means a joint tenancy and "and" means a tenancy in common. If you intend a joint tenancy, do not rely on the mere conjunction; say so by using the title "as joint tenants." A particular offender with the "or" versus "and" wording is bank passbooks, which are doubly confusing because the passbook is not the real document of title in the first place. True title is stated on the signature card which you sign when you open the account, and that card must be examined if you need to determine true title. That card is a miniaturized, pre-printed contract between you and the bank, and it states the true title. Joint-tenancy bank accounts are a bit different from other joint-tenancy properties because by banking rules in most states, each joint tenant may at any time withdraw all funds in the account. Many people do not know that and too casually put someone else's name on their accounts as a joint tenant.

Probate And Tax Factors

There are various probate and tax factors which bear on the advisability of holding property in the joint tenancy form. It is well known that joint tenancy avoids probate; the reason it does and the consequences of probate avoidance will be examined in chapter five. The tax factors and all other information will be brought together in later chapters; at this point I just want to give you the information as to what joint tenancy is.

Tenancy by the Entirety

From here on in this chapter, I will discuss forms of ownership where the co-owners must be married to each other. The first of these, which does not exist in community property states and has been abolished in several of the other states as well, is the **tenancy by the entirety**. Basically, this is similar to a joint tenancy between spouses and is established by using the words "George and Alice Jones, Tenants by the Entirety." Its main feature is the right of survivorship in the surviving spouse. That survivorship, just like in a joint tenancy, occurs automatically and can not be defeated by the decedent spouse's will. So it is a form of title holding which guarantees that the surviving spouse will "inherit" the decedent's interest to the exclusion of any of his other heirs. But it differs from a true joint tenancy in several respects. Its survivorship feature can be undone only with the consent of both spouses, whereas in a joint tenancy any one co-owner can cause a severance and thereby undo the survivorship feature. Originally, only the husband had control of property held as tenants by the entirety, and he was entitled to all of the income from it. Some states have modified that aspect, but if that aspect has not been altered, it differs from a joint tenancy where each co-owner is entitled to an equal share of income. Tenancy by the entirety is getting to be more and more an archaic form of holding title.

I will now turn to an examination of marital property, which concerns the right that one spouse may have in the property of the other, or in their mutual marital property. These marital rights have a profound effect upon estate planning because they determine the very power that a spouse may or may not have to control who will inherit some or all of that property after his or her death. If you are in a common law state (see below) you may be tempted to skip the material concerning community property, and vice versa. While you are certainly free to do that, remember that in our increasingly more mobile society people are finding that their estates may touch both systems. A common example is the corporate executive who is transferred into and out of community property states, or the person who spends his working life in one type of state but retires in the other type of state. Such people may find that their accumulated property bears characteristics of both marital property systems, and so you may want to be informed as to both systems.

FORMS OF PROPERTY OWNERSHIP: EVERYTHING FLOWS FROM THIS

Marital Property in the 42 Common Law States

The **common law states** are all states except Arizona, California, Idaho, Louisiana, Nevada, New Mexico, Texas, and Washington. The history of marital property in the common law states traces directly back to feudal times in England when a wife was nothing more than a piece of property owned by her husband. A man might own a cow, a plow, some furniture, and a wife; it was as simple as that. It should not be surprising that, originally, everything she owned or produced belonged to him. Of course, we have come a long way since then, but the historical beginnings explain the starting point for the law's evolution and still leave us with traces of older theories. Marital property laws are currently in a particular state of flux due to the women's rights movement, and so developments in your state should be watched closely. Also, should the Equal Rights Amendment to the United States Constitution ever be ratified, we might see further changes in marital property laws.

Concept Of Separate Property

Both common law and community property states operate under a concept similar to what the latter states call **separate property.** This is all property owned by either spouse before marriage, plus any gifts or inheritances received by that spouse even after marriage, and usually includes the income produced by that property as well as all growth in value of that property. Such property belongs entirely to the owning spouse and passes at death under his or her will or under state law if that spouse did not leave a will. But in most states the form of title holding is all important because if the inheriting spouse or the spouse with pre-marital property places the other spouse's name on the title, many changes will occur. Example: if George Jones had separate property but titles it in the name of George Jones and Alice Jones, that would create a tenancy in common, there will be a gift of one-half to Alice, and if Alice dies, her one-half interest will pass under her will (or by state law if she left no will). If a joint tenancy or tenancy by the entirety had been created, then the survivorship provisions of that title will control. A gift tax may be payable, and George would have given up the ability to pass one-half of that property at his death.

Aside from separate property, the common law states are divided as to who owns property acquired from the post-marriage earnings of the spouses. In some states which have not evolved far from the original English law, the husband owns all such property even though the wife worked and contributed her earnings to their present property holdings. In other common law states, each spouse owns the proceeds of his or her own earnings. Under either system, if the husband is the only spouse who has ever worked, then all of the post-marriage property which is not the wife's separate property belongs to him. The differences between states arise if the wife has also worked and has had earnings of her own. See Table 2-1 for an example of a not untypical estate.

TABLE 2—1.

GEORGE AND ALICE JONES ESTATE, ILLUSTRATING OWNERSHIP OF PROPERTY OWNED BEFORE MARRIAGE AND ACQUIRED DURING MARRIAGE.

	George's Separate Property	Alice's Separate Property	Marital property: husband's in a common law state, community in a community property state.
1. George was worth $54,000 prior to marriage in 1940; assume that property now worth $120,000.	→ $120,000		
2. Alice was worth $40,000 prior to marriage; assume that property now worth $95,000.		→ $95,000	
3. Thirty years ago, George inherited a $100,000 ranch, now worth $350,000.	→ $350,000		
4. Twenty-five years ago, Alice inherited stocks worth $100,000. She sold them to invest in a company that is now in bankruptcy, and she has been told that she's likely to receive 20 cents on the dollar.		→ $20,000	
5. Twenty-three years ago, George was given stocks worth $50,000. He changed the title to "George and Alice Jones"; stocks now worth $120,000.	→ $60,000	→ $60,000	
6. Twenty years ago, Alice's mother died, and bequeathed property then (and still) worth $100,000 to George and Alice Jones.	→ $50,000	→ $50,000	

TABLE 2–1. (continued)

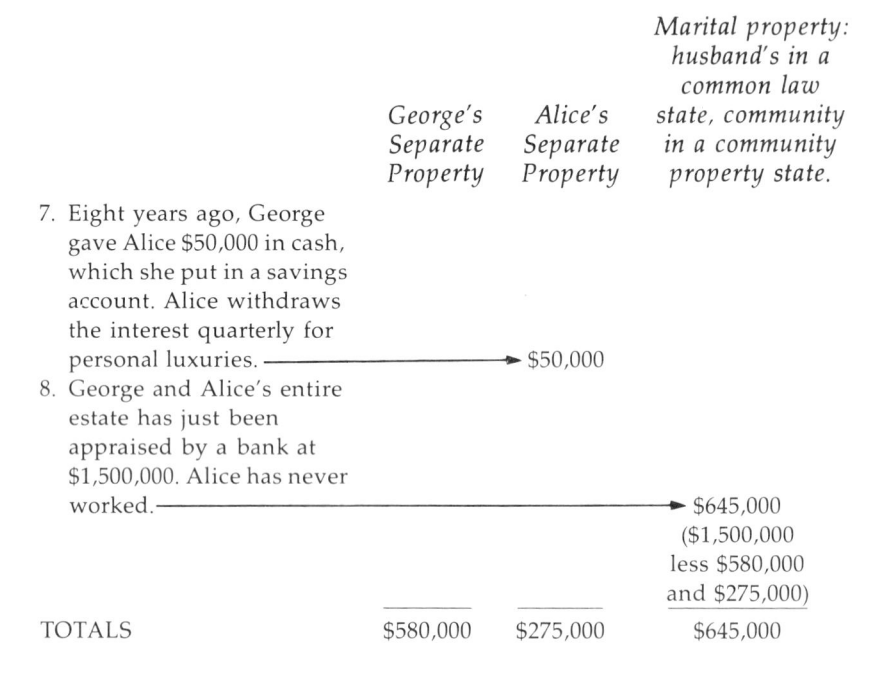

	George's Separate Property	Alice's Separate Property	Marital property: husband's in a common law state, community in a community property state.
7. Eight years ago, George gave Alice $50,000 in cash, which she put in a savings account. Alice withdraws the interest quarterly for personal luxuries.		$50,000	
8. George and Alice's entire estate has just been appraised by a bank at $1,500,000. Alice has never worked.			$645,000 ($1,500,000 less $580,000 and $275,000)
TOTALS	$580,000	$275,000	$645,000

Dower And Curtesy Rights

However, not all the marital property will pass at death under the owning spouse's will or under state laws if he dies without a will. The reason is that the surviving spouse is usually entitled at the death of the first spouse to a certain percentage of the decedent spouse's post-marriage, non-separate property. Although the percentage varies, it is usually either one-third or one-half. Also, the type of right it is varies from state to state, particularly as to whether it is a right to absolute ownership or just a right to use such property for the balance of the surviving spouse's life (called a **life estate;** see page 49).

In some states these rights only accrue in real estate, while in other states they accrue in all marital property of whatever type. These rights are often called **dower** when the survivor is the wife and **curtesy** when the survivor is the husband, patterned after ancient concepts left over from the English common law. Many states are now referring to these rights simply as **statutory shares.** The important point is that the dower or curtesy rights can not be defeated by the will of the first spouse to die, since the surviving spouse has an absolute right to this share. The balance of the marital property does pass pursuant to the decedent spouse's will or under the intestacy laws if there was no will. So these rights cut into the power that the decedent spouse has to pass some of the marital property to anyone other than the surviving spouse.

In the states of Arizona, California, Idaho, Louisiana, Nevada, New Mexico, Texas, and Washington, the situation is quite different. Most community property law migrated from Spain by way of Mexico, and Spain had a totally different system than did England. The basic concept in the community property states is not that the wife is a possession of the husband, but rather that the marriage is indeed a community between the spouses in which they have equal rights similar to an equal partnership. Accordingly, most community property states say that the wife at any given moment (not just at death) owns a **present, existing and equal** ownership interest in all of the marital property, which is of course called community property in those states. If the wife absolutely owns one-half of such property and the husband should die first, he obviously cannot in his will dispose of the half that she owns, no more than any person in a will can dispose of another person's property. Clearly, this creates a whole different set of concepts for estate planning purposes. The laws of the community property states differ in greater or lesser degree, particularly Louisiana, which has a totally unique legal system based on a mix of the English common law, the French Napoleonic code, and the Spanish community property system. But several general concepts can be stated.

Marital Property in the 8 Community Property States

Determining Community Versus Separate Property

The key inquiry in community property problems is usually the determination of how much of the property is **community property** and how much is **separate property.** Remember, the latter is property owned before marriage, plus any gifts or inheritances received even after marriage. Community property is all property acquired after marriage which is not separate property. Therefore it does not matter which spouse worked or had earnings because all the earnings of either of them are by definition community property (in some states, income earned by separate property is also community property). Note that all property of anyone not at the moment legally married is by definition separate property, and this includes never-married persons as well as divorced or widowed persons. Although a person may have been married previously, upon divorce or the other spouse's death, that person is no longer married and therefore all of his or her property is separate property.

But defining separate and community property is only the

first step. In the nature of things, married couples often **commingle** all their property, both separate and community, making the problems caused thereby among the most difficult to unravel. The commingled property is often unraveled by a doctrine called **tracing,** which is emminently fair but causes extreme complexities. Tracing means that once you determine the original character of a piece of property as either separate or community, you are obliged to follow its entire history through gains, losses, transformations of form, re-investments, additions, and every other conceivable alteration. The current property traceable back to the original will still retain the same character, in whole or in part, of the original. Complexities arise when opposite character properties are all tossed into the pot so that the current property contains elements of both. Determining what amount of the current property is allocable to the separate property of one spouse and what amount to their community property, is a legal and accounting problem of the first magnitude.

Rights Of Management

An important factor in determining the proper allocations between separate and community property is knowing whether both spouses have the right to manage the community property, or only one spouse does. If only one spouse has the right to buy, sell, take out loans, and otherwise manage, that spouse may not jeopardize or diminish the rights of the other spouse, and so some of the commingling might be held against that spouse's interest whenever it becomes necessary to trace back through the commingling. Many of the community property states have undergone a recent major change in this regard. Originally in our male-dominated culture, it was thought that dual management would lead to chaos, and in choosing one of the spouses as manager the choice quite automatically was the husband. Many rules grew up regarding what he could not do by way of management to disadvantage his wife's equal interest; for instance, he could not give the community property away without her consent, and if as manager he did so anyway, she had various methods to retrieve it. Under the impetus of the women's rights movement, several states recently changed their law so that both spouses now have equal management rights. Each community property state has a subtly different set of statutes regarding management and control, and so few generalities are possible.

The right of management bears on the problem of unraveling a commingled estate by using the doctrine of tracing. This is because assistance in tracing is provided in several states by a series of presumptions, and some of these presumptions are based on the right of management. All such presumptions may be overcome by actual evidence to the contrary, but in the absence of any evidence these presumptions are sufficient to determine how much property is separate property and how much is community property. They also provide a guide for understanding the way tracing works.

Significance Of How Title Is Held

One set of presumptions derive from the way title is held on the appropriate document of title, such as a deed, a stock certificate, etc. Prior to the change of law regarding management, since the husband was the manager, any property standing in his name alone was presumed to be the community property of both spouses. As a corollary, any property standing in the wife's name alone was presumed to be her own separate property, unless a different intention was expressed in the document; the same was true for any property she held in common with persons other than her spouse. After the change to equal management rights, the presumption regarding the husband's holdings remains the same (community property), but the presumption regarding the wife's holdings has been abolished. Although replaced with no new presumption, it seems clear from the legislature's intention that property in the wife's name, either alone or in common with others, is also presumed to be community property and not her own separate property as it was before. But each state's particular laws must be consulted for fully accurate determinations.

You may wonder how a spouse should hold title if the property is in reality his or her separate property. The recommended form is in that spouse's name, with the addition of the wording "As her sole and separate property." Further, since spouses in community property states have the power to make agreements as to how their property is held, the safest thing would be for such an agreement to exist in which the property is explicitly stated to be the separate property of one of them. If the spouses deliberately intend for property to be held as community property and do not wish to rely on the rebuttable presumptions, the recommended form is "John and Mary Jones, Husband and Wife, as Community Property."

The Problem Of Community Property Funds In A Joint-Tenancy Purchase

One of the most vexing problems occurs when the spouses invest admitted community property funds in a new purchase, but take title to that purchase as joint tenants. Several states hold that joint tenancy is entirely different from community property, and also that community property and joint tenancy can not co-exist in the same piece of property. In those states, the purchase referred to above can not be community property in any way, and must be the totally distinct form of joint tenancy. Because the title to the purchase is in joint tenancy, the invested funds have lost their community property character. This switch has great impact upon both probate and tax consequences, and after the death of one spouse sometimes leads the survivor to allege that the property really was community. That allegation has been a possibility because some states will recognize even an oral agreement regarding the status of property, and the surviving spouse might establish an oral agreement that the property was really intended to be community property notwithstanding title in joint tenancy. This possibility has confused matters even further and has led to problems with the Internal Revenue Service over matters we will examine in later chapters. These problems have led most estate planners to recommend that spouses make a clear decision as to whether they prefer joint tenancy or community property, and then the title is structured to reflect that decision without relying on any suspicious oral agreement. Which of these forms of ownership is the most beneficial depends on several factors we will discuss and then bring together in a later chapter.

Apportionment Theory

Another set of presumptions deals with the time when property was acquired. As would be suspected, any property acquired before marriage is presumed to be separate property, whereas any property acquired during marriage is presumed to be community property. Not only can these presumptions be rebutted by contrary evidence, but also they do not tell the whole story. For instance, assume a person buys a $6000 car prior to marriage by giving a down payment of $1500, but thereafter he marries and the balance is paid off with post-marriage earnings, which are therefore community property. Some states would hold that the entire automobile is separate property simply because it was separate at the time it was acquired. But others follow the apportionment theory, which results in the car being twenty-five percent separate property and seventy-five percent community property of both spouses. Again, very fair but quite complex, making it necessary to look not only to the time of original purchase but also to the source of the funds used to make every installment payment.

The apportionment theory leads to perhaps the single most complicated problem in community property law. This occurs when prior to marriage a person invests some money to start a business, and after working in it awhile, he marries. After marriage more and various kinds of capital are contributed to the business by either or both of the spouses, and furthermore he continues to work full time in it. Many years later the business is worth a fortune, and upon either death or divorce, it becomes necessary to figure out what portion of it is his own separate property and what portion community property. You can see how, upon divorce, this is a very loaded issue because he will keep that portion which is his separate property but must split with his spouse that portion which is truly community property. Another fair but difficult to evaluate factor is thrown into this problem because most courts hold that his efforts after marriage are a community property contribution no less than the investment of community property funds. The courts have evolved two different methods of solving such a problem, one of which basically favors the community property and the other favors the separate property. The one favoring community property is used when the spouse's efforts factually were the most important factor contributing to the growth of the business, such as in almost any professional practice or where the spouse was the magnet which drew the customers. But the separate property is favored when the growth of the business was more due to the natural enhancement of the particular business, which was first acquired as separate property. Examples might be in land sales companies where rapid appreciation in land values was much more important than the spouse's salesmanship of land owned before marriage, or where all businesses of the type owned before marriage appreciated greatly due to general economic factors (automobile dealerships after World War II, electronics companies in the early sixties, etc.). Litigation over such matters often takes weeks and involves squads of competing accountants, appraisers, and economists all trying to be convincing on behalf of one spouse or the other.

Yet another series of presumptions arises when property is originally purchased, in whole or in part, with borrowed funds. Generally, the character of such property is determined by the character of the property to which the lender looked for his security. Thus, if one spouse mortgaged some inherited property in order to purchase an investment, that amount of it allocable to the borrowed funds would be separate property.

Finally, there are a series of presumptions arising if one spouse contributes one kind of property to improve or enhance the other kind of property (example: wife's separate property cash used to build a building on community property vacant land). In this area, the concept of gifts enters in because in allowing the improvement, one spouse is in reality making a gift to the owner(s) of the underlying property. The use of community property funds

TABLE 2—2.

ESTATE OF BUDDY AND KIKI JONES OF BEVERLY HILLS, COMMUNITY PROPERTY SPOUSES; AN INEXACT BUT ILLUSTRATIVE EXAMPLE.

	Buddy's Separate Property	Kiki's Separate Property	Community Property
1. Upon the settlement of Buddy's divorce from his 3rd wife the morning he married Kiki, Buddy was awarded property worth $100,000.	→$100,000		
2. In the adjacent courtroom, Kiki was awarded $240,000 upon her divorce from her 4th husband.		→$240,000	
3. A few weeks later, the studios paid Buddy $100,000 for a script he had finished before he married Kiki.	→$100,000		
4. Kiki's first husband died and left her $50,000 in his will.		→$50,000	
5. From his 3rd marriage, Buddy brought his condominium worth $150,000 which stands in his name alone. Since the marriage, he has paid off the $100,000 mortgage out of his earnings, and it is now worth $300,000.	→$100,000 ($50,000 equity shares pro-rata in the increase)		→$200,000
6. From his 3rd marriage, Buddy brought his clothing store worth $50,000. Kiki invested $100,000 she inherited from her mother to remodel the store. Buddy's abilities and drawing power have turned the business into a chain of 8 stores, worth $800,000.	→$75,000 (assumed increase in value of original interest)	→$150,000 (assumed increase in value of her contribution)	→$575,000
7. Buddy's father died and left him a vacant lot in Palm Springs worth $50,000. Kiki's father died and left her $100,000. Buddy borrowed $100,000 using his interest in the last store he opened as security, and they have just finished using the $200,000 to build a weekend retreat.	→$50,000 →$100,000 →$100,000		(gift from Kiki) (usually considered a gift from the community, but the community may have a claim for reimbursement.)
TOTALS	$625,000	$440,000	$775,000

to improve one spouse's separate property yields different results than formerly in those states where the spouses now have equal management rights in the community property.

Summary

It is probably pretty clear by now that this is quite a complex area of law, which is certainly true. Most community property/separate property problems can be resolved only on the basis of the particular circumstances surrounding them. Many genuine experts remain confounded concerning the interaction of community property and joint tenancy, so do not feel badly if by this point you are unclear as to all the interactions. Sometimes all the types of presumptions mentioned above will apply to a given matter, often in conflicting manners, and then only experts or a court can come up with a solution. See Table 2-2 for an inexact but illustrative example of a community property estate.

Quasi-Community Property

As if all the above complexities were not enough, some states have seen fit to add another (though for very good reasons). This crops up when a married couple acquires an estate in a common law state and then move to a community property state; what is the status of such property? The legislatures quite properly desire that all their residents ought to be treated alike, and so laws were passed saying that if the property had been acquired in a foreign state under such circumstances that, if acquired in the community property state, it would have been community property, then such property becomes community property when the owners become community property state residents. That law was held unconstitutional when it was applied under old divorce laws and resulted in taking from the husband and awarding to the wife a good chunk of the property which was "his" in the common law state. As we shall see in chapter four, a state does have the power to dictate what shall happen to property upon the death of one of its residents, so the law was re-enacted to apply only at that time. Accordingly, all such property of new residents is treated upon death as if it were community property (hence "quasi"-community property), meaning that the surviving spouse owns one-half of it and the first spouse to die can not defeat that right in his or her will.

Quasi-community property is of course very frequently observed, since so many people move from common law states into community property states. Its presence, along with pure community property acquired after the move plus genuine separate property of either or both of the spouses, presents the most complex estate possible for estate planning purposes. The reason is that the estate tax law treats quasi-community property as if it were separate property, not community property, and so it must be handled appropriately for tax purposes (as we shall see) while still adhering to local community property law.

What, if anything, should one do concerning all these complexities? There is really not much one can do, for the facts relevant to the estate speak for themselves. The serious problems arise when it becomes necessary to ascertain what the factual situation really is. Good record keeping is immensely valuable, and often one of the major things accomplished by estate planning is to convince the spouses of the need for it. Another major goal of estate planning is to unravel a badly commingled estate, to make informed decisions as to how property should be held, and then to set things straight. It is much more advantageous and feasible to do so while both spouses are here to contribute the history, rather than having courts, disgruntled heirs, or Internal Revenue Service (IRS) agents attempt it to their own advantage after the one who best knows the history is no longer here. An agreement between spouses can outline all of the history and the consequent current status of their estate, and from there on that agreement, together with continued good record keeping, will set the estate in its most advantageous position.

APPLICATION

1. Determine the *true* title of each of your assets. Examine deeds, stock certificates, and particularly the signature cards governing your bank deposits.

2. If married, list all property which you or your spouse has inherited, has received by gift (including from each other), or owned before marriage. Identify it; assign it a value as best you can at the date of inheritance, gift, or marriage; and then trace it to your current holdings. Remember that income such property produces, any appreciation in its value, and reinvestments into other property usually still carry with them the original character.

3. For spouses in the 42 common law states, seek a local determination of each spouse's ownership rights under the particular law of your state. Your lawyer can tell you in a five minute phone call, or you might ask your local bar association for the information. If the wife's earnings are hers alone, determine the *net* amount of such earnings still present among your holdings.

    a.) also determine the statutory share which a surviving spouse is entitled to in your state.

4. For spouses in community property states, after having completed number two above, identify which assets contain the remaining values, which ought to be your community property.

But be cautious, and perhaps obtain local advice because in some community property states the income produced by separate property is community property. Identify assets where commingling has occurred.

    a.) for all joint tenancy property, determine whether it was purchased with community property funds.

5. If you have moved to a community property state from a common law state, find out whether your new state has "quasi-community property." If so, identify what amount of your property is quasi-community.

6. After having completed the above, and after having finished this book, discuss with your advisors whether to alter any titles and also whether to set down any of the facts in a contract between spouses concerning the character of their property.

3

intestacy: if you leave no will

Glossary For This Chapter

Domicile
Escheat
Intestate
Issue
Per Capita
Per Stirpes
Personal Property
Real Property
Residence
Right of Representation
Testate

To appreciate what can be accomplished by proper planning, it is necessary to understand what will occur if there is no planning at all. The ultimate in no planning occurs if you leave no will, a situation called **intestacy.** The term is centuries old, when a will for technical reasons had to be titled "Last Will and Testament," so that one who had a will would die **testate** and one without a will, **intestate.** In an intestacy, there really is an estate plan, but it is one imposed by the governing laws of the state. Certain tax, probate, and inheritance results necessarily follow from the law-imposed plan. You ought to be aware of those results so that you can decide whether you are content with the plan provided by the state.

Which State's Laws Will Govern Your Estate?

But first there is a preliminary question: The law of which state? Assume a person, residing in New York, dies intestate and possesses the usual residential and other personal property within New York. But assume he also owned a hunting lodge in Michigan; a ski chalet in Switzerland; shares of stock in a Delaware corporation, which are traded on a regional exchange in Chicago, and the certificates for which are kept by his son in Florida; and an interest in a logging business with principal offices in Oregon. Which state's law will impose this person's involuntary estate plan?

Two Kinds of Property: Real and Personal

To determine the solution, you must first know that there are two types of property and that often different laws will apply to each. One type is **real property,** which can be roughly defined as real estate and anything growing on it or permanently connected to it (buildings, etc.). The other type is **personal property** and is essentially all else, whether tangible property which you can pick up and move (jewelry, furniture, cars, machinery, etc.), or intangible property such as contract rights, employee benefits, business interests, bank deposits, and even shares of stock and stock rights.

The laws of the state or country where real property is located will dictate the inheritance of an intestate's real property, while the laws of the state or country where the intestate was domiciled will dictate the inheritance of his personal property no matter where that property might physically be located. In the above example, Michigan law would dictate the inheritance of the hunting lodge, Swiss law would govern the inheritance of the ski lodge, and New York as the state of domicile would determine the inheritance of all the intestate's personal property wherever it may physically be.

Domicile Versus Residence

The matter of a person's true **domicile** is itself often a matter of great importance, and sometimes of dispute. Domicile is not necessarily the same as **residence** or current physical presence. It is usually defined as the place where a person intends to make his permanent home, and the place he intends ultimately to return to if he is away. Thus, service in the armed forces, or transfer to another state or country by one's employer, does not necessarily change domicile. During life, one can testify as to domicile, but if a question is raised after death, the matter can become quite difficult to solve. It is then that all the various possible pieces of evidence will be reviewed to try to demonstrate the person's intention. Although many people believe that where one votes is conclusive, that is actually only one of many possible pieces of evidence, though a very important one. Others are things such as any direct or inferential statements of the deceased on the subject, where state tax returns were filed, where a car is registered, where property is owned, and many other things. The common statement of residence in the lead paragraph of a will is therefore useful as evidence of the decedent's intention, but in an intestacy there is of course no will.

How State Laws Overlap

The same rules of real property, personal property, and domicile govern the validity of wills, so that if you want to leave out-of-state real property by a will valid in the state where the property is located, you would have to examine the law of wills in that state and not rely on the laws of the state of your domicile. The interrelationships of the laws of several states on a particular problem is a fascinating and murderously complex field of law known as **conflicts of laws,** and these conflicts arise more and more as our multi-state society gets even more mobile. A different type of example: Say an Arizonan rents a car from a California corporation at its branch office in Oregon, where the car is registered. While driving the car in Idaho, he has an accident with a car registered in Colorado, which is being driven by a resident of Utah; passengers residing in Wyoming and Montana are injured. In the event of a lawsuit, which state's laws will govern the trial? The same types of "conflicts" problems often appear in matters of inter-state ownership of property, how wills and inheritances apply across state lines, and how multi-state taxation affects estates with contacts in more than one state. If your situation falls within that kind of problem, you should surely seek counsel in order to determine which law will apply.

Once you have determined which state's intestacy laws would apply, you would then have to consult that particular state's law because each of the fifty states has laws slightly different from every other. Since most of those laws have evolved from the English common law and so bear a good deal of similarity to each other, it is meaningful to examine the general patterns.

General Patterns of State Intestacy Laws

Intestacy laws will apply to whatever property the intestate is considered to have owned and which consequently passes from him at his death. There are no complicating factors if an intestate is unmarried because all of the property will pass pursuant to the proper state's intestacy laws. But if an intestate is a married person, only that amount of marital property which does not automatically go to, or belong to, the surviving spouse will be subject to the intestacy laws. For a common law spouse, that portion of the marital property not subject to dower or curtesy rights will pass pursuant to intestacy laws if either spouse dies without a will. For community property, if one spouse dies intestate, most such states provide that the decedent's half of the community property goes entirely to the surviving spouse, which is very simple providing that you can identify which of the property is truly community property. The intestate's separate property, though, passes under the general intestacy laws described below.

Inheritance By Spouses and Descendants

The general rules of inheritance from an intestate depend entirely upon which relatives survive the decedent. The following rundown indicates the general outlines of a typical intestacy system, although each state will probably differ in some degree.

If an intestate leaves a surviving spouse and only one child, one-half of the property goes to the spouse, and one-half to the child, if living; if the child is not living, then to that child's **issue** (meaning lineal descendents). If there is a spouse and more than one child, the spouse will receive one-third, and the children (however many there are) will share the other two-thirds equally. If any child has died and left surviving issue, those descendants would take the share their deceased parent would have been entitled to, called **taking by right of representation.** This means that the issue represent the parent by standing in his shoes and taking his share; in a will it is often called **per stirpes,** which is Latin and roughly translates as "by stocks," but many modern lawyers are trying to eliminate such stilted language and will use plain English instead.

This is all perhaps more easily understood by assuming that an intestate left property worth $300,000 and left a wife surviving him along with two children, X and Y. The wife, X, and Y would each get $100,000. But if X had died before his father and had left two children, A and B, the latter would each get $50,000 by right of representation, splitting the amount their deceased parent would have been entitled to. Now assume that Y had also died and had left three children surviving. Do these three children also share their parent's $100,000 ($33,333 each), and if so isn't that unfair when A and B would be entitled to more ($50,000 each) by the mere accident that their parents didn't have as many children? Most states say it would be unfair, and so where the persons who inherit are in an equal degree of relationship to the decedent (here, they are all grandchildren standing in the second degree of relationship to the decedent), they all take equally (**per capita**) rather than by representation. So each of the decedent's five grandchildren would receive an equal $40,000 share. Right of representation is used only when any of those entitled to inherit are not in the same degree of relationship as all the other heirs entitled to inherit.

If no spouse of the intestate survives, but if the intestate left lineal descendants (child, grandchild, etc.), the descendants would take everything in equal shares if they are all in the same degree of relationship to the decedent, otherwise by right of representation.

Inheritance By Other Relatives

If there are no lineal descendants but there is a surviving spouse, the spouse does not get everything, but rather only one-half. The other half goes to the decedent's parents, and if there are none, then to his brothers and sisters (or if a brother or a sister is deceased, then to their descendants by right of representation). Only if there are no parents, no brothers or sisters, and no descendants of any deceased brothers and sisters, will the surviving spouse get everything. If you do not approve of that result, then you are obliged to make a will to direct differently.

If there is no spouse and no lineal descendants, then the entire estate goes first to the intestate's parents, or if none, to the brothers and sisters or to their issue by right of representation. And if there are none of those close relatives in existence, then the estate will pass to the nearest relatives of the decedent. Here is where we get into counting degrees of relationship, because if one heir is in a closer degree than any other claimant, that one will inherit everything to the exclusion of all the others. If there is more than one heir in the same degree of relationship to the decedent, those heirs will inherit equally, or their issue will split their shares by right of representation if one or more has already died but left issue surviving. Taking the shares of a predeceased heir by right of representation, plus the complexities of proving degrees of relationship, make for juicy newspaper reading about lengthy lawsuits which result in a long lost ninth cousin suddenly becoming heir to a fabulous fortune.

Escheat

If no relatives of any degree can be found, then the property of the intestate will **escheat**—pass to the state. Surprisingly, this is not an unusual occurrence, as millions of dollars escheat to each state each year. There is usually an extended period of years during which undiscovered heirs may show up to claim escheated property, before the state gets irrevocable rights to it. For this reason, some private detectives or other persons attempt to locate missing heirs of escheated property, making a deal with any discovered heir for a nice percentage of an otherwise unknown inheritance.

See Table 3-1 for a chart of a typical succession pattern.

It is not unusual for a person to die intestate; in fact, quite the contrary. It has been variously estimated that between fifty and seventy percent of persons die without a will. Part of the reason for this is undoubtedly an emotional reluctance to think about a will, either as a denial of mortality or perhaps some holdover of primitive superstitions that thinking about something might cause it to happen. Only a psychiatrist could meaningfully comment on that, but it is wise to die without a will only if you are content with the state imposed plan, which carries with it the probate and tax consequences we shall examine in later chapters.

Other Problems With Intestacy

There are many and various other problems connected with the matter of intestacy. For instance, what of adopted children? In most states, they are treated in every respect as are natural-born children. An adopted child's inheritance rights from his natural parent are almost everywhere cut off by adoption, so he may not inherit even if he is the natural parent's sole survivor. As for rela-

TABLE 3—1.

SUCCESSION TO $300,000 ESTATE OF AN INTESTATE
UNDER TYPICAL INTESTACY PATTERN DESCRIBED IN TEXT
[BUT EVERY STATE DIFFERS IN GREATER OR LESSER DEGREE].

	Spouse	Children	Grand-children	Parents	Brothers and Sisters	Nephews and Nieces	More Distant Relatives
Spouse and one child.	$150,000	$150,000					
Spouse, sons Jon and Sam, (or more)	$100,000	$200,000 equally					
Spouse, son Sam, children of predeceased son Jon	$100,000	$100,000	$100,000 by right of representation				
Spouse, no children surviving, 2 sons of Sam, 3 sons of Jon.	$100,000		$200,000 equally				
Spouse, no children, no issue. Parents.	$150,000			$150,000			
Spouse, no children, issue, or parents. Brothers and sisters.	$150,000				$150,000		

TABLE 3–1. *(continued)*

	Spouse	Children	Grand-children	Parents	Brothers and Sisters	Nephews and Nieces	More Distant Relatives
Spouse, no children, issue, parents, brothers, or sisters. Nephews and nieces.	$150,000					$150,000	
Spouse, no children, issue, parents, brothers, sisters, nephews, or nieces.	$300,000						
No spouse. Children.		$300,000 equally, or if one had predeceased, to his children by right of representation, etc.					
No spouse, children, issue. Parents, brothers, and sisters.				$150,000	$150,000		
No spouse, children, issue, or parents. Brothers and sisters.					$300,000		
No spouse, children, issue, parents, or brothers and sisters. Nephews and nieces.						$300,000	
No spouse, children, issue, parents, brothers, sisters, nephews, or nieces. More distant relatives.							$300,000 by right or representation.
No relatives in any degree, anywhere in the world.	—ESCHEAT TO STATE—						

tives of the half blood, in most states they inherit equally with whole blood relatives in identical degrees of relationship to the intestate, subject to certain subtle exceptions.

Many states have remains of the old feudal property rules. In those states, if the second spouse to die leaves no will and has no children surviving, any property inherited from the estate of a previously deceased spouse (by will or intestacy) must go back to blood relatives of that previously deceased spouse. This curious effect can be entirely avoided if the second spouse would but leave a will.

And what of the millionaire who is bumped off by his closest relative in order that the latter may inherit his estate? All through the law runs a doctrine that one may not profit by his own wrong, and so the ploy will only serve to jail the relative without any inheritance. This doctrine has led to several fascinating trials, usually instances of semi-accidental killings in a blind rage, often of one spouse by the other, where the sole issue in the trial is whether the crime is a homicide for purposes of this non-inheritance rule. Usually, involuntary manslaughter is not considered a homicide under this rule, and such a verdict would mean that the accused could inherit from the deceased (or, as is often the case, receive the proceeds of the deceased's life insurance policies).

There, then, is a general outline of everyone's estate plan. If it does not appeal to you, or you suspect that it can be improved upon, then you should give your attention to the following chapters.

APPLICATION

1. If the situation concerning your domicile is at all confused, obtain advice or take other steps to determine the state of your legal domicile. Consider further steps to make a record of your intentions about your domicile, and perhaps change any of your acts (such as voting, etc), which may be confusing the picture.

2. Determine the intestate succession laws of your state. A lawyer can outline them to you in five minutes, you might be able to find out through your local bar association, or you could go to your county law library and ask the librarian to give you the statutes on this subject.

    a.) Decide whether or not you are satisfied with the intestacy laws of your state.

    b.) If you are satisfied, do not yet make a decision to not have a will, at least until you have read more of this book about the administrative persons you can appoint in a will (executor, guardian for your children, etc.) and the tax consequences of having your property go outright to your heirs under the intestacy laws.

4
all about wills

Glossary For This Chapter

Administration
Administrator
Codicil
Devise and Bequeath
Executor
Fee Simple
Heir
Holographic Will
Joint and Mutual Will
Legacy
Life Estate
Life Tenant
No Contest Clause
Nuncupative Will
Personal Representative
Remainder
Remainderman
Republish
Residuary Clause
Residue
Reversion
Revive
Testamentary Capacity
Testator
Will
Will Contest

Although the will is not the only instrument of an estate plan, it is more often than not the key instrument. Contrary to what you probably expect, making a will and leaving property to heirs is not one of the inalienable rights of citizenship. The reason it is not is purely historic, dating back to the Middle Ages when only feudal lords owned property, and no one even imagined property rights for anyone else. As the feudal system died out, people began to demand ownership rights in what they managed to acquire, followed by demands for a way to leave acquisitions to their heirs. Finally the English Parliament granted permission to pass property by will, but only if a person did so in a very formal document complying with quite a set of technicalities. To this day it remains true that making a will and leaving property to heirs is merely a privilege granted by the legislature, exercisable only if we strictly comply with the rules granting the privilege. Undoubtedly any modern attempt to withdraw the privilege would never be allowed to occur, but the historical facts help make clear why we must still put up with the many technical rules regarding wills.

Types of Wills

There are three different types of wills, and different states allow anywhere from one to three of them. The types are: nuncupative, an oral will; holographic, a handwritten will; and the formal witnessed will. The first is severely limited, and the second is potentially dangerous. The witnessed will is thus the most recommended form, and offers the greatest security. A closer look at these three wills follows.

Nuncupative Will

This is the only form of oral will allowed. However, its use is very restricted. Many states say it can be used only by someone during his last illness and in immediate peril of death, often only a certain minimum number of days before death. Other states restrict it to persons in the armed forces who are dying from battle injuries. Almost all states restrict its effectiveness to personal property and then usually in a very minimum amount (such as $1000). It is not an estate planning factor.

Holographic Will

The second type, the **holographic** will, is allowed in roughly half the states. This type is written entirely in the **testator**'s (definition: the person who writes a will) own handwriting and usually requires a date and a signature, but not witnesses. The major problem in guaranteeing its legality is the usual requirement that it be written entirely in the testator's own handwriting. Lawsuits have invalidated holographic wills written on printed letterhead, wills containing a rubber stamped word within their body, wills where anything at all was typewritten on the paper, and similar rulings. Although such results may seem silly, since writing a will is a privilege and many legislatures have specified "entirely" handwritten, we must comply. In those states which permit them, a holographic will is a perfectly legal document of no lesser standing than a formal, witnessed will—as long as the rules can be met.

Although legal in many states, a holographic will has two inherent dangers which have nothing to do with its validity. One, as the Howard Hughes mess proved, is that there can be problems of authenticity. The second is that the testator is not trained to write for the judges, lawyers, and tax officials who will be interpreting the will. A frequently seen problem is that, although the testator knew what he meant, what he has written turns out to be full of ambiguities. That can lead to significant challenges or other problems, with consequent added expenses of resolving the problem, and also can lead to adverse tax consequences. For this reason alone, one should be very careful about using a holographic will, and perhaps it is best to avoid them entirely.

Formal, Witnessed Will

The third type of will is the **formal, witnessed** will, which must comply with all the legal formalities. Since state laws differ, it is essential to get local counsel in any given state, but typical formalities include the following points:

The will must be "subscribed" at the end by the testator either signing it or making his mark, or by someone doing so in his presence and at his direction (thus, both illiterate and physically handicapped persons can execute wills). The subscription must be done in the presence of the witnesses, who must see it done. The testator must declare that it is his will and that he is asking the witnesses to witness his signature, though they need not read the will. Some states require only two witnesses, but most require three; each of the witnesses must sign at the end of the document at the testator's request and in the presence of both the testator and all the other witnesses. Usually, the witnesses also sign their addresses to facilitate locating them when the time comes for them to attest that all the necessary formalities were observed.

Many attorneys have both testator and witnesses either sign or initial each page of the will. Normally this is not required, but the purpose is to have those signatures or initials appear on all the pages so that it will be more difficult for anyone to substitute pages without the testator's knowledge. Some lawyers also exclude one spouse from the room when the other spouse signs a will, in order to give the signing spouse one last chance to express any doubts while out of the presence of the other spouse (who just might be bringing pressure as to the terms of the will). Nothing requires both spouses to have identical wills, so a final moment of confidentiality might be appropriate.

Spouses could request one will for both of them, which would state their wishes as to what should occur at either death. This is called a **joint and mutual will,** and most attorneys believe it is extremely ill-advised and should be avoided like the plague. It can have disastrous tax consequences (for reference to a future chapter—it can lose the marital deduction), it can foul up the normal probate process, and it can easily lead to disputes concerning whether the survivor has the power to revoke the will and make a new one, or conversely whether the will was a contract between the spouses not to revoke it and to leave their property as specified therein. It is almost always better that each spouse have his or her own will, which can be identical if they wish.

Witnesses and Other Matters

In most states at least one witness must supply a written declaration for the opening of the testator's probate, attesting that all the formalities were complied with when the will was executed. This suggests that they be persons of roughly the same age as, or younger than, the testator. But even more important is that they be persons who will be easy to locate years later when their written declaration (or, in the event of a contest, their verbal testimony) will be required. A person who will vanish into the fabric of society is not the most recommended witness. The lawyer who drew the will, plus his office personnel, are excellent witnesses because professional directories can almost always be used to track them down. If witnesses all vanish or all predecease the testator, there are still methods built into every law for proving the will, although at the cost of some additional time and perhaps expense.

Some states are now allowing the witnesses' declaration written into the will itself to be used in an uncontested probate. In those states, the selection of a witness is therefore less important.

A Witness Should Not Benefit From The Will

The law has always been concerned about witnesses who benefit from a provision in the will they are witnessing, on the theory that if they benefit they will be less likely to reveal an error in the formalities of execution. Most state's laws therefore provide that a gift in a will to any of the witnesses is void, except that if the witness would have taken a share by intestacy if the testator had died intestate, then such a witness may inherit at least his intestate share. Accordingly, anyone beneficially mentioned in the will must not be used as a witness. If it is impossible for a lawyer to supervise the formalities of execution (which lawyers much prefer to do as part of their responsibility to their client), the testator will be told that no one whose name appears in the will can be a witness. Even though that statement is a bit overly broad, it will protect the testator's wishes.

Protect Your Will And Keep It Safe

Once a will is executed, it has no operative effect during the lifetime of the testator; it is merely a piece of paper, not governing in any way what the testator may or may not do with his property. However, it is a very important piece of paper, because if it is not revoked, it will be the document which will one day take effect. It should be protected against the off chance that some devious person will wrongfully alter it, perhaps by substituting pages or scratching things out, but more importantly, it should be safe from fire. A fireproof vault is best, and this should usually be either a safe deposit box in a bank or an attorney's vault. Many states impose a freeze on any safe deposit box carrying a decedent's name, but only until the state tax authorities can inventory the box for the legitimate purpose of making sure that the estate accounts for all the contents on the death tax return. In some states the bank will allow you to remove the decedent's will even prior to such an inventory, but in others you must wait until the tax people can schedule the inventory. Keeping a will in an attorney's vault eliminates the need for such a wait, since the attorney's vault will not be frozen. Other than that, there is no advantage except convenience in having the lawyer keep it.

Some attorneys advise executing duplicate originals of wills, while others advise having only one original with all others being conformed copies. The latter course seems best, since having only one executed original will lessen the potential confusion if a deceitful person gets hold of and alters one of the duplicate originals. Even if the sole original is lost, there are methods in every state to prove the validity of a lost will, so having more than one original to protect against loss is not a compelling argument. The sole original should just be very carefully protected. There can then be as many copies for reference as the testator wishes, each one conformed to show date, signature, and witnesses, and none of those will have any claim of being the actual original.

Testamentary Capacity and Will Contests

To execute a valid will, not only must the statutory formalities be observed, but also the testator must possess the legal ability (called **capacity**) to make a will. Without such capacity, the state simply says that the writer does not have any legal power to make a will. The area of testamentary capacity is the source of **will contests,** which are lawsuits challenging the validity of all or part of a will. Only rarely do contests challenge the correct performance of the formalities required for executing a will, especially if the execution was supervised by an attorney. Most will contests allege that a testator did not possess the required testamentary capacity.

Elements Of Testamentary Capacity

One element of such capacity is **age.** The minimum age to execute a will is usually either eighteen or twenty-one, depending upon the state. In these days of wealthy rock musicians, athletes, and other well-off young people, the age limit seems a bit old fashioned, but that's the way it is.

Another element of testamentary capacity is **mental capacity,** often called being "of sound mind." It is much easier to satisfy this requirement than most people think. For one thing, the necessary capacity needs to exist only as of the time the will is made, it being irrelevant if the testator might have been of unsound mind at a time either earlier than or later than the making of the will. A person under psychiatric treatment, or even institutionalized for treatment of mental illness, can be capable of possessing testamentary capacity if the illness does not affect the legal requirements for such capacity. These generally require only that the testator remember and comprehend his relatives, remember and comprehend his property, and be able to understand the nature of the act of making a will. It is clear that a person could be mentally ill and under treatment for disabilities not at all affecting those particular capabilities. For these reasons, lawyers are often forced to discourage potential contestants who think they can successfully overturn old Uncle Elmer's will just because he was a bit batty.

A further element of testamentary capacity is that the testator must be **free from fraud, menace, duress,** or **undue influence** when he composes and executes his will. A will might be made due to fraud if someone had made a misrepresentation to the testator with the intent to induce him to make a will, and if the will or some part of it was a direct result of the fraud. A classic example is that of the marital adventurer, who goes around purporting to marry wealthy widows or widowers in order to benefit from their wills, often when he or she has not bothered to procure divorces from several earlier victims. A will might be made under undue influence if another person were in some sort of confidential relationship to the testator, the confidant then took some active part in getting the will made, and in the end, the confidant profited unduly from the will. An example might be the elderly lady who had three children, two of whom had predeceased her, who is pressured by her surviving child to re-write her will leaving everything to him instead of one-third shares to her grandchildren from the predeceased children.

A testator in his will often states that he is "of sound mind," and free from fraud or undue influence. However, that is a mere self-serving statement and will not protect the testator if the true facts reveal the opposite. Therefore such language might just as well be omitted.

Will contests are classic opportunities for jury trials, as juries might be swayed by various tales of woe. Perhaps forty or fifty percent of such cases yield favorable jury verdicts to the contestants, but such verdicts are invariably appealed, and only a very small percentage of the victories are upheld on appeal. There are therefore very long odds on ultimately being successful in a will contest which, when coupled with the relative ease with which testators may possess testamentary capacity, makes a will contest an extremely long shot indeed.

No Contest Clauses

Many wills contain clauses to the effect that if anyone even brings a contest against the will, the testator bequeaths to such person the sum of one dollar, and no more. The theory of these **no contest clauses** is that they will discourage a potential troublemaker by convincing him that even if he wins the contest, he will only get one dollar; however, their true effect is considerably less than that. Some states allow these clauses to be effective, while others don't. Where valid, such a clause only discourages a contestant if two conditions are met: he is a beneficiary named in the will, and he loses the contest. Then and only then will the clause operate to deny him the inheritance specified in the will and give him one dollar instead. If he wins the contest, then the entire will including the no contest clause is invalid, and so its punishment can never occur. But any person not a beneficiary under the will takes nothing from it anyway and so has nothing to lose by bringing a contest. Note that a will contest only helps someone who stands to inherit under the intestacy laws, for only such persons receive anything if the will is voided by a successful contest. So, such clauses offer protection only under specified circumstances, but they are otherwise harmless and usually used in wills written in states which permit the clauses.

Codicils and Revocation

A will may be changed as often as the testator wishes, usually by a simple document known as a **codicil,** which is an amendment to an existing will. A codicil is executed with all the same formalities as are required of a will, and in states where holographic documents are permitted, a holographic codicil may amend a formal will and vice versa, since both types are of equal legal validity.

When Should You Use A Codicil And When Should You Rewrite Your Will

A testator often wonders whether he should rewrite his entire will, or just make a change by codicil. Good judgment should control the decision, with the general feeling being that only simple and minor changes should be made by codicil. When there get to be too many codicils, simple good housekeeping would recommend that the entire will be rewritten instead. The goal to be achieved is one of clarity, for things will be confusing enough without the testator being there to explain what it was that he really meant or wanted. It seems foolish to confuse things any further by a codicil which makes too major a change, or by a series of codicils which make reading the documents overly difficult. If in doubt, it's probably a good idea to rewrite the entire will.

Revocation

A new will automatically **revokes** all prior, inconsistent wills. Since you wouldn't be writing a new will unless there was something inconsistent you wanted to provide, normally any will is revoked by a subsequent will. Although wills often recite that they revoke all prior wills and codicils, that really is not necessary. However, revoking a will revokes its codicils, but revoking a codicil does not revoke the will.

Aside from a subsequent will, other ways to revoke a will are by acts done to the document itself. Such acts include burning it up, tearing it up, defacing it, and other similar things. Although one can revoke a portion of a will by scratching out the offending portion, one cannot provide a substitute direction by merely writing it in. All testamentary statements must be made in properly executed wills, so such written-in changes (called interlineations) do not qualify because they were not witnessed and done with all the other proper formalities. They also do not qualify as holographic codicils because they aren't dated and signed, and the document is not "entirely" in the testator's own handwriting. In short, a change can only be made by a properly executed codicil or by a new will.

It is possible to revive a will which has been previously revoked. Most states only allow this to be done by a written document which expressly declares the testator's intention to revive a formerly revoked will. The document reviving a will must be executed with all the same formalities required of a will itself.

Which Will Governs?

It is clear that only the testator's "last" will is the one which will be operative. If several wills are offered for probate, only the one last in time will be accepted because all former ones are automatically revoked by their successsors. It is better practice to destroy any former wills after a subsequent one has been executed in order to avoid any potential parade of wills with different dates, or any allegations that older wills had been revived.

What a Will Contains

As to what should go into a will and how it should be written, the short answer is to consult an attorney, tell him what you desire, and leave it to him to write it properly. But over and above the short answer, it is useful to know what can and can not be accomplished by a will.

There is a lot of unnecessary language historically found in wills that is not really required. The title "Last Will and Testament" is one; the only effective will is the last one written, and it doesn't help to say so. A will and a testament in olde England disposed of different kinds of property, and the two documents were often combined into one; since the distinction no longer applies, the title "Will" is sufficient. I've mentioned a few other unnecessaries earlier; it doesn't help to declare that you are of sound mind and free from fraud or undue influence, and it is not necessary to specifically revoke earlier wills and codicils. Many wills contain directions to pay the decedent's "just debts and funeral expenses as soon as can conveniently be done"; since this is the obligation of the executor in any case, it is unnecessary to state it. Statements as to the character of the testator's property (such as, in a community property state, that it is all community property) are superfluous, since the will is a mere self-serving declaration and can not change the actual facts. Therefore, many modern wills omit all types of statements just mentioned and keep the language as short and simple as possible.

Wills can be as unique and even as humorous as the testator wishes; there is no law against originality, cynicism, or satire. The well-known German poet Heinrich Heine left all of his property to his wife on the condition that she remarry, "Because then there will be at least one man to regret my death." One testator said "To my wife (who is no damned good) I leave $1." A rather wealthy individual left the following will: "To my wife I leave her lover, and the knowledge that I wasn't the fool she thought I was. To my son, I leave the pleasure of earning a living. For twenty-five years he thought the pleasure was mine. He was mistaken. To my daughter, I leave $100,000. She will need it. The only good piece of business her husband ever did was to marry her. To my valet, I leave the clothes he has been stealing from me regularly for ten years, also the fur coat he wore last winter while I was in Palm Beach. To my chauffeur, I leave my cars. He almost ruined them, and I want him to have the satisfaction of finishing the job. To my partner, I leave the suggestion that he take some other clever man in with him at once if he expects to do any business."

One well-known industrialist wrote a lengthy will, entirely in his own language, disposing of a large fortune—with the approval and assistance of his lawyer. He started out by saying that he was of sound mind, and went on, "Some lawyers will question this when they read my Will; however, I have my opinion of some of them, so that makes it even." So do not hesitate to express your own personality, views, or comments in your will, even though this is probably not done enough. Not only is it pleasing to leave a personal message, but also it is likely to be of helpful psychological assistance to those you leave behind.

If You Want To Leave Out Your Spouse Or Children

In most states, a testator is not required to leave any property to his spouse or children and may **disinherit** any or all of them so long as the omission is intentional. As to a spouse, the ability to disinherit applies only to that amount of the marital property which the decedent can control by his will. In a common law state, a decedent spouse can not defeat the legally granted statutory share of the surviving spouse (often archaically called dower or curtesy), but is not bound to leave the survivor any amount in excess thereof. In a community property state, the decedent spouse can of course do nothing by will to defeat or infringe on the surviving spouse's ownership rights in one-half of their community property.

If an omission appears to be unintentional, most laws protect spouses and minor children by granting them a percentage of the estate. If one intends a disinheritance of a spouse or child it is advisable to say so specifically, sometimes softening the impact by adding, "Since they are already well provided for," or some such phrase. The statutory percentage for an unintentionally omitted spouse makes it necessary to rewrite your will if you remarry, for if never done, the new spouse will qualify as unintentionally omitted and will receive a percentage share, often contrary to the real wishes of the testator.

How To Describe Property

It is usually inadvisable to list all of your property in your will because that would necessitate a codicil every time you changed an asset by sale or reinvestment. Specific items need only be mentioned if you want to make a specific gift of that item. And in many states it no longer matters whether such gifts are called **bequests, devises, legacies,** or just plain **gifts.** Historically, legacies were of cash, bequests passed personal property, and devises passed real estate, but those distinctions hardly matter any more.

Residuary Clause

Most well-drawn wills contain a **residuary clause,** in which the testator states the disposition of "all the rest, residue, and remainder" of his propery which is left over after all specific gifts have been made. It is usually the major gift in the will and disposes of all remaining property, whatever it may be comprised of as of the date of death. The residuary clause also takes care of any specific gifts which may lapse for one reason or another, usually because the testator says they should if the designated recipient predeceases him. The residuary clause is thus the testator's main protection and final wrap-up.

Life Estates and Remainders

A testator (and also the donor of a lifetime gift) has a good deal of power to control the future ownership of his property. Property owners can place time limitations on the ownership or use of property which they give away, sell, or bequeath. Those time limitations govern both the commencement and duration of future interests in their property. This is equally true for personal property as well as real estate. You should be sure that you fully understand the material which follows, because it will continue to be important for the balance of this book, and because it is a key concept around which estate planning benefits principally revolve.

If a person owns property outright and without any time limitations applicable to his full ownership of that property, it is called owning in **fee simple.** The owner is said to have the fee, and although the term technically applies only to real estate, the identical concept also applies to personal property. A fee owner may do anything he wishes with his property, including giving it away, selling it, or bequeathing it in his will. I will focus on bequeathing it by will, but you should remember that the owner can also do the things we will be discussing during his life, such as by gift or sale.

A fee owner may specify in his will that an heir is to have only a temporary ownership interest in the property during which time the heir would have the right to use, possess, and take the income from the property. The time period may be defined by common time frames such as a week, a month, a year, or a number of years (which is all that a lease is if done during life for installment payments, which we call rent). Or the time period may be defined by somebody's lifetime—anybody's life, so long as that person can be located, for then the lifetime is simply the measuring stick for the temporary interest. Most often the measuring life is that of the person who receives the temporary interest, in which case it is called a **life estate.**

The fee owner has the further right to specify who will get the property after the temporary interest has run its course. If the fee owner were still alive, he could specify that the property should come back to him, in which case the interest following the temporary one is called a **reversion.** Or, he could specify that the property should go on to someone else. The owner could create further temporary interests. (However, he can't keep doing this for an unlimited time; the Rule Against Perpetuities limits his power in this regard, and we shall discuss that rule at page 108.) Or the owner could specify that after one or more temporary interests have run their course, someone shall be entitled to the final outright fee simple interest, in which case the final interest following the temporary ones is called a **remainder.** The person who owns the life estate is called the **life tenant,** and the person who will be entitled to the remainder is called the **remainderman.** The terms life estate, life tenant, remainder, and remainderman should be thoroughly understood and should become a part of your vocabulary.

Included in the power of the fee owner is the power to make these future interests **vested** (certain to arise) or **contingent.** Contingent interests have often been used to impose some family, social, or religious condition, such as, "My daughter gets the remainder only if she marries," or "To my son so long as liquor is never consumed on the premises." Such restrictions have traditionally been well within the legal power of the fee owner, but in recent decades the Supreme Court has struck down racial restrictions upon the use or ownership of property as being inconsistent with modern society.

Life estates, remainders, and reversions are property, just as much as anything else one owns. Vested ones can be sold, mortgaged, given away, and, except for life estates (which automatically expire on the life tenant's death), bequeathed or inherited. They can be levied on by creditors, and they pass into a bankrupt's estate for the benefit of his creditors. This is all true even if a person does not yet have the present possession of the property, but only has a present and vested right to a future interest.

These interests can be very valuable, although a contingent one cannot be assigned any monetary value because no one knows whether the contingency will or will not occur. But the value of a vested remainder can be easily determined, depending upon the terms of any prior temporary interest and, usually, the age of the life tenant. How would you like to own the vested remainder interest to all the rents from a forty-story office building after the death of a life tenant who is now ninety-years-old? There are tables to value life estates and remainders, based upon the present discounted value of the right to get something after a person of a certain age and sex dies. Those tables combine mortality tables for males and females with interest factors under current conditions. For one life estate and one remainder, the sum of the factors for each will always equal one hundred percent, and there are also tables for more complex situations. Obviously, the remainder in the office building mentioned above will be very valuable due to the advanced age of the life tenant, whereas if the life tenant was thirteen, you would have a long time to wait and so the valuation would be very low (although the life tenant's interest would be valued very high). Some examples taken from the tables are shown in Table 4-1.

Life estates and remainders are very common things. When a testator tells his attorney that he wants his wife to live in his house for the rest of her life and thereafter he wants his daughter to have the house, he is really saying life estate and remainder, and his will will be drawn in precisely that form. But except for simple situations like the family home, life estates and remainders are tremendously cumbersome in our modern economy. The reason is that both the life tenant and the remainderman have certain rights, and neither can do anything to infringe on the rights of the other; the hundreds of legal rules about that effectively make a pure life estate an unworkable and unrecommended device. Instead, if the life estate concept is what a testator wants, he will al-

TABLE 4—1.

PRESENT WORTH OF A LIFE ESTATE AND A REMAINDER. MULTIPLY VALUE OF PROPERTY BY PERCENTAGE FIGURES LISTED.

Sex of Life Tenant:	MALES		FEMALES	
Age of Life Tenant	Life Estate	Remainder	Life Estate	Remainder
10 years	.94598	.05402	.96365	.02890
15	.93069	.06931	.95314	.04686
20	.91403	.08597	.94021	.05979
25	.89445	.10555	.92375	.07625
30	.86750	.13250	.90259	.09741
35	.83255	.16745	.87593	.12407
40	.78923	.21077	.84281	.15719
45	.73808	.26192	.80269	.19731
50	.67997	.32003	.75476	.24524
55	.61776	.38224	.69859	.30141
60	.55052	.44948	.63226	.36774
65	.48212	.51788	.55803	.44197
70	.41294	.58706	.47540	.52460
75	.34194	.65806	.38833	.61167
80	.27098	.72902	.30177	.69883
85	.21070	.78930	.22441	.77559
90	.15922	.84078	.16241	.83759
95	.12535	.87465	.12535	.87465
100	.10087	.89913	.10087	.89913

most always be advised to create a trust and to give his heirs life interests and remainder interests in the trust.

Creating a Trust By Will

For the reason just mentioned many testators will want to create a **trust,** which is a device whereby a designated person, called the **trustee,** manages and invests the property placed into the trust for the benefit of persons, called **beneficiaries,** who have life interests and remainder interests in the trust itself. A trust can be created while the property owner is still alive, or it can be created in his will. If the latter, all the terms and conditions of the trust are contained in the owner's will, and it is called **testamentary trust** because it is established in the owner's testament. In this case, the trust does not come into existence until after the property owner dies.

Trusts have many tax advantages as well as practical advantages, and they are a vital part of estate planning. Chapter six will be devoted to them, so further discussion will be put off until then. What you need to be aware of at this point is that a person's will can contain all the terms and conditions of a trust which he wishes to put into effect following his death.

Administrative Clauses

Following the dispositions of all the testator's property, either by outright gift or in trust, various administrative clauses are found. If a trust is used, the trustee and perhaps several alternate trustees will be named, and their administrative powers will be granted. A clause with great significance is one which directs whether each gift in the will should bear its own percentage portion of death taxes, or whether all taxes should be paid out of the estate without charging each beneficiary for his or her share. If the latter, the effect is that specific gifts are tax-free (that is, free of death taxes; inheritances are not taxable income), and the people who inherit the residue in effect pay all the taxes. Each testator must decide which tax result he desires.

Most states have statutes addressing the problem of who is deemed to survive whom if two people die together under circumstances where there is no way to know. In a will, a clause may be drafted to alter the statutory formula and to state who is deemed to survive whom. This may be very important, both for practical purposes, and also because certain beneficial tax results will only occur if one person (usually a spouse) survives the other. Where qualifying for the marital deduction is important (see page 231), it is usually advisable to have the will create the presumption that the spouse who does not own the bulk of the marital property survives the one who does.

The will also names the person charged with managing the estate during probate, called the **executor**. Naming one or more alternate executors is advisable, in case the primary nominee either can not or does not want to serve. An executor can be either an individual, including any of the beneficiaries themselves, or the trust department of a bank.

Appointment of Executors, Attorneys, and Guardians

The Choice Between An Individual And A Bank

Whether to name an individual or a bank is often the subject of much discussion, but the choice always boils down to the personal decision of a given testator in the light of his particular circumstances. There are literally scores of arguments in favor of banks and just as many in favor of individuals. You might want to correlate what we say here about that choice with all the material in the balance of this book concerning the frightening complexities added to the executor's job by the 1976 Tax Reform Act. Those complexities may now more strongly encourage the use of a professional executor than was formerly the case. Over and above such matters, the general advantages cited for banks include personnel professionally trained for the task, the fact that banks never die or go on vacation, and highly efficient (often computerized) record keeping services which make estate accountings a snap. Among disadvantages cited for banks are the inevitability of their charging a fee, impersonal treatment of the testator's family, and management conservatism bordering on stodginess. Some advantages cited for individuals are greater personal attention and empathy for the testator's family, the likelihood that a family member will waive the executor's fee, and perhaps greater expertise in managing a particular asset comprising a large part of a given estate. Disadvantages of individuals include the facts that they do die, get sick, or go on vacation; that they possess less training in both managing assets and handling the often complex record keeping required; and that it may be unwise or unfair to saddle them with the responsibilities involved. And then the counter arguments begin: If an individual is appointed executor, the estate's attorney often does all the work anyway, so why not try to save the executor's fee by naming an individual who will waive that fee; banks realistically must be more standardized and less individualistic in their handling of an estate in view of the large number of estates they are handling at any one time. The arguments are endless, and this book takes no position one way or the other because the decision must be personalized for each situation. Perhaps none of the above arguments apply to a particular bank in your city or to a particular individual you may have in mind; perhaps all of them will apply.

What About Co-Executors?

Co-executors are a possibility, but you must consider that if two executors are named, you are setting up the distinct possibility of a stalemate which might be solved only by appealing to the probate court. Too often testators avoid the hard choice between an individual and a bank by naming one of each to serve as co-executors, but this method of avoiding a difficult decision may be unwise. Often the conflict in methods between an individual and a bank as co-executors may prove so disruptive to the smooth functioning of a probate that the estate would have been far better off had the testator chosen a sole executor of either type.

If an individual is named, most states will allow the testator to **waive the bond** which will otherwise be required as security for the faithful performance of the executor's duties. Such a bond means that a bonding company will make up any loss caused by a negligent or criminal executor. Assuming confidence in the executor, it is usually a good idea to waive the bond, as it saves the expense of annual bond premiums. However, no bond is required of a bank, as they possess sufficient assets to protect an estate even in the unlikely event of a loss.

The Estate's Attorney

Some wills contain clauses purporting to nominate the attorney who drew the will to be attorney for the estate. And many people believe that the attorney who drew the will must be appointed as the estate's attorney. Although many lawyers will probably not appreciate this information being revealed, that is not required, and in many states such clauses will be completely ignored. "Attorney for the estate" is really a misnomer anyway, for it is the executor who needs a lawyer, and like every other client, he is entitled to choose his own lawyer. Common sense may well dictate that the testator's lawyer ought to be employed, particularly if he served the testator for many years and has thorough knowledge of the testator's affairs. But it is strictly up to the executor.

Some executors may toy with the idea of acting as their own attorney. This is quite permissible, but the danger of it in the complicated legal jungle that is probate will be indicated in the next chapter. Most attorneys feel that probate is the last field in the world where anyone should attempt to act as his own attorney.

Many people are annoyed because a bank, if named to be executor, will in most cities "return the favor" by naming the lawyer who drew the will to be its attorney for probate purposes. But that practice is not necessarily open to criticism. Banks do not use their own legal staffs when probating an estate for which they have been named executor, and so they must choose some attorney to represent them. As stated, there is perfectly good logic for the choice of the testator's own attorney. The only criticism would be if the attorney who drafted the will influenced the testator to name a bank as executor rather than the testator's real preference for an individual, for the sole reason that the bank would later name that lawyer as the probate attorney (thus insuring the probate attorney's fee). It is clearly unethical for a lawyer to influence a client out of the lawyer's personal financial motive. On the other hand, it is proper for an attorney to comment impartially on his client's reasoning in choosing an executor of one type versus the other.

Naming Guardians For Minor Children Is Crucial

In an additional extremely important clause, most states will allow a testator to name a **guardian** for any of his minor children. A surviving parent of minor children will automatically be their natural guardian (even if the parents were divorced and the parent with child custody dies), so that a nomination of a guardian takes effect only in the event of a common disaster, or upon the death of the second parent. It is obvious that for parents, this is one of the most vital things that can be done in a will and is the major reason for young marrieds to have a will even if they have yet to accumulate any significant amount of property.

Most states do not attempt to dictate who the parents may choose as guardian, and so the parent's best judgment can be utilized. There are really two aspects to guardianships, control over any inheritance coming to the minor from his parents' will and control over the person of the minor (the parent substitute function). These functions can be split between two different appointees, and while the property function leads to the choice of a capable property manager, the parent substitute function is even more vitally important to the welfare of the children. If no guardian is named by will, a court will usually resort to the closest blood relative satisfactory to the court, but this might be the very person you do not want for that function. Often, close friends will be the best choice, and so a will must be used to avoid the court appointment of the wrong person. Some parents with particularly strong feelings even go so far as to state who they do not in any circumstances want as guardians.

One further word. It is a gross injustice to all concerned to name guardians without first consulting them. Although one can resign from an unwanted guardianship, feelings of guilt or responsibility will often prevent the nominee from resigning even though he would really prefer to do so. It isn't wise to put anyone in that spot, and since the only real concern is the welfare of the children involved, their best interests cannot possibly be served by thrusting them into the care of unwilling guardians.

APPLICATION

1. For goodness sake, reread your will to see whether you are still satisfied with it. Get in the habit of doing so every year or two. Get a codicil made to effect simple changes.

2. Determine whether one or all of the witnesses may have died or can no longer be located and whether a simple codicil with new witnesses, or even a new will, is advisable.

3. If the circumstances surrounding the making of your will could even appear to an unfriendly outsider that you were subject to undue influence, fraud, or duress, or were of "unsound mind" at the time you wrote it, consider executing a new will under more favorable circumstances.

4. If you have married or remarried and have not made a new will or codicil dated after the marriage, consider doing so at once in order to avoid allegations that your spouse was unintentionally omitted. Similarly, if a child has been born or adopted who is not either specifically or generally ("to my children") mentioned, consider a codicil or new will to mention that child in whatever way you want.

5. Are you still satisfied with your choice of executor, trustee, or guardian? Ask yourself this question again after you have completed this book, in light of all the new burdens of the 1976 Tax Reform Act.

6. Be certain that you understand life estates and remainders, and the definition of a life tenant and a remainderman. These concepts will continually reoccur throughout this book, and you will be missing a lot of the impact which estate planning can make if you do not have a good grasp of these concepts.

5
probate: that hateful thing examined

Glossary For This Chapter
Accounting
Administration
Administrator
Alternate Valuation Date
Bond
Chancery Court
Creditor's Claim
Deficiency
Election
Family Allowance
Fiscal Year
Homestead
Income
Letters Testamentary
Notice to Creditors
Orphan's Court
Personal Representative
Preliminary Distribution
Probate
Probate Court
Surrogate Court
Uniform Probate Code

Probate is a subject which infuriates a great many people. Because of that deep-seated public sentiment, many insist that the greatest estate planning achievement is avoiding probate. Due to that prevailing attitude, it is important to rationally discuss the reasons why probate exists, the disadvantages and even possible advantages of it, and above all to analyze its costs. You can then have a basis for determining whether there is any value being received for the costs and inconveniences incurred.

Probate is that period of time following a person's death when certain portions of his estate are administered under the supervision of a court. That administration will continue until all the various obligations the law imposes on an estate have been satisfied, at which time the probate will be terminated and the estate distributed to the decedent's heirs. The term probate comes from an old French word meaning "to prove," and originally probate examined the decedent's will to prove only that it was duly executed and was indeed the last document so executed. If so, the will was "admitted to probate." The modern functions go far beyond that, and the period of time is more properly called the period of **administration** of a decedent's estate.

Probate matters are usually handled in a particular department of any state's normal trial court. This is more for convenience than anything else, and usually that court has no different jurisdiction or powers than any other state trial court. Even though there is no specially constituted court for these matters, the place where the particular judge sits who is handling probate matters is popularly called the probate court. Different states have different names for that place; some call it probate court; some, surrogate court; some, orphan's court; and some, chancery court.

During the period of administration, a **personal representative** of the decedent is needed to manage the decedent's affairs and attend to his post-death obligations under supervision of the court. The decedent in his will may appoint such person, in which case he is termed an **executor** (**executrix** if female). If no executor was named, either because there was no will or because all the persons named in the will can not or will not serve, then the court will appoint the personal representative and he will be referred to as the **administrator** (female: **administratrix**).

Why Probate Continues to Exist

Most people probably think that probate is unnecessary and serves no useful function. Or at least that, since it is so universally despised, it ought to be abolished. But to understand probate, you must remember one basic fact: the United States is a capitalistic, creditor-oriented economy. Many provisions of our laws are designed to protect creditors, who enable our type of economy to function. If the law failed to grant creditors reasonably adequate protection for their business risks, our economy as we know it would surely grind to a halt. You have probably heard of *caveat emptor* ("let the buyer beware"); can you imagine *caveat creditor*? The most basic justification for probate in our modern legal system is that it gives creditors the opportunity to present their claims against a decedent's estate and to have those claims fairly determined and then paid. Chaos would surely result if there were no probate system to enable the post-mortem collection of debts by everyday business creditors (such as retail charge accounts, bank credit cards, oil company charge cards, utility companies, finance institutions, and many others). Every creditor would demand medical examinations of every applicant for credit, no one with grey hair would get credit, and probably no credit would be extended to anyone older than about thirty-seven years of age!

Although that is the key reason why no legislature even considers abolishing probate, the process does have several other functions. It determines the last will or lack thereof, and if there is a will, it ensures that the decedent's wishes are followed. Since reasonable people can and do differ, it provides a forum where, within a reasonable period of time, any disputes which might arise can be resolved, after which the decedent's heirs will no longer be bothered. And in a most important function, it provides a court order on which institutions may rely in transferring legal title to heirs. The latter is often the reason why a family estate with no other conceivable problems must nevertheless be probated. After all, if your father died and you knew you were his sole heir, no bank would cheerfully hand over all his money to you just because you stroll into the bank one day and tell them that your father died. Neither will a stock transfer agent reissue all your father's stock in your name upon your mere say-so, nor will a title company blithely transfer real estate title to someone you sell to if your father's name still stands of record as the owner. The probate court's decree of final distribution is the document necessary to convince all such institutions that you are now entitled to be treated as the legal owner.

Probate Expenses

There are certain expenses of maintaining probate, and these costs are what anger so many people. But assuming that probate is either socially desirable or necessary (which is our present legal policy) and further assuming that in our society some expenses are justifiable to pay those who perform the required functions, the major issues are the amount of those costs and deciding who should rightfully bear them.

Who Pays The Costs And Why

On the latter point, the current policy is to have the decedent's estate pay them, thus reducing the inheritances of the various heirs and effectively passing on the costs to them. Whether payment by the heirs is the equitable solution is open to differences of opinion, but that is the current law. After all, the heirs are now receiving a "windfall" in acquiring property that they neither earned nor, before the decedent's death, had any legal right to, and so the legislatures have little sympathy if those heirs bear the costs of transferring such property to themselves.

No alternatives seem feasible. You might argue that since the state requires probate, it should pay, but in these times of strangled state budgets and high taxes to fund current programs, political and budgetary reality tells us that this will never happen. You might then argue that since probate benefits creditors, they should pay. However, unsolvable administrative nightmares and inequities prevent any such solution. Consider this inequity: the sole creditor with a five-hundred-dollar claim in A's one-million-dollar estate pays all the probate costs, but in B's one-hundred-thousand-dollar estate, eight creditors with ten-thousand-dollar claims each divide the considerably lower costs of that estate. Obviously A's creditor will decline to present his claim, thereby forfeiting his rightful five hundred dollars and leaving no one to pay for A's probate. Such a system would be unworkable and inequitable. Better, say the legislatures with considerable logic, that the "windfall" recipients pay.

What The Probate Costs Are

Consider now the amount of the probate costs. Although there are several minor charges, the biggest elements (usually over 90% of most probate expenses) are really only two. One is the **fee to the personal representative** to pay him for his efforts in managing the decedent's affairs. The other is the **fee to the personal representative's attorney,** paying him for his legal services to the estate. Since most would agree that in our society workers should be paid for work done, the vital issue is simply the fairness of their compensation.

In an attempt to provide fair compensation while at the same time preventing anyone from gouging estates by charging unreasonable fees, many states set the amount of the fees by statute. These fees are usually based on a percentage of the value of the estate, on the logical theory that the more valuable the estate, the more work will have to be performed on it. In order for there to be a state-wide standard, the fees must be in arbitrary amounts. Inevitably, in some estates those paid earn more per hour of time spent than do others, and sometimes they even "lose" money based upon how they usually value their time. Conversely, estates may pay "too much" in one instance, and "too little" in another. Any arbitrary standard utilizes an average point, and inevitably that exact average point is hardly ever hit right on the nose. Unfortunately for clarity and the ease of understanding, the fees set by the fifty states vary widely. Table 5-1 shows what the statutes of each state say about the amount of the personal representative's fee in that state. But that table is only a basic introduction and guide to the fee structure in your particular state. Not only will these fees change as inflation increases, but also the statements in the table do not begin to tell the complete story. For instance, even though some twenty-two states say something along the lines of "reasonable compensation," the fact is that in most of those states the reasonable fee is determined by local custom and is quite stan-

TABLE 5–1.
STATUTORY STATEMENTS IN 50 STATES PLUS DISTRICT OF COLUMBIA AS TO COMMISSIONS OF THE PERSONAL REPRESENTATIVE. CAUTION: STATUTES CHANGE OVER TIME. ALSO, MANY STATES PROVIDING "REASONABLE COMPENSATION" IN PRACTICE FOLLOW CUSTOMARY AMOUNTS WITHIN A GIVEN COUNTY OR IN THE ENTIRE STATE AS A WHOLE; LOCAL ADVICE MUST BE SOUGHT.

Alabama	Just and fair, not exceeding 2½% on receipts and 2½% on disbursements.
Alaska	Reasonable compensation.
Arizona	Reasonable compensation.
Arkansas	On personal property: 10% of the first $1000, 5% of the next $4000, 3% of the balance. On real estate: as the court may allow if substantial services performed.
California	On entire estate accounted for, plus income: 4% of the first $15,000, 3% of the next $85,000, 2% of the next $900,000, and 1% of the balance over $1,000,000.
Colorado	Reasonable compensation.
Connecticut	As claimed if found to be reasonable. In practice, a fixed percentage of the gross asset value.
Delaware	Set by rule of court.
District of Columbia	Fixed by probate court within limits of 1% to 10% of the inventory value.
Florida	Reasonable compensation.
Georgia	2½% on money received and 2½% on money paid out. On property delivered in kind, court may allow reasonable fee up to 3%.
Hawaii	Reasonable compensation.
Idaho	Reasonable compensation.
Illinois	Reasonable compensation.
Indiana	Just and reasonable compensation.
Iowa	Reasonable compensation not in excess of 6% of the first $1000, 4% of the next $4000, and 2% of the excess.
Kansas	Reasonable compensation.
Kentucky	May not exceed 5% of personal assets and 5% of income. For services regarding real estate and taxes, reasonable compensation as determined by the court.
Louisiana	2½% of inventory value.

TABLE 5-1 *(continued)*

Maine	Not exceeding 5% on the amount of the personal assets.
Maryland	Not to exceed 10% on the first $20,000 and 4% on the balance, excluding real estate but not excluding the income thereon. Up to 10% on real estate sold by the executor.
Massachusetts	As the court may allow. No set rate, but the following are customarily considered not unreasonable: 2½% to 3% of the personal estate up to $500,000, and 1% of the balance.
Michigan	5% of the first $1000, 2½% of the next $4000, 2% on the balance over $5000.
Minnesota	Reasonable compensation.
Mississippi	In the discretion of the court, but not to exceed 7% of the entire estate.
Missouri	On value of personal property and real estate sold: 5% of first $5000, 4% of next $20,000, 3% of next $75,000, 2¾% of next $300,000, 2½% of next $600,000, and 2% of excess over $1,000,000.
Montana	3% of first $40,000 and 2% on the excess over $40,000.
Nebraska	Reasonable compensation.
Nevada	On personal estate: 6% on the first $1000, 4% on the next $4,000, and 2% on the excess over $5,000. Sales, and services concerning real estate and estate management, are extraordinary services.
New Hampshire	Executor's claim on his accounting is allowed if reasonable.
New Jersey	On estate including real estate: 5% on first $100,000, and not to exceed 5% on the excess. 6% on income. Up to 1% more for each additional executor.
New Mexico	Reasonable compensation.
New York	4% of the first $25,000, 3½% of the next $125,000, 3% of the next $150,000, and 2% on the excess over $300,000. Where executor required to collect rents and manage property, one fee of 5% of gross rents. If multiple executors: on estate over $200,000 up to three full fees; on estate between $100,000 and $200,000, up to two full fees; on estate under $100,000, only one fee.
North Carolina	In discretion of court, not exceeding 5% of receipts and expenditures.
North Dakota	Reasonable compensation.

TABLE 5-1 (continued)

Ohio	On the personal property, income, and proceeds of real estate sold: 6% of first $1000, 4% of next $4,000, and 2% on balance over $5,000. 1% on real estate not sold and on non-probate property reportable for tax purposes.
Oklahoma	On entire estate: 5% of first $1,000, 4% of next $4,000, and 2½% on excess over $5,000.
Oregon	On all probate property plus income and realized gains: 7% of first $1,000, 4% of next $9,000, 3% of next $40,000, 2% on excess above $50,000. 1% on non-probate property, except life insurance proceeds, reportable for tax purposes.
Pennsylvania	No statutory fee, depends upon services performed. In practice, 5% on both principal and income in small estates, 3% in large ones, but no dividing line between small and large.
Rhode Island	In the discretion of the court.
South Carolina	2½% on appraised value of the personal assets received and paid out.
South Dakota	On assets including real estate sold: 5% of first $1,000, 4% of next $4,000, 2½% of excess over $5,000. Just compensation for real estate not sold.
Tennessee	Reasonable compensation.
Texas	5% on all sums received in cash and 5% on all sums paid in cash; never more than 5% of the gross value of the estate.
Utah	5% of first $1,000, 4% of next $4,000, 3% of next $5,000, 2% of next $40,000, 1½% of next $50,000, and 1% on excess over $100,000.
Vermont	$4 per day; more if unusually difficult administration or unusual responsibility assumed.
Virginia	Reasonable compensation, usually 5%, but may be reduced or increased depending upon performance.
Washington	What the court deems just and reasonable.
West Virginia	Reasonable compensation, usually 5% on receipts.
Wisconsin	2% of inventory value less mortgages or liens, plus corpus gains.
Wyoming	10% of first $1,000, 5% of next $4,000, 3% of next $15,000, and 2% of excess over $20,000.

Source: *Martindale-Hubbell Law Directory*, Vol. VII, *Law Digests*. Martindale-Hubbell, Inc., 1978.

dard in a particular county or even over the whole state. Readers in those states will still have to find out what "reasonable" really means in their locale.

Even in those states where a definite percentage is indicated, an equally important question is: percentage of what? In some of those states the percentage is computed on real estate only if the property is sold during probate, in others there is a completely different percentage for real estate not sold during probate, and in some states the stated percentage applies to the entire estate including real estate. Where real estate is included, many states figure its value at the full fair market value and not on its net equity value (which would be full value less any existing mortgages). Although the estate's equity in the property might be low, the theory is that if the property is (for example) a seventy-seven-unit apartment house that just happens to be mortgaged to the hilt, nevertheless the representative is going to have to spend all the time necessary to oversee a seventy-seven-unit apartment house.

Another factor is that in many states, the fee is computed on the income received during probate, while in others the fee includes the amount of all funds paid out during probate. The final word is that, as with so many other things, you are simply going to have to ask local experts about what really occurs in your state.

To complicate matters still further, some states allow an individual representative the same fee as if a bank were the representative, others allow an individual only a portion thereof, and some only allow an individual his or her expenses while awarding the full fee to the bank. The states also differ regarding the fees of multiple executors. In some, if there are co-executors, the normal fee is not increased, and the executors must share the fee as they may agree. If they can't agree, then the probate judge will allocate the fee based upon the work performed by each of them. But in other states, naming co-executors will serve to increase the probate costs; some allow multiple executors two full fees, and others may go even higher than that (see the listing for New York in Table 5-1).

So far we have only been discussing the personal representative's fee and not the attorney's. But the **attorney's fee** is at least half of the costs of probate, and in some states it is considerably more than half. California, Iowa and Missouri require that the attorney's fee be the same as the personal representative's fee. Arkansas has a precentage schedule which is different than that for the personal representative, and in Montana the attorney gets one and a half times the representative's fee. In other states the statutes say only that the attorney's fee shall be "reasonable" or shall be approved by court, or else the statutes say nothing at all about attorney's fees. As a practical matter, though, custom and practice in a particular locale often provide a normal fee for probate attorneys. So on this subject, local information is even more necessary than for the representative's fee.

Where fee schedules are provided for either the representative or the attorney, the schedules are usually for **ordinary services** only. Those services are sometimes set out by statute, and they encompass most of the usual tasks required. However, if either the representative or the attorney perform **extraordinary services,** they are entitled to additional compensation. The amount of extraordinary compensation is within the jurisdiction of the probate judge and is usually determined at the time of final termination of the estate. In many states, the probate judges are very strict about allowing extraordinary fees, and they demand a full accounting showing that the services were necessary and that the requested compensation is reasonable. At that, many judges will still cut down the request somewhat in a general effort to save money for estates. Common examples of legitimate extraordinary services are attending to sales of estate property and making out the federal estate tax return if one is required.

The other expenses of probate are usually either court costs or fees paid to others who do work on and for the benefit of the estate. For instance, accountants may have to be employed, as may property appraisers. Some states appoint inheritance tax referees on a round robin basis, and they both appraise the estate and determine the state's inheritance tax. Some people think that the appraiser has an incentive to value estate assets as high as possible since his fee will be based on their values. But in reality, a typical referees's fee is only one-tenth of one percent of the asset values, so except in cases of huge assets there is only a few cents difference in his fee, and the appraisers do not appraise in a self-serving manner. Attorneys are generally quite grateful for this system, for nowhere else can they get appraisal services (which will be necessary in valuing the estate for federal estate tax purposes) as cheaply as one-tenth of one percent.

Methods of Saving Probate Costs

There are several potential methods of saving probate costs by reducing or eliminating one or both of the fees mentioned above. As in every other matter in American courts, the personal representative is free to represent himself and not hire a lawyer. However, probate is such an immensely technical area, with all kinds of statutory requirements to be fulfilled and notices to be given or published at statutory times, that it really seems foolish in the extreme for someone with an executor's responsibilities to risk wading through this legal jungle without the services of a trained attorney. One mistake can cost far more than the attorney's fee. Another method of cost saving is for the testator to get the potential executor or attorney to agree by contract that he will charge a certain amount less than the normal probate fee. In most states that is perfectly legal, and all you have to do is find a competent person who is willing to act under those conditions, usually not an easy thing to find.

A more feasible method is to name a good friend or a family member as executor, on either the hope or understanding that he will **waive the executor's fee.** If a beneficiary under the will is named executor, he will often be advised to waive his executor's fee. The reason is that the receipt of inheritances is not taxable income, whereas executor's fees are payment for services rendered and therefore are taxable income. So by taking the fee, an executor/beneficiary is turning an income tax free inheritance into taxable income to the extent of the fee, which is usually silly. But sometimes even that isn't so silly because the executor's fee is a deduction against the estate and inheritance taxes. If the estate tax bracket is considerably higher than the executor/beneficiary's own personal income tax bracket, there will be a net saving in taxes if the executor takes his fee.

If an attorney is asked to serve as executor, in many states the attorney is not allowed to represent himself and claim both the executor's and attorney's fee. He could hire another attorney to represent him, but to do so would be a gross waste of estate funds, which the probate judge would likely disallow. In states where attorneys can not claim both fees, naming an attorney as executor would be a potential manner of saving one-half of the probate expenses. Often however, many estate attorneys will not agree to this arrangement for the simple reason that they want to practice law and not become full-time executors; also, many commendably confess that they are not trained or skilled as executors.

Delay and Publicity

Aside from the cost factor, there are two other disadvantages of probate: delay and publicity. **Delay** is inherent—it protects creditors by allowing them sufficient time to present their claims. Without a reasonable time to do so, their protection would be a mere sham. The **publicity** factor is also inherently necessary and ties into the same protection for creditors because the creditors must receive some reasonable public notice that an estate exists before they can be expected to present claims. It is too much to expect that every creditor, particularly ones in far away locales, will in fact come to know of every probate. So the law does not require the impossible, puts some burden on the creditors to keep themselves informed, and simply requires what is known as "constructive notice." This usually takes the form of a posting of public notice at the courthouse and a publication for a certain period of time in a newspaper of general circulation. As a practical matter, most daily newspapers do not carry the scores of such notices required every day; rather, in most metropolitan areas, a special legal newspaper exists, the chief function of which is to carry all these notices. The general public may not even be aware of the existence of such papers, but all firms in the business of extending credit examine such papers carefully every day. With posting and publication, constructive notice is satisfied, and the fact that a given creditor may not actually receive notice will not delay the estate beyond normal time limits.

The public has other fears about the delay and publicity factors. While most people are not too terribly concerned about the delay imposed on distant relatives who may inherit, they are genuinely concerned about a surviving spouse and children. There is a largely irrational fear that these dependents will be left without financial support or a place to live while all the property plods through the probate process. This fear springs from a misunderstanding of the probate process, which is merely a time period requiring judicial supervision and not something that renders the estate's property unavailable for use or for the production of income. In almost every state, a surviving spouse and minor children are entitled to remain in the family home during probate, and often for as long as the lifetime of the surviving spouse (if the home is not otherwise bequeathed to him or her). They are also entitled to have a family allowance paid to them out of the assets of the estate, based upon the family's normal standard of living. These family rights are usually superior to the rights of most creditors, who may only make claims on whatever property is left after these rights have been satisfied. As for other heirs, they will indeed have to wait, as it is more important that creditors be enabled to satisfy their just claims than to give more distant relatives a quick inheritance.

Since probate files are a public record, people who have either a rational or irrational need to assure secrecy for their estates may well wish to avoid probate for this reason alone. But it turns out that strangers do not make a practice of snooping through probate files, so that everyone's automatic reaction of assuring their own privacy is hardly ever threatened in reality by probate. For those with newsworthy morsels to their estates, various manners of assuring privacy can be found, and avoiding probate is indeed one of them.

How To Avoid Probate

It's simple. There are **three kinds of property** which do not pass under your will and consequently **do not go through probate.** So to avoid probate, all you have to do is hold your property in one of, or a combination of, these three forms. The reason they each avoid probate is that in each case you are not considered to have owned the particular type of property as of the moment of death.

Joint Tenancy With Right Of Survivorship

The first of these three types you will undoubtedly remember from chapter two: the **joint tenancy** with right of survivorship. Since the property automatically by legal definition belongs to the survivor at the very moment of the decedent's death, the decedent is not considered to own it any longer, and it does not pass pursuant to a will. Since probate originally dealt only with wills and the property passing under them, there was never any need for joint tenancy property to be subject to probate, and so it has remained to this day.

Trusts Created During Life

The second form of property that avoids probate is property that you have during your lifetime placed into a **trust created during life.** As will be seen in chapter six, the trust itself is the legal owner of such property, and therefore the decedent can not be considered the owner. Trust property passes under the terms of the trust and not according to the decedent's will, which has no effect on trust property just as it has no effect on joint-tenancy property. So probate of such property is unnecessary. There is also no probate if the trustee dies, because the trusteeship is an office and an office never dies even though the current holder of it may die.

Proceeds of Life Insurance Policies

The third type of property that avoids probate is **proceeds of life insurance** policies and other contractual payments which are payable to a beneficiary designated by the decedent. The reason is simply that the decedent never owned such proceeds; he only had a contractual right to have them paid to a person of his choice. A will does not affect such proceeds because they pass under a contractual designation of beneficiary and not according to a will.

Therefore the "how" of avoiding probate is exceedingly simple. Whether you should avoid it is a deliberate choice for the informed person to make, based upon the costs discussed, the advantages we have yet to discuss, and the tax consequences of holding property in a form that avoids probate versus holding property in a form that deliberately incurs probate (to be discussed later).

In some states, you don't even avoid all probate expenses by holding property in joint tenancy or other probate-avoiding forms.

For instance, in Ohio and Oregon, the executor is entitled to a fee of 1% of the value of non-probate property which is nevertheless taxable (as we shall later see, most non-probate property is taxable). And in New Jersey, the executor is entitled to a reasonable fee on similar property.

The Relationship of Avoiding Probate with Avoiding Taxes

There is none! This is a dangerously common fallacy, and perhaps the failure to understand this complete lack of relationship is one of the reasons why so many are so intent on avoiding probate. **Probate and taxes have absolutely nothing to do with each other.** Probate is simply a time period. Court supervision is necessary, and unfortunately it does have some costs associated with it for the reasons previously discussed. But these costs are fees to individuals, not taxes to any government. The tax law is a completely different subject and inquires into whether the decedent owned property and in any way exercised his right and power to pass it on at his death to persons of his choice. Taxation, as we shall see, depends upon the latter inquiry, and this has not the slightest thing to do with whether or not there is a time period when the supervision of a court is required. So try to keep that distinction firmly in mind, and never confuse the question of avoiding probate with avoiding taxes. In reality, what avoids probate does not usually avoid taxes.

The fact that taxes are not avoided by probate-avoiding property means that not all the costs or delays associated with probate can be eliminated by simply avoiding the probate process. And this is true even in those states that do not specifically allow a statutory fee to the representative for including non-probate property on the tax returns. When taxes are due, an attorney or accountant will usually have to be hired to make out the appropriate tax returns. Therefore some costs will be incurred in fees to such persons, and those fees are not regulated by any law, as probate fees are. Although there should be no delay in the continued operation and income payments under an already established trust, there is often a delay in the transfer of joint tenancy title and the payment of life insurance proceeds. As to the latter, most insurance companies will not pay the proceeds until they can be assured that all tax obligations have been satisfied, which often involves securing a document of release from the state's inheritance tax department. Joint tenancy property can also not be transferred until a release or consent is obtained, so in either case, the payment or transfer is delayed until the tax work is completed and the inheritance tax department satisfied.

While there are no formalities beyond the inheritance tax releases for living trusts or life insurance proceeds, joint tenancy property entails a further step. In order for the surviving joint tenant to have a freely transferable asset in his or her name alone, the name of the decedent must be removed from the record title. As to stocks, each stock transfer agent has its own requirements, often involving several mailings back and forth until all the required documentation is completed. As to real estate, there must be an appropriate change noted on the Recorder's records. In many states this can be accomplished in one of two ways, the first being a court decree which can be obtained after a short court proceeding. It is often called a Decree Establishing Fact of Death, and it can be recorded. The other is a simplified affadavit, which is recorded along with a copy of the death certificate and the release or consent of the inheritance tax department. In either case, some delay is encountered to accomplish this, and some costs are involved. So it is a total fallacy that avoiding probate avoids all costs and delays.

Probate and Community Property

In a community property state, when the first spouse dies, he or she only owns one-half of whatever property is actually the community property of the spouses. It might therefore seem that only the one-half belonging to the decedent spouse would be subject to probate. But the matter is not quite that simple, and in fact turns on the management rights of one or both of the spouses, which were discussed at page 22.

If only the husband is the manager of the entire community property, this means that only he can subject both halves of it to debts. If the wife is manager only of her half, then she can subject only that half to debts. Since probate has largely to do with debts and creditors, the probate results often parallel the right to subject the community property to debts. Each community property state has subtly different statutes regarding the management powers of the spouses, and so the probate effect in each of those states must be individually analyzed. The management powers in most community property states originally were those stated at the beginning of this paragraph, and so when the husband died, the entire community property went through probate in order that the creditors be allowed to satisfy their claims out of all of it. This also meant that the probate fees were computed on the entire amount of the community property. But when the wife died first, only her half was subject to probate since that was all that she could subject to debts, and so the probate expenses were cut in half.

In recent years, several community property states have changed their management laws so that now each spouse is the manager of the entire community property and can consequently subject all of it to debts. A logical result would therefore be that the entire community property would be subject to probate no matter which spouse died, which would increase the probate costs all the way around. But, to mention one example, California reformed its probate laws at the same time, and instead the opposite tack was taken. Now, only the decedent's half of the community is potentially subject to probate, no matter who dies first. The reform then went even further by saying that if community property passes directly from the decedent spouse to the surviving spouse (by intestacy or under the decedent's will), then probate is abolished for such property! But to escape probate, the community property cannot pass to anyone other than the surviving spouse, and also if it passes to the surviving spouse in trust, it must still be probated (because it is not now passing to her "directly").

Since title companies, stock transfer agents, and the like will still demand some court decree authorizing the transfer of title to the survivor, a short form procedure to confirm the community property transfer to the survivor was devised. No executor is necessary, and so any representative's fee is eliminated, but no statutory fee schedule was enacted for the attorney. Most courts are allowing attorneys' fees based on the time they spend on the matter, which often amounts to approximately one third of what the statutory probate fee would have been. So the probate expenses have been greatly reduced by this procedure.

The Problem Of Creditors

There is a matching problem with creditors, though, who are now denied an opportunity to present their claims against such property in probate. To deal with this factor, the right to avoid probate for all or a portion of the community property was made **elective** with the surviving spouse. If he or she elects to avoid it entirely or to probate only the decedent's half, then she takes the non-probated portion subject to the claims of creditors (which means that they can enforce their claims against her personally in the correctly apportioned amount). While the effect just stated is badly simplified, it will have to do for our purposes; any surviving spouse would have to get thorough legal advice as to the options.

Along with the right to elect to avoid probate for such community property, the surviving spouse was also given the right to probate (in the old, normal manner) either the decedent's half of such property, or even all of it, including the surviving spouse's half. These elections have technically placed the survivor's estate attorney in a position of conflict of interest, because his fees will be either 100%, 50% or zero, depending upon how much of the community property the survivor decides to probate. It well may be that the survivor ought to seek independent legal advice as to which elections he or she should exercise. Then no one could accuse the estate attorney of coloring his advice so as to set himself up for a handsome fee.

Why in heaven's name would a survivor elect to probate the entire community property, and thereby pay a 100% probate fee on it? Obviously it would be to avoid personal liability on the creditors claims, and the situations where that might arise depend solely on the circumstances of the couple involved. But consider the spouse of a deceased surgeon; he or she might elect a full probate in order to place some limitations on the potential malpractice claimants and avoid full personal liability for such claims.

Timetable and Procedures of a Probate

Although state laws vary considerably in this regard, basic probate procedures can be indicated. An outline of these procedures is given in Table 5–2, and in the following paragraphs, I'll fill out that outline a bit. But bear in mind that the precise procedures, and the names of them, might be quite different in your state.

Some states have enacted all or parts of the Uniform Probate Code, an extensive project of a national group of probate scholars. This code substantially cuts down on the involvement of the court in a probate procedure subject to that code and has the effect of both simplifying probate and sometimes making it less costly. But many states are still wallowing in remarkably ancient probate procedures. Often change is resisted because certain groups like things just the way they are, usually for reasons of financial self-interest. You would be wise to try to acquire objective information as to the cleanliness and modernity of the probate system in your state, so that you can intelligently evaluate how important it might be to avoid probate in your state. In some states from which some pretty horrible stories have emerged, avoiding probate might be a very good idea indeed.

A Probate Timetable: What Is Done

In order to give you something by way of example, presented below is a fairly typical timetable of probate procedures. While your state might have procedures generally resembling some of the procedures noted below, you must not assume that any particular thing applies in your state.

After the death of a decedent, any interested person may file a petition for the probate of a will or for the administration of an intestate's estate. There is usually no required time limit when this must be done, and it has often been known to occur many years later when a problem crops up which can only be solved by a probate decree (usually concerning title to property). After a petition has been filed, a hearing date is set, and notices must be given both publicly, and directly to heirs under an intestacy or to persons named to receive benefits in a will.

Table 5–2. Outline of an average probate, with time periods for accomplishment of each task. CAUTION: state laws vary widely as to the particular tasks and the particular time period.

Task	Usual Time Period
File Petition for Probate of Will, or for Letters of Administration if intestacy	0–30 days after death
Publish or post Notice to Creditors	Immediately upon granting of Petition for Probate
Apply for Family or Widow's Allowance, or Probate Homestead	Immediately upon granting of Petition for Probate
Gather assets and prepare formal Inventory of estate; present to Appraiser if required	Promptly after Representative assumes his office
Notice to Creditors period elapses	Varies widely; normally from 2 to 6 months after first publication or posting
Sell estate property to raise cash for taxes of distribution	Any time after Representative is appointed
Make preliminary distributions	Usually after Notice to Creditors period elapses
Prepare and file state inheritance tax papers	Usually from 6 to 9 months after appointment of representative
Alternate valuation date for federal estate tax purposes	6 months after date of death
Where no federal estate tax return required, make final accounting and distribution, and close estate	Approximately one month after Notice to Creditors period elapses, and state taxes paid
File federal estate tax return, and pay federal estate taxes	9 months after date of death, unless extensions applied for and granted
Where no wish to wait for audit of federal return, make final accounting and distribution, and close estate	Approximately one to two months after estate tax paid
Keep estate open until federal return is audited, or audit period elapses	3 years after estate tax return is filed
When audit period elapses, make final accounting and distribution, and close estate	One to three months after audit period elapses
To keep securing income tax advantages of probate estate, keep it open	As long as possible
Gigantic or extraordinarily complex estates	May stay open for many years

Probate is one of many areas in the law where concessions are made to administrative problems of crowded court calendars and too few judges. In many modernized probate systems, the required notices are treated as opportunities for interested parties to submit objections, and if none are received, the matter will be granted without any actual court hearing taking place or even the attorney physically appearing before the judge. So in many states, the vast majority of probate procedures are handled by mail, with a court commissioner reviewing all matters for compliance with the applicable statutes, and the judge signing the requested order if no objection is made in a timely fashion. However, once an objection is received, then the matter is handled in an actual hearing where the judge allows each side to present whatever evidence it wishes. Such things as will contests, objections to distribution plans, and claims of heirship are therefore guaranteed their day in court. Contested probate matters are a specialized field in themselves, and of course anyone involved in such things must seek individual counsel, but for our purposes I'll assume that no objections were entered and the matters will be validated in a streamlined fashion.

Appointment Of Personal Representative

Assuming the file is in order and (if there was a will) a written declaration of at least one of the subscribing witnesses has been submitted (testifying to all the required formalities of will execution), the will is admitted to probate and the personal representative appointed to his office. As evidence of his authority to do all acts in the name of and on behalf of the decedent and his estate, he is issued a document called Letters; **Letters Testamentary** if there was a will, and **Letters of Administration** if there was not.

Notice To Creditors

The immediate first step is to publish **notice to creditors** for the prescribed number of times in a local newspaper, and this is of course the way creditors are informed that they must present their claims. The date of first publication of notice to creditors is a benchmark date for the estate. Within a specified time from that date, several things must occur if they are to occur at all; that time varies from state to state; in my state it is four months. Creditors must file their claims within those four months, any will contest must be brought within that time, and preliminary distributions of estate assets may thereafter be made without any expensive bonding requirements being imposed on the estate. Even if there are no creditors and everybody knows it, the notice period for creditors must still run, and so this (in my state) four months outlines the minimum time period over which a probate must exist. Figuring roughly one month to get things together and file for probate, and one month after the four months period to get the final distribution ordered and accomplished, six months is really the minimum possible duration for a probate in my state.

Family Allowance And Homestead

While waiting for the notice to creditors period to elapse, a lot is going on. If a **family allowance** (see Glossary) or probate **homestead** (see Glossary) is required for the surviving spouse and minor children, it is applied for and commenced (usually retroactive to the date of death). The executor is gathering together all of the decedent's known assets, which is often not as easy as it sounds and in a complicated estate can take many months or even years. Some form of formal Inventory and Appraisement is submitted, and in some states the appointed inheritance tax referee appraises all of the estate's property. These are the values on which the probate fees as well as the state inheritance taxes will be based, and so when the appraisal is completed, the executor examines it very carefully. If the executor is not satisfied with the valuation of one or more assets, he can resolve it informally with the referee, or if an agreement can not be reached, he may petition the court to hold a formal hearing with valuation evidence being presented so that the court may render the final valuation. Thereafter, in many states the referee assesses the state inheritance tax, a rather complex matter under the state's own particular rules of taxation, and again if the executor disagrees, he may ask the court to hold a formal hearing and determine from the evidence presented what the final tax should be.

Limitation On Creditors' Claims

A very significant thing has occurred when the estate reaches the end of the notice to creditors period. Not only can no will contest now be brought against the estate, but also any creditor who was required to file a claim and did not do so by then will be forever prohibited from collecting on that claim against the estate or the distributee of any of the decedent's property. And virtually all creditors, including even those with contingent claims, are required to file claims within the notice period or be forever barred. So this limitation acts just like a very short statute of limitations as far as creditors' claims are concerned, and in fact creditors are sometimes tripped up by this requirement, to the benefit of the estate.

It should be apparent that here is the first major advantage of probate, not only in the potential elimination of some claims, but also in the mere fact that claims must be received within a reasonable period of time at the end of which the heirs will know all the estate's liabilities. They will also know that there can never be any further reductions in their inheritances by reason of claims from creditors. Avoiding probate means avoiding that statute of limitations, so that the heirs who succeed to the decedent's non-probate property might continue to be pressed by his creditors for as long as the state's general statute of limitations runs on the particular type of claim involved.

Executor's Powers

During probate, the executor has many powers to deal with the estate's property, powers that are conferred by state law but may be increased by a specific grant of additional powers in the will. In an intestacy, of course, the decedent has forfeited the possibility of granting any additional powers. The essence of the executor's power is to conserve and protect the estate for eventual distribution to the heirs, but except in doing so, the executor can not invest the estate or try to make it grow in value. Common powers of executors are the right to sell, lease, borrow money, continue a business, etc. Traditionally any move made by the executor in the exercise of his powers could be taken only with court permission, and accordingly, an executor in a complex estate is constantly filing petitions for authority to do one thing or another. If necessary to raise money or to facilitate distribution, real estate or personal property may be sold during probate, subject to the later confirmation of the court. It is on such occasions where one sees bidding by prospective buyers in the probate courtroom because part of any confirmation procedure is the opportunity for anyone to enter increased bids for the property. A final and very handy procedure often invoked by a personal representative is to ask the probate court for its instructions on anything about which the representative may be in doubt, such as his authority or the propriety of any action he is considering. When a probate court grants an order of instructions or any other regular order, it operates as a court decree which protects the personal representative from any later accusation that he exceeded his authority or made an improper move.

Most states have not adopted the Uniform Probate Code; others have liberalized their probate procedures along some of the general lines proposed by that code. In the latter states, except for a certain few things where court approval is specifically still required (such as sales of estate property, for one), the executor is free to take many actions without petitioning the court for authority to do so. He need only give notice to the various heirs of his proposed action, and if they fail to object, he may proceed. Using the new procedure is up to the executor if he has received the original authority to proceed under it, and in every instance, he is free to petition the court for authority just as he used to, if he values the protection of a court decree. Needless to say, many conservative executors with proper regard for their potential responsibility to heirs, particularly banks, still petition the court for authority in many cases.

Federal And State Death Taxes

No probate may be terminated and the assets of the estate distributed to heirs until both the state and federal death taxes have been paid. Federal taxes are due nine months after the date of death, as are most state inheritance taxes. The federal law (but not many state laws) provides an **election,** where all of the assets in the estate can either be valued for tax purposes as of the date of death, or as of the **alternate valuation date,** which is six months after death. For this reason, virtually every estate where a federal estate tax return is due will wait until the alternate date rolls around in order to examine the values of its assets and determine whether any tax saving is possible. Because of that, most federal estate tax returns are not filed until very close to the nine months limit, and consequently the nine months marks the next usual benchmark for how long a probate will last. With some time to open probate and some time to close it after the taxes are paid, one year is a very normal duration for an estate that requires a federal estate tax return. As we shall later see, the new Tax Reform Act substantially reduces the number of estates that will require an estate tax return, thereby providing the additional benefit of faster probates.

However, it is not at all unusual for a probate estate to last much longer than one year. For one thing, it may be either impossible or a severe hardship to come up with the tax money within nine months, particularly if many assets have to be sold to raise the tax money, and so the federal government allows extensions of time within which to file and pay. Since no estate can be closed until the taxes are paid, the probate will remain open until that time.

If the personal representative distributes most of the estate assets in a preliminary distribution, but the federal government audits the estate tax return and later assesses an estate tax deficiency within the statute of limitations period allowed to it (three years after filing the return), the personal representative is personally liable for the deficiency if the heirs have squandered the property or are otherwise unable to pay the deficiency. Since the personal representative is actually the estate attorney's primary client, the attorney often advises his client to keep the probate open until the three years has run, in order to protect himself against potential personal liability. Many conservative executors gratefully accept that advice, and so such period provides a final and extended benchmark for the continuation of a probate. Often the problem is solved by a written agreement among the heirs to share in any deficiency assessed, and in a family situation with a family executor this often suffices. But in more complex situations, even such an agreement may not satisfy the conservative executor.

It should at least be mentioned that, of course, some estates are so complex that it takes years to resolve them.

The Attorney's Influence On Length Of Probate

It seems very common for heirs to complain that the attorney has unduly prolonged the duration of probate. Sometimes this is due to the heirs not understanding the various time limits involved and just plain becoming impatient. But sometimes the complaint is unfortunately true. What can I say here? Hopefully this only occurs infrequently. It is of course a matter for the attorney's own conscience, but if the attorney is truly guilty he can be discharged by his client as can any attorney in any kind of matter. In states with statutory fee schedules, there is no personal advantage to the attorney to string out the probate, as he can earn no greater fee thereby; in fact, usually he has an incentive to terminate it because only then can he get his fee.

My state has initiated a new procedure whereby if an estate is not terminated within twelve or eighteen months from the date of death, depending upon whether a federal estate tax return is required, any person may call the attorney or executor into court to explain. The court may then either allow continued delay if it is found necessary, may order the estate terminated by a given time, or in cases of genuine neglect of duty may reduce the executor's and attorney's statutory fees. That should help.

Terminating Probate

When it is finally time to terminate a probate estate, the personal representative must submit a final accounting of all his acts and transactions, including details of all items of income and all items of outgo. At the same time, a petition for final distribution is prepared which details the property on hand to be distributed, the heirs entitled to the distribution under either the intestacy laws or the decedent's will, and the representative's proposed distribution plans. This is the final chance for any interested person to object to anything that has gone on during probate or to the proposed manner of distribution. After the appropriate notices are given, the personal representative's accounting is approved and distribution is ordered. After the receipts of the heirs have been filed, the executor receives a final discharge from his office. If the distribution is to a trust established in the decedent's will, all the terms of the trust will be set out in the decree of distribution, and this court order then becomes the actual document legally establishing the trust. Income earned during probate is distributed to the heirs in proportion to their inheritances from the estate, and if a trust is the main beneficiary, all the probate income goes to the trustee to distribute it according to the terms of the trust.

The decree of distribution can then be presented to all those responsible for titling the decedent's property, and they will accept it as authorization to issue new title to the heirs named in the decree. If real estate is involved, its legal description is set out in the decree, and a certified copy of the decree is then recorded in the County Recorder's office. This decree acts as a deed to the heir and places record title in his name; upon any later transaction, a title search will reveal the probate decree, and title will be established in the name of the heir so that he can thereafter freely sell the property or otherwise deal with it as his own.

The final reason why probate may be continued for quite a period of time may be (believe it or not) because it is advantageous to do so.

The Advantages of Probate: Lowering Taxes

Many of the advantages of probate concern income earned by the estate during probate. The reason is that when the probate status is established, a probate estate becomes a **separate taxpaying entity,** the same as a corporation, a trust, etc. Conventional income tax wisdom is that it is always preferable to spread a given amount of taxable income among as many different taxpaying entities as possible. The reason lies in the graduated rate structure of the income tax.

As a taxpayer's brackets go up, the impact of the tax on that taxpayer increases. Therefore, it is always better to pay two taxes on one-half each than to pay one tax on the whole. Due to the graduated rate structure, a tax on the whole is more than double (often substantially more than double) the total of two taxes on one-half each. Also, for each taxpayer there is an exemption eliminating the first portion of income from tax, and if income can be broken down among more taxpayers with more exemptions, the lowest rates of tax apply several times instead of just once. For example, the tax on income of $40,000 at the joint return rates is

$12,140. But by breaking that income into two $20,000 halves among two taxpayers, the tax is only $4380 each, or a total of $8760 and a saving of $3380.

While it is generally true that it is best to divide any given amount of income among several taxpayers, this generalization must be related to the tax brackets of the income recipients. If one of the persons getting half of the income referred to above were in the 70% bracket, there would of course be no actual savings involved.

Managing The Calendar Year For Paying Taxes

A probate estate offers several advantages due to its arrival on the scene as an additional taxpaying entity. First of all, whenever a new taxpayer is created, it is entitled to choose the twelve-month year on the basis of which it will pay its taxes. This can either be a calendar year or a **fiscal year** ending on the last day of any month during the calendar year. That possibility can be used to the advantage of everyone interested in the estate because it can squeeze out an extra set of exemptions and can lower all the tax brackets.

It is easiest to deal with a hypothetical example. Assume the executor and attorney estimate that the probate will take eighteen months, and the decedent died in early July. If they stick with a calendar year, their first tax year will be of six months duration ending on December 31, and their next tax year will be twelve months. They will therefore get two sets of exemptions and will have six months income taxed once, and twelve months income taxed once. But if they choose a fiscal year ending September 30, they will then have a first fiscal year of three months, a second of twelve months, and a third of three months. The result is that they get three sets of exemptions instead of only two, and they get two taxations of only three months income each at the lower brackets applicable to lower amounts of income, as opposed to one taxation of the greater amount of income earned over six months (which will naturally be at a higher overall tax bracket).

Nature And Timing Of Income

A clever executor and his advisors will also consider the **nature and timing of the income that is received.** Assume our decedent died in May, and assume he operated a resort hotel, which past history shows takes in 70% of its income during June, July, and August. The clever executor will elect a short fiscal year ending August 31, in order to freeze the summer's receipts into a taxable year when no other income will be added to it to increase the tax brackets applicable. Thereby the tax bracket for the summer's receipts is kept as low as possible, and the income earned over the next nine months is also taxed at a low bracket since it is not inflated by the summer's earnings. Or, a July 31 fiscal year might be elected in order to divide the summer's receipts between two fiscal years. This executor will be well-advised to terminate the probate by May of the following year so that the second fiscal year of nine or ten months will not catch the next year's summer receipts.

The taxation of probate or trust income is extremely complex when talked about in technical terms because of a maddening tax concept called "distributable net income." Essentially, the probate pays tax on all income it receives and keeps during that tax year, but it does not have to pay tax on any such income it distributes to beneficiaries in that tax year. The latter comes about by means of a deduction for such distributions, which then must of course be included in the taxable income of the beneficiaries in the year they receive it. This leads to two potential advantages. One is a **tax deferral advantage,** which can be seen by assuming a January 31 fiscal year for the probate estate. Assume that the estate distributes all or a great part of its income to the estate beneficiaries between January 1 and January 31; it then has no tax for such distributions due to its deduction for them. Although the beneficiary has to pay tax, he, as an individual, is on a calendar year basis and will not have to pay the tax until some fourteen months after receipt (April 15 of the following calendar year). Presto; income earned by the estate in (perhaps) February of 1979 is distributed to the beneficiary in January of 1980, and no tax will be paid on it until April of 1981. There is always some advantage to tax deferral, particularly for those who correctly compute into the equation the earning power of the funds before the tax is due.

Tax Brackets Of Beneficiaries

The second advantage deals with the various **tax brackets of the beneficiaries** when related to the concept of preliminary distributions of estate assets. Assume an estate owns many thousands of shares of a security that, via dividends, produces $100,000 of income each year. Assume the securities were willed to the decedent's four children equally, and that their individual income tax brackets are 20%, 30%, 50%, and 70%. Assume further that the tax bracket of the estate itself is 70% if the entire income is taxed to it in any given year but only 40% if half of such income is taxed to it. The clever executor will apply to the court for the preliminary distribution of all or a portion of the shares (or the income earned by those shares) allocable to the 20% and 30% bracket heirs in order to have the income taxed to them at their lower brackets and also to lower the estate's own brackets. Income held in the estate which is actually allocable to the 50% and 70% heirs will have had its tax paid at the estate's lower bracket and will later be distributed to them as principal upon the final distribution of the estate. The even more clever executor will, if the nature and amount of the assets make it feasible, string the estate out for as long as possible and continue to parcel out various amounts of the assets in such fashions as to keep everyone's tax brackets as low as possible.

The ultimate rub in these situations is that the income tax advantages can be so attractive that it is the heirs who desire the continuation of the probate estate for as long as possible, and the IRS, which has a whole set of rules about length of probate, dictates when an executor must terminate a probate in order to cut off these tax advantages! This is a far cry from those who believe that probate is totally disadvantageous. It is apparent that the advantages are greater when the estate is quite large and has a lot of income producing assets, but the same principles apply to an estate of any size. In the smaller estates it may be even more dramatic to save some tax dollars for the family because no one has money to burn in such a situation.

Other Options

There are other elections and options available to a probate estate which can improve the family's income tax picture. Many of these involve elections as to when or on which type of tax return to take various deductions, or when and how to take various items of income. Competent tax advisors can brief any executor on such effects.

Community Property States

A final tax effect of probate involves the community property states. Assume that the decedent spouse wills all the community property to the survivor, and that under the applicable state laws the decedent's half of the community is subject to probate. This is an **automatic splitting of the income** earned by the community property into two halves and two taxpayers, one being the estate and the other the surviving spouse. Each of their brackets is thereby lower, there are two sets of exemptions, and it is to the surviving spouse's tax advantage to delay the day when she is taxed on all of the income. Since the surviving spouse is going to get all the community property anyway, it is to her advantage that the probate estate continue for as long as possible in order that it pay taxes on one-half the family income at its lower bracket. The after tax income from the probate half will eventually be distributed to her as principal. This may be an additional and valid reason why the surviving spouse under the new liberalized probate laws of some community property states may elect to probate the decedent's half of the community property. The probate fee necessitated by that election may be far less than the total taxes which can be saved, and the probate fee is deductible anyway (on either the estate tax or income tax return, but not on both).

Obviously, avoiding probate eliminates all these advantages. The advantages and disadvantages of avoiding probate versus incurring probate are summarized in Table 5-3. No income splitting for community property spouses, no fiscal year elections, no tax deferral, and no allocation of income among the various tax brackets according to where the taxes will be the least. Avoiding probate also avoids the various non-tax advantages discussed in this chapter, chief among which is the short statute of limitations on creditors claims and will contests. A further factor stems from the often family-wrecking disputes that can come up in an inheritance situation. Only a psychiatrist could comment on the emotional

Should Probate Be Avoided?

TABLE 5—3.
ADVANTAGES/DISADVANTAGES OF INCURRING PROBATE VERSUS AVOIDING PROBATE.

INCURRING PROBATE

Advantages	*Disadvantages*
Provides clear title	Expense (see Table 5–1)
Short statute of limitation on creditors' claims	Delay (see Table 5–2)
Forum to hear disputes	A public record
Permits family allowance	Involves attorneys
Permits probate homestead for spouse and children not willed the family home	State probate system may be corrupt
Provides income splitting between estate and eventual beneficiary	
Choice of fiscal year may be able to reduce income taxes	
Use of preliminary distributions to lower total family income taxes	
Fees deductible against highest bracket tax return	
Permits property to pass by will and be subject to wishes expressed in estate plan	
May be required in order to obtain estate tax savings discussed in chapter eleven	

TABLE 5-3. *(Continued)*

AVOIDING PROBATE

Advantages	Disadvantages
Avoids probate fees	Still incurs some expense for tax work and title clearing work
Speeds up process of settling decedent's affairs	Fees for tax work and title clearing work not set by statute or subject to court scrutiny
No public record	
Minimizes involvement of attorneys	Still suffers some delay due to tax work and title clearing work
Avoids involvement of a possibly corrupt court system	No short statute of limitations on creditors' claims; heirs may remain personally liable
Avoids possibility of someone contesting a will	No provision for family allowance or probate homestead
	100% of income taxed to survivor who receives property outside of probate
	No maneuvers available to reduce income taxes
	Property not subject to wishes expressed in decedent's will
	May cause large increases in estate taxes compared to estate plan which goes through probate; see chapter eleven

needs that compel people to get embroiled in such issues, but if that kind of a dispute arises, the family may be much more secure if there is an orderly probate forum to hear such a dispute, as well as court protection afforded to the personal representative who can easily be caught in the middle.

In chapter eleven we will begin to examine some of the techniques for avoiding or minimizing the impact of both federal and state death taxes. For the reasons to be discussed in that chapter, those savings may only be possible if probate is deliberately incurred. In that chapter, we will analyze the amount of the savings, but at this point it is enough if you are aware that there may be far greater total savings available by deliberately going through probate rather than by avoiding it, even aside from the income tax savings referred to above.

However, the advantages are not the whole story. The disadvantages of probate must likewise be weighed. Perhaps the probate system in your state is shockingly corrupt; I happen to practice in an extraordinarily clean system where the advantages of probate look attractive. Perhaps you can not tolerate the delay and publicity factors for a reason completely personal to you. Even if those factors do not deter you, still you must evaluate the probate costs in your state. The real issue should be: Are the costs and advantages worth it to me when I consider what I am getting in return, particularly when I also consider the costs and delays inherent even for non-probate assets, and can I tolerate the disadvantages? That is a question which only you and your advisors can answer.

APPLICATION

1. Compute your "probate estate" by eliminating all assets held in joint tenancy or tenancy by the entirety, assets subject to a living trust, or insurance proceeds. Then assign a realistic fair market value to the remaining balance of your assets; for valuation information, see page 131.

2. Determine the representative's fees and the attorney's fees charged by statute or custom in your state. Using Table 5-1 as a start, get accurate information as to the actual charges in your area.

3. Find out whether using a bank as executor, or using co-executors, will increase the probate costs in your state.

4. Reduce the costs you have so far arrived at by any fee-saving device you have in your will or can arrange, such as using a family member as executor who will waive his fee, obtaining contracts to serve for reduced fees, or combining the functions of executor and attorney for just one fee instead of two.

5. Try to inform yourself as to the speed, procedures, and freedom from corruption characterizing the probate system in your state. Speak with court personnel, attorneys whom you trust, bank trust officers, and acquaintances who have experienced probate in your state. Ask the local bar association for any available literature; banks may also have such literature.

6. Determine whether any of the advantages of probate mentioned in this chapter do or do not confer any realistic benefit in your own personal situation.

7. Reserve final decision on avoiding probate until after you have finished this book, when you can compare the estate and inheritance tax effects of holding property in probate-incurring form with those of holding property in probate-avoiding form.

6

trusts: flexible tools of many uses

Glossary For This Chapter

Accounting
Beneficiary
Corpus
Court Trust
Discretionary Trust
Fiduciary
Fiduciary Income Tax Return
Funded Trust
Grantor
Income
Inter Vivos Trust
Irrevocable Trust
Life In Being
Living Trust
Non-Court Trust
Pour Over Trust
Principal
Principal and Income Act
Res
Revocable Trust
Rule Against Perpetuities
Settlor
Spendthrift Clause
Sprinkling Trust
Testamentary Trust
Throwback Rule
Trust
Trustee
Trustor
Unfunded Trust

Trusts are an essential part of estate planning because a great many estate planning benefits involve their use. Not only is it important to understand and appreciate trusts for that reason, but also to clear away a frequent suspicion that a trust locks up property against a beneficiary's use and so shows no faith in that person. Nothing could be further from the truth, as creating a trust usually shows the deepest concern for the welfare and security of a beneficiary. A trust also provides a flexible way to meet the uncertain future.

A trust is an entity with full-fledged legal existence, as are other legally authorized entities such as corporations, partnerships, probate estates, etc. The chief identifying feature of a trust is that one person or institution, called a **trustee,** owns, manages and invests the property contained in the trust not for his own benefit, but for the benefit of the **beneficiaries** of the trust. The trustee is placed under very strict standards of performance when he accepts his role. The trust carries on

87

a legal existence much the same as any other owner of property, in that it has power to manage its own property, it assumedly earns income from that property, and it pays income taxes on what it earns. The trustee is the actual person who performs all those functions. The beneficiaries receive the benefits of what the trustee accomplishes by way of distributions of income from the trust, growth in the value of their property if the trustee invests wisely, and periodic distributions of the property contained in the trust.

Trustor, Trustee, Beneficiary: The Relationships

The person who creates a trust is variously called the **trustor,** the **grantor,** or the **settlor;** we'll use the term **trustor.** The property contained within the trust is usually called either the **principal** or the **corpus,** although occasionally you will see the Latin word **res.**

People often ask whether trustor, trustee, and beneficiary must be three different people, or whether two or more of these roles can be filled by the same person. The latter is true, and any confusion in grasping those dual roles can be reduced by understanding that creating a trust brings into existence entirely new and unique legal relationships concerning both people and property. So long as a property owner's legal status regarding his property is changed when a trust is created, he is permitted to hold dual functions. For instance, he could declare himself trustee of his own property for the benefit of another person, in that manner changing his status regarding the property which he previously owned solely for his own benefit; he would thereby be both trustor and trustee. Or, he could declare someone else the trustee of his property, but for his own benefit; he would thereby be both trustor and beneficiary, but he has altered the legal status regarding his property by creating a new legal owner bound to administer the property under trust rules. Can he be all three: trustor, trustee, and beneficiary? Such an arrangement gets dangerously close to not changing anything about his status over his own property, in which case the supposed trust would simply be ignored as, at best, a sham. But with proper drafting, a property owner might make himself trustee for his own benefit for the rest of his life, so long as at the same time he makes someone else the person who will benefit after he, the trustor, has died. That would alter his status concerning his own property, for he would no longer own the fee simple (defined at page 49).

How a Trust Is Created

A trust is created by a property owner subjecting particular property to the special trust relationship. It is ordinarily done in a detailed, written document within which the trustor sets out all the terms and conditions under which the trust is to operate. Various kinds of documents can set up various kinds of trusts. These types are summarized in Table 6–1 and are more fully explained in the following paragraphs.

Living Trusts and Testamentary Trusts

These trusts are similar, but just describe different times when the trust was created. A living trust is often called an **inter vivos trust,** which is Latin for "during life," and describes the fact that the trust was established and began legal existence during the trustor's lifetime. On the other hand, a trust may be created only in the trustor's will (hence, testamentary trust), in which case the trust does not begin operating until after the trustor's death. The many necessary trust provisions of a testamentary trust are found within the trustor's will and not in any separate trust document. Upon final termination of the trustor's probate estate, the property will be ordered distributed to the newly born trust, rather than distributed to an individual heir.

Recall at this point that **living trusts are not subject to probate,** because the trustee and not the decedent is the legal owner of the property. There is no probate even if the decedent is also the trustee because the trusteeship is an office and offices don't die even though their current occupant might. When a trustee dies, the trusteeship continues uninterrupted, and a successor trustee assumes the office.

Court Trusts and Non-court Trusts

In most states a testamentary trust is subject to the ongoing jurisdiction of the probate court, and so it is often called a **court trust.** The trustee of such a trust must make periodic accountings to the court covering all trust income and all expenditures. While many people consider this a nuisance to be avoided, it affords the trustee several protections which can later become valuable. When an accounting has been submitted and approved, a court judgment is issued which ratifies, confirms, and approves all the acts and transactions of the trustee covered by the accounting. This judgment protects the trustee from liability for any acts or omissions covered by the accounting and approved by the court.

An additional advantage to a court trust is that the trustee may voluntarily go to court for instructions concerning any difficult or doubtful action. The trustee will then receive a court judgment, instructing him to do or not to do a given thing. This provides the trustee with protection against any future allegation of wrongdoing or of exceeding his authority.

TABLE 6–1.

TYPES OF TRUSTS

Name	Major identifying fact
Living trust	Established during trustor's lifetime
Testamentary trust	Established in trustor's will; takes effect only after his death
Court trust	A testamentary trust which is subject to the continuing jurisdiction of the probate court
Non-court trust	A living trust which is not subject to probate court jurisdiction
Revocable trust	A living trust which may be revoked, altered, or amended at any time
Irrevocable trust	A living trust which may not be revoked, altered, or amended
Pour over trust	A living trust designed to receive property to be "poured over" from the trustor's will via his probate estate
Life insurance trust	A trust designed to receive the proceeds of life insurance, and sometimes to also own life insurance
Clifford trust	A trust lasting a bit more than ten years, for tax reasons to be explained in chapter thirteen
Charitable trust	A trust which has a charity as its beneficiary
Support trust	A trust designed to provide the funds necessary to support a beneficiary
Accumulation trust	A trust which retains all the income it earns, as opposed to distributing it
Discretionary trust Sprinkling trust	Trusts where the trustee has the power to retain or pay out the income earned in whatever proportions he deems best
Spendthrift trust	A trust the principal of which is protected from a beneficiary's creditors

NOTE: Several of these terms may apply to a single trust, such as a "revocable living pour over discretionary trust."

On the other hand, in most states a living trust is not subject to the continuing jurisdiction of any court. In those states, the trustee of such a **non-court trust** may not even voluntarily submit an accounting or seek instructions because the courts have no jurisdiction in those matters. This of course prevents the trustee from being protected by the court judgments described, but it also saves going to court with periodic accountings. Many people are primarily concerned with saving the nuisance and expense of periodic court appearances, and are also more interested in not blocking their beneficiaries from holding the trustee accountable for his actions than in affording the trustee the protections of court judgments. For such objectives, the non-court trust is the type to use. It very much depends on whether one's focus lies in making the situation secure and acceptable for the trustee, or giving the beneficiaries opportunities to hold the trustee accountable. As in most things, the rights of both parties (trustee and beneficiary) must be protected, and not affording any protection to the trustee may result in the inability to find anyone willing to serve as trustee.

Some states have begun to modify these traditional aspects of court versus non-court trusts. For example, in California the courts can now entertain accountings and requests for instructions begun voluntarily by either the trustee or any beneficiary. And even more recently, unless the trust instrument provides otherwise, the ongoing jurisdiction over testamentary or "court" trusts has been reduced from mandatory to the same voluntary basis as now exists for living trusts. In this case, the choice of living or testamentary trust can turn on factors other than concerns over court jurisdiction. But California is unusual among the states in this regard.

Sometimes a decedent who is a resident of one state will name as trustee a person who is a resident of another state. Though by no means impossible, it is often considered inconvenient for an out-of-state trustee to periodically account to a probate court of another state. Where those considerations are important to the parties involved, a living non-court trust is indicated. Some states do not permit out-of-state persons to be trustees of a testamentary trust, in which case the choice is either a local trustee or a living trust using the out-of-state trustee.

Another difference between the two types of trusts is that a testamentary trust is subject to the trust law of the state whose probate court jurisdiction it falls under. But laws pertaining to living trusts generally permit the trustor actually to choose, by one means or another, the state law he wishes the trust to be subject to. Disadvantageous trust laws of a particular state can thereby be avoided, whereas with a testamentary trust one is stuck with the trust laws of the state having probate jurisdiction.

Revocable and Irrevocable Trusts

These distinctions apply only to living trusts, for with a testamentary trust the trustor is by definition no longer alive to do any revoking. A living trust is made either revocable or irrevocable by a clause in the trust document stating which type the trustor wants it to be. A few states have a law that a trust is revocable unless it is expressly made irrevocable by its terms. This seems to be a prudent law because it prevents a trustor from unintentionally creating something he can never undo. But many states say that for a trust to be revocable, the document must expressly declare that it is revocable. If you are contemplating a living trust, you should certainly find out which type of state you are living in.

A trustor can always get out of a **revocable trust,** in whole or in part. He can revoke it in its entirety, or amend it in particular parts, or change beneficiaries, or otherwise alter it in any way during the remainder of his life. In contrast, an **irrevocable trust** is a very serious step, for it means precisely what it says. The trust and all of its terms are never revocable, never amendable, and never changeable no matter what the reasons might be. So the trustor can never change his mind, either due to whim or due to some pressing necessity or change of circumstance he never imagined when he created the irrevocable trust (as, for instance, divorce). Obviously, there ought to be good and pressing reasons for the creation of an irrevocable trust, and it ought to contain only property that the trustor will never conceivably need. We will later examine why anyone would ever take such a serious step, and as you may suspect, it has mostly to do with tax reasons.

The Pour-Over Trust.

This trust is also by definition a living trust. The terminology is merely a nickname for the fact that the trust does not, during the trustor's lifetime, contain all of his property, but after his death his remaining property is willed to the trust and is therefore **poured over** from his probate estate into the already existing trust. It is a technique for avoiding court jurisdiction after probate over the bulk of the testator's property (because that property ultimately winds up in a non-court living trust), while at the same time not putting that property into trust during the trustor's lifetime. With this plan, the trustor can continue his outright ownership and control of his own property for the rest of his life, unencumbered by any of the trust rules. The technique involves placing only minimal property in the living trust upon its creation, such as $100, and in some liberal states, the trust can even contain nothing at all. But the trust document spells out all of the trustor's desires for the operation of the trust after his death, the same as would a testamentary trust. Then the trustor writes a very simple will which leaves all or most of his property to the already existing trust. Note that this is not a probate-avoiding mechanism, since the property must pass through probate on its way to the pour-over trust, but it does enable outright control of the trustor's property during the rest of his life. Since it is a non-court trust, the pour-over trust may also be easily moved from state to state if an out-of-state trustee is used.

Life Insurance Trusts.

These are also living trusts, describing a trust whose property is either the ownership of a policy of life insurance, or else only the fact that the trust has been named to be the beneficiary of a life insurance policy. The purpose is to have the proceeds of the policy subject to management by a trustee, as well as to have those proceeds obtain the various tax advantages which trust ownership affords (see chapter fourteen). Other reasons are to ensure the planned use of life insurance proceeds in the payment of taxes and expenses and also to protect those proceeds by preventing them from going outright to an individual who might waste them. Life insurance trusts are perhaps the most common form of pour-over trusts, where the only asset of the trust during the trustor's life is the policy on his life, or just the beneficiary rights under it. But after death, all the other assets will be poured over into the same trust, thus putting both insurance proceeds and all other property under one management umbrella, as well as giving the trustee maximum investment flexibility and leverage.

In those states retaining the difference between court and non-court trusts, sometimes a **reverse pour-over** is used when a trustor purposely wants the protections afforded by a testamentary trust. With this device, the life insurance proceeds pay to a living trust, but upon the conclusion of probate all other assets go into a testamentary trust, and then the life insurance trust pours over into the testamentary trust. This also gets all assets under one management umbrella, but winds up with a court trust instead of a non-court trust. This device is becoming less important now that life insurance companies seem willing to name the person designated as testamentary trustee in the insured's will as the beneficiary of the policy; in the past companies would often refuse to do so. That type of beneficiary designation also gets the life insurance proceeds into a testamentary, or court, trust.

Life insurance trusts are often referred to as being either **funded** or **unfunded.** This means that they either do (funded) or do not (unfunded) contain other income-producing property the income from which is enough to pay the premiums on the life insurance. If a life insurance trust is unfunded, the insured simply continues to pay the premiums just as if no trust existed.

Clifford Trusts

This type of trust has specific tax motives, and discussion of it will be deferred to chapter thirteen where we will review the tax and planning implications of various kinds of trusts. It is a trust which only exists for a bit over ten years, and the reasons why will be explained in that later chapter.

Other Types of Trusts

There are many other descriptive terms used to describe the function of a trust. A **charitable trust** is simply a trust which has a charity as its beneficiary.

Support trusts are ones whose income is specifically designated for the support of one or more beneficiaries. **Accumulation trusts** are ones whose income is accumulated within the trust and is not distributed to any beneficiary, at least not until some later time when it may be distributed as principal. **Discretionary trusts** or **sprinkling trusts** are really terms more applicable to clauses within trusts, although the entire trust often takes on this name. They describe trusts where the trustee has the discretion to allocate the income among the various beneficiaries in whatever amounts he sees fit, rather than in specified amounts dictated by the trustor; thus, he has the power to "sprinkle" the income.

Spendthrift trusts also more accurately describe a particular clause within many other kinds of trusts. In a desire to protect the beneficiary against "spendthrift" tendencies, trustors may want to restrict the beneficiary's ability to make economic moves which might harm his trust interest, as well as restrict the ability of his creditors to take his interest away. Such a clause usually provides that the beneficiary's interest will not be part of his estate if he goes bankrupt, and that the interest is not subject to levy or execution by a creditor who may have obtained a judgment or other claim against him. The beneficiary is further prohibited from selling, assigning, or giving away his interest in the trust and also from borrowing against his trust interest or pledging it as security for a loan. In some states such clauses are completely valid and very effective to protect the beneficiary, and in others they are only valid in some respects or not valid at all. So local law will have to be consulted.

The Flexibility Of Trusts

The many types of trusts indicate the flexibility which the trustor has in choosing the type best suited to his needs and the needs of his beneficiaries. In fact, flexibility is the keynote to trusts. There is great flexibility available in the choice of a trustee, in the many powers a trustor may grant to or withhold from the trustee, and in the directions set down for the continuing management and administration of the trust. By these various means, the trustor can provide the most flexible possible device to meet the many economic and family uncertainties which may arise over the entire future period during which the trust will exist. Because of these important flexibilities, in modern day usage a trust is almost universally used when one wants to create a life estate in property. Although a life estate (defined at page 49) can legally be created without the use of a trust, it is an extremely ponderous and limited thing. There are many questions about what a life tenant can or cannot do (sell the property, borrow against it, give it away, etc.,) because the remaindermen (defined at page 50) have rights which cannot be taken away from them by the life tenant. So a trust is usually the answer, with life interests and remainder interests in the trust rather than in the underlying property itself, thereby giving the trustee the flexibility to do many things that a life tenant is not able to do.

Selecting a Trustee

In any estate plan where a trust is indicated, choosing the trustee may well be the single most significant decision a trustor will make. It may not be readily apparent why this is so, but a moment's reflection should point up the reasons. All the decisions which minimize the tax impacts and in combination result in the final estate plan usually revolve around one paramount consideration: namely, the concern that the testator/trustor has for the persons who are his beneficiaries, and his wish to provide the most favorable possible climate for their long-term security. All the testator/trustor can do is make those decisions, but where a trust is involved it is the trustee who actually carries them out and shoulders the day-to-day responsibility over the difficult economic realities. If the trustor is a success in his decisions, but the trustee is a failure in carrying them out, the net result will only be failure of the estate plan as a whole. If so, it is the persons most dear to the trustor, his beneficiaries, who will suffer the most. In an all-too-common absurdity, trustors often give only a few moments thought to the choice of trustee, just tossing off the selection with a cavalier remark such as, ". . . Oh, I guess Mr. X would be pretty good."

Naming An Individual Versus A Bank

The initial puzzlement when contemplating the selection of a trustee usually concerns naming an individual versus naming a bank. As with the choice of an executor, it is a matter which often arouses strong feelings. Some people have what amounts to a virtual prejudice against banks, and others have almost prejudicial inability to recognize any benefits to using an individual. In such a significant matter demanding rational decision-making, all such quasi-prejudices ought to be recognized for what they are, and put aside. Once that is done, a difficult choice is still faced, for there are scores of reasons favoring the choice of one and scores favoring the choice of the other. The crucial task is to determine which way the balance falls in one's own personal situation.

If there is one almost cliche-like truism which will be more and more a theme of this book as you read on, it is that estate planning is an intensely personal matter. Any materials you read or lectures you might attend can only state the rules and the considerations by way of generalities. It would be foolish and irresponsible for any general text or lecture to presume to tell you what you "should" do; that can only be determined by analysis of an individual situation and all its unique factors. So it is with the choice of a trustee, and whether an individual or a bank is preferable. Dogmatic thinking, whether on the part of an advisor or his client, is no service to anyone, and ought to be viewed with just a bit of suspicion. I have worked through situations with many clients where we have been completely comfortable with a bank as trustee, and I have worked through many situations with clients where we have been completely comfortable with an individual as trustee; I can state no preference or recommendations, for the ultimate answer is truly: "It depends." But having said that, here are a few of the factors which ought to be weighed in arriving at the choice.

Banks are in the business of being highly professional trust managers, and they bring trained, experienced, and thoroughly professional management to bear. As they are fond of saying in their promotional literature (statements which are nevertheless completely valid), banks never die, never go on vacation, never become ill, and their attention to the trust never wanes. Most of the major banks are now utilizing sophisticated automation techniques, and thus they can quickly present a full accounting of income and outgo. The latter can be a great convenience (as well as economical when compared to accountings done by hand) and in appropriate situations is reason enough to use a bank.

On the other hand, the trust department of a bank is understandably and of necessity a volume operation which, while never remotely neglecting its duty, can admittedly not give the same type of personal involvement with the beneficiaries' lives as can an individual. Theirs is a business relationship and not a personal or family relationship; they cannot spend long bouts of time on the phone discussing various persons' health, trials and tribulations, and recent restaurant experiences. To wish a bank to do so is to misunderstand its true function.

A bank is often hesitant to operate a going business left by the trustor or to actively manage those kinds of real estate investments which need constant personal attention. A bank often instinctively wants to convert such holdings to more liquid and easily manageable funds. For those reasons, sometimes the nature of a trustor's assets will go a long way towards dictating the choice of trustee.

It is only equitable that a trustee be paid for its services. A bank, being in business specifically to earn such fees, will most assuredly charge an annual fee, whereas an individual may charge less or even nothing at all depending upon his degree of closeness to the beneficiaries. In most states there are no mandatory trustee fees set out by statute; however, in order not to engage in price-cutting wars, most banks in a given state or other appropriate locale will charge roughly the same fees. In my area at the time this is written, the standard fee seems to be three-quarters of one percent of net asset value per year for ordinary services in managing easily managed types of assets. However, for assets more difficult to manage or for extraordinary services, the fees are subject to upward negotiation between the trustee and the beneficiaries, often subject to court approval if the trust is a court trust.

Most of the larger banks have a minimum size for the trusts they will normally agree to handle. Their reasoning is simple: below that minimum size, experience tells them it is uneconomical both for themselves and for the trust itself to have them act as trustee. That minimum size varies with geography, and also varies with the size of the bank and its aggressiveness in seeking new trust business. In my area, most banks would have to be convinced of unusual circumstances to undertake a trust much under $100,000, and many of the larger ones would prefer to start closer to $250,000. They will, however, consider smaller trusts, often upon adjustment of their normal fee structure, and they are always open to discussions with potential trustors and/or beneficiaries. It is always a good idea to discuss a potential trusteeship with the bank concerned. They often have very good suggestions for trust provisions and sometimes have requirements which must be drafted into the trust in order for them to accept the trusteeship. If they are not consulted in advance, the trustor runs the risk that the named bank may decline to accept the appointment or may resign during the course of its administration. For the latter reason as well as several others, it is always a good idea to specify one or more alternate trustees should the initial trustee selected become unable or unwilling to serve.

Banks may often suggest (and it may well be a good idea even if they don't) that a clause be inserted whereby if the trust dips below a certain amount in total value, the trust at that time be discontinued. The reason is the same as given above; below that figure it is just too uneconomical for everyone concerned to continue operating the property as a trust.

Certainly one factor in the question of whether to appoint a bank or an individual is whether a qualified individual is available to the trustor. Being a relative or close friend does not necessarily qualify someone for the task; that statement is ridiculously obvious, but it is amazing how many people are prone to ignore its message. A major factor here, which the trustor must soberly consider, is the responsibility, obligation, and even burden that being a trustee puts upon an individual. It ought to be a major question in the trustor's mind whether he wishes to lay that burden on the life of a given potential trustee. It is of course more than appropriate to discuss the matter with the potential trustee, test his willingness to assume the obligation and his own assessment of his abilities to manage property, and obtain his agreement to serve. The latter goes beyond a mere matter of courtesy; it is better that the trustor himself know of any reluctance so that the trustor can choose another trustee of his own choice. In many cases, the burden felt by a trustee, rationally or irrationally, can be an awesome one. Both parties should seriously consider whether the proposed selectee is genuinely willing to accept that burden.

The Surviving Spouse As Trustee

Many trusts exist in the context of a married couple, with property being placed in trust to benefit the spouse who survives. If the surviving spouse is the lifetime beneficiary of the trust, can or should the survivor be his or her own trustee? Legally, the beneficiary can of course be the trustee, but whether he or she should be is another matter entirely. In subsequent chapters you will see some tax reasons why it may be less advantageous for the surviving spouse to also serve as trustee. At the very least, if the survivor is both trustee and beneficiary, the trust must be drafted very carefully in order not to run afoul of some major tax traps. It often happens that by using an independent trustee (that is, one who is not also one of the beneficiaries), the trust can operate in a much more flexible manner. On the other hand, many spouses chafe at the idea that any outside person or bank will take over control of their property just because one of them has died; in such cases, even a more restrictively drafted trust using the survivor as trustee may best satisfy the parties. However, you must consider that surviving spouses may not be the most trained or capable persons to serve as a trustee. Then too, there is the same factor mentioned above concerning the burden and responsibility placed upon a surviving spouse who acts as his or her own trustee. As with so many other things in this increasingly complicated world, the whole matter is a dilemma and a paradox; each couple will simply have to decide what is best for them.

Co-Trustees

There are literally scores, even hundreds, of other considerations which may crop up in any given situation concerning the choice of a trustee. In what often appears as desperation, people may "solve" the problem by requesting **co-trustees,** usually a bank and an individual. It must be immediately recognized that a co-trusteeship raises the possibility of a difference of opinion between the trustees. Since they each have equal authority, an inability to solve the matter may quite literally hamstring the trust in a tie vote. When you think about it, such divisions of opinion are even more a probability than a possibility. While co-trusteeships most definitely have their place where they are clearly indicated, there ought to be some compelling reason for them in order to outweigh the possible problems. There can be many sources of such compelling reasons, including very valid emotional ones. Where indicated, some kind of dispute-solving mechanism might profitably be drafted into the trust; some banks are hesitant to accept a co-trusteeship unless such a mechanism is present in the trust document. Many times they approve of a mechanism which allows the individual trustee, particularly if he or she is also one of the beneficiaries, to have the dominant vote and thereby the ability to break the tie. In larger trusts, which would justify such an arrangement, a simple solution would be to use three trustees, or some other uneven number.

As you read on and see some of the sophisticated problems and elections of being a trustee, think about the type of trustee able to knowledgeably carry out the various duties. And also think about the responsibility, obligation, and burden of doing so.

Powers and Duties of a Trustee

The administrative responsibilities of a trustee are unique because they are not to be exercised for his own benefit but rather for the benefit of other persons. A property owner is free to do whatever he wishes with his own property, even including throwing it away, but the standards of managing property for someone else's benefit are entirely different. The standard of conduct a trustee is subject to is known as fiduciary duty, and a trustee is often called a **fiduciary.** There are many other fiduciaries in the law, including executors, guardians, directors of a corporation, and several others;

they are all held to the highest possible standard of care and conduct. This implies the utmost good faith and the highest possible degree of loyalty to those for whose benefit a fiduciary is acting.

The fiduciary standard can be compared to the standard to which public officials are now held in this post-Watergate era, where we have discovered from painful experience that the appearance of wrongdoing by persons in certain sensitive positions is just as bad as any actual wrongdoing itself. It is all a matter of public confidence and trust, even over and above the need to prevent actual wrongdoing; so too it has always been with fiduciaries. Thus, fiduciaries are traditionally not allowed to put themselves into any position where there can be even an appearance of wrongdoing. No dealing for his own account with the trust assets or with the beneficiaries is allowed: the trustee is traditionally not allowed to sell any of his own property to the trust even at a fair price, to purchase property from the trust at a fair price, loan money to or borrow money from the trust, be a joint owner of any asset with the trust, or scores of other things designed to prevent suspicious appearances.

The subject of the duties and powers of a trustee is easily the subject for a multi-volume legal work. Naturally, that is not our purpose and no such thing will be even slightly attempted. Any trustee or other person interested in these subjects will simply have to seek individual advice. For our purposes it is important to know that the trustee is subject to the strict fiduciary duty and that he is granted certain powers to perform that duty. Generally, he is given by law those powers necessary to do all things which a prudent man would do in the preservation and management of property held for the benefit of others; this is the famous **prudent man standard** where a trustee's action can theoretically be tested by reference to what the mythical prudent man would do. This standard is the source of the so-called approved list of trust investments, which still has some relevance in certain states, whereby certain types of investments are considered to be non-prudent and therefore disallowed to a trustee. Commonly found among unapproved investments are such things as unproductive or underproductive property, investments in new or speculative enterprises, investments in second mortgages, and the like. The prudent man standard is also the source of the general rule that a trustee ought to diversify the investments of a trust.

Of overriding importance, however, is that modern trust law allows the trustor to reverse the normal rules by either permitting or disallowing particular powers. Perhaps the primary overriding concept of modern trust law is that the intention of the trustor will be carried out. It is for this reason that most well-drafted trust documents contain lengthy lists of the powers the trustee may have in the administration of that particular trust. Once the trustor has permitted or restricted a function, there is no further chance that the trustee will run afoul of the often archaic and restrictive general trust law. Many times a trustor will want a trustee to be able to make speculative investments, in which case he merely needs to say so. Conversely, he may want to restrict the trustee to investments even more conservative than those permitted by general law, and if he expresses this intention in the trust document, his directions will be upheld.

Most trust draftsmen feel that, if the trustor has absolute confidence in his trustee, considering the uncertain economic world in which we now live and which may only get more uncertain as the decades roll by, optimum economic flexibility will be assured by providing the trustee with the broadest possible powers. The trustor is also wise to specifically authorize what would otherwise be breaches of the fiduciary standard if he knows in advance that such situations are desirable and will inevitably arise. An example might be where several family members all have ownership interests in the same business, and now one of them is to become a trustee over his brother's interest; of course there will now be common ownerships between the trust and the trustee individually, and probably certain cross-dealings as well, so the trustor must specifically authorize them to enable that trust to function.

The trustor may also specify restrictions greater than those otherwise imposed by law, perhaps due to the nature of the assets involved, or perhaps due to the personal philosophy of the trustor. In one well-known case, a trustor who had successfully weathered the Depression imposed extremely restrictive conditions upon any investments his trustee might make. When all the beneficiaries and the trustee joined together years later to seek relief from these restrictions, on the ground that the trust was thereby prevented from participating in the post-war economic boom, a court denied any relief. That case indicates two things: the sanctity of the trustor's directions, and the need for every trustor to very thoroughly think through his instructions and their effect on what may occur in the unknown future.

The Income of a Trust

One of the chief goals when creating a trust, and one of the chief responsibilities of the trustee, is to provide sufficient **income** for the normal needs of the beneficiaries. The trustor is concerned with their long-term security and ability to maintain their standards of living, so the trustee will be investing the trust property in income-producing assets to provide that income. Such income can be provided by interest on bank deposits or bonds, dividends on stock, or income from real estate investments or businesses, among many other sources. The income so produced is usually visualized in standard time periods, such as annual, quarterly, or monthly, and then distributed in whatever way the trustor has directed in the trust document. There are several choices.

Ways To Distribute Trust Income

The income can be entirely paid out monthly, quarterly, or annually to one or more beneficiaries for a certain number of years; often, the time span is the rest of the beneficiary's life, which is the essence of having a life interest in a trust. Or, the income could be entirely **accumulated** (held within the trust by adding it to the principal), although that alternative is becoming less attractive than it previously was because of the income tax reason soon to be mentioned. As a third alternative, the trustee may be granted the discretion either to accumulate all or any part of the income or to pay out all or any part of it to one or more beneficiaries; this is the so-called **discretionary or sprinkling trust.** An inexact but illustrative example of the tax results produced by each of these three methods of allocating the trust's taxable income is shown in Table 6-2. Then there are all kinds of positions in-between. A set annual sum could be provided for the beneficiary, with any balance being either accumulated or paid to someone else. Although a set sum might fail to take account of inflation, it could be supplemented by a well-thought-out escalator or cost-of-living clause increasing the amount each year. Or, the trustor could set down certain conditions restricting the use of income, such as for health emergencies only, to pay all necessary expenses of someone's education, or whatever.

A discretionary or sprinkling power in the hands of the trustee has two primary benefits. First, it provides the greatest amount of flexibility to meet any changing circumstances of the beneficiaries and/or the economy. Secondly, it has an excellent income tax effect. A trust is a **separate taxpaying entity** which files an annual income tax return on Form 1041, the Fiduciary Income Tax Return, covering the income it earns. The trust gets a small exemption, and then pays income taxes at the rate of a single person on any net income retained in the trust at the end of its taxable year. But a beneficiary will pay income taxes at his own tax bracket on whatever income is distributed to him from a trust, and the trust gets a deduction for that distributed income to ensure that such income is not taxed twice.

If all the annual income of a trust is distributed, the distributions deductions will cancel out the income, and the return will be only an informational return (which must still be filed) showing no tax due. Due to the operation of those tax rules, a trustee with a discretionary power over income has the power to effect tax results

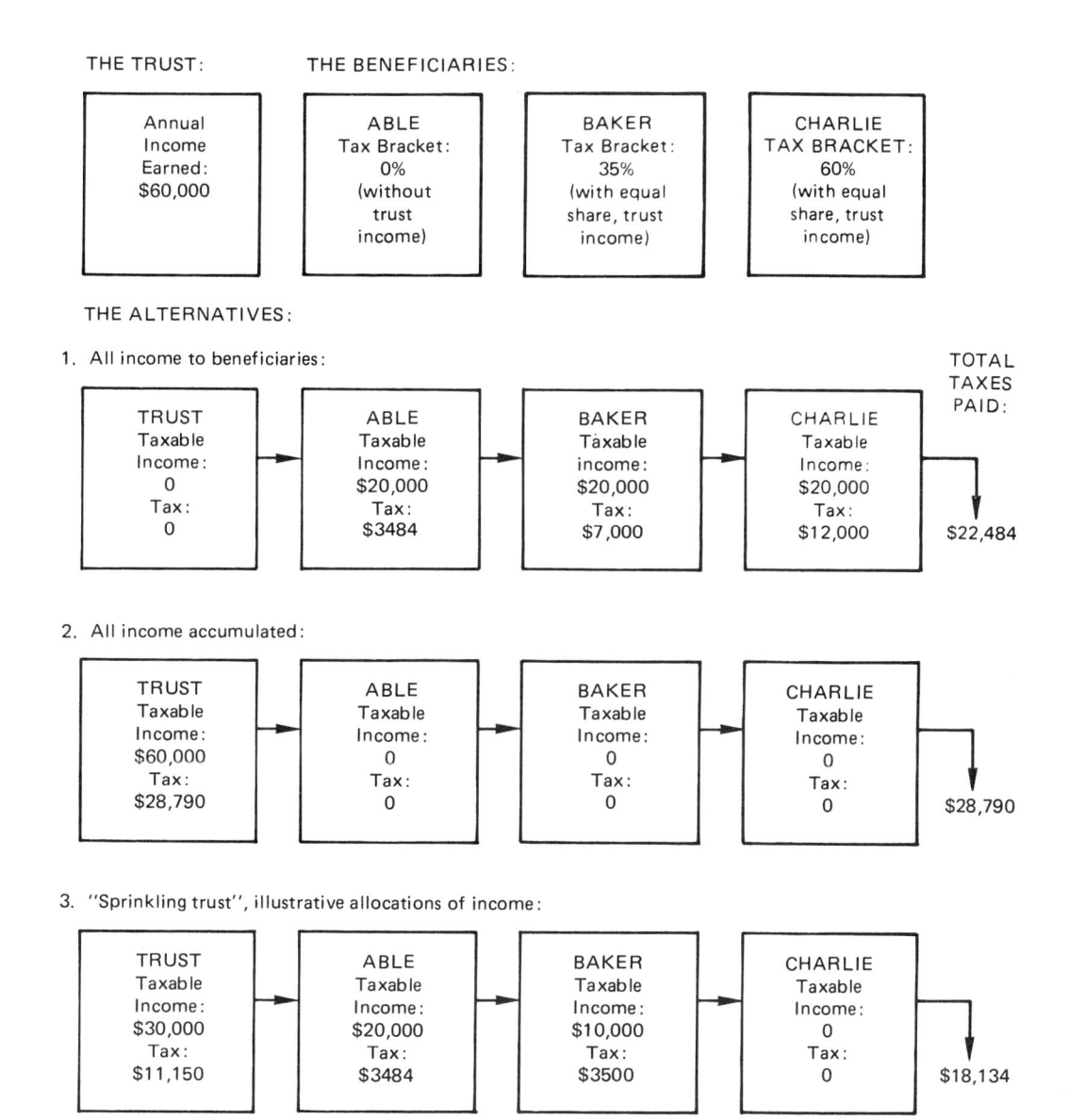

Table 6–2. Inexact illustrations of income tax results for different types of trusts.

THE TRUST:

Annual Income Earned: $60,000

THE BENEFICIARIES:

ABLE Tax Bracket: 0% (without trust income)	BAKER Tax Bracket: 35% (with equal share, trust income)	CHARLIE TAX BRACKET: 60% (with equal share, trust income)

THE ALTERNATIVES:

1. All income to beneficiaries:

TRUST Taxable Income: 0 Tax: 0	→	ABLE Taxable Income: $20,000 Tax: $3484	→	BAKER Taxable income: $20,000 Tax: $7,000	→	CHARLIE Taxable Income: $20,000 Tax: $12,000

TOTAL TAXES PAID: $22,484

2. All income accumulated:

TRUST Taxable Income: $60,000 Tax: $28,790	→	ABLE Taxable Income: 0 Tax: 0	→	BAKER Taxable Income: 0 Tax: 0	→	CHARLIE Taxable Income: 0 Tax: 0

$28,790

3. "Sprinkling trust", illustrative allocations of income:

TRUST Taxable Income: $30,000 Tax: $11,150	→	ABLE Taxable Income: $20,000 Tax: $3484	→	BAKER Taxable Income: $10,000 Tax: $3500	→	CHARLIE Taxable Income: 0 Tax: 0

$18,134

by minimizing the overall tax impacts. If a beneficiary is in a high income tax bracket, the trustee may do well to pay no income to him, as it would only increase his tax burden and be taxed at very high rates. The trustee might do better by keeping the income in the trust and paying income taxes on it at the trust's (presumably) lower income tax bracket. If there are several beneficiaries all in different income tax brackets and with differing needs for income, the trustee can wisely distribute the annual income in completely different amounts among the various beneficiaries. A wealthy son in a high income tax bracket might get little or no income, another son just starting out in business and having little taxable income might get a goodly proportion of it, as might a daughter finishing up her education with no other income at all. From the viewpoint of a beneficiary earning substantial taxable income from sources outside the trust, a discretionary trust is really the **perfect tax shelter,** since it makes it possible for him not to receive any income he doesn't really need or want.

Trustees Who Should Not Have Discretionary Power

Not every trustee should have a discretionary power over income, and sometimes the advisability of giving a discretionary power to the trustee will dictate the choice of trustee. For instance, if one of the beneficiaries who is entitled to share in the income is also the trustee, he can not be given a discretionary power; the tax law provides that in such a case all of the income would be taxed to him no matter who actually got it, simply because he possessed the discretionary power. Therefore, a discretionary power is only useful if an independent (non-beneficiary) trustee is used. A surviving spouse cannot serve as trustee and also have a discretionary power over income, for to so structure the trust would destory the income tax savings the trustor would be seeking to achieve.

Taxes Make Accumulation Trust Unattractive

As mentioned earlier, recent changes in the tax law have reduced the tax benefits of **accumulation trusts** (where income is retained in the trust and taxes are paid by the trust at its own tax bracket). From the point of view of the government, they presented too great an opportunity for income tax avoidance. The reason is that a payment of trust income to a beneficiary is taxable income to him, but a distribution of trust principal is generally not taxable income. When income is accumulated within a trust and taxes are paid on it by the trust, the amount remaining after taxes becomes a part of principal. Therefore, if income in year number one is retained in trust and added to principal, but the identical amount of money is distributed to the beneficiary in year number two and called a distribution of principal, you can see how income taxes could be reduced if the trust were in a lower income tax bracket than the beneficiary. To prevent that ploy, we have what is known as the **throwback rule.** If income is accumulated and if at any time in the following years it is distributed as "principal" to a beneficiary, the tax brackets of the trust and of that beneficiary for the year in which the income was earned have to be compared, and if the beneficiary's bracket was higher, the appropriate amount of extra tax is collected. The just described ploy is thereby made meaningless because the throwback rule will cause taxes to be paid at the beneficiary's higher rate in any case.

One result is that an accumulation trust imposes an immense recordkeeping burden on the trustee, and since the tax advantage of the accumulations has been greatly reduced by the unlimited throwback rule, accumulation trusts are less frequently used. To avoid the throwback problem, all income of a trust must be distributed to someone each year, or else the income will have to qualify under one of the two exceptions to the throwback rule.

The two exceptions are rare advantages doled out to taxpayers by the 1976 Tax Reform Act. One eliminates the throwback rule for any accumulations of income on behalf of a beneficiary during those years when the beneficiary was unborn or was under the age of twenty-one. This is a most welcome and realistic piece of relief, because it is usually unwise to distribute any substantial amounts of income to children under twenty-one just to avoid a tax rule such as the throwback rule. The other happy change eliminates the throwback rule for capital gains taxes, so that if there is a later distribution of proceeds from a sale on which the trust itself paid the capital gains taxes (because it retained the proceeds beyond the end of the taxable year), no excess capital gains taxes will now result.

Despite the throwback rule, accumulation trusts can still be used to advantage in particular situations. The complexities of this rule are the province of a sophisticated tax accountant or attorney, and there are several opportunities to advantageously plan with the two exceptions to the throwback rule.

Allocations Between Principal and Income

In a frequent trust scenario, there are one or more income beneficiaries who get all the annual income in a given year, and there are remainder (i.e., principal) beneficiaries who will at some future time receive distributions of the principal after the income interests have ended. These two sets of beneficiaries have conflicting economic interests. To illustrate, assume the trust is sued or sues someone and in a given year there are legal fees of $20,000. If those fees are charged entirely against income, there will be much less net income for the income beneficiaries, and they will therefore be paying all of those legal fees. But if the fees are charged entirely against principal, then the remaindermen will be paying the fees, and the income beneficiaries will pay none of them. What is equitable? Or, assume the trust holds stock in a small corporation which goes through a complex merger, and the trust receives a check for $100,000 as one of its payments in the merger. If that check is properly all income, one set of beneficiaries will get it all, but if it is properly principal, the other set will get it all. What is equitable? The inconsistent interests of the two sets of beneficiaries create a grave problem for the trustee. What should he call stock brokerage commissions? The expenses of remodeling a building owned by the trust? Stock dividends received? Gains on the sale of trust assets?

There are two different ways to guide the trustee in this problem. Most states have passed a statute known as the **Uniform Principal and Income Act,** which lists scores of usual and unusual items of expense as well as items of receipt, and which states whether such items are properly principal or income. The trustor can provide in the trust document that the trustee should make decisions in this area by reference to that statute. Or, the trustor could provide that the trustee may make allocations between principal and income "in his sole and absolute discretion." The latter grants the trustee tremendous flexibility in adjusting and controlling the amounts to be received by the different beneficiaries. It can also in some instances allow the trustee to adjust the income tax results. The IRS has some overriding rules in many such areas, but you can see that where the IRS is bound to follow the trustee's decisions as to what is income and what is principal, the income tax results will also follow those decisions. Needless to say, this is a subtle, sophisticated, and technical matter.

It should be noted that not all trustees should possess the power to allocate between principal and income, sometimes due to the abilities of the particular trustee, but more often due to restrictions contained in the tax law. Several instances exist where granting this broad power to any trustee under a given trust will result in adverse tax consequences and may perhaps even destroy a principal tax reason for creating the trust in the first place. A knowledgeable advisor will be able to help you weigh the tax considerations.

Invasions of Principal

It is usually considered foolish for a trustor to lock up the principal of a trust so that it is unavailable for an emergency or other appropriate needs of the beneficiaries. In some cases, the annual income of a trust will not be enough to cover either regular or extraordinary expenses of a beneficiary. In other cases, the trustor may wish to provide occasional or emergency access to the trust principal for persons who are not the beneficiaries of annual income. For instance, if all the income is to be paid to the trustor's surviving spouse during his or her lifetime, the trustor may still wish to provide access to the trust principal for designated purposes on behalf of the children. All such situations can be handled if the trustor writes into his trust powers to use the principal, often referred to as **invasions of principal.** Indeed, it can generally be said that almost all trusts ought to contain such provisions.

The power to invade principal may be granted only to the trustee, or it may also be granted to one or more of the beneficiaries. Depending upon the wishes of the trustor and what he specifies in the trust document, such powers may be either unlimited and at the virtual whim of a trustee or beneficiary, or these powers may be restricted to only those specified circumstances allowed by the trustor. In the latter case, the trustor may specify anything he deems appropriate, which may be restrictive or liberal. Common conditions under which the use of principal is allowed include the health, education, support or maintenance of the beneficiary. Sometimes the trustee is directed to take into account the beneficiaries' other sources of income and funds, whereas in other cases the trustee might not be so directed; it all depends on whether the trustor wants the trust funds liberally available or only for situations approaching emergencies. The trustor can also provide for very specific instances where invasions may be allowed, such as for a child opening a business or purchasing a home, as a graduation stipend, or whatever.

Again, the tax law has many things to say about such powers of invasion and in certain trust structures will effectively limit or prohibit what the trustor might otherwise wish. In some cases, to allow the beneficiaries any powers of invasion would defeat the very tax purposes the trustor is trying to achieve, and often the tax law requires that the invasion powers be quite restrictive. Further, tax rules have a great deal of impact on the invasion powers allowed to a trustee who is also one of the beneficiaries, and because of tax considerations, it may be (and often is) appropriate that an independent trustee be used; that is, a trustee who is not also one of the beneficiaries. The tax law's impact on powers to invade principal will be covered in chapter eight.

A 1976 Tax Reform Act Change

One specialized change wrought by the 1976 Tax Act deserves mention. It introduces a new tax factor which operates in ways analogous to the throwback rule, and was inserted to prevent what Congress saw as certain abuses. This change specifies that if a trustor creates a living trust and transfers to the trust a piece of property worth more than what the trustor paid for it, if that property is sold by the trust within two years after the property was so transferred, then the capital gains taxes will be assessed at the tax bracket of the trustor and not at the tax bracket of the trust itself. Obviously, trustors had been using the former law to reduce their capital gains taxes where those taxes at the bracket of the trust would have been less than at the trustor's own bracket. But now, the trust will have to hold the property for at least two years in order for the capital gains taxes to be assessed at the trust's own bracket.

Termination of Trusts

Trusts normally terminate according to their own terms, at whatever time the trust instrument specifies. But there is a very important, centuries-old rule which specifies the maximum duration a trust will be permitted to exist before it must be ended. That rule is known as the **Rule Against Perpetuities,** or more notoriously, as just "The Rule."

The Rule Against Perpetuities

The precise language and effect of it vary from state to state, but the basic restriction is the same for all states. Its purpose is to prevent a property owner from creating successive life interests in perpetuity, which he might otherwise do to keep his property in his family forever. This rule carries out a social purpose of breaking up large family holdings which might otherwise go on forever, by requiring that ownership of property must eventually pass to someone, outright and free of usual trust restrictions. In that way, the outright owner would have the ability to sell some or all of it, give some of it away, or develop it. This tends to recirculate the property within the general economy, and benefits everyone.

Unfortunately, The Rule is perhaps the single most confusing thing in all of law. It is not important to our purpose for you to understand what The Rule means or how it works (if that were even possible; legal scholars have devoted lifetimes to it without fully grasping its every twist). Instead, it is only important that you realize that The Rule exists, that you see what it says so that you will have some awareness of the time period it covers, and that you be able to recognize provisions in trusts which are there because The Rule exists.

Here is what The Rule says (don't worry if this doesn't make total sense; I just want you to see what it says): For a trust or other disposition of property to be valid, the property must vest, if at all, within a life then in being plus twenty-one years from the date of the trust or gift. But if, considering every conceivable possibility which might prevent vesting within the time described, it can be shown that the property might not vest, the trust or gift is absolutely void. That's the source of the confusion, because some of the "every conceivable possibilities" are pretty wild indeed.

Vest means, essentially, receiving the fee simple (see page 49), outright and free of any trust, within the time specified. A "life in being" includes only those people whom the trustor names as beneficiaries of the trust, or specifies should be the persons against whom the time period should be measured (although there are limitations of reasonableness on the trustor's specifying such persons). As to the "every conceivable possibility" business, there are many bizarre and often humorous examples of dispositions which can run afoul of this element. There is no point in confusing you with examples which can be constructed. It is sufficient to say that whenever any trust or other property disposition contains several generations, or whenever one contains a qualifying age for the outright receipt of property which is greater than twenty-one years of age, a lawyer inevitably thinks of The Rule. It is for this reason that a lawyer may have to advise a client that a desired condition in a trust or other gift is not possible. But it is worth noting that gifts to charities, including charitable foundations, are generally exempt from The Rule (this being one of several legal policies designed to encourage charitable giving).

Perpetuities Savings Clause

In some but not all states a clause known as a **perpetuities savings clause** is valid. This is mentioned because, if you see one in a will or trust, you may be puzzled at the appearance of this strange sounding clause. It typically appears after all the conditions for the final termination of a trust have been stated, and often begins ". . . notwithstanding any of the above, this trust shall end . . . (within a time period sounding very much like The Rule)." People are often bewildered why, after all the elaborate provisions have been stated, a clause should appear that seems to reverse everything previously done. It really doesn't reverse previous provisions, but only puts an outside limit on them and assures that the terrible Rule will not be violated.

Within the limits of The Rule, a trustor may specify any time for trust termination. That time could be defined as an absolute number of years, it could be dependent upon the length of a given beneficiary's life, or it may be dependent upon any number of external conditions. Where the ultimate beneficiaries are or may be youngsters, a common condition is to provide for outright distribution only when each of them attains a certain age or series of ages. In chapter eleven I will discuss further some of the considerations concerning appropriate ages at which financial maturity is likely.

Terminating Revocable And Irrevocable Trusts

A revocable trust can of course be terminated at any time while the trustor is still alive. Most revocable trusts automatically become irrevocable when the trustor dies, since the trustor is no longer alive to revoke them, so after that occurs the trust can normally not be prematurely terminated in advance of the time specified in the trust instrument. Testamentary trusts are of course irrevocable since no one is alive to revoke them, and hence they too can normally end only by their own terms.

The parties to an irrevocable trust would sometimes prefer premature termination of that trust, but that is available only in very limited circumstances. If the parties can convince a court that the entire purpose of the trust is being frustrated by keeping it in existence, the laws of many states will allow premature termination by judicial decree. Sometimes this involves a total breakdown in the working relationship between trustee and beneficiaries, where the only alternative to chaos is the requested termination. If the trustor is alive, most states allow the trustor, trustee, and all beneficiaries the power to prematurely terminate the trust so long as they all agree and obtain court approval. A major problem on this score is that all beneficiaries must agree, including minors and even potential unborn beneficiaries (who after all have distinct property rights in the trust). There are legal mechanisms available where a disinterested person can represent the position of minor and unborn beneficiaries, but sometimes even those mechanisms prove impossible to implement and so everyone is stuck. If an irrevocable trust can be terminated prematurely, the property does not revert to the trustor, but rather it is distributed to the proper beneficiaries under the terms of the trust instrument. The only way for the trustor to then get the property back would be by gift from the beneficiaries. That is why an irrevocable trust is such a serious step and should be undertaken only upon a conviction by the trustor that under no conceivable circumstances will he ever again need the trust property.

APPLICATION

NOTE: This Application will assume that you have decided to create a trust. The reasons behind such a decision are contained in the later chapters of this book, so you might want to return to this Application section after you have finished the book.

1. Determine whether your situation generates more reasons for a testamentary trust, or a living trust.

2. If a living trust, decide whether it should be revocable or irrevocable, and determine your state's law concerning how to make a trust either revocable or irrevocable.

3. If a living trust, consider whether to fund that trust with some or all of your assets during life, or only a nominal amount of assets.

4. Consider whether to name a trust the beneficiary of your life insurance.

5. Give careful thought to the choice of both a trustee and an alternate trustee, weighing the advantages and disadvantages of banks versus individuals. Ascertain the willingness of a proposed trustee to assume the responsibility of serving. If you are leaning towards an out-of-state trustee, determine your state's laws concerning their ability to serve. If you are considering your spouse as trustee, thoughtfully consider his or her financial management abilities and experience, as well as the responsibility which being a trustee will impose. Be sure that your choice is capable of coping with the many tax law complexities of trusts. Be confident that your choice understands the nature of fiduciary responsibilities, and that you view your choice as a person capable of fulfilling them.

6. Do not gloss over the powers you grant to your trustee. Consider whether you wish to expand or restrict his usual powers. Be sure to specifically authorize something that you wish to permit but which, if you don't authorize it, would not be permitted by the general trust law of your state (such as mutual ownerships, self-dealing, etc.).

7. Determine whether the annual trust income should be entirely paid out, entirely accumulated, or whether the trustee should have the power to sprinkle the income among the beneficiaries according to their needs and tax brackets.

8. Determine what powers the trustee should have to invade trust principal, and whether those powers should be narrowly drawn or liberally drawn.

9. Give instructions or directions to your trustee, in writing within the document, on any subject you wish to comment on. The law allows you to express whatever it is that you want; exercise that right.

10. Give a good deal of thought to the time, or series of times, when trust beneficiaries should receive outright distributions from the trust. Consider the ages, needs, money-handling abilities, and financial maturity of each of the beneficiaries.

part two
estate and gift taxes

7

estate and gift taxes: rates and exemptions

Glossary For This Chapter

Annual Exclusion
Deductions
Deficiency
Estate Tax
Exemption
Gift Tax
Gross Estate
Inheritance Tax
IRS (Internal Revenue Service)
Orphan's Exclusion
Unitary Transfer Tax

Many people are furious at the idea of estate taxes. After having paid income taxes on what has been earned all during life, they don't see why the sad occasion of death cruelly causes still another tax. From that point of view, the tax is indeed distasteful. But it exists neither to be cruel nor primarily to raise revenue. Along with the Rule Against Perpetuities (page 108), it fulfills a much broader societal purpose, which is to break up and recirculate large concentrations of wealth. The Rule does so by making property freely transferable within a maximum period of time, while the estate tax does so by making certain wealth-concentrating devices futile, as well as by channeling taxes collected from wealth into the economy via government spending. A recent study indicated that without these two devices, all the wealth of our rather young nation would by now be held by less than one-hundred families. If that study is even approximately accurate, the estate tax is justified. Otherwise we would have created a modern day feudal society, we would all be

115

working for the one hundred owners, and there would be no incentive for any of us but the chosen one hundred.

Estate and Gift Taxes Are Excise Taxes

All excise taxes are taxes on a privilege. The federal government and some of the states levy an **estate tax** where the privilege being taxed is that of leaving property to one's heirs. As noted earlier, this is not an inalienable right of citizenship but rather is a grant of privilege from the legislature which the government may tax. The amount of an estate tax is determined by the amount of property a decedent owned, since that is what is subject to the privilege he is exercising. The tax is levied against the decedent's estate and is not concerned with who inherits the property nor in how many shares, but only with how much property the decedent owned.

Some of the states have a different tax system for their death duties, called an **inheritance tax.** This is also an excise tax on a privilege, but here the privilege being taxed is that of inheriting property. Therefore such a tax is very much concerned with how much each heir inherits and usually also with the degree of relationship of each heir to the decedent because different rates and exemptions apply to different degrees of relationship.

The **gift tax** is also an excise tax, on the privilege of giving and is measured by the amount of the gift. The gift tax was originally inserted into the law not to produce revenue, but rather to protect the estate tax. Without the gift tax, the estate tax could be easily evaded simply by giving away all that one owns. After recent revisions in the tax structure, the gift tax assumes a different posture, as we shall soon see.

The Federal Tax Is By Far The More Important

Except in isolated instances, we shall not be saying much about any state's death duties or gift taxes. The reasons are several: the federal tax is vastly more significant in dollar impact, often as much as ten times more so than any state tax, and so arrangements seeking to minimize the federal tax will have by far the greater impact. Also, the principles behind both federal and state taxes are roughly the same, so that if you understand something of the federal tax you will also understand most aspects of any state's tax. And finally, since each state differs in its particular system (and one state, Nevada, doesn't even have such a tax), it is best to have each reader learn matters of local significance from local advisors. Otherwise this book would be a fat reference encyclopedia containing fifty state's laws, which is not its purpose.

The federal estate tax is structured along lines similar to the income tax. When you make out your income tax return, you add all items includible as income to arrive at gross income, you take all itemized or standard deductions to arrive at taxable income, you apply the tax rates to arrive at the tax, and finally you take any credits available directly against the tax itself. For the estate tax, you also add up all the items which are includible (i.e., taxable) to arrive at the **gross estate,** where there are two general issues: taxability and the proper valuation of what is taxable. From the gross estate, all available **deductions** are taken to arrive at the taxable estate. The **tax rate** table is then applied against the taxable estate, although its application is quite a bit more complex than is the income tax rate table. Finally, all available **credits** are taken directly against the tax.

Just as the pattern of both income and estate tax returns is the same, so too they are both **self-reporting systems.** The taxpayer reports the property which is includible in the gross estate as well as the valuation assigned to it, although of course the taxpayer is not the decedent, but rather the decedent's personal representative or heir(s). If the IRS (Internal Revenue Service) disagrees with either taxability or valuation, it has three years after filing to audit the return and assess any deficiencies in the tax. It is out of such audits that, when a settlement can not be negotiated, tax litigation ensues.

The Unitary Transfer Tax: Its Rates and Exemptions

A dramatic change was made in the federal estate and gift tax system by the 1976 Tax Reform Act. Previously, there were two separate transfer taxes, the estate tax for transfers at death and the gift tax for transfers during life. That structure presented several advantages to taxpayers who could afford to make substantial lifetime gifts (a separate exemption and cheaper rates). The 1976 Congress determined that the former system was inequitable, primarily because only wealthy persons could afford to take maximum advantage of the tax structure.

Effects Of The 1976 Tax Act

As a result of the 1976 Act, even though the former terminology and distinctions still retain importance in determining how the new system works, essentially both the estate tax and the gift tax were abolished. In their place we now have the **Unitary Transfer Tax,** which taxes any transfer of property, whether made during life or at death, under a unitary system with the same rate of tax and with only one exemption. Happily, that exemption was raised in the 1976 Act, although it is now technically a credit subtracted directly from the tax due. But mathematics can transform the credit into an equivalent exemption, which is much easier to grasp because it indicates the amount of property exempt from the tax, and so I will continue to refer to it as an exemption.

The new exemption was gradually phased in over a five-year period. Note that it is available for each decedent, so that a husband and a wife, or any two people of whatever relationship, each have the identical exemption available against their own estate taxes:

Decedent dies in:	Credit	Equivalent Exemption
1977	$30,000	$120,666
1978	34,000	134,000
1979	38,000	147,333
1980	42,500	161,563
1981	47,000	175,625

The new rates yield a bit less tax for estates under approximately $1,200,000, just a bit more tax for estates between that figure and $5,000,000, and a bit less tax for those estates over $5,000,000 because the very top rate was reduced. Table 7–1 shows the tax rates. The table says "the amount with respect to which the tentative tax is to be computed." This is Congressional gobbledygook for the method adopted to tax both lifetime gifts and deathtime bequests at exactly the same rate. The same rate occurs because the tentative tax is based on the sum of the taxable estate from the estate tax return plus the total amount of lifetime gifts over $3000 per person per year made by the decedent after December 31, 1976 (when the new law took effect; gifts made before that date are simply ignored for these purposes). The tax is "tentative" because, after arriving at it, you subtract the amount of the credit referred to above for the year in question. (To be complete, it should be mentioned that the tax base will sometimes include one more item, a "gross up" factor for gifts in contemplation of death, a subject we will address in the next chapter). The point to remember is that the tax base on which the tentative tax is computed includes all lifetime gifts over $3000 per person per year after December 31, 1976, plus all transfers made at death. We will discuss these $3000 gifts later in this chapter.

Transfer Tax: Lifetime and Deathtime

To compute any transfer tax applying at the time of a lifetime gift, the tentative tax is based on the lifetime transfers made up to and including that time. The exemption is applied to the first transfers subject to the new Act in a chronological sequence, so that lifetime gifts will first use it up, and only such of it as remains thereafter will be available against the deathtime transfers.

TABLE 7—1.

UNITARY TRANSFER TAX RATE SCHEDULE. THE "EQUIVALENT EXEMPTION" IS NOT TO BE APPLIED TO THIS TABLE; IT IS A FIGURE CONSTRUCTED PURELY FOR CONVENIENCE. THE TRANSFER TAX CREDIT IS NOT SUBTRACTED FROM COLUMNS 1 OR 2, BUT IS SUBTRACTED FROM THE TAX RESULTING FROM THE APPLICATION OF THIS TABLE.

If the amount with respect to which the tentative tax to be computed is:

Tentative tax is:

From	To	Tax	+	%	On Excess Over
0	10,000	0		18	0
10,000	20,000	1,800		20	10,000
20,000	40,000	3,800		22	20,000
40,000	60,000	8,200		24	40,000
60,000	80,000	13,000		26	60,000
80,000	100,000	18,200		28	80,000
100,000	150,000	23,800		30	100,000
150,000	250,000	38,800		32	150,000
250,000	500,000	70,800		34	250,000
500,000	750,000	155,800		37	500,000
750,000	1,000,000	248,300		39	750,000
1,000,000	1,250,000	345,800		41	1,000,000
1,250,000	1,500,000	448,300		43	1,250,000
1,500,000	2,000,000	555,800		45	1,500,000
2,000,000	2,500,000	780,800		49	2,000,000
2,500,000	3,000,000	1,025,800		53	2,500,000
3,000,000	3,500,000	1,290,800		57	3,000,000
3,500,000	4,000,000	1,575,800		61	3,500,000
4,000,000	4,500,000	1,880,800		65	4,000,000
4,500,000	5,000,000	2,205,800		69	4,500,000
5,000,000	. . . .	2,550,800		70	5,000,000

Note: the estates of **Nonresident Aliens** are taxed pursuant to a different schedule, with only a $3,600 credit. That schedule is:

0	100,000	0		6	0
100,000	500,000	6,000		12	100,000
500,000	1,000,000	54,000		18	500,000
1,000,000	2,000,000	144,000		24	1,000,000
2,000,000	. . . .	384,000		30	2,000,000

Just so there can be no mistake about it, there is no danger of a lifetime transfer being taxed twice. Lifetime gifts are only "added back" for purposes of computing the estate's transfer tax bracket. That bracket is based upon the totality of all transfers the decedent had ever made at any time after December 31, 1976, so "adding back" lifetime gifts over $3000 per person per year is only for the purpose of coming up with that total amount. If the transferor's exemption had been entirely used up by his lifetime gifts, any "gift taxes" paid on them during life will be subtracted from the tentative tax computed at death. If lifetime gifts had only used up a portion of the exemption/credit, the remaining amount will still be available after death. All this should demonstrate that lifetime and deathtime transfers are taxed at exactly the same rate, and also that there is no such thing as "saving the exemption" in order to use it after death; since the credit and the rates of tax are the same, it makes no mathematical difference whether the credit is used during life or after death. There is, though, a special gift tax marital deduction for gifts between spouses, which is discussed below.

Note from Table 7-1 that the minimum estate tax rate after 1979 is 32%, because that is the first year that amounts in excess of the exemption fall into that bracket. This minimum rate at which an estate "enters the tax structure" is much higher than under the old law. When Congress raised the exemption, it did away with all the lovely low tax brackets. The effect is that any property not sheltered by the exemption, even the very first dollar, is now subject to tax at a high rate.

The Orphan's Exclusion

The 1976 Act introduced a completely new exclusion from the estate tax, based upon a Congressional decision that orphans under age twenty-one should be entitled to some special tax relief when their last surviving parent dies. The law now provides a deduction for each underage orphan if (and only if) the decedent's death orphans any of his children under age twenty-one. The deduction is $5000 multiplied by the number of years the child is under twenty-one. So a twenty-year-old orphan would entitle the estate to a $5000 deduction, but a one-year-old orphan would entitle the estate to a $100,000 deduction. If bequests are drafted in terms of this exclusion in order to qualify the maximum property for it, an often undesirable result occurs because younger children will receive more than will older children. And some tricky drafting may be needed because it is only necessary to qualify for this exclusion for amounts of the estate in excess of the estate's regular exemption; this may yield a complicated formula clause similar to the marital deduction's formula clauses we will discuss in chapter twelve.

As is reasonable to expect, the exclusion only applies to the extent that the excluded property is left to the orphan (or for his benefit), and not if the decedent's property goes to someone else. Further, in a move that many people think is an unnecessary complication, in order to qualify for the exclusion, the property must be left to the orphan in a particular manner. That manner is virtually identical with the way in which property must be left to a surviving spouse in order to qualify for the marital deduction, an extremely important subject I shall examine in depth in chapter nine. So as not to repeat the same material twice, I will refer you to that topic for the applicable rules; since that topic is generally much more significant, it is best to cover those rules when discussing the marital deduction. Suffice it to say that in order to qualify for the orphan's exclusion, property must be left to the child in such a way that the property will be taxed in the orphan's estate when the orphan dies (assuming he were still to own that property). In some estates, the orphan's exclusion will grant substantial relief from tax, and so a testator to whom it is important should receive specific advice ensuring that his estate will qualify for it.

Filing Estate Tax Returns, and Audit Odds

Whether or not an estate is required to file a federal estate tax return is determined by the size of the gross estate and not by the size of the net taxable estate after all deductions have been subtracted. As of 1981, the minimum gross estate requiring the filing of a return is $175,000 (not $175,625). If you have an estate over that amount but it is clear that appropriate deductions will reduce the taxable estate to below the minimum, an estate tax return indicating this must be filed anyway.

But remember the discussion on lifetime gifts over $3000 per person per year, and the fact that they are now to be added to deathtime transfers to compute the estate's transfer tax bracket. If taxable lifetime gifts had been made after December 31, 1976, when the new Act took effect, the amount of such gifts must be added to the value of all property remaining at death in order to determine whether an estate tax return must be filed. This is consistent with the unification of lifetime and deathtime transfer tax rates. Example: if in 1981 or thereafter there is a gross estate of $170,000 remaining at death (below the minimum filing amount), but the decedent had made $100,000 of lifetime transfers after December 31, 1976 (thereby using up his unitary exemption in that amount), then all his transfers total $270,000, and an estate tax return will have to be filed because $270,000 is greater than the minimum filing amount.

The new Act does, however, eliminate both the nuisance and the cost of filing estate tax returns for many estates. But the corollary to that benefit is the rather obvious fact that many more of the estate tax returns which now must be filed will be audited. The IRS has not revealed its intentions, but it only stands to reason

Gift Taxes

It should be clear from the above discussion that the old separate lifetime exemption from gift taxes no longer exists. For any gift made after the beginning of 1977, the unitary transfer tax, with its single lifetime/deathtime exemption, applies.

Note that under the new Act one is able to make large lifetime transfers tax free. Under the old law, the lifetime exemption was $30,000 per donor, whereas after 1980 it is $175,000. This should make possible those transfers which the donor genuinely wants to make during life but which might formerly have been inhibited because the donor encountered the gift tax after $30,000 of gifts.

Note carefully that because lifetime gifts (either within the exemption or taxable if the exemption has been used up) are added to property left at death, the former rationale of saving estate taxes by "getting property out of your gross estate" has now been negated. Since there is only one exemption against one unitary rate of tax, mathematically it doesn't make any difference whether the transfer is made during life or after death (except for certain $3000 annual gifts, which we'll discuss in a moment). This is precisely what Congress intended. Be sure you understand and retain this point, because it affects a lot of post-1976 estate planning, and I will be noting this effect on several future occasions. There are still several advantages to making lifetime gifts, which I'll detail in a later chapter.

The Gift Tax Marital Deduction

In addition to a donor's regular exemption, there is a further **gift tax deduction for gifts between spouses.** Under the old law, one-half of the gifts from one spouse to the other, no matter what their value, were deductible and therefore not taxable. Under the 1976 Act, the first $100,000 of such gifts made after December 31, 1976, even if previous inter-spousal gifts have been made, are totally free of tax. However, the next $100,000 of such gifts are fully taxable, and inter-spousal gifts over $200,000 are subject to a marital deduction of one-half (the other half being fully taxable). The effect is that if inter-spousal gifts are desirable, for the first $100,000 of such gifts it now costs no gift tax to make them. By the time $200,000 of such gifts is reached, the new law is the same as the old.

There is a bit of penalty for utilizing the gift tax marital deduction. There also exists a marital deduction against the estate tax, and that deduction will be somewhat adversely affected by using at least the first $200,000 of the gift tax marital deduction. I will examine that adverse effect in the section concerning the estate tax marital deduction (page 159); I apologize for referring you somewhere else for the information, but there is no perfect order in which to present this material. No matter what is presented first, some references must be made to later material, so please bear with me.

The $3000 Annual Gift Tax Exclusion

There is a **$3000 annual exclusion** from gift taxes, making small gifts possible without any tax consequences. Many people are not clear as to how this exclusion works, so it bears a bit of explanation. Every donor is entitled to the exclusion, and it is **annual, per donee.** That means that in each and every calendar year, each donor may give up to $3000 to as many different people (per donee) as he wishes. Contrary to the belief of some, the donees do not have to be relatives, and you could give $3000 to every person listed in your telephone book if you wanted. And you could do so every calendar year. Since it is available to every donor, a husband has one such exclusion and so does a wife. Therefore, a married couple could give up to $6000 to one person each year, $3000 from each of them. And if a married couple gave to another married couple, they could give $12,000 each and every calendar year.

Married persons can consent to have half the gifts made by their spouse considered to be made by the spouse who is not the actual donor. As an example, if under the applicable laws of the state of her residence a wife owns no property at all, any gift made by her husband out of his own property can be considered to be made one-half by her if she so consents on his gift tax return. That way, he could give $6000 of his own property to one person tax-free in a given year, since one-half could be considered to have been made by his wife, and they would each use their $3000 annual exclusion to avoid any gift taxes. The same is true of much larger gifts which require the use of the exemption each has under the 1976 Act. That is, a husband could give (in 1981 and thereafter) up to $350,000 of his own property free of transfer tax so long as his wife elected to have one-half of it considered made by her; they would both thereby use up their $175,000 exemption.

For gifts of community property, the spouses each own one-half due to their state's property laws, so the division is automatic. But the spousal consents referred to above (called **gift splitting**) are available for gifts of the separate property of one of the spouses to which the other spouse consents.

By the way, many people are unclear as to whether the donee of a gift must pay income taxes when he receives it. The donee need not, because gifts are not taxable income by definition. They are also not deductible to the donor, so any gifts must be made with property which has already been income taxed.

There is an extremely important qualification on the $3000 annual exclusion, again something not clearly understood by many. To be allowed this exclusion, the gift must be of a **present interest** and must not be of a future interest. That is, the gift must give the donee outright and absolute present control of the money or property given. If it does not, then the donor (who is the person primarily liable for the gift tax) may not claim the $3000 annual exclusion.

Handing over a check for $3000 is obviously a gift of a present interest. But gifts in trust are usually gifts of a future interest, which do not qualify for the annual exclusion (gifts to a trust are considered to be made to the beneficiaries of the trust). They are future interests because most trusts postpone outright and absolute control over the funds until some future time, by the very nature of what a trust is. However, if the beneficiary has a present right to the income from the trust, then a portion of the gift might qualify for the annual exclusion because it is a present gift of at least the income from the gifted property; that's getting pretty technical, and expert assistance is called for.

The future interest rule presents a real problem when one desires to make gifts to a minor child because normally one does not want to give outright control of money or property to a minor. The tax law recognizes this and provides two specific statutory exceptions to the future interest rule so that certain types of such gifts may be made to minors with the donor still qualifying for the annual exclusion. One is for gifts made under the Uniform Gifts to Minors Act, where someone acts as Custodian for the minor. The other is a special kind of trust for the benefit of minors. I will examine both these devices in chapter fifteen.

Gift Tax Returns for Lifetime Transfers

Unlike any other kind of tax return, gift tax returns must be filed quarterly, within 45 days of the end of the calendar quarter during which the gift was made. The 1976 Act makes these requirements a bit easier because a quarterly return during the year of the gift will now only be required when gifts for that year exceed $25,000 within a calendar quarter. If $25,000 has not been reached before the end of the year, then the return must be filed by February 15 of the following year. And if $25,000 has been once reached during the year, a return is then due, but another one is not due until additional gifts exceed an additional $25,000.

The $3000 annual exclusion technically excludes that amount from the workings of the tax, and so normally a return is not even required. But a return may well be advisable, due to the rules governing the IRS's three-year statute of limitations within which a return may be audited and more tax assessed. That statute normally (in the absence of fraud or other very serious derelictions) cuts off the IRS three years after a tax return has been filed, but if a return has not been filed, the statute never begins to run. If the statute never runs, the IRS may at any later time (even after the donor's death) open up an issue. If the IRS is successful in assessing past due taxes many years later, all kinds of interest and penalties may have accrued. Although there is some argument, most attorneys believe that only a return showing a taxable gift will start the statute of limitations running.

It may well be important to start the statute running, as can be illustrated by the following example. Assume you have a family corporation and that you value the shares of stock at $100 per share. You desire to make a tax-free annual gift to your son, so you give him 30 shares and do not file a gift tax return since the gift totals $3000. But who says you are accurate in your valuation of the stock? The IRS is entitled to argue the point, and if you have not started the statute of limitations running against them, they can forever afterwards bring up the issue. Many years later they may do so, alleging that the true value of the stock at the date of the gift was $500 per share. If they win, you or your estate may be liable not only for the tax, but also for interest over all those years and probably for penalties for failure to file as well. It would be better if you gave your son 31 shares of stock, showing a taxable amount of $100 on a gift tax return, thereby giving the IRS the opportunity to challenge your valuation. If they fail to do so within three years, you are home free, at least as to that year's gift tax return.

It is always necessary to file a gift tax return in order to claim all or a part of your transfer tax exemption. You must show the taxable gift, and then claim the exemption against it, which also serves to start the statute of limitations running. So in the example given above, there would be no tax due because the taxable portion you reported would be wiped out by your exemption.

Many people ignore gift tax returns, figuring that there is no way for the IRS to discover that they had made a gift. But this is not necessarily true, particularly where the donor's estate is large enough to require an estate tax return after his death. There are several questions on the estate tax return designed to reveal lifetime gifts, and the executor must sign that return under penalty of perjury. Unless he wants to commit perjury, the executor must tell the truth about lifetime gifts. In that way, the IRS may discover a gift on which no gift tax return had even been filed, thus exposing the estate to back taxes, interest, and penalties, or at the very least to perhaps a major reduction in the estate's exemption on account of that unreported gift. At the new tax rates, that reduction would cost the estate a minimum of 32% of the unreported gift in taxes, and for that reason it may well be that the IRS will now even more vigorously seek to challenge past valuations where no taxable gift started the statute of limitations running against them, or no gift tax return was ever filed.

State Death Taxes

Every state except Nevada has some form of a death tax, but those taxes take different forms in different states. Some are estate taxes as is the federal (although at lower rates), while others are an inheritance tax taxing the recipients of inherited property. The tax bite under an inheritance tax is much more complicated to figure out than under an estate tax, because we must know how much the decedent is leaving to each of his various beneficiaries, and what relationship each of them is to him. Since exemptions apply to each beneficiary who inherits, rather than having just one exemption for the decedent's entire estate, and since those exemptions are in differing amounts depending upon the blood relationships, we need to know the facts of a decedent's will before we can estimate the tax bite. The rates of tax are also different for each inheriting beneficiary, depending upon his blood relationship to the decedent, so that further complicates matters. So, it is literally impossible to quote any state inheritance tax rates even to a group of people who are all residents of a single state, to say nothing of a general readership comprised of people residing in all fifty states. Sorry.

A problem which has become more serious since the 1976 Act is the matter of conformity between the federal law and a state's death taxes. Some state legislatures favor conformity (making state laws identical to federal laws) and try for it whenever possible, while others don't even try. But for those which do, the frequency with which federal changes have been taking place presents a timing problem in the effort to achieve conformity. A few states have attempted to conform to the changes wrought by the 1976 Act, although of course there is a lag in time before the state legislature can get conformity into effect. Then too, some states will attempt to conform only selectively; California has recently pulled one of its worst stunts, by conforming to all the bad (expensive) parts of the 1976 Act, but deliberately failing to conform to all the good (tax-reducing) parts of that Act. As this book was being written, Congress was debating a Technical Corrections Act to alter some of the obvious technical mistakes and oversights contained in the 1976 Act, but also inserting a few very substantive changes. That Act is now law, so a state which seeks conformity will try to conform to it. Assuredly Congress will be debating some new change even as that state is trying to conform to the change they just enacted. You can see why some states don't even attempt conformity.

I might add that major changes in the federal law will probably not occur for many years; after all, it took Congress several decades to decide on enacting the major changes of 1976. But cosmetic changes will undoubtedly continue spewing out of virtually every Congress.

APPLICATION

1. Be sure you thoroughly understand the fact that the unitary transfer tax taxes the combined total of all transfers you have ever made after December 31, 1976, at exactly the same rate. This includes both transfers made at death and lifetime gifts over $3000 per donee per year.

2. If your death will make orphans out of any of your children aged twenty-one or younger, try to qualify bequests to them for the orphan's exclusion. Tell your advisors that you wish to do so.

3. Determine whether there are good reasons for making substantial lifetime gifts to a particular donee or donees, and if so consider doing so, since the higher exemptions will allow you to make these gifts without tax.

4. Determine whether there are family reasons for making gifts to your spouse, and if so, consider doing so under the new provision allowing $100,000 of such gifts tax free. But read the material on page 159 about the partial loss this will cause in the marital deduction which is available to you at death, and have one of your advisors compute where the greatest benefits lie for you.

5. Give some thought to the pros and cons of making $3000 per donee gifts this year and in future years, and whether to increase the amount to $6000 by having your spouse consent to the gift on your gift tax return. Before making any decision about such annual gifts, read the material starting on page 159 now, or else defer any decision until after you have read that material.

6. Consider whether it might be advantageous to make gifts of slightly more than $3000, in order to start the statute of limitations running.

7. Determine the rates and structure of your state's inheritance tax law.

8
property subject to estate taxes

Glossary For This Chapter

Alternate Valuation Date
Appointee
Ascertainable Standard
Closely Held Corporation
Contemplation of Death
Contribution Theory
Default Taker
Disclaimer
Donee
Donor
Fair Market Value
Five By Five Power
General Power of Appointment
Incidents of Ownership
Individual Retirement Accounts (IRAs)
Insured
Joint and Survivor Annuity
Owner (of Insurance)
Pension and Profit-Sharing Plans
Power of Appointment
Special Power of Appointment
Special Use Valuation

The estate tax burden for any given estate depends upon how much of the property owned by a decedent is subject to tax. The tax bite will be determined by two things: which of his property is **includible in the gross estate** (i.e., taxable) and the propery **valuation** of that property. I will examine the various types of property which are taxable, and along the way I'll say a few things about valuation.

Property in Which the Decedent Had an Interest

The tax law's first statement defining the gross estate is all-inclusive. It says that the gross estate shall include all property, wherever situated, in which the decedent **had an interest.** Estate tax will be payable on all property the decedent owned outright, as well as his fractional or other interests in property owned with others, wherever in the world that property might be.

Since that one sweeping statement so all-inclusively taxes everything the decedent

129

owned, you may wonder why any other categories are even addressed. Those other categories deal with ambiguous situations, or else reach out beyond everything the decedent owns to tax even property he once owned but now no longer does. Thus, the estate tax will reach everything you own, and then some.

A Key Factor In Estate Planning

An extremely important concept hidden within the first sweeping statement must be identified, as it is a key to estate planning. That concept can best be illustrated by the following situation: assume that a father dies, leaving all of his property in trust to benefit his wife for the rest of her life with the remainder after her death going equally to their children. When the father dies, all his property will be included in his gross estate because it was property in which he had an ownership interest, and the estate tax doesn't care that he carved it up into a life estate and a remainder.

But now assume that his wife has later died, and her estate taxes must be figured. Is all the property held in the trust to be included in her gross estate? After all, she did indeed have an "interest" in the trust property because she had the lifetime use of it and the income from it. Although the law's first sweeping statement would seem to tax such an interest, in the early history of the estate tax, certain legal and constitutional arguments were immediately raised against that possibility. Recall that the estate tax is an excise tax on the privilege of leaving property to one's heirs at death; in the assumed situation the surviving wife had not really done so. In fact, the father had really made two gifts of his property, a **life estate** (defined at page 49) to his wife and a **remainder** (defined at page 50) to his children. Thus, the children get their remainder not from their mother, but directly from their father. Their mother is not leaving the trust property to them, so it would be constitutionally inappropriate to impose any privilege tax on her because she is not exercising any privilege whatsoever.

If it is possible to pinpoint any such thing, this may well be the **single most key factor around which estate planning revolves.** Namely, that when the owner of a life estate granted by some other person dies, the property in which the decedent had the **life estate is not estate taxed.** Anytime there is something that says you may have certain property rights without their causing estate taxation, estate planners make great use of such a device. Be sure you understand this point, and retain it. The 1976 Act made a modification in this area with its "generation skipping tax," which we'll examine in a later chapter, but the Act did not destroy the estate planning key as some Congressmen were threatening to do.

Returning to our hypothetical example to illustrate a final point, assume that the surviving wife is still living but that one of the children dies before her. Should that child's share of the trust property in which he has a remainder be included in his gross estate? Is it property in which he had any interest? A remainder is a present property right which can easily be valued by appropriate tables (see Table 4–1, page 51). If the remainder was contingent and the contingency had not yet occurred, then the child had no certainty of acquiring the remainder and neither did any of his heirs, so there would be no estate tax should he die before his mother. But if the remainder was not contingent on anything, the deceased child's heirs will get it either by will or intestacy, and so it will be subject to estate tax. This situation can be a real trap for the unwary, particularly if the remainderman is a youngster or other person whose estate would not contain sufficient funds to pay the resulting tax. The havoc that can be caused by the imposition of tax liens should not be allowed to occur, and the remedy is to write the remainder in such a way that it will not be taxed should the remainderman predecease the life tenant. More about this in later chapters.

Valuation

The valuation of property included in the gross estate is at least as important to each taxpayer as is the issue of taxability in the gross estate, but much less can be said about it by way of general remarks. This is because accurate valuation depends so much upon the precise facts surrounding a particular asset or piece of property. In fact, disputes over valuation account for a very large percentage of all disputes between taxpayers and the IRS.

Fair Market Value

The standard for valuation is **fair market value,** which is legally defined as the price which a willing buyer would pay a willing seller if neither of them was under any compulsion to either buy or sell. In other words, what property would bring in a free market. That is easy enough to state, but difficult to arrive at in the absence of market activity or an actual sale between willing parties. Valuation is the business of appraisers, and also of accountants who are involved because the figures pertaining to a given piece of property are very relevant.

For federal estate tax purposes (but not under many state's inheritance tax laws, so watch out), the executor is entitled to an election concerning the date on which estate assets will be valued. He can elect either to value all of the assets as of the date of death, or else have all of those assets valued as of an **alternate valuation**

date six months after the date of death. Note that the executor may not pick and choose as to each asset making up the estate; his only election is to value all of the assets as of one date or the other. It is obvious that most executors are well advised not to file the estate tax return until after the alternate valuation date has passed, in order that they may check the market values on the latter date and perhaps save a large amount of tax if values had dropped a great deal.

Some assets are quite easy to value, such as cash, bank deposits, certificates of deposit, etc. It is also simple to value any stock or bond which is traded on any recognized stock exchange, where the appropriate valuation is not the stock's closing price on the day in question, but rather the average between its high and low during that day. It is much less simple to value various items of personal property, such as valuable furniture, antiques, jewelry, and (particularly) art. For such items, an appriasal is usually necessary.

Valuing An Interest In A Business

The most difficult property of all to value is an interest in a business, whether it be a sole proprietorship, a partnership, or a corporation which is not traded on any recognized stock exchange. The latter are often referred to as **closely held corporations** because their stock is not held by the public at large but is held by some smaller "close" group, often a family. Since there is no established market for such stock, the only accurate approach is to value the underlying business as a whole, an involved and exceedingly difficult process.

A famous IRS revenue ruling says that primary consideration will be given to the earnings of a business. That alone gets complex, because the various methods which the firm's accountants use to arrive at earnings have a major effect on whether the earnings reported for income tax or dividend purposes are either high or low. Often those reported earnings must be readjusted for the purposes of estate tax valuation. Other important factors set out in the revenue ruling are the firm's capacity to pay dividends (not the dividends it has actually paid), the book value or net asset value, and comparisons with stock market quotations of publicly held corporations engaged in the same business.

In many cases, the value assigned to closely held corporate stock by the process described is then reduced by the application of one or more **discount factors** which the law recognizes. A principal one is the discount for minority interests, on the reasoning that someone who would purchase a non-controlling interest would not pay as much as would someone purchasing a controlling interest. Another discount is for lack of marketability, on the reasoning that a purchaser would not pay as much for stock which is not readily marketable as he would for stock traded on a recognized stock exchange. A third is known as blockage, which means that if it is a very large block of stock that is being valued, recognition must be given to the reality that if the entire block were put up for sale the market price (if there were one) would immediately become depressed. The latter may not seem particularly logical, but it is in fact what happens when large blocks of stock are marketed. Other potential factors are that if there is no market, in order to sell the stock a brokerage firm may have to be paid commissions to effect the sale, so a discount for that factor is appropriate; that there may be restrictions on transferability imposed by the terms of the stock itself; and that the stock may be burdened with a large amount of inherent capital gain. All in all, one or several of these discounts may apply to reduce the real value of the stock in question.

These valuation discounts present a planning opportunity, because they can substantially lessen the costs of making any lifetime gifts, as well as the cost of estate taxes. The discounts are primarily applicable to shares of stock in closely held corporations, so a planner might sometimes recommend that some or all of a person's holdings be incorporated simply and only so that these discounts can become applicable. The client may then be advised to undertake a program of giving away some of these shares, and if the attorney or accountant is successful in his negotiations with the IRS over valuation discounts, whatever transfer tax consequences there are will be encountered at discounted values. The amount of the discount is a matter for the negotiating talent of the attorney or accountant, but it can be a very major saving and is validly looked upon as a pertinent part of estate planning. You might want to remember this discussion for later chapters, when we talk about estate planning techniques.

Valuing Real Estate

The other type of property that is difficult to value is real estate, such as residential property, real estate used as farmland or used in a going business, and real estate held for development or speculation. There are several recognized appraisal techniques, and often the final valuation becomes some combination between them. The most common techniques are **comparable sales** (where the problem is to locate a truly comparable piece of property which sold quite recently) and the **income method.** The latter determines the net income that the property produces and then assigns a multiplication factor to try to arrive at the price a buyer would pay for that income-generating ability (such as "eight times earnings," or whatever). The IRS can quarrel with the methods used to determine the earnings, and can of course argue long and loud about the appropriate multiplication factor to be used.

Real Estate Used as a Farm or in a Business

The 1976 Act has introduced a new election, applying only to real estate, and only if it is being used as a farm or as part of a going business. Prior to 1976, the very definition of fair market value led to valuation of real estate at its **highest and best use,** since this is in reality what property will bring on the open market. To illustrate the adverse impact of that valuation, assume a person is farming his 500 acres as a growing city spreads out closer and closer to his property. Soon he is surrounded by shopping centers, subdivisions, and high rise apartment complexes. As farmland, his property might be worth $1000 per acre, but to a developer it might be worth $50,000 per acre. When that farmer dies, "highest and best use" valuation would value the land at $50,000 per acre, and the astronomical estate taxes resulting therefrom would force the heirs to sell in order to raise the cash necessary to pay those taxes. The increasing frequency of such occurrences was not only disastrous for the family concerned, but also not good for the nation as a whole because a great deal of productive farmland was being lost to such forced sales.

Accordingly, the 1976 Act allows the executor to **elect** to value real estate used as a family farm or in a family business at its **value for such actual use** as opposed to its highest and best use. While that appears to be a marvelously beneficial reform, unfortunately the reality falls considerably short. The reason is the incredibly convoluted, complex, confounding, and close to insane manner in which our Congress has written this supposed reform. The restrictions, rules, and regulations necessary to qualify for this rather simple concept are literally causing estate planners to recoil. Many nationally prominent experts have flatly declared these rules to be so awful that they will never recommend that clients use them! Now what kind of a reform is that?

Just a few examples from the jumble of rules: The farm or business real estate must comprise 50% of the decedent's "adjusted" gross estate, and this new election cannot reduce the gross estate by more than $500,000. The property must have been used by a "qualified member" of decedent's family in a "qualified use" (both terms have detailed technical definitions) for five of the eight years preceding death, and such use must continue for the fifteen years following the decedent's death. If anyone ever slips up during that time, or any of the property might have to be sold, or changing economics might force a change in use, the IRS returns to enforce a special lien on the property which recoups the estate taxes saved by the use of the new method compared to highest and best use valuation. Note that this recapture possibility virtually forces the executor to make the highest and best use appraisal anyway. The record keeping and other severe restrictions that must be imposed on the decedent's survivors for the subsequent fifteen years, during most of which they won't be under an expert attorney's scrutiny, are so frightening as to be reasons for not using this supposed "reform." If you have such property you will have to explore with your own advisors whether your family can live with the restrictions, and whether the benefits make the complexities worth it to you and your family.

Marital Property

Returning now to the property which comprises the gross estate, a few words should be said about marital property. In a common law state, recall that the husband is usually the owner of all or a goodly part of the marital property, although his wife is entitled to some percentage of that property at his death by way of "dower." Should all of the marital property therefore be included in the husband's gross estate, or only that portion in excess of his wife's statutory share? The law requires the inclusion of all the marital property, although the wife's statutory share can be made non-taxable if the husband properly qualifies for the extremely important marital deduction. I will examine the crucial marital deduction in depth in the next chapter; it is crucial because it is really the essence of marital estate planning in the common law states.

In the eight community property states, only the one-half of the community property owned by the spouse who died will be included in his or her gross estate. Since there is no federal property law, federal taxes are based upon the ownership rights of taxpayers as defined by the laws of their own state. And since the community property laws define the ownership interest of the deceased spouse as but one-half of the community property, that is all that can possibly be taxed.

It may seem inequitable that a community property husband will have only half the marital property taxed in his estate, while a husband residing in a common law state will have all or most of the marital property taxed in his estate. This seeming inequity is in fact removed by the marital deduction, the primary function and purpose of which is to equalize the treatment given to residents of common law and community property states.

But what if the wife dies first? In community property states, that fact doesn't make the slightest difference because she owns exactly the same amount of community property as does her husband. But in a common law state there may well be a difference. In states where the husband is considered to own all the marital property, if the wife dies first there will be no marital property to include in her estate, since under state law she doesn't own any Of course, any property she owns separately from the marital property, such as property she inherited or acquired by gift, will usually be included in her gross estate. And in those states where a wife does have some ownership interest in some of the marital property, often in her own earnings, then that property would be included in her estate.

It thus might seem that a common law couple is better off than a community property couple should the wife die first, since there will be little or nothing included in her estate. But for reasons which I will more fully develop in chapter eleven when I examine the arithmetic of the total estate picture, we will see that in reality the exact opposite may be the case. The simple explanation is that it is almost always mathematically preferable to have the estates of the husband and the wife be equal so that one-half of the total marital property will be taxed at one death, and one-half at the other. Often a major thrust of estate planning in common law states is to arrange the marital ownerships, usually via gifts, to achieve that equality. More of this later.

Gifts in Contemplation of Death

The law would be foolish if it allowed a decedent to completely escape estate taxes by the simple expedient of giving away all his property shortly before his death. (You may instantly say that such a ploy would no longer do any good under the single tax rate of the unitary transfer tax, but read on to see where this subject still makes a difference.) The government quite obviously has the right to protect its revenues from any such circumvention, but the problem is in defining what "shortly before death" is. Any definition must incorporate some arbitrary standard, and a period of **three years prior to death** was chosen to define gifts in contemplation of death. This means that the value of any gifts made within that three-year period will nevertheless be taxable in the decedent's estate, even though he had given away the property covered by the gift. Prior to the 1976 Act, his estate was allowed to argue that the decedent's motives for the gift might be such that its value ought not to be taxable in his estate. This possibility caused a great deal of argument between the IRS and executors of estates, arguments which distressingly often found their way into the already overburdened courts.

Accordingly, Congress thought it advisable to remove those controversies from the courts, by altering the law so that the issue would not arise. This they did in the 1976 Act, but from a taxpayer's viewpoint they did it backwards. That is, they did not abolish the attempt to tax gifts made within three years of death;

rather, they legislated that for decedents dying after January 1, 1977 all gifts made within three years of death would now automatically be included in the decedent's gross estate regardless of motive, age, health, or cause of death. But Congress certainly succeeded in removing such controversies from the courts!

Since all post-1976 gifts are included in the computation of deathtime transfer taxes, why does this contemplation of death business matter any more; in fact, couldn't the whole category now be dispensed with? No, because of several additional factors. For gifts made within three years before death, not only the gift, but also the money used to pay the gift tax will be taxed in the estate; this is called the **gross up rule.** But for gifts made more than three years before death, the gross up rule will not apply, so that the gift tax dollars themselves will not be included in the estate, and thus those dollars will never be taxed at any point.

Another continuing disadvantage of gifts in contemplation of death is that such gifts will be included in the taxable estate at their **values as of the date of decedent's death,** whereas gifts made more than three years prior to death will be added to the estate (to compute the estate's tax bracket) only at their value on the date of the gift. With most values continuing to rise, being forced to use the later date of death value will most likely result in a higher tax.

A final remaining significance of gifts in contemplation of death concerns the $3000 annual exclusions from gift taxes, and here the 1976 Act has conferred one of its infrequent benefits. The **$3000 annual gifts are now specifically excluded** from the clutches of the contemplation-of-death rule, which means that a donor may make such gifts even within the three years prior to his death without either gift tax or estate tax cost. This relief provision will mean that deathbed gifts of up to $3000 per donee will now actually be encouraged, since those gifts are now freed from the estate tax. But to meet a subtle IRS technicality, one must be very certain that all gifts to a particular donee each year within the final three years prior to a donor's death, even gifts of small objects for birthdays or at Christmas, do not exceed a total value of $3000 per year. Otherwise, the new benefit can be lost, meaning that all those gifts would be estate taxed at death under the usual automatic contemplation of death rule.

Transfers With Retained Interests

As soon as the estate tax became law, attorneys and their clients instantly tried to find legal methods of avoiding it. (By the way, that's perfectly proper. A couple of court-approved tax cliches to remember are these: Only tax evasion is a crime, and there is nothing wrong with tax avoidance; in fact, by writing the law the way it does, Congress permits tax avoidance in qualifying circumstances. Also, every taxpayer has the legal right to reduce his taxes to the minimum by all legal means available.) Since the estate tax was imposed on all property in which the decedent had an interest, the only way to escape that tax was to not have any interest in a particular piece of property; or, stated in the usual way, to give property away. But a serious flaw in gift giving is that the property owner may not wish to lose the economic benefits he enjoys from property ownership, including the possession of it, the income from it, and the control over it. Human nature nevertheless compelled taxpayers to try various methods of getting property out of their gross estate by "giving" it away while still retaining either secret or even obvious economic interests in their "former" property.

Attempts To Avoid The Estate Tax

There were many devices created by taxpayers in hopes of avoiding the estate tax. Many were attempts to "get property out of your gross estate" either under gift tax exemptions, by paying the formerly cheaper gift taxes, or sometimes even without any gift taxes at all. But the motive behind many of those devices is largely obsolete after the 1976 Act because under the unitary transfer tax there is no longer the same advantage to "getting property out of your gross estate." This is because the tax rates are identical for lifetime gifts and deathtime transfers (with the exception of the $3000 gifts, which are completely free of tax at any time). Nevertheless it is still important to recognize what it is about those devices which subjects the property involved to estate taxes.

Another good tax principle to remember is that the IRS is at least as smart as the taxpayers, and it quickly reacted to the various tax avoidance techniques. Over a history of legislative counterattacks and many court decisions, one thing became quite clear: a property owner would not be allowed to escape estate taxes if he gave away his property but **retained "the possession or enjoyment of, or the income from"** such property. A simple but helpful analogy has grown up over the years, concerning the fruit and the tree. You may have given away the tree, but if you kept even a tiny amount of the fruit you had not thoroughly enough given away the property to escape estate taxes. You could indeed have given away property so that you had no retained interest in it at death, and under prior law you might therefore escape estate taxes, but to do so you must have given away the fruit and the tree; you must have completely severed all of your economic rights in, and economic enjoyment of, that property. If you had not, your death would serve as the ultimate transfer of those rights to your chosen beneficiary, and the privilege tax could appropriately tax you at that time.

Enjoyment Of The Property

The key phrase in the statute is the one concerning "enjoyment" of the property because if you could be said to have retained any of the **economic enjoyment** from the property you have not given it away "good enough" to escape estate taxes. Examples: you may not give away property and still retain either the legal right to the income earned by that property, or be actually receiving the income from it even via some very informal arrangement with the new owner. The reason, of course, is that getting the income is one of the prime elements of economic enjoyment. Perhaps I ought to say that you may legally do such things; it's just that you do not escape estate taxes if you do so.

You may not give away residential property or other real estate, even by a delivered and recorded deed, and still live in the property, farm it, or do anything else on it which in reality is the economic enjoyment of it. It is therefore useless to attempt the common ploy whereby the parents deed the house to their son, on the understanding that the parents may continue to live in the house for the rest of their lives.

You may not give away property, in trust or otherwise, and have the income from it used to satisfy your legal obligations of support. For after all, satisfying those legal obligations is truly one of the economic enjoyments one gets from one's property. You may not give away property and retain the right to get it back again at some future time, for the right to have it back is surely one piece of economic enjoyment. And you may not give away property, usually in trust, and still retain the right to **alter, amend, revoke,** or **terminate** the terms of the gift. Those four words have a great impact, and you should not pass over them lightly: alter, amend, revoke, or terminate. This is why any lifetime transfer which even had hopes of escaping estate taxes had to be irrevocable, itself a rather frightening move to make when you consider the uncertain future and what your security needs may become. In setting up a gift or a trust with the intention of avoiding estate taxes, you had to state irrevocably all the terms and conditions at the time of making the gift because you could by definition never again change any of those terms (alter or amend), get the property back (revoke), or decide that the donee wasn't really worthy of receiving the property after all (terminate).

Irrevocable trusts will continue to be used even though the 1976 Act has destroyed most of the estate tax advantages of them, because of their income tax advantages. In a correctly drafted irrevocable trust, the income tax will be paid by the beneficiary or divided among several beneficiaries. This will lower the total income taxes payable on the income generated by the property, compared to taxing 100% of it to the trustor at his bracket. The cumulative income tax savings can be dramatic. But there is a tax cost to be weighed against the advantages, which is that any irrevocable transfer will trigger a gift tax, or at least use up some of the donor's exemption. The estate tax and the gift tax usually operate in tandem; what is estate taxable is not gift taxable, but what escapes estate taxes (such as an irrevocable transfer) is gift taxable. Still, the 1976 Act may have the effect of encouraging more income tax saving irrevocable trusts, since (after 1980) any trustor can create such trusts up to $175,000 worth of his property without any transfer tax cost. That amount can increase to $350,000 if his spouse joins in the gift under either the gift-splitting rules or the laws of community property.

You can see how all-encompassing are these matters of retained economic enjoyment, often called retained life estates. Whereas life estates created by someone else escape estate taxes in the estate of the life tenant, life estates in your own property created by you for your own benefit will definitely not escape estate taxes.

Annuities and Employee Benefit Plans

Most annuities disappear at the death of the annuitant, since they are usually contracts to pay him a certain sum monthly for life. They thus leave nothing to be estate taxed. But there is one type of annuity which will be taxed in the gross estate. That is the **joint and survivor annuity,** where an insurance company contracts to pay the annuitant a periodic stipend for the rest of his life and, following his death, to continue to pay the stipend to a survivor whom the annuitant designates. The joint and survivor annuity is estate taxed because the annuitant realistically retains the economic enjoyment of the funds used to purchase the annuity by ensuring that a chosen survivor can continue to receive their benefit. The annuitant's death transfers the benefit to the chosen survivor, an appropriate incident for the privilege tax to apply.

Many companies and self-employed persons have pension, profit-sharing, or other forms of benefit plans under which the employee is guaranteed a periodic stipend after retirement, often with a further guarantee that upon his death a stipend will be paid to a survivor designated by him. This looks like a joint and survivor annuity, and indeed it is. However, many of these employee benefit plans are "tax qualified," meaning that if they meet many rigorous standards imposed by the tax laws, all kinds of tax advantages are extended to those plans. They are widely referred to as **qualified plans,** and can be corporate plans, the so-called Keough Plans of self-employed persons, or Individual Retirement Accounts; the latter allow a person not covered by any other retirement plan to deposit up to $1500 (in some cases, $1750) per year and qualify for the various tax advantages, including the deduction of the annual contribution from the contributor's income tax. One of the tax advantages of such plans is that the joint and survivor annuity feature is exempt from estate tax to the extent of contributions made by the employer (but not to the extent of contributions made by the employee himself), if certain conditions are met.

Under the Revenue Act of 1978, in order to qualify for the estate tax exemption the survivor's benefit can be paid out either as a lump sum or as an annuity, providing that an irrevocable election is made not to compute the income taxes payable on the benefit when it is received under certain favorable options. Those options allow a special ten-year averaging for the income taxes payable, and a special capital gains provision. If the loss of the income tax options is too serious in any given case, then the alternative is to have the survivor's benefits paid out in either a lifetime annuity or in periodic installments extending over at least thirty-six months following the decedent's death. The latter course will preserve the estate tax exemption of the survivor's benefits at the cost of receiving the benefits in installments rather than in one lump sum. These conditions apply to all pension and profit-sharing employee benefit plans, whether corporate, Keough, or IRA. Due to these conditions, it may be necessary for you to alter the method of payout to your survivors if you want to qualify for the most favorable tax treatment.

Joint Tenancies and Tenancies by the Entirety

We have already seen that revocable living trusts, one of the two most popular devices for avoiding probate, do not avoid estate taxes because the revocation power is the retention of an important bit of economic enjoyment. Now we see the same result with joint tenancies, the other most popular method of avoiding probate. This discussion also covers tenancies by the entirety, but to avoid extra language I'll only speak of joint tenancies even though the law (including the 1976 change applicable to these tenancies) is equally applicable to tenancies by the entirety.

Joint Tenancies Are Estate Taxed

The reason why joint tenancies are estate taxed is that, consistent with factors previously discussed, you retain a great deal of economic enjoyment when you utilize a joint tenancy. For one thing, you retain the possibility that you will acquire one-hundred-percent ownership if your joint tenant predeceases you. Also, you retain the power to revoke a joint tenancy, due to the right to apply to a court to have the property partitioned as well as the possibility that you will do something to sever the joint tenancy (and as to joint tenancy bank accounts, because any joint tenant may withdraw all the money at any time). Your death is the event by which you exercise your privilege of "leaving" the joint tenancy property to your chosen survivor, whereas prior to that moment no one knew whether you'd get it all, or he would. So estate taxation is appropriate.

To be consistent, only your interest in the joint tenancy ought to be subject to tax. The gross estate includes only such proportion of the joint tenancy's value as is attributable to the decedent's contribution to it. This **contribution theory** means that if the decedent contributed nothing to the joint tenancy, nothing will be taxed in his estate. But if the decedent contributed all of the purchase price and all subsequent improvements, then the entire property will be included in his gross estate. Note that if one person contributed 100%, there may well have been a taxable gift when that contributor put another person's name on the property as a joint tenant. There often is such a gift, though it sometimes depends upon some subtleties of your state's law, so it has to be checked. But under most state's banking laws, the one-hundred-percent contributor to a joint-tenancy bank account does not make a gift upon opening the account because he could withdraw all the money the very next day. However, if the non-contributing joint tenant withdraws some money, then at that moment there is a completed gift from the contributor, a very sneaky gift particularly if the withdrawal is months or even years after the account was set up.

In community property states, if community property funds are used to purchase the joint tenancy, then under state property law each spouse has contributed one-half. So at the death of either, only one-half the value of that joint tenancy will be included in his or her gross estate.

What The 1976 Tax Act Did

The 1976 Act instituted a change in the area of tenancies by the entirety and joint tenancies between spouses, which appears to be meaningful only to spouses in common law states. To eliminate the need for such spouses to prove who had contributed how much to the joint tenancy, under certain conditions tenancies created by spouses after January 1, 1977, will be treated as if each spouse had contributed one-half (exactly the same treatment afforded community property spouses). To qualify, personal property must have been a completed gift, and upon creation of a tenancy in real property, the spouses must elect in a timely filed gift tax return to treat the creation as a taxable gift if one spouse actually contributed more than one-half. If this new provision appears advantageous to spouses already owning the described tenancies, they may destroy the old tenancy and re-create it after January 1, 1977, so long as they make the election referred to. That is, they must treat the re-creation as a taxable gift and be certain to file a gift tax return on time (a late return will disqualify the election). But if the spouses file a gift tax return prior to the end of 1979, they do not even have to go through the mechanical steps of severing the old joint tenancy and re-creating it.

There can be some very delicate problems of who contributed what and how much to a joint tenancy, particularly in trying to allocate the correct proportion of growth in the property's value to the respective contributors. That problem is beyond our scope, but specific analysis may be necessary in many cases.

Powers of Appointment

You have not yet been introduced to these devices, so let's first define them and then discuss how they are taxed. A power of appointment is a power given to any person to designate who shall receive property, or in what shares it shall be divided. It can be created either by the will of a decedent or during lifetime by way of gift. It is used when the testator or donor does not himself want to make those decisions, or when he thinks it advisable that someone else make them, usually after he has died. It is usually involved with a life interest in property or in a trust because it is a manner by which the persons who receive the property after the life interest is over can be decided upon. It is often given to the person who also has the life interest, although it can just as easily be granted to someone else.

How An Appointment Works

A common example of its use is called **taking a second look.** A testator might leave a life interest to his wife, but rather than personally make a second gift to named remaindermen (defined at page 50), he may say instead that the remainder shall go to those persons whom his wife **may appoint.** This enables her to observe how their children, or any other persons, are developing as they reach adulthood, what their needs are, or how they handle property.

The testator is called the **donor** of the power of appointment, and the person who has the power is called the **donee** of it. The persons to whom the property might be appointed are called the **appointees.** The donor can add that if the power is never exercised, then the property shall go to specified persons or charities, who are then termed the **default takers** (because they take "in default of appointment").

Just as the creator of a life estate and remainder legally makes two separate gifts, a life estate to one person and a remainder to another, with a power of appointment the creator is also making two distinct gifts. He gives a life interest to a definite and named person, but he also gives a remainder, except that the taker of the remainder is an indefinite and unnamed person. Because of that, the donee of the power does not herself make a gift of the remainder to anyone; she is merely the agent of the donor in making that decision, while he is the maker of the gift itself.

Types Of Powers Of Appointment

The donor can make several decisions about what type of power it shall be. It can be exercisable by the donee during the donee's lifetime (called an **inter vivos power**) or only by the donee's will (called a **testamentary power**). More importantly, powers are either **general powers of appointment,** or **special powers of appointment.** With a general power, the donee can appoint to anyone at all, including even to himself, to his creditors, or to his own estate. But with a special power the donee is restricted to appointing among a group or class of persons specified by the donor. Often, a donor will specify that a power is exercisable only among his children, his nieces and nephews, his relatives, etc.

As with many things in the law, unwilling recipients are not irrevocably stuck with unwanted powers. The donee can, promptly upon discovery of the power (promptly often means within nine months), **renounce** it. If the donee does not renounce a power, he exercises it in the manner specified by the testator.

Returning to the estate tax law, we must consider the effect on a decedent's taxable estate if he even possessed a general power of appointment without exercising it. Possessing a general power of appointment is tantamount to owning the property covered by the power, for by the mere stroke of a pen you can just take the property for your own. It is therefore not surprising that merely possessing such a power will cause the value of the **property subject to that power** to be taxable in your gross estate. If you are given such a power and don't desire the tax consequences of it for your estate, your remedy may be to renounce the power by a document called a **disclaimer.** The 1976 Act specified that to be effective for tax purposes, disclaimers must be executed within nine months of discovery of the unwanted power or property, but the Act confusingly failed to correlate its provisions with state laws of disclaimers. So here again, local advice will be a necessity.

As to special powers to appoint only among a designated group, none of which is yourself, the possession of such a power will not cause the value of the property subject to the power to be included in your gross estate. This is because such a power does not meet the definition of a taxable general power of appointment, and naturally estate planners are most interested in this non-taxable power. You might want to remember it for later discussions.

Non-Taxable Powers

The estate tax law specifically excludes from the definition of a taxable general power of appointment two other carefully defined powers which, since they are non-taxable, are most interesting to us. One is the power given to a designated person, who may or may not be the beneficiary of a trust, to withdraw from trust principal such amounts of money or property as are necessary for that person's **health, education, maintenance, or support in his or her accustomed manner of living.** This is widely known as the **ascertainable standard,** and the words quoted are the precise words of the law and regulations. Those exact words are necessary to keep the power non-taxable, and using even one other unpermitted word to define the power holder's rights can make all the property subject to the power taxable under the estate tax. People are forever trying to sneak in additional words such as comfort, happiness, well-being, and the like, but the lesson is by now clear that even one such extra word will cause unwanted taxation. This is an example of how carefully, knowledgeably, and technically estate planning documents must be written.

The other permitted type of non-taxable power is one granted to a trust beneficiary to withdraw annually from principal an amount not to exceed either $5000 or 5% of that principal, whichever is greater; note that 5% is often far greater than $5000. (This is one of the only times the tax law says "whichever is greater"; it usually says whichever is lesser.) That power to withdraw need not be for any purpose at all and can be at the mere whim of the power holder, thereby giving the beneficiary some flexibility to obtain a few luxuries. As stated, this power must be annual, so that if it is not exercised in a given year it must disappear at the end of that year and will not authorize $10,000 or 10% in the following year. For a beneficiary to have this power, it must be authorized in the trust document.

While that so-called **five by five power** may seem like a boon, it is by no means universally used. For one thing, in the year the holder of such a power dies, it will be a general power of appointment as to the greater of $5000 or 5% of the trust principal since the beneficiary could indeed have appointed that amount to himself in that year. So it will definitely cause estate taxation of at least 5% of the trust value, but many people think the flexibility it gives is worth that price. Another potential negative about this power concerns the income taxation of the annual trust income, where the existence of this power can in some circumstances cause unwanted income taxation for the beneficiary. More of this later, but you should realize that the five by five power is not always recommended.

Life Insurance

The final type of property included in a decedent's gross estate is insurance on his life. Many people are confused about the estate taxation of life insurance, primarily because they do not fully understand the nature of life insurance. Therefore let's examine it, which can best be done by examining the "cast of characters" involved in life insurance.

The Basics Of Life Insurance

A life insurance policy is nothing more or less than a contract, whereby one party promises to pay a sum of money to a person the other party designates when a certain event happens; namely someone's death. That contract could easily be between any two persons, if they were both willing and could agree on the price, except that for the protection of the public, laws now provide that only certain well-financed corporations may issue such policies. The company's agreement of course has a price, and purely as a matter of convenience, the price is usually paid in installments, which have come to be known as premiums.

The person upon whose death the company will pay the agreed upon sum is known as the **insured.** The person who undertakes to pay the annual installments is known as the **premium payer.**

The person who has all the various ownership rights in the policy is known as the **owner.** He possesses all the **incidents of ownership,** which usually include, among others, the following: the right to name the beneficiary, the right to change the beneficiary, the right to cancel the policy, the right to turn it in and receive its cash surrender value (if any), the right to borrow against the policy, the right to give the policy away, the right to convert term insurance into permanent insurance, etc. There is absolutely no reason in either law or logic why the owner need be the same person as either the insured or the premium payer, and indeed these can easily be three different persons. Just because they so often are one and the same person should not obscure the fact that they don't have to be.

The final character in the cast is the **beneficiary,** who of course is the one who will receive the agreed-upon sum when the insured dies. Again, he can be the same or a completely different person than the owner or the premium payer, but for obvious reasons he could not possibly be the same person as the insured. Often we find that these four different functions are held by four different persons.

While it is common in a family situation for the father to be the insured, owner, and premium payer, with the mother or children being the beneficiary, it by no means has to be so.

How do you tell from the policy who is the insured, owner, premium payer, and beneficiary? The policy will always state who is the insured and who is the beneficiary, but the other two functions are often not set out in the policy itself. The premium payer function need not be specified, as the company will gladly accept the premiums from anyone who wishes to pay them. While in my opinion all policies should state who is the owner, most do not unless an endorsement has been added at someone's specific request. If no such endorsement or other indication appears, usually the person who applied for the policy is the owner. That applicant might be the owner, but might not be the insured.

Estate Taxation Of Life Insurance

Now, remembering what's been discussed about economic enjoyment, and about property in which the decedent had an interest, on whom do you think estate taxation will fall: insured, premium payer, owner, or beneficiary? It should be pretty obvious that it falls upon the **owner,** who is the one with the economic interests and rights in the policy. Many people erroneously believe that there is no estate taxation on life insurance, but that is incorrect. Perhaps the confusion comes about because the receipt of life insurance proceeds is usually not taxable income for the beneficiary as far as his own income taxes go, but that does not mean that there is no estate taxation. Also, in several states there is a specific exemption from state death duties for life insurance, but that is not true of the federal estate tax.

It makes a tremendous difference whether or not the owner who will be hit with estate taxes is or is not the insured. If the owner is the insured and he dies, then the amount taxable in his gross estate is the full amount of the policy's proceeds. If the owner is not the insured, we need to look at two situations. In one, the insured who is not the owner dies; nothing will usually be taxable in his estate, a complete reversal of the tax consequences when the insured is the owner and dies. Second, the owner who is not the insured dies before the insured; his ownership interest is indeed taxable in his estate, but only at its value, which is the cash surrender value of the policy (if any) and not the full amount of the proceeds (technically, something a bit different than cash surrender value, though we need not be concerned with the difference). But all of this must be cross-referenced with the transfers in contemplation of death rules, to which life insurance policies are equally subject. If the insured transferred his ownership rights to someone else, but he died within three years of the transfer, then the full amount of the proceeds will still be automatically taxable in his estate. You should begin to see some planning possibilities here, which we will talk about in depth in a later chapter. You might also note that term insurance has no cash surrender value, and neither does a whole life policy which has been borrowed against to the hilt.

For persons in community property states, life insurance just like any other piece of property can be community property so long as it was acquired under circumstances making it an item of community property under state law. Normally, this means by paying the premiums with community property funds. If the policy is in fact a community property item and the insured spouse dies, consistent with community property law only one-half of the face amount of the policy will be included in that spouse's gross estate. And if the policy was community property but the non-insured spouse dies, he or she under state law has one-half of the incidents of ownership, so one-half of the cash surrender value (if any) will be included in the non-insured spouse's gross estate.

Two Charts To Help You

A chart showing in synopsis form how a life insurance policy is taxed under varying conditions of ownership is given as Table 8-1.

It should be obvious that by placing the incidents of ownership in someone other than the insured, much of the impact of estate taxation can be avoided. This is one of the factors which makes life insurance a unique asset, and I shall examine the hows and whys of planning with it in chapter fourteen.

To conclude this chapter, before going on to a discussion of the deductions and credits available against the estate tax, Table 8-2 summarizes most of the types of property which are taxable in a decedent's estate.

APPLICATION

1. Be sure you understand the estate planning key; namely, that a life estate is not taxed upon the death of the life tenant (unless it runs afoul of the generation skipping tax, which will be discussed in chapter ten).

2. Use Table 8-2 to compute your current gross estate. Assign realistic fair market value figures to the property listed; human nature leads most people to value their property a bit on the low side.

3. For any of the property listed in Table 8-2 which is community property, reduce the value by one-half.

Table 8–1. Estate Taxation of a Life Insurance Policy under varying types of ownerships.

APPLICATION

The Insured: George Jones
Face Amount: $100,000
Cash Surrender Value: $6,000

Varying Conditions		Amount Taxable in George's Estate
Owner:	George Jones	$100,000
Owner:	George Jones and Alice Jones, as Community Property	$50,000
Owner:	George Jones and Alice Jones, as Tenants in Common	$50,000
Owner:	Alice Jones, and premiums are paid with community property funds	$50,000
Owner:	(In a community property state) Alice Jones, as her sole and separate property, and premiums are paid from Alice's separate property	-0-
Owner:	(In a common law state): Alice Jones	-0-
Owner:	Children, or any other individual other than George or Alice	-0-
Owner:	An irrevocable trust with neither George nor Alice serving as Trustee	-0-

		If Alice Jones dies first, amount Taxable in Alice's Estate
Owner:	George Jones	-0-
Owner:	George Jones and Alice Jones, as Community Property	$3,000
Owner:	(In a common law state): Alice Jones	$6,000
Owner:	(In a community property state) Alice Jones, and premiums are paid with community property funds	$3,000
Owner:	(In a community property state) Alice Jones, and premiums are paid from Alice's separate property	$6,000

Table 8-2. Synopsis of property which is estate taxable.

PROPERTY	COMMENTS

Real Estate
   a. sole ownership
   b. interest as tenant in common
	Located anywhere in the world

Stocks, Bonds and Other Securities	Includes foreign securities
Cash, Bank Deposits, Notes Receivable, and Mortgages Receivable	Includes foreign bank accounts and other items located abroad

Certain Property Transferred During Life
   a. all property given away within three years of death, except gifts of $3000 per donee per year
   b. transfers with retained income, retained possession, or retained economic enjoyment
   c. transfers, including living trusts, over which decedent retained right to revoke, alter, or amend
	Valued as of date of death, not date of transfer
	   a. estate also included gift taxes paid on gifts made within three years of death, except $3000 gifts

Joint and Survivor Annuities a. includes death benefits under pension and profit-sharing plans, Keough plans and IRAs if benefits payable in a lump sum	Employee's contributions to "qualified plans" not included if death benefits paid out over more than 36 months
Joint Tenancies and Tenancies By Entirety	Taxation based upon how much the decedent contributed; includes all types of property held in joint tenancy, or by the entirety.

Business Interests
   a. sole proprietorships
   b. decedent's interest in partnerships and joint ventures
   c. closely held corporate stock included with other securities
	The most difficult assets to value.

Miscellaneous
   a. decedent's funds in "in trust for" bank account
   b. decedent's gifts under Uniform Gifts to Minors Act if decedent was the custodian
	Includes personal effects, cars, jewelery, furniture, art, antiques, collections, etc.

Powers of Appointment	General powers taxable even if never exercised

Life Insurance
   a. on decedent's own life
   b. on someone else's life, if decedent was the owner
	Proceeds taxable if decedent was the owner
	"Cash surrender value" taxable

9
estate tax deductions, credits, and payment plans

Deductions Reducing An Heir's Inheritance

Glossary For This Chapter

Charitable Foundation
Charitable Remainder Annuity Trust
Charitable Remainder Unitrust
Closely Held Corporation
Credits
Deductions
Flower Bonds
Marital Deduction
Pooled Income Fund
Prior Taxed Property Credit
303 Redemption

One set of deductions from the gross estate has a common reason for existing, which is that the decedent's heirs should not have to pay estate taxes on expenditures which reduce the amount of property actually being transferred to them. This set of deductions includes expenses of administration, debts of the decedent existing at the date of his death, certain taxes accrued and owing at the date of his death, and unreimbursed losses of estate property. Later, I shall examine the extremely important charitable and marital deductions, which have different reasons for being.

Expenses of Administration

Expenses of administration are all the probate expenses incurred in administering a decedent's estate. Primarily, these include the ordinary and extraordinary fees of the personal representative and of the attorney. Note, therefore, that due to the deduction, the government is paying part of those fees, to the extent of the tax bracket involved. If the tax bracket is 40% and the fees total $10,000, the heirs are really only paying a total of $6000 in probate fees, since $4000 of the tax is saved by the deduction. So the true expenses of probate are only the portions of those expenses in excess of the tax bracket against which they are deductible. Other common deductible expenses of administration are court costs, appraiser's fees, and accountant's fees.

The executor has several **elections** available as to the tax return on which the deductions for expenses of administration will be taken. They could of course be taken on the estate tax return to reduce estate taxes. Or, by election, they can be taken on the estate's own income tax return to reduce the income taxes owned on income earned during probate. Or, they could be passed through to the heirs for use on the heirs' own individual income tax returns, to reduce their own income taxes. The latter can only be done if the expenses are paid in the final tax year of the estate's existence, because the method by which the estate's final year income is taxed (to the distributees who receive it) will pass the deductions on to the heirs. Two things are clear: these deductions can only be claimed on one such return or allocated among those returns in amounts not to exceed the total deductions available, and the decision regarding which return should claim the deductions is based on the comparative tax brackets for each of the three tax returns mentioned.

Deductions For Debts Of The Decedent

Deductions for **debts** of the decedent are limited to amounts owed by the decedent at the date of his death. Those amounts reduce the totality of "his" property, and therefore reduce the amount that will be transferred to his heirs. One beneficial exception is for funeral expenses, which are not really debts the decedent himself owed before he died, but which are expressly allowed as deductions by statute. And although the statute does not specifically say so, cases have also allowed deductions for the decedent's last illness expenses. Other debts which the decedent actually owed, whether common ones like charge accounts or utility bills, or uncommon and specialized borrowings or debts, will also be allowed as deductions. Due to the deductibility of debts, it is clear that only the decedent's equity in real estate or any other property on which a loan is outstanding will be subject to estate taxes. Although the full fair market value of such property will be included in his gross estate, any mortgages, deeds of trust, margin accounts, or other loans against the specific property will be allowable deductions.

Taxes That Are Deductible

Taxes to be deductible must have been legally owing at the date of death. Federal income taxes are only deductible to the extent of taxes on income received by the decedent prior to his death; if a joint return will be filed with the surviving spouse (which may be done for the full year of the decedent's death), then only the decedent's portion of the taxes relating to pre-death income will be deductible, and not the spouse's share of such taxes. The same is true of state income taxes. The other common deduction for taxes concerns real estate or other property taxes, where deductibility completely depends upon the "lien date" for such taxes under local law. If those taxes were a lien before death, then the decedent legally owed them, and any amount unpaid by him but later paid by his estate is an appropriate deduction.

Note that the estate is not allowed a deduction for the amount of the estate taxes themselves, even though the heirs will not be receiving the funds used to pay those taxes. In reality, the heirs are paying a **tax on a tax;** if there is a $275,000 taxable estate which after 1980 would result in a $32,300 tax, the tax is figured on the full $275,000 and not just on the $232,700 that the heirs will receive after taxes.

Deductions For Losses

A deduction for **losses** is rather uncommon, and it resembles the casualty loss deduction allowed on your income tax return. It would arise if estate property is lost through fire, theft, or other means and the amount is not recovered by insurance; the heirs will therefore receive neither the property itself nor the insurance proceeds. But if the loss is covered by insurance, then the amount so covered is not a deduction.

Probate And Non-Probate Property

Recall that some of the property taxable in the gross estate goes through probate, but some of the taxable property avoids going through probate if its title was arranged in a probate-avoiding manner. The estate tax return allows deductions both for property going through probate and for such expenses as are actually incurred in working on property that avoids probate. Such expenses would include those related to clearing the title to joint tenancy property and doing the necessary tax work on any property that avoids probate but which is still estate taxable.

Deductions And Community Property

The deductions allowable on returns of decedents who own community property are affected by the state law regarding responsibility for debts and other expenses. If under state law the decedent's half of the community property is only responsible for one-half of the debts, then it follows that only one-half of all amounts just discussed will be deductible against the decedent's estate taxes. But if by state law the decedent's share of the community property is fully responsible for all such payments, then the full amount is deductible. Some community propery states have passed laws making the decedent's share one-hundred percent responsible for certain items, often funeral and last illness expenses, with the obvious purpose of qualifying the entire amount for deductibility on the decedent's estate tax return. It is clear that a community property resident will have to investigate the appropriate laws in his or her own state.

How To Avoid Estate Taxes (The Charitable Deduction)

To further the national policy of providing incentives for charitable contributions, a decedent's estate is allowed a **full one-hundred-percent deduction** for any bequest to a qualified charity. The percentage limitations for charitable deductions on the income tax return do not apply in the estate tax area. Charitable bequests are therefore the complete answer to "how to avoid estate taxes."

There are many problems and technicalities with the charitable deduction. One may be valuation and another may be a problem of authenticity, as the IRS will make you prove that it is indeed a Van Gogh painting or a Chippendale desk.

Remainder Interests That Qualify As Charitable Deductions

Often, a testator may leave property, usually in trust, to his spouse or to some other person for life, with the remainder thereafter going to a charity. A major issue is whether the estate may claim a charitable deduction for the value of that remainder bequest. Recent statutory changes have reacted to many decades of perceived abuse in this area, where decedents would set up such a trust, but the trust would typically contain all kinds of powers to invade the principal for the benefit of the individual beneficiary. These invasions could seriously diminish or even eliminate the amount ultimately left over for the charity. Not a bad gimmick, if a decedent's estate could obtain a hefty charitable deduction for the value of the remainder, while at the same time the decedent had advised his trustee and beneficiary to consume the entire trust so that the charity would never actually receive any property. The IRS said that in order to qualify for the deduction, the deductible amount must be certain to belong to the charity eventually. Even this wasn't airtight enough, and so recent statutory changes have sharply restricted the types of trusts under which a remainder interest will qualify for the charitable deduction.

Under present law, there are only three types of situations where a remainder will qualify for the deduction if a trust is used. One is called a **charitable remainder annuity trust,** another is the **charitable remainder unitrust,** and the third is a **pooled income fund.** The latter is a fund maintained by a charitable organization to receive contributions from many different donors, wherein each particular life beneficiary receives a percentage of the fund's annual income based upon a comparison of the value of what was contributed to the value of the fund at the time of the contribution. The principal cannot be invaded on behalf of the life beneficiary, and upon his death, the charity becomes the outright owner of the contributed amount. Due to the prohibition on invasions of principal, the amount which the charity will receive can be computed with certainty.

The two forms of charitable remainder trusts qualifying for the deduction of the remainder interest's value have several things in common. The designated beneficiary is to receive a predetermined amount from the trust every year for a period of either his life or for not in excess of twenty years. There can normally be no invasions of principal for anyone's benefit (except sometimes to make up deficiencies in the predetermined amount). In the charitable remainder **annuity trust,** the beneficiary must receive a stated and identical sum each year, which sum can be an absolute dollar amount or else can be phrased in terms of a fraction or percentage of the fair market value of the trust. Further, there is a general rule (with some highly technical exceptions) that the guaranteed annual amount must be a minimum of 5% of the beginning fair market value of the trust. The charitable remainder **unitrust** differs only in that the guaranteed amount, which is also subject to the same 5% rule, can be a fixed percentage of the fair market value of the trust assets as that value is determined annually (as opposed to at the commencement of the trust in the case of an annuity trust). As you can imagine, an entire book could easily be written on the technicalities of such trusts. It is likewise clear that expert advice must be sought if anyone is interested in employing such trusts.

If the trust qualifies, the charitable deduction is the net fair market value of the property in the trust, reduced by the present discounted value of the life interest annuity in the case of an annuity trust. What it is reduced by in the case of a unitrust would make your hair stand on end if I told you, so let's just ignore the complex accounting calculations and reams of tables necessary to figure it out. But valuing the charitable deduction is no simple task.

Charitable Foundations

Another very difficult subject is **charitable foundations,** and to preserve your sanity and mine I am making an author's decision to just tell you what the problem is without attempting to describe how the problem is dealt with. You'll just have to seek personal advice on this matter if it interests you. Charitable foundations are organizations, usually corporations, which exist to disburse their annual income in various charitable pursuits. As bona fide charitable organizations, bequests to them qualify for the estate tax charitable deduction. This has led many super-wealthy families to organize their own foundation, often bearing the family name, and attempt to qualify bequests to it for the estate tax charitable deduction. The bequest would often consist of all or a controlling portion of the interest in whatever business was responsible for the family fortune, and the bylaws might require or suggest that family members be in control of the foundation. As charitable organizations they were exempt from the Rule Against Perpetuities, so what evolved were organizations maintaining perpetual family control of a business or a fortune where future generations of family members were assured of foundation jobs, often at lucrative salaries. You can imagine how the IRS reacted against that, and the recent infuriatingly complex legislation was the result.

The whole area of the charitable deduction is a fertile field for disputes between taxpayers and the IRS, and a major portion of estate tax litigation occurs in this area. The obvious lesson to any careful planner or client is a warning to proceed with caution, at least where using anything other than an outright gift to a charity.

The Marital Deduction

The marital deduction permits no tax to be due on a portion of the decedent's marital property. It was put into the estate tax law in order to equalize the treatment afforded spouses in common law states with that afforded spouses in community property states. That objective has in great measure been realized, and it is helpful to remember that purpose when considering how the deduction operates.

Community property residents should *not* skip this section, even though only one-half of the community property will automatically be taxed upon the death of the first spouse to die, and the marital deduction is unnecessary to make that happen. The marital deduction applies in community property states in three different areas: it applies (and therefore can result in reduced taxation) to **separate property** (defined at page 18), it applies to **quasi-community property** (defined at page 27), which is treated for estate tax purposes as if it were separate property), and it can actually apply to **some of the community property itself.**

At the death of a common law spouse who under the law of his state owns all or a large portion of the marital property (usually the husband), we have earlier seen that the entire amount of that property must be included in his gross estate even though his wife may have her dower right to a percentage of it. In community property states, only one-half the property is included in the decedent spouse's estate because under state law that is all he owned. That appears to be an inequity, and the remedy is to allow the common law spouse a deduction that will equalize the tax treatment.

When a community property spouse dies, the surviving spouse owns his or her half outright. When the survivor later dies, that half will be subject to estate tax, since the decedent owned it. So to be fair, the marital deduction must ensure that the common law spouses come out in the same place; namely, that such amount as qualifies for the deduction, thereby reducing the tax bite at the first death, will belong to the survivor in a fashion which ensures that it will be taxed when the survivor dies. The need to ensure that equality of treatment is what leads to most of the technicalities concerning the marital deduction.

To be equal with community property where only one-half is taxed at the death of the first spouse, the maximum amount which can qualify for the marital deduction is one-half of the decedent's estate. (That amount has been a bit expanded by the 1976 Act, but that is a special circumstance we will consider shortly.) To qualify, the deductible amount must go to the surviving spouse and to no other person. And to qualify it must not pass from the surviving spouse to a third person after the mere lapse of time. Stated another way, it must go the survivor in such a fashion that it will be taxable at the survivor's later death. She is, though, allowed to use it up, or spend it, or even give it away. The pertinent requirement is that she must receive it in a manner giving her absolute control over it so that, if she does still have it at her death, it will then be taxable.

Of course, bequeathing the property to the survivor outright qualifies, as do other specific situations allowed by law. One allows periodic distributions from the proceeds of a life insurance policy on the decedent's life so long as one of several allowable methods are used for such payouts, sometimes in tandem with the survivor's general power of appointment over the proceeds. The existence of the general power would guarantee the estate taxation in the survivor's estate, which is what the IRS is after. The allowable methods for such payouts cover most of the methods one might wish, and their technicalities can be checked out with any knowledgeable advisor. The second specific situation allowed is a bequest to the survivor conditional upon her surviving the decedent by a period no longer than six months. This is the reason for the commonly used **six-month survivorship clauses** found in many wills, which have the added benefit of avoiding another probate if the survivor does in fact die within six months of the decedent. The third and most important specific situation allows the bequest to be made in trust with the survivor having a life estate (clearly a terminable interest), but if and only if the survivor has to get all the annual income of the trust, and if the survivor also possesses a general power of appointment over the trust property. The latter will guarantee that the trust property will be taxed in the survivor's gross estate.

Qualifying for the marital deduction is the essence of estate planning for married couples in common law states. The tax savings to the family as a whole are substantial, due primarily to our graduated rate system of taxation. That system necessarily tells us that two taxes on one-half each are always less than one tax on the whole amount. You can prove this to yourself by examining either the income tax rate tables, or the estate tax rate tables. In the first portion of chapter eleven I'll examine the mathematics proving that result, and there will be some dollar examples demonstrating the effect.

So it is normally almost mandatory for common law spouses to qualify for the marital deduction. This involves using either an outright gift, or by being very sure that you qualify for one of the specific situations mentioned. The latter is not quite as easy as it seems, as I will examine in greater detail in chapter twelve where we will discuss the estate planning devices used to insure qualification. I will also discuss in that chapter the problem of qualifying the exactly correct amount of property for the deduction, neither too much nor too little, and I will explore the effects of qualifying too much of it.

The $250,000 Deduction

There is now an election to take a marital deduction of up to $250,000 or one-half of the adjusted gross estate, whichever is greater. This can prove beneficial to family estates with a total value of less than $500,000 (for estates worth more, the usual one-half maximum amount which the 1976 Act retains is more beneficial than the new amount). In a $400,000 estate, whereas the normal marital deduction is limited to one-half, or $200,000, now the decedent can leave up to $250,000 to the surviving spouse and have that amount deducted from his taxable estate. But the person concerned with saving the most taxation for the total family might not elect the new higher amount. The reason is that the absolute minimum in family taxation will result if exactly one-half the property is taxed in the husband's estate and exactly one-half in the wife's. For the husband in the $400,000 estate to obtain a deduction for $250,000, he must leave that amount to his wife in a form insuring that it will be taxed at her death. If he does, her estate will then total $250,000, which is more than exactly half of the $400,000 marital property. The tax on $250,000 at her death will be more than the total taxes on each spouse's estate if exactly one-half the property ($200,000) had been taxed in the estates of each of them; the tax will total $23,800, whereas if half the property had been taxed at each death, the two taxes would total $15,600, for a saving of $8,200.

Many people will elect the new, increased marital deduction amount even with the full knowledge that it can increase the total family tax bite. They will reason that there is both an economic and an emotional benefit to **tax deferral,** and they would rather pay little or no tax at the first death even at the price of paying more total tax at the second death. With this choice, the maximum property is sheltered from the first estate tax and is therefore available for the security of the surviving spouse. The advantage would be obvious in the case of a marriage between an 80-year-old and a 20-year-old; since there will likely be very many years elapsing between the two deaths, paying the least amount of tax at the first death will leave the greatest amount of property to earn income and grow by appreciation over the long life span of the surviving spouse. That income and growth should pay for the increased tax bite at the survivor's death many times over.

In order to ensure that common law spouses do not now acquire an advantage over community property spouses, the special $250,000 marital deduction now applies to community property for the first time. If the same $400,000 family estate were all community property, even though the first spouse to die only owns $200,000, his estate will still be allowed to elect the $250,000 marital deduction and pay estate taxes as if all the decedent owned was $150,000. But for the same reasons expressed above, the estate might not elect to do so.

Recall from the discussion of lifetime gifts between spouses (see page 122) that there is a penalty for utilizing the gift tax marital deduction for gifts to a spouse up to a value of $200,000. The marital deduction which is available against the estate tax must be reduced, in an amount by which the gift tax marital deduction used by the spouses exceeds a theoretical deduction of fifty percent of the actual gift between the spouses. Once such gifts exceed

$200,000, that penalty becomes meaningless because the deduction actually used by that point is limited to fifty percent. If $100,000 of totally tax free gifts from one spouse to the other have been made after 1976, only $50,000 would have been tax free under the theoretical 50% deduction, so the estate tax marital deduction must be reduced by the $50,000, which is the extra tax free marital deduction.

For inter-spousal gifts between $100,000 and $200,000, it takes a good deal of arithmetic to compute the amount of the penalty to the estate tax marital deduction. Assume an inter-spousal gift of $150,000; the first $100,000 is completely tax free, and the second $50,000 of the gift is fully taxable. But a theoretical 50% deduction for the entire $150,000 gift would be $75,000, leaving $75,000 taxable. So the reduction in the estate tax marital deduction will be the $25,000 difference between the $50,000, which was actually taxable under the new law, and the $75,000, which would have been taxable under a theoretical 50% marital deduction from gift taxes.

A Note on Tax Law Complexity and on Future Reform

This ends our discussion of the gross estate and the deductions from it. Are you by this point becoming annoyed at the complexity of the new law? If so, you have a lot of company. And you haven't even heard all of it yet; wait until you read the next chapter about the two real gems, carryover basis and generation skipping transfers. It is this kind of complexity, as Congress piles one year's "reforms" on top of many previous years' "reforms" plus all the special interest sections of the law, which is beginning to lead to a clamor that the tax law ought simply to be thrown in the wastebasket, and we ought to start all over again. In the opinion of many persons, that would be the only sane way out of the intolerable mess the tax has now gotten into. Whether political and lobbying pressures will ever allow such a sane thing to happen seems highly problematical under our system of government, but we can always hope. It is said that constituency pressure on Congressmen really does work. Maybe someday people will just have had enough of this kind of complexity and will refuse to take it any longer.

Credits Against the Estate Tax

Credits are marvelous. They are subtracted directly from the tax, dollar for dollar, whereas **deductions** (whether from the gross estate or from gross income) are only as good as the applicable tax bracket. A deduction against a 32% tax bracket only saves 32% of the amount of the deduction, whereas a credit saves 100% of the amount against the tax itself.

There has always been a credit for gift taxes paid on property nevertheless included in the gross estate, such as gifts in contemplation of death and the like. That credit has been effectively abolished by the way in which the new system works. Gifts in contemplation of death are now automatically included in the gross estate, and any gift tax paid on them is also "grossed up" by including the tax amount in the gross estate along with the gift itself. But for taxable gifts made more than three years before death, even though they are added back to compute the estate's tax bracket, the law now automatically allows a "credit" for the gift taxes previously paid. Therefore, taxes will never be paid twice on the same property.

Credit For State Death Taxes

There is a **credit for state death taxes paid,** which is the lesser of the actual amount of those taxes or an amount determined by a particular table based upon the size of the estate (Table 9-1). In many instances it is a false credit, for many states have cleverly enacted statutes which reclaim for the state the amount of federal taxes saved by the use of the credit. Some states call this the **pick-up tax,** and wherever such statutes are found the federal credit is actually just a subsidy to the states in the amount of the credit (since the state, instead of the federal government, gets those dollars). Each reader will have to determine for himself whether his state has such a statute.

Credit For Prior Taxed Property

Another **credit, for prior taxed property,** is more helpful and shows the government's concern that the same property not be taxed too often. As with contemplation of death, a purely arbitrary time was selected to define "too often," in this case **ten years.** If a current decedent had inherited property from a prior decedent whose estate had been taxed within the previous ten years, the credit will be allowed in a declining amount over the ten-year period as the second estate gets farther and farther away from being taxed "too often." The credit is the smaller of the estate taxes on the inherited property in the first decedent's estate, or the estate taxes on it in the second decedent's estate. The credit starts at a full 100% of such taxes if the second decedent dies within two years of the first decedent, reduces 20% for every two years after the first decedent's death, and disappears after ten years. It is not necessary that the inherited property be identified in the second decedent's estate, or even that it be in existence at the second death, so long as it was taxed in the first estate and was inherited by the second decedent. And the inherited property need not even be taxable in the second decedent's gross estate; for instance,

TABLE 9—1.

THE CREDIT FOR STATE DEATH TAXES AVAILABLE AGAINST FEDERAL ESTATE TAXES.

Taxable Estate

From	To	Credit =	+ %	Of Excess Over
0	100,000	0	0	0
100,000	150,000	0	.8	100,000
150,000	200,000	400	1.6	150,000
200,000	300,000	1,200	2.4	200,000
300,000	500,000	3,600	3.2	300,000
500,000	700,000	10,000	4.0	500,000
700,000	900,000	18,000	4.8	700,000
900,000	1,100,000	27,600	5.6	900,000
1,100,000	1,600,000	38,800	6.4	1,100,000
1,600,000	2,100,000	70,800	7.2	1,600,000
2,100,000	2,600,000	106,800	8.0	2,100,000
2,600,000	3,100,000	146,800	8.8	2,600,000
3,100,000	3,600,000	190,800	9.6	3,100,000
3,600,000	4,100,000	238,800	10.4	3,600,000
4,100,000	5,100,000	290,800	11.2	4,100,000
5,100,000	6,100,000	402,800	12.0	5,100,000
6,100,000	7,100,000	522,800	12.8	6,100,000
7,100,000	8,100,000	650,800	13.6	7,100,000
8,100,000	9,100,000	786,800	14.4	8,100,000
9,100,000	10,100,000	930,800	15.2	9,100,000
10,100,000	....	1,082,800	16.0	10,100,000

property in which the first decedent granted the second decedent a life estate will qualify even though there will be no tax on it in the second decedent's estate. An illustration of this credit is shown in Table 9-2.

Credit For Foreign Death Taxes

There is one other credit potentially available—for **foreign death taxes** paid under specialized circumstances where foreign taxation would be assessed under foreign laws and still the property must be included in the domestic federal return. You can seek specialized advice if that situation should arise.

Normal Payment Times and Extensions

The federal estate tax return is due, and the tax payable, **nine months** after the date of death. There are only a very few provisions giving any relief from that deadline.

In complex estates it is often quite difficult to gather the necessary information and complete the valuation of all assets within

TABLE 9—2.

ILLUSTRATION OF THE CREDIT
FOR PRIOR TAXED PROPERTY.

FACTS: George Jones inherited property worth $200,000 from his father, Paul Jones. That property bore estate taxes of $60,000 in Paul Jones's estate.

George Jones dies:	Amount of Credit Available
1 year after Paul Jones	$60,000
2 years later	$60,000
3 years later	$48,000
4 years later	$48,000
5 years later	$36,000
6 years later	$36,000
7 years later	$24,000
8 years later	$24,000
9 years later	$12,000
10 years later	$12,000
11 years or more later	-0-

nine months. The law has always contained provisions allowing for an **extension of time,** but those provisions have been phrased and administered in differing ways. Now, the test is whether there is "reasonable cause" to grant an extension. It seems to be the policy that a three-month extension will be almost automatically granted if any reasonable cause is shown, and without too much additional effort, a second extension to six months after the normal due date will be granted.

It should be noted that there are two distinct extensions available, an extension of time to file the return, and an extension of time to pay the tax. If the request is only for an extension of time to file, then the tax, or the taxpayer's best estimate of it, must nevertheless be paid by the due date. A request for an extension of time to pay, however, will delay the need to pay by the due date in circumstances where the return is not yet ready to be put into final form. The granting of an extended time to pay will eliminate the assessment of any penalties for failure to pay on time, although it was never intended to and does not stop the necessity to pay interest on the tax amount for the period of time covered by the extension. The rate of interest payable is no longer a fixed amount, but an amount which fluctuates with the prime rate. The interest rate will be periodically redetermined as the prime rate moves up or down.

Needless to say, a request for an extension of time to file or to pay, or both, should be made prior to the due date of the return and the tax, giving the IRS time to act on it prior to the due date.

Otherwise, an IRS refusal to grant the requested extension may leave the estate in a bad position when it finds out after the due date that the request had been denied.

Flower Bonds

These bonds can be turned in to the Treasury in the payment of a decedent's estate taxes and can represent a method of paying some or all of the estate tax liability at bargain rates. The reason is that they are certain special issues of United States government securities which the Treasury has authorized as acceptable payment, but the economic realities of the bond markets give them an added value when they are so used. Most government bonds or notes are given a $100 par value, but they almost all sell at a discount from that value; generally, the farther the bond or note is from its maturity date, the greater is the discount at which it will sell. Thus, a $100 par value bond due, for example, thirty years hence might sell on the bond market for only $70, which is a 30% discount. Only a very few issues of United States government bonds or notes are **flower bonds** redeemable in the payment of estate taxes, but those that carry such authorization are redeemable at full par value ($100) in the payment of those taxes. They are called flower bonds because they "flower," or become worth more, in the payment of estate taxes. They may have been purchased at $70 each, but all of a sudden they are worth $100 for the limited purpose of paying estate taxes.

When Are Flower Bonds Useful?

Flower bonds are one of a series of devices that are often recommended when we either know or suspect that someone is near death. It may then be recommended that such bonds be purchased for the decedent. It is not normally recommended in other circumstances, because in the opinion of most persons these bonds are poor investments due to their very low interest rates. Thus, one does not normally want to have them sitting around in one's portfolio for years. To be redeemable in the payment of estate taxes, the bonds must have been owned by the decedent prior to death, so if the purchase is made it must be done in such a manner that the bonds will be registered in the decedent's own name (or specified kinds of trusts for his benefit), and the purchase must be completed before his death; it does no good for the family to rush down to buy some after he has died. And in a community property state, if they are purchased with community funds and stand in such name or names as under state law they will be held to be community property, then only one-half of them can be redeemed at par in the payment of the decedent spouse's estate taxes. It is thus often advisable, in community property states, to arrange the purchase and titling so that the bonds will, if possible, be the decedent's separate property.

If they are purchased at, for example, $70 but are worth $100 in the payment of decedent's estate taxes, not only must they be included in his gross estate because they were property he owned, but also the appropriate value on the estate tax return is $100; after all, that's what they are now really worth. But even though estate taxes must be paid on the difference between purchase price and par value, only a percentage of that difference will be lost to estate taxes (depending upon the applicable tax bracket), and the estate is still money ahead.

Flower Bonds Are Becoming Obsolete

Two recent events have made flower bonds much less attractive, and by the end of this century they will be a vanishing phenomenon. One is that in the early 1970s Congress ordered the Treasury to stop issuing flower bonds. Although no more will be issued, those already issued are still available and are perfectly valid. But as we get closer and closer to their final maturity dates around the turn of the century, they will sell on the bond markets for smaller and smaller discounts, until finally they will sell at or very near their par value. So the bargain will slowly disappear, although for a few more years the bargain element will still be present. The other event lessening their attractiveness is the 1976 Act's changeover to carryover basis, the meaning and mechanics of which will be explained in the next chapter. I need only note at this point that prior to the change, using flower bonds at par in the payment of estate taxes did not generally cause any capital gains tax, but that after the effective date of carryover basis, turning them in at par in the payment of taxes will cause a capital gains tax. This added tax cost coupled with the reducing amount of the bargain element inherent in them will in a few years kill them off as an attractive tax device. You might want to remember the capital gains tax point concerning flower bonds, and after you have read the next chapter you should understand why capital gains taxes will now be assessed.

Installment Payments for Closely Held Businesses

The tax law recognizes a special hardship when a large part of a decedent's gross estate is comprised of an interest in a closely held business (defined at page 132). There may be a significant amount of tax due, but very little in the way of liquid assets with which to pay the tax. Many estates have little liquidity to meet large tax obligations, and their only remedy is to sell estate assets in order to raise the necessary cash. But it is usually either difficult, disadvantageous, or impossible to sell a closely held business in order to raise the necessary cash; furthermore it may be totally counterproductive as far as the decedent's family is concerned. The tax law recognizes such factors and has built into it several options for meeting the tax obligation without being forced into sales of the business. Forced sales under pressure from tax obligations would often have to be made at distress or sacrifice prices since buyers have a habit of knowing and capitalizing on such factors, and no useful social or economic policy would be served by forcing estates into such a position.

One relief provision has been to allow the estate tax attributable to the business interest (not the entire estate tax) to be paid in **ten annual installments,** together with interest on the unpaid amounts. Such relief enables a family to retain ownership of the business for their own security (and hopefully also for the economic good of society) while meeting the tax obligations out of the continuing earnings of the business. Qualification for the installment privilege is governed by rules that were altered by the 1976 Act, and in fact the former single relief provision has been expanded into two different relief provisions.

The first provision, essentially retained from the prior law, allows for ten equal annual installments of the estate tax attributable to the business. Interest is added, at the then going rate for interest on tax payments. A qualifying closely held business is either a proprietorship, a partnership if it has 10 or less partners or more than 20% of the partnerhsip's capital is included in the decedent's gross estate, or a corporation if there are 10 or fewer shareholders or 20% or more of the value of the voting stock is included in the decedent's gross estate. The qualifying closely held business interest must, in order for the installment election to apply, comprise either 35% of the decedent's gross estate or 50% of his taxable estate. There are several other technical requirements which must be checked in each particular case, but the above are the main qualification requirements. However, if 50% or more of the decedent's interest is withdrawn from the business, or is sold, then it is assumed that there will be sufficient funds to pay the full amount of the tax, and that entire amount will then become due. So the family's future actions in relation to the business interest must be carefully watched.

The second provision, for **fifteen year installments,** also allows ten equal annual installments, but if the estate can qualify for this provision, those installments need not begin until the sixth year following the filing of the estate tax return. In the first five years, only interest on the deferred amount is payable, and this interest is specified to be only 4% on the tax applicable to the first one million dollars worth of the qualifying business interest; any excess will bear interest at the regular rate. The qualification for this new 15-year-installment privilege at the advantageous interest rate is similar to that for the ten-year privilege, but is not strictly identical. Partnerships can have up to 15 partners, and corporation up to 15 shareholders. The closely held business interest must comprise 65% of the adjusted gross estate, which is the gross estate less all deductions except the charitable and marital deductions. If only one-third of the value of the interest is withdrawn by the family, or is sold, the entire deferred tax then owing will become immediately payable. As usual, competent advice will be needed to investigate whether or not all the technical requirements can be met in any given factual situation.

One sometimes difficult problem under both installment privileges is whether the decedent's activities constitute a "business" for purposes of qualifying for these privileges. Farming has always qualified, and the new 15-year-installment privilege now also includes most of the residential buildings located on the farm. The recent drift of tax cases seems to indicate that investing is not a "business" for these purposes, and that the receipt of investment income is not sufficient to qualify (for instance, by a landlord of income-producing real estate).

Either of these privileges is obtained by an election made no later than the date for filing the estate tax return, including any extensions that have been duly granted. The privilege does not attach automatically, and the election is necessary to obtain it.

Redemptions of Stock to Pay Estate Taxes (Sec. 303)

I apologize for throwing numbers at you, but these are so commonly known as **Section 303 redemptions** that you might as well know what that reference means. These devices also provide relief designed to meet the same hardship as are the installment payment provisions; namely, that of a large part of the gross estate being comprised of a non-liquid interest in a closely held business. One major difference is that with the redemption provisions the business interest must, by definition, be a closely held corporation and not a proprietorship or a partnership. To understand the relief provided, it is necessary to explain briefly what a redemption is and what its tax consequences normally are.

What Is A Redemption?

Income earned by a corporation is taxed to it at the corporate income tax rates, and if that after tax income is then distributed to the shareholders in the form of dividends, the shareholders will also have to pay an income tax on that dividend income. This is the familiar **double tax on corporate earnings,** and to avoid it, owners of closely held corporations often retain the earnings within the corporation so that those earnings will only be taxed once. If the owner sells the corporation, he will pay capital gains tax on the sale, so that if the sale included the retained earnings he will only have to pay the lower capital gains tax instead of the higher ordinary income tax which he would have had to pay if he had taken the earnings as dividends. Instead of selling, though, he may just reason that he can sell his shares directly to his own corporation and obtain the capital gains tax treatment; it is this sale to the corporation itself that is known as a redemption, for the corporation is in actuality "redeeming" its own shares. The tax law recognizes the potential for tax avoidance implicit in such redemptions, and so it provides that a shareholder can only obtain capital gains treatment if the redemption covers all of his ownership in the corporation; if it is a redemption of only part of his ownership, then he must pay the same ordinary income taxes as if he had taken the earnings out as dividends.

If the shareholder dies, the corporation may possess sufficient cash to pay off his estate taxes, but if the family wants to retain an interest in the business they will want only a partial redemption in an amount sufficient to cover his estate taxes. The normal tax rules make that prohibitively expensive, since partial redemptions are taxed at ordinary income tax rates. So in recognition of the special hardship imposed by the expenses of a shareholder's death, a special relief provision, Section 303 of the Internal Revenue Code, permits a partial redemption to pay off those expenses at capital gains rather than ordinary income tax rates.

Advantages Of The 303 Redemption

One tremendous advantage to a 303 redemption (as they're called) is that the amount of cash which can come out of a closely held corporation at capital gains rates is not limited to just that portion of the estate tax computed on the value of the corporation in his estate. Rather, it can cover the entire amount of the federal estate taxes, the entire amount of the state inheritance or estate taxes, and the entire amount of both funeral and administration expenses. This advantage is so strong that estate planners would often recommend that an individual's enterprises be incorporated simply and only so that a 303 redemption could ultimately be used. Further, a sophisticated life insurance salesman might sell the corporation a life insurance policy on the shareholder's life, so that when the shareholder dies, the policy proceeds will be payable to the corporation and the necessary amount of cash will be available to make the 303 redemption possible.

How The 1976 Tax Act Harmed 303 Redemptions

In an extremely unfortunate move which strikes me as completely without justification, Congress in the 1976 Act tightened up the relief provision which they had previously granted so that it is no longer nearly as much of a relief. It used to be that to qualify for a 303 redemption, the closely held corporate stock had to comprise at least either 35% of the gross estate or 50% of the taxable estate; now, it must comprise 50% of the adjusted gross estate (gross estate less all deductions except charitable and marital). Don't ask me why. Furthermore, it used to be that the 303 redemption could be made from anyone receiving the shares from the decedent regardless of who under state law bore the responsibility for paying the decedent's estate taxes or other expenses. Now, the redemption can only be made from someone whose interest in the shares received from the decedent will be reduced under state law by his or her responsibility for those taxes and expenses. Many wills contain tax clauses that specify which beneficiaries, or the estate itself, are to be responsible for taxes and expenses; now, where a 303 redemption is contemplated, that tax clause may have to be revised, and you may want to consult your advisors if this applies to you. An interesting provision of 303 redemptions, however, is that the cash obtained from the corporation by the redemption does not have to be actually applied to the payment of the taxes and expenses. Accordingly, a 303 redemption is a pretty neat way to get locked up cash out of a corporation at the lesser capital gains rates where a shareholder has died.

But the overwhelming disadvantage visited upon 303 redemptions by the 1976 Act has to do with the new carryover basis provisions, which unfortunately for the sake of continuity will be explained in the next chapter. You might make a note to review the matter of 303 redemptions after you have read that chapter, and then you will be able to understand what the blow has been. In short and without explanation at this point, under the former "stepped-up basis" provisions explained in the next chapter, a 303 redemption could be pulled off at either no capital gains tax whatsoever, or with such little capital gains tax as not to matter very much. Now, however, a 303 redemption will trigger significant capital gains tax, thus adding another large cost to the other expenses the decedent's estate and family already have to face. It is doubly unfortunate that Congress did not allow the amount of those capital gains taxes to also qualify for 303 redemption treatment, so that means that the cash to pay the capital gains taxes must be found in some other source. None of this means that 303 redemptions will no longer be used. It is just that they are now considerably more expensive than formerly and also more difficult to qualify for.

The increased difficulty of qualifying for the important 303 redemptions due to the higher 50% of the adjusted gross estate test suggests certain estate planning considerations. For instance, if a shareholder has been in the habit of giving away stock to his family members on an annual basis, perhaps within the $3000 per year gift tax exclusion, he might now stop doing so in order that he preserve more than 50% of his net worth in closely held stock. He might want to substitute gifts of other assets instead. Also, if he owns two or more closely held corporations, he must own 75% of the value of each such corporation as an additional requirement to qualify for a 303 redemption. That might indicate adjustments in his normal gift giving patterns, or it might indicate a merger or other reorganization among his several corporations so that he winds up with just one corporation which is able to meet the 50% test.

APPLICATION

1. If you live in a common law state and are married, reduce the amount of your gross estate computed by the use of Table 8-2, page 150, by one-half. If the amount of your gross estate is $500,000 or less, you are entitled to reduce it by either one-half, or $250,000, whichever is greater. The above assumes that you are willing to leave that amount of property to your surviving spouse.

2. If you live in a community property state and are married, you can reduce the amount of all of your separate property and quasi-community property included in your gross estate by one-half of such property or $250,000, whichever is greater, if you leave such property to your surviving spouse.

3. If you live in a community property state, are married, and have an estate of $500,000 or less which is comprised entirely of community property, you are entitled to a deduction of one-half of the property or $250,000, whichever is greater, if you leave that property to your surviving spouse.

4. Reduce the amount of your gross estate per Table 8-2 by expenses of administration, debts (including mortgages), and taxes (including real estate taxes) owing, as well as by any charitable bequests you intend to make.

5. Compute the tax on the amount you finally arrive at, by using Table 7-1 on page 119, and then subtracting the appropriate credit listed on page 118.

6. From that tax, subtract the state death tax credit, Table 9-1 on page 162, as well as any credits for prior taxed property or for foreign death taxes that may be available.

7. If you own an interest in a business, determine whether its value comprises a great enough percentage of your estate to qualify for any installment payment of estate taxes, or (if a corporation) for a 303 redemption. If not, consider altering the mix of your assets, or even incorporating, in order to obtain those benefits. Perhaps judicious use of gifts will successfully alter the mix of your assets so that you can qualify for one of these benefits.

10

two nasty innovations of the 1976 tax reform act

Glossary For This Chapter

Basis
Capital Gain
Carryover Basis
Deemed Transferor
Fresh Start Adjustment
Generation Skipping Tax
Minimum Basis
Stepped-Up Basis
Younger Generation Beneficiary

1. Carryover Basis

Carryover basis applies to all property inherited or received from a decedent who dies on or after January 1, 1980. The initial change to carryover basis was made in the 1976 Act, and was designed to be effective January 1, 1977, but a tremendous outcry arose against carryover basis in the first eighteen months of its existence. As a result, in a later tax act Congress postponed the effective date of carryover basis to January 1, 1980, ostensibly to give Congress time to study its effect and consider alterations.

The carryover basis provisions are undoubtedly the most expensive provisions of the 1976 Act. The additional revenue that will be raised from them seems to be the price Congress exacted for raising the basic estate tax exemption. Comparing the gigantic cumulative costs of carryover basis to the smaller savings effected by the increased exemption indicates that the Treasury came out the winner on that exchange. Obtaining the highest basis possible is a crucial part of estate planning, and to ensure full understanding of it I will start with an explanation of what basis is.

What Is Basis?

All property which you acquire has a **basis,** and upon acquisition a property's basis is its **cost.** I'll use a share of stock as an example; assume you had purchased it for $10, and its value had risen to $100 at the time you sell it. You have a **capital gain** of $90, computed by comparing the selling price of $100 to the stock's cost basis, which is the $10 you paid for it. Although initial cost basis can be adjusted upwards or downwards by many things, the latter are beyond our purpose and so I will just consider basis as being the cost of an item. The comparison of basis with selling price yields **gain** or **loss,** which may be either **short-term** or **long-term** depending upon the holding period for the asset. Property must be held for one year in order to qualify any gain as a long-term gain, or loss as a long-term loss. Short-term gains are fully taxed at the ordinary income tax rates, whereas only 40% of long-term gains are taxed at the ordinary income tax rates. The amount of long-term capital gains tax depends upon your income tax bracket, and after the 1978 changes in the capital gains tax rates that tax can exceed 28% in federal income taxes alone.

Stepped-Up Basis

Still considering the same stock you purchased for $10, assume that when its value had risen to $100, you died. The stock will be taxable in your gross estate at its fair market value of $100, and estate taxes will be paid on it based upon that value. But that having been said, the next question is what should be the basis of the stock in the hands of the heir who inherits it, for the purposes of computing his capital gains tax whenever he may sell it. Before the 1976 Act, Congress recognized that an estate tax had already been exacted on the stock at its appreciated $100 value and felt that it would therefore be unfair to exact another tax on the same $100 value when the heir sells the stock and becomes liable for capital gains tax. So the heir was granted a new basis for the inherited stock identical to the value at which the stock was estate taxed, known as the **stepped-up basis.**

In our example, since estate taxes were paid at the $100 value, that would be the stepped-up basis of the stock in the hands of the heir. This was immensely important because it could completely wipe out the capital gains tax allocable to all pre-death appreciation. Even if the stock had appreciated after the death of the original owner to $150 when the heir decides to sell, the heir's capital gain would be only $50 (selling price over the stepped-up basis of $100), so the potential capital gains tax allocable to the pre-death appreciation from $10 to $100 would be permanently eliminated. If the heir were in a high income tax bracket so that capital gains taxes might approach the maximum rate, stepped-up basis could provide significant tax savings to the heir, and estate planning would certainly want to take such savings into account in planning the decedent's estate. A common and crucial situation might involve the residence of a married couple, perhaps purchased for $30,000 and worth $150,000 at death. If after the death of the first spouse the survivor no longer wanted to live in the property, a sale could imply large capital gains taxes. But if a stepped-up basis for the house in the survivor's hands could be ensured, all capital gains tax on the $120,000 of pre-death appreciation could be wiped out.

For almost a decade, Congress had been aiming its guns at the stepped-up basis; you might wonder why, since the rationale stated above seems logical and fair. But there was a growing Congressional feeling that only the wealthy could take advantage of stepped-up basis since they were the only ones likely to have appreciated property. Also, Congress felt that the stepped-up basis encouraged people to hang on to assets for artificial tax reasons instead of treating their property according to their other best interest. The latter had a great deal of truth to it, for if a 90-year-old proposed selling a stock portfolio that had cost $50,000 and was now worth $500,000, any knowledgeable tax advisor would have strongly urged retaining the stock until death in order to give the heirs the stepped-up basis. If the elderly person sold, the profit would be diminished by the capital gains tax, and what remained thereafter would be diminished still further by the estate taxes payable at death. Holding until death would have incurred only one tax instead of two.

Note carefully that because Congress postponed the effective date of carryover basis, the beneficial rules of stepped-up basis continue to apply to all property inherited or received from a person who dies through December 31, 1979.

The Change To Carryover Basis

For several years, the proposed remedy was to impose a capital gains tax on the pre-death appreciation at the time of death, and then an estate tax on the deathtime value of the property reduced by some complicated credits lessening the full impact of the double taxes. That would have been even more costly to heirs than the change Congress did enact.

Instead, the new Act requires that the heir take over the decedent's basis in any asset acquired from a decedent who dies after December 31, 1979, leading to the term **carryover basis.** This had always been the situation with regard to property acquired by gift, where the donee took over the donor's basis with one upward adjustment in the amount of any gift taxes payable on the gift. Gifts had never had a stepped-up basis, and Congress merely applied the same concept to property acquired by a deathtime gift from a decedent. So the elimination of all potential capital gains taxes on pre-death appreciation of inherited property is no longer available to an heir. Now the widow selling the family home after her spouse dies will be faced with a capital gains tax. That's why this is such an expensive change.

Nothing Congress did in the 1976 Act is uncomplicated, and the complications of carryover basis are, unfortunately, extremely important. There are several exceptions and adjustments to "pure" carryover basis, each of which I must now discuss.

Exclusion for Personal and Household Effects

By an election on a timely filed estate tax return, **personal and household effects** of the decedent can be excluded from carryover basis property, **up to a value of $10,000.** The effect of this exclusion is that such property will not have to carry over the decedent's basis, but rather will acquire a full stepped-up basis as it did under the old law. Accordingly, if an item which qualifies as such property has appreciated a great deal, capital gains taxes on its later sale can be reduced or eliminated by putting that property within the excluded portion.

The Fresh Start Adjustment: First Adjustment

When an heir inherits a piece of property, his basis will be the same basis as the decedent had in the property, but only after four different adjustments have been made to the decedent's basis. These adjustments are to be applied in the order presented and are extremely important, particularly this first one called the **fresh start adjustment.** Tax laws are never supposed to operate retroactively, so it would have been grossly unfair and perhaps even unconstitutional to simply repeal the stepped-up basis. Instead, the fresh start adjustment essentially preserves the stepped-up basis for the appreciation that occurred prior to the effective date of the 1976 Act, which was December 31, 1976. The fresh start adjustment says that for any asset actually owned by the decedent on that date, or which he acquired from a trust, by a gift, or in a tax-free transaction from a person who owned the asset on that date, for the purposes of computing gain but not loss, the heir's basis will be stepped up to the asset's value on December 31, 1976. However, that adjustment cannot increase the basis higher than the asset's fair market value on the date of the decedent's death. Even though carryover basis does not take effect until January 1, 1980, when it takes effect, the date for applying the fresh start adjustment will still be December 31, 1976 (not 1979). Unfortunately for taxpayers, that date was not changed. It is just that Congress decreed a three year "moratorium", after which the law as originally written in the 1976 Act is the effective law.

It is therefore crucial to determine the value of property as of December 31, 1976. But while still deliberating the Act, Congress realized that there weren't enough appraisers in the entire world to appraise all property in the United States before that date. Not only would such appraisals cost billions, but the IRS would probably just argue with those appraisals anyway. So a method was devised to avoid the need for appraisals, which is the following.

If the asset is any stock, bond, or other marketable security traded on a recognized exchange, then its actual value (average between high and low) for December 31, 1976, will be utilized for the fresh start adjustment. Several fat pamphlets are available which list the value of all traded securities on that date.

If the asset is any other type of property, then no actual appraisal will be recognized, and even if one had been prepared it will be ignored. Instead, an automatic "straight line" type of appreciation formula was adopted, which comes up with a percentage figure. That percentage is arrived at by comparing the number of days (not weeks or months) from purchase date to December 31, 1976, with the number of days from purchase date to date of death. The resulting percentage will be applied to the property's appreciation (the difference between the decedent's basis and the property's fair market value at date of death), and the result will be the fresh start adjustment. Example: if property were purchased on December 31, 1956, and death occurred on December 31, 1986, the resulting percentage is exactly two-thirds. The heir will be entitled to a fresh start basis which equals the decedent's basis plus two-thirds of the property's appreciation. Computations of the fresh start adjustment are illustrated in Table 10-1.

Carry over basis only affects heirs who inherit property; it has no effect on the basis of property in the hands of the person who owned it on December 31, 1976. The increase in basis provided by the fresh start adjustment can only be used for computing gain to the heir, and not for computing any loss. Thus, an asset will really have two bases in the hands of the heir, carryover basis as adjusted by the fresh start rule for computing gain, but

TABLE 10—1.
COMPUTATIONS OF THE FRESH START ADJUSTMENT FOR VARYING TYPES OF PROPERTY.

	1.	2.	3.	4.	5.	6.	7.	8.	9.	10.	11.	
Asset	Purchase Date	Decedent's Basis (same as Price at #2)		Date of Death	Value at #4	Appreciation to #4	Days From #2 to #4	Days From #2 to 12-31-76	% #8 Bears to #7	#9's % Applied to #6	Value on 12-31-76	Basis to Heir after Fresh Start Adjustment (#3 + #11, or #11 for stocks)
A. Traded Stock	7-9-67	$50,000		7-9-87	$98,000	$48,000	Not Applicable to Traded Stock				assume $72,000	$72,000
B. Traded Stock	7-9-77	$50,000		7-9-87	$98,000	$48,000	"				—	$50,000
C. Traded Stock	7-9-67	$50,000		7-9-87	$40,000	$ -0-	"				assume $72,000	$40,000
Examples of Property Other Than Traded Stock:												
D. House	7-9-67	$50,000		7-9-87	$116,000	$66,000	7305	3444	47.15	$31,119	$31,119	$81,119
E. House	7-9-77	$50,000		7-9-87	$116,000	$66,000	7305	-0-	-0-	-0-	—	$50,000
F. Investment	7-9-67	$50,000		7-9-87	$40,000	$ -0-	7305	3444	47.15	-0-	—	$40,000

Reasons for Results

Item A. Listed securities take actual value on December 31, 1976.
Item B. Property purchased after December 31, 1976, does not qualify for fresh start adjustment.
Item C. Fresh start adjustment cannot increase heir's basis higher than value at date of death.
Item D. Illustrates application of the "automatic formula" for computing fresh start adjustment.
Item E. Same reason as B.
Item F. Same reason as C.

pure carryover basis without that adjustment for computing an heir's loss. And remember that the fresh start adjustment cannot increase basis higher than an asset's fair market value at the date of death. Further, if the heir can depreciate the asset he inherits, he can use the higher fresh start basis as the value on which he computes his depreciation.

Who is hurt and who is helped by the way in which the automatic formula operates for figuring the December 31, 1976, value? If property had actually had most of its appreciation prior to that date and does not appreciate much after that date, the heir is hurt by the automatic rule because the benefit of the high actual December 31, 1976, value is being constantly reduced thereafter. But if the property had not appreciated very much prior to that date and appreciates greatly thereafter, the heir is helped by the automatic formula because he will obtain a higher new basis under it than if actual December 31 values had been utilized.

The fresh start adjustment makes the change to carryover basis not too disadvantageous for heirs inheriting property only a few years after the end of 1979 because the fresh start rule will give them an increased basis that will include most of the appreciation accruing to the property. But as the years roll by and property continues to appreciate, the heir will be faced with more and more capital gains tax when he sells the property because the fresh start rule will do him less and less good. If the stock I used as an example had been worth $100 on December 31, 1976, and death had occurred in 1980 when the stock was worth $104, the fresh start rule would give the heir a $100 basis and very little capital gains tax if he quickly sold for $104. But if the decedent does not die until 1990 when the stock is worth $900 per share, the fresh start carryover basis is still $100 and upon a later sale by the heir for $900, there will be a large capital gains tax.

Note again that the fresh start rule applies only to property owned by a decedent on December 31, 1976. For any property acquired by him thereafter, the fresh start adjustment is not applicable when his heir later inherits such property. The heir will simply take a pure carryover basis; namely, whatever was the decedent's basis will be the heir's basis. After a few decades have gone by, the fresh start adjustment will fade into virtual oblivion because little property will exist which was owned on December 31, 1976, by anyone dying in those later decades.

If a husband owning all of the marital property under the laws of a common law state dies, all of such property is included in his gross estate. Accordingly, it all qualifies for the fresh start adjustment, even though up to one-half of it may not bear any estate taxes due to the marital deduction. In order that community property spouses be placed in an equal position, the old law provided that even though only one of the community property owners had died, the entire community property, including the surviving spouse's half, received a full stepped-up basis. It remains clear under the 1976 Act that even though only one such spouse dies, both halves of the community property will receive the fresh start adjustment to carryover basis.

A piece of property is entitled to only one fresh start adjustment, even though property owned on December 31, 1976, may pass through several estates. If Mr. Jones owned a ranch on that date, upon his death with a will leaving everything to Mr. Scott, the ranch will qualify for the fresh start adjustment. But when Mr. Scott dies and leaves all his property to Mr. White, the ranch will not qualify for another fresh start adjustment even though it was owned by someone on December 31, 1976.

Mention should be made of the interplay of carryover basis with special income tax rules concerning residences. If the proceeds from the sale of a taxpayer's principal residence are reinvested within eighteen months in another home costing at least as much as those proceeds, then there will be no capital gains recognized, nor capital gains tax due, on the sale of the previous home. However, the basis of the first home is carried over as the basis of the second home, so the second home's basis is therefore not its actual cost. Even though the home owned by a decedent may have been purchased after December 31, 1976, if the tax-free provisions had applied to that home, and the original home which started the chain was purchased before December 31, 1976, the decedent's home will still be entitled to the fresh start adjustment. This effect is due to some beneficial technicalities of the law, and is illustrated by Figure 10–2.

Purchase Date	Purchase Price	Basis	Sale Date	Sale Price	Capital Gain
12-31-46	$ 17,000	$ 17,000	7-19-58	$ 46,000	-0-
11-16-58	$ 46,000	$ 17,000	9-13-66	$ 67,000	-0-
1-13-67	$ 67,000	$ 17,000	8-16-72	$ 91,000	-0-
12-31-72	$ 91,000	$ 17,000			

ASSUMED VALUE 12-31-76, per formula: $130,000
                                   9-29-80 $192,500   -0-
| 11-7-80 | $192,500 | $17,000 | | | |

DECEDENT DIES 12-31-88
                 $130,000   12-31-90 $250,000 $120,000

Figure 10–2. Illustration of Fresh Start Adjustment available to residence even though purchased after 12-31-76, where proceeds of previous sales continuously reinvested.

Adjustment for Federal and State Death Taxes: Second Adjustment

This is the second beneficial adjustment to carryover basis. That portion of the federal and state death taxes which is allocable to the appreciation element in each carryover basis asset increases the basis of that asset in the hands of its heir. The adjustment is not for the entire tax on the asset involved, but is only for that portion of the tax which represents the asset's appreciation over its basis after the fresh start adjustment has been made. An illustration of this adjustment is provided in Figure 10–3.

Each carryover basis asset is entitled for these purposes to its own pro rata share of such taxes, and when there are many such assets in the estate, a formula must be applied to each one in order to determine the correct adjustment for each asset. This particular adjustment can be made only to property which is subject to tax, so property qualifying for the marital or charitable deductions, or the survivor's half of the community property, is not entitled to this upward adjustment in carryover basis.

$60,000 Minimum Basis: Third Adjustment

In the third adjustment, all the carryover basis property distributed from a given estate is entitled to a total **minimum basis of $60,000** if that figure has not yet been reached after having applied

FACTS:

Asset: family business
Purchase price: $100,000
12-31-76 value (per automatic formula): $300,000
Date of death value: $400,000

Pure carryover basis:	$100,000
Frest start adjustment:	$200,000

Basis after first adjustment: $300,000
Assumed federal and state death taxes on the asset: $130,000
Amount of those taxes allocable to the appreciation after the first adjustment was made ($100,000/$400,000 = 25%; 25% of $130,000 = $32,500)
Adjustment for death taxes: $32,500

BASIS TO HEIR AFTER 1st AND
2nd ADJUSTMENTS HAVE
BEEN MADE: $332,500

Figure 10–3. Illustration of Adjustment for Federal and State Death Taxes.

the first two adjustments. Assume that an estate having two assets (which together cost the decedent a total of $10,000 in 1970) was worth $30,000 on December 31, 1976, and $80,000 at the decedent's death in 1990. The heir's new basis will be a total of $60,000 under the minimum basis adjustment, and the allocation of that minimum basis between the two assets will be determined by formula. Remember that if the executor had elected to do so, $10,000 of personal and household effects can be completely excluded from treatment as carryover basis property, so that the $60,000 minimum basis can be allocated to other assets over and above the excluded personal effects.

This adjustment only applies if the total bases of all carryover basis property is under $60,000. Carryover basis property is defined to include cash, and even though cash hardly ever appreciates, its presence can ruin the application of the minimum basis adjustment. If, in the example used in the preceding paragraph, there had also been $50,000 of cash or bank deposits, the minimum basis adjustment would have been unavailable because the fresh start adjustment for the two "other" assets we assumed would be $30,000 and the basis of the cash would be $50,000. That would be more than the minimum $60,000 in basis ($30,000 + $50,000 = $80,000), so the two appreciated assets would lose the benefit of the minimum basis step-up. In an appropriate situation, prehaps pre-death planning could have altered that disadvantageous result.

State Taxes Paid by Heir: Fourth Adjustment

This adjustment, the fourth and last, is virtually identical to the second, but it applies where the heir or transferee himself is liable under state laws to pay the state inheritance or estate taxes. Many state laws are cast in that form, and so this adjustment seeks to do the same thing in those circumstances as does the second adjustment. All the same rules, formulas, and exclusions apply.

Basis of Gifted Property

The 1976 Act made a technical but disadvantageous change in the rules concerning the **basis of property acquired by lifetime gift.** Prior to the Act, such basis was increased by the amount of the gift taxes paid on the gift (if any). Now, that basis will only be increased by the amount of the gift taxes allocable to the appreciation portion of the gift as computed on the date of the gift, and not to that portion of the taxes allocable to the donor's basis in the property.

Unknown Basis

It can and will happen that upon a decedent's death, his executor and his heirs will be unable to locate appropriate records to show what the decedent's basis was. Without that information, how can carryover basis be determined? If such information is lacking, then the decedent's basis will be assumed to be the fair market value of the asset on the date, or the approximate date, when the decedent acquired it. It is quite clear that even that information can be very difficult to obtain, but the law at least gives the interested parties something to work with in their search for a satisfactory solution. The danger, of course, is that the IRS, with its vast resources, will be able to track down an assumed acquisition date and an assumed fair market value on that date, and the IRS solution may be the one that is disadvantageous to the heirs concerned.

At this point enters a tax rule which makes me more angry than any other, and which I consider to be totally backwards and unfair given the disparity in staff and budgets between the IRS and taxpayers. That rule says that anything the IRS proposes is presumed to be correct, and the taxpayer has the burden of proof in any attempt to prove the IRS wrong. No further comment. But you can see the problems this can pose for the heir when the decedent has failed to leave accurate records. An immensely important part of estate planning after the 1976 Act is to convince everyone to preserve accurate records. Even if the records are unavailable, it will be far better to exercise your recollection to the best of your ability now, and then sign a memorandum or affidavit that hopefully will be binding under state law. If binding, it will fix the facts so that the IRS can not disadvantage your heirs, and even if not binding, it will likely be accepted by any fair minded IRS agent or at least go a long way towards coming close to the real facts.

Congress made things a bit easier regarding tangible personal property (stocks and bonds are intangible, not tangible, property; the word tangible generally refers to objects that you can pick up and move, such as jewelry, art, machines, etc.). If the cost of such property cannot be reasonably ascertained but it is known that the decedent owned it on December 31, 1976, then a formula is provided for figuring out its carryover basis. The fair market value of the object on the date of the decedent's death is first determined, and then approximately 8% per year is subtracted back to December 31, 1976 in order to determine the asset's fresh start adjustment and therefore its carryover basis. That should help a bit as far as complexity goes, but it may prove to be disadvantageous where the asset did not really appreciate by 8% per year from December 31, 1976 to the date of death.

Computation and Information Requirements of Executors

The new Act provides that every executor (or if there is none, then whoever is in possession of the decedent's property) must furnish carryover basis information to both the IRS and to each heir who inherits such property. This information will enable the IRS to keep track of the basis history of each item of property inherited from a decedent and will also enable each heir to knowledgeably compute his later capital gains taxes when he sells such property. The information, in writing, will include the carryover basis of each asset with all of the adjustments to it made by any of the four adjustments we have discussed.

Note one thing very carefully. There is nothing in the new Act saying that carryover basis only applies in situations where the decedent's estate was required to file a federal estate tax return, and there is nothing exempting the executor or other person from these requirements if there is no such return. So this imposes a completely new burden in instances where no federal return is required, and an obligation which is most likely to be missed by many. What's worse, there are penalties for missing it, as follows:

For failure to furnish the required information to the IRS, a penalty of $100 for each such failure, up to a total fine of $5000. For failure to supply the written information to each recipient of carryover basis property the penalty is $50 for each such failure up to a total penalty of $2500.

It should be apparent from reading the above rules concerning carryover basis and the various adjustments to it that many more computations will now have to be made. The executor or other person concerned will have to know the decedent's basis, the value of listed securities on December 31, 1976, the date of death value, and the value on the alternate valuation date six months after death. The four adjustments will have to be made for purposes of the information requirements referred to, and complete information to the heirs must show the heir's basis for purposes of computing his gain as well as a different basis for purposes of computing any loss he may incur. The question this raises is whether or not persons ought now to consider appointing more professional executors than they formerly might have. No judgment is meant on that issue, and the answer can certainly be no, but it is worth thinking about.

Flower Bonds and 303 Redemptions

Do you now see why flower bonds and 303 redemptions are less advantageous after December 31, 1979 than they formerly were? When a flower bond purchased for $70 is turned in at $100 in payment of federal estate taxes, that is clearly a $30 capital gain. Formerly, the bond would have acquired a stepped-up basis of $100, its estate tax return value, so no capital gain would have been inherent in transaction. But with carryover basis, the $30 capital gain will have to be recognized, and tax paid on it.

As for 303 redemptions, the relief provided by that section extends capital gain treatment to partial redemptions made for the purposes discussed. Formerly, the shares of stock redeemed would have acquired a stepped-up basis equal to their estate tax return value so that, when they were redeemed at that value, the "capital gain" would be zero because the redemption price would have equaled the stepped-up basis. But with carryover basis, the redemption price will be in excess of the heir's basis, and that will cause a capital gains tax to become due. Section 303 does not allow the cash necessary for paying the capital gains tax to be also included in the amounts for which the redemption can be made, so such cash will have to be found elsewhere, and the entire maneuver is now considerably more expensive than it formerly was. Which of course severely diminishes the relief that section 303 was enacted to provide in the first place.

The Outcry Against Carryover Basis, and Possible Changes

Congress has been literally deluged with protests concerning carryover basis, to the effect that it is entirely unworkable. The many computations that must be made at so many stages of planning and post-mortem administration are tremendously confusing, in their interplay if not each one alone. Congress has caused a rather hefty increase in the costs of administration because professionals must be paid for the many hours they must devote to meeting all the requirements. One well-known commentator speaks for all of us by saying that carryover basis doesn't seem so bad on the surface, but the more you know about it the worse it becomes.

A standard goal of tax policy is that tax laws should not unduly intrude into daily affairs, in order that economic decisions can be made on their merits as opposed to their tax consequences. But carryover basis violates that goal by intruding on virtually every decision with which a planner and an administrator are faced, often confusing and hamstringing the process to the point of breakdown. I'll consider some of those planning points in a later chapter where I'll be discussing many planning devices in one convenient place.

Many bills have been introduced in Congress to repeal carryover basis, and many more to reform it in one of several ways.

There is a good deal of sentiment in Congress favoring outright repeal, but to date there has not been quite enough constituency protest to carry the day, although such protest must surely be credited with convincing Congress to pass the three year moratorium and to study further alterations. So there is still a strong possibility that the obnoxious carryover basis will be further whittled away or repealed altogether.

The Treasury opposes outright repeal, although it seems willing to make three major concessions. One is to allow the fresh start adjustment for purposes of computing loss as well as gain, thus doing away with the ridiculous concept of having two different bases. Another is to increase the minimum basis adjustment from $60,000 to $175,000. That would not only be of great monetary benefit to many heirs who inherit from moderately sized estates, but it would also completely remove the need to go through all the computations and comply with all the reporting requirements whenever no federal estate tax return is required. The third concession is to simplify the immensely complex adjustment to basis for federal estate and state succession taxes. This would be accomplished by eliminating the adjustment for state succession taxes (a very welcome simplification) and in exchange, the adjustment for federal estate taxes would be computed differently. The basis adjustment would be at the highest estate tax bracket instead of at the average estate tax bracket as it now is. We can only hope that these changes will be enacted, and it is very accurate to say that Congressional willingness to consider outright repeal or major changes has come about because of the many protests from constituents.

Should repeal ever occur, carryover basis could be replaced by something not yet even dreamed up. Or, hopefully, we could just go back to stepped-up basis as it existed prior to the 1976 Act. Basis considerations have been and always will be an extremely major part of estate planning, but estate planning will be different (and much easier) if we go back to stepped-up basis, as opposed to continuing with carryover basis.

The Generation Skipping Transfer Tax

If you were about to be devoured by a pack of man-eating tigers, it would be pretty useless to worry about which one of them was the worst. In the mess that Congress has thrown at us called the 1976 Act, it serves little purpose to worry about which of the new provisions is the worst. However, for difficulty of understanding, the generation skipping provisions clearly take the cake. Congress should certainly be flunked on this one and sent back to the 10th grade for a remedial writing course. I bring this up simply to alert you to the jungle ahead, and to offer my sympathies in advance for your attempt to digest this stuff. A whole new language has been created, although most primitive languages make more sense. I do not propose to lead you into the technicalities of this area, for it would serve no real purpose; your own advisors will be better able to explain to you the significance of these rules as applied to your own particular situation. At least one book and countless lengthy articles have already been written in the attempt to educate professionals in this new language, and I don't need to add to it. What I will do here is to try to indicate to you why this new tax was enacted, and what it attempts to do. The technicalities of how it does that, and how it acts on a given estate plan, are beyond our scope. Hopefully, you will be able to see how it affects estate planning in general.

As with many new tax provisions, the **generation skipping tax** was enacted to correct a perceived abuse. Calling something an "abuse" simply announces Congress's conclusion. Here, the conclusion was that the economic benefits of too much property were being enjoyed by too many successive generations without the payment of enough estate taxes. That could occur because of the estate planning key; namely, that a life interest in property left to you by someone else would not be taxed in your gross estate. So long as successive life estates could be used, estate taxes could be avoided. The only limit placed upon the use of successive life estates was the Rule Against Perpetuities (see page 108), but for an older trustor/testator with two or even three generations of living descendents, the Rule would not prevent him from setting up successive life estates which could run for 100 years or more. If a trustor had great-grandchildren living, he would have three generations of living descendents who could all fit within the time period allowed by the Rule. He could create a life estate in his property for his wife, then his son, then his grandson, and then his great-grandson, with remainder to his great-great-grandchildren. After the elderly decedent had paid his tax, no further estate tax would be due until the death of the great-great-grandchild.

To prevent such schemes, Congress enacted a brand new tax, called the generation skipping transfer tax. The new tax does not prevent all usage of life estates, recognizing that some are desirable within a family structure; the tax is imposed when the succession of life estates gets a bit out of hand. That is done by imposing a tax on the transfer of benefits in a trust which is identical to what the estate tax on it would have been if no life estate had been used and a bequest of that property had been given directly. To define when this new tax should apply, Congress felt forced to create a new language of technical definitions which would spotlight the occasion when the new tax should apply.

The way in which the new tax works is tied into many definitions, the first set having to do with **younger generation beneficiaries.** A person and his spouse are always considered to be in the same generation, no matter what their actual ages are, so there is never any problem with the new tax for transfers for the benefit of one's spouse. A person's lineal descendents (children, grandchildren, etc.) are younger generation beneficiaries, and the generational levels are what you would expect: one generation for one's son, the next lower generation for one's grandson, etc. The spouses of younger generation beneficiaries are in the same generation as the person to whom they are married, no matter what their age differences are. Brothers and sisters are in the same generation with respect to each other. Any heirs not included within the category of spouse, descendants, spouses of descendants, or brothers and sisters are assigned to generations based upon their ages as compared to the decedent or other person who created the interest under scrutiny. A person born within twelve and one-half years of the decedent is in the decedent's generation, a person born between twelve and one-half and thirty seven and one-half years of the decedent is assigned to the first generation younger than the decedent, and a lower generation is assigned for each successive twenty-five years of age difference. Assignments to generations are illustrated in Figure 10-4.

That takes care of the definition of generations, but not of the definition of beneficiaries. A **beneficiary** is anyone with an **interest** or a **power** (almost always in a trust). Each of those terms is very technically defined, one of the complications I'll avoid. It is enough to say that not only do rather normal economic interests make one a beneficiary, but so can mere powers in the trust; the latter carries a loud message about who should and who should not be the trustee of a trust, since trustees by definition have many powers. Some common trustee powers may be enough to cause the trustee to be stuck with the tax label of beneficiary, which in turn can cause some bad tax consequences under this new tax even if the trustee has no other interest in the trust. Repeating the familiar refrain, expert advice is called for, though it does seem certain that a corporate trustee (bank or trust company) could never be a beneficiary for these purposes.

The new tax only applies to any **generation skipping trust** or "generation skipping trust equivalent," so what are they? Dealing only with trusts, which are the most commonly used device, a generation skipping trust is one that has younger generation beneficiaries belonging to more than one generation. The latter point is crucial, because it points out that the new tax only falls on trusts where the **benefits of the trust are split or shared between two younger generations.** If the benefits are not split or shared, you

Life Beneficiary	Remainder Beneficiary	Results
Spouse	Children	NO
Spouse	Grandchildren	NO
Direct bequest to grandchildren, in or out of trust		NO
Spouse, then life interest to children	Grandchildren	YES
Spouse	Children, but to their children if a child dies before becoming entitled	YES, as to amounts passing to grandchildren
Brother	Nieces and nephews	NO
Brother	Brother's grandchildren	NO
Brother, then life interest to his children (your nieces and nephews)	Brother's grandchildren	YES
First cousin (uncle's son)	Second cousin (uncle's grandson)	NO
Friend 10 years younger than you	Friend 40 years younger than you	NO
Friend 15 years younger than you	Friend 40 years younger than you	YES

YES = Is a generation skipping trust.
NO = Is not a generation skipping trust.

Figure 10-4. Examples of application of generation skipping tax to trusts created for various beneficiaries.

simply do not have the type of trust that will attract the new tax. A trust with a life estate to the decedent's spouse, remainder after her death to their children, is not a generation skipping trust because the wife is assigned to the same generation as the decedent and so the trust does not have two younger generation beneficiaries; it has only one, which is perfectly permissible. The same would be true of a trust with a life estate to the surviving spouse, remainder to their grandchildren, because here too there are not two younger generations splitting or sharing the trust's benefits. And of course a direct bequest to one's grandchildren, nephews or anyone else in younger generations is not subject to the tax because no interest is being split between anyone. But a trust to benefit the decedent's children for their lives, remainder to the decedent's grandchildren, is a generation skipping trust since the children and grandchildren are two younger generations in respect to the decedent, and they are splitting the interest in the trust. And unfortunately, the following common set-up is potentially a generation skipping trust: to the surviving spouse for her life, remainder to the children when they reach a specified mature age, but if one of the children dies before reaching that age then his share to go to his children. If a child does die before that age we have a generation skipping trust as to the share of the child who died.

Although we may have a generation skipping trust with younger generation beneficiaries, we won't have a generation skipping tax unless specified happenings occur. Those specified happenings carry some of the most highly technical definitions contained in the Act, and this is another technicality I will avoid. It is sufficient to mention that the generation skipping tax will only occur if there is either a **taxable distribution** from, or a **taxable termination** of, a generation skipping trust. What this means is that the new tax will apply when the economic benefits of the trust are transferred by "distribution" or "termination" from one younger generation beneficiary to the next lower younger generation beneficiary of the trust. Not only are the definitions of these two terms highly complex, but also there are several provisions which postpone the need to pay the new tax until the last of a series of distributions or terminations contained in the trust are made. But even interim distributions, for instance of principal during the run of the trust, can be taxable distributions or terminations under the definitions, and the generation skipping rules are laden with land mines all set to explode in the face of the unwary.

When a taxable distribution or termination occurs so that the tax is now payable, who pays the tax and on whose estate is it figured? It is the **deemed transferor** on whom the tax is figured, and of course that raises another highly technical definition. The deemed transferor is, in essence, the younger generation beneficiary whose interest now stops and is being succeeded to by the next younger generation beneficiary, by means of a taxable distribution or termination. Example: life estate to son, remainder to grandson, and son dies; that's a taxable termination of the son's interest, so the son is in that case the deemed transferor. Remember that the main reason behind the new tax is to tax a transfer of benefits in a trust in the same estate and at the same rates it would have been taxed had the transfer been made directly instead of in trust. In our example, the tax is computed as if the son had owned the trust property outright and had willed it to the grandson at death; if so, the property would have been included in the son's gross estate and taxed at the son's estate tax rates. That's precisely how the generation skipping tax works. The son is the deemed transferor, and the tax is computed at the son's estate tax rates by assuming that the trust property is added to the other property contained in the son's gross estate. If the property remains in trust, the tax is paid by the trust itself out of trust assets, but if the property is actually distributed to the grandson, then the grandson or the son's estate is liable for the tax; in either case, the tax is computed as indicated.

The Grandchildren Exemption

There is only one meaningful exemption from the generation skipping tax, and it only applies where any interest in the decedent's property passes via a generation skipping trust to his grandchildren. The amount of the exemption is $250,000, but you must very carefully note the rules and restrictions of this exemption. First, it is not per grandchild. Rather, it is per deemed transferor (usually, the trustor's child), for transfers to his own children. Thus, if a decedent had three children and nineteen grandchildren, the total exemptions will only be $750,000 because there is only one such exemption per child of the decedent. If, in that example, one of the decedent's children was childless and all grandchildren came from his two other children, the total exemptions would be reduced to $500,000 because the childless deemed transferor can not be transferring any property to his children (since he doesn't have any). Also, the rules are written so that the exemption only applies to one transfer from the deemed transferor to his own children, preventing double exemptions where some of the property the deemed transferor is deemed to be transferring came to him from his father and some of it from his mother. The exemption is not per decedent at the level of his mother and father, but only per deemed transferor at the child's own level, so he only gets one $250,000 exemption.

Another important factor to keep in mind is that the $250,000 is computed as of the date of the taxable termination or distribution, at property values at that time. This makes the exemption almost impossible to plan with, in view of inflation. If assets are in any way appreciating, it would do little good for a decedent to leave his son precisely $250,000 in a generation skipping trust in hopes of qualifying for the grandchild exemption when the son's life interest terminates. With inflation in values, those assets will be worth more than $250,000, and very few decedents can guess how long their son is going to live so as to be able to compute the rate of growth in value. The exemption will prove beneficial in moderate-sized estates or where there are many children to serve as deemed transferors so as to multiply the exemptions. But in larger estates we can only gratefully accept the exemption, though we cannot really plan with it in any precise manner.

Effective Dates

Since tax laws are not supposed to apply retroactively, some provision had to be made for pre-existing trusts and estate planning documents. If a trust was irrevocable on June 11, 1976, the generation skipping tax will not apply to terminations or distributions from it unless the property being distributed was added to the trust after that date. If a will or revocable trust was in existence prior to that date, a five-year grace period was provided. For anyone dying before January 1, 1982, the generation skipping tax will not apply to any generation skipping transfer so long as the will or trust was not amended after that date in a manner that creates or increases a generation skipping transfer. Such documents may be freely amended in other respects, though. For persons dying after January 1, 1982, the generation skipping tax will hit all generation skipping transfers coming from a will or revocable trust no matter when it was made. And finally, it will also hit any such transfer coming from a will or trust, whether that trust was revocable or irrevocable, if the document was made after June 11, 1976.

APPLICATION

1. It is now crucial for you to carefully save all records concerning the cost of any asset you own, including (for real estate) all improvements. A journal or other record book containing the cost basis of all assets will be an immense help to your executor and to your heirs.

2. If cost records are unavailable, honestly exercise your memory to the best of your ability and make some memorandum thereof. If you are married, consider executing a written agreement with your spouse in which you both agree as to the facts concerning the cost basis of your assets.

3. Completely informed estate planning will now include considerations of how carryover basis and capital gains will affect your heirs. To be fully informed, compare the current values of the assets you owned on December 31, 1976, against their value on that date (actual value for listed stock and bonds, assumed value per the automatic formula for any other asset). If an asset was purchased after December 31, 1976, compare current value with your cost.

4. Review any wills or trusts you currently have (or are thinking about creating) to determine whether they are generation skip-

ping transfers. If they are, determine whether you want to go ahead with them anyway, or whether you want to adopt any alternatives.

5. If you have any trusts or estate planning documents which existed on June 11, 1976, be cautious about adding property to any such existing trust or amending any such existing documents. It may be preferable to create a new trust, rather than add more property to an irrevocable trust which existed as of June 11, 1976.

part three
estate planning techniques

11

the estate planning key: saving the second tax

Glossary For This Chapter

By-Pass Trust
Review:
Ascertainable Standard
Five By Five Power
Income
Life Estate
Powers of Appointment, both General and Special
Principal
Remainder

If you had an estate of $350,000, would you rather pay estate taxes of $57,800, or zero? If you had an estate of $600,000, would you rather pay estate taxes of $130,700, or $40,800? This chapter will tell you how to achieve the lower taxes.

We have already seen that the estate tax hits everything you own, and then some. We have also seen that, aside from the $3000 annual gifts, gift giving no longer serves to eliminate property from your taxable estate. So it might seem that estate planning cannot do much good as far as saving taxes goes. But the savings mentioned in the first paragraph are available via good estate planning, and I will focus on how that can be achieved in the face of apparent tax obstacles.

An Overview of Estate Planning

To understand how those tax savings can be achieved, though, it is necessary to direct your thinking to views taken by estate planners. Each individual person normally, and quite understandably, thinks only about his own estate and his own taxes. But an estate planner thinks in broader terms when considering various planning opportunities and focuses on either a generation as a whole or on a unit such as an entire family. He asks: What will be the cumulative effect of the estate taxes on my client's generation before his property passes to the next generation, and what will be the sum total of the taxes which the family as a whole must pay? It is within that extended focus that estate planning can achieve dramatic results.

It is inevitable in our economic system that when you acquire property by your own labors, it will be taxed when you die. However, it need not be taxed more times than necessary, nor at higher than necessary rates. But for your heirs, the tax system permits you to separate the property they will inherit from you from whatever property they will acquire by their own labors; the latter type will inevitably be subject to estate taxes when they die. Estate planning may be able to save taxes on the inherited portion, though, and it is this focus that you should adopt in order to understand and appreciate the savings estate planning can achieve.

But I immediately and strongly emphasize that **tax savings are not the only benefits of estate planning.** In fact, in my personal opinion, they are not even the major part of what you should be seeking from estate planning. Family security, family harmony, and expert management of assets for the benefit of your chosen heirs ought really to be the major part. As I proceed from this chapter onwards, I will be discussing both tax and non-tax facts. Although you ought to keep the non-tax factors uppermost in your mind, of course both tax and non-tax factors are important, and for a moment, let's focus only on some tax factors.

When Taxes Begin to Apply

For purposes of demonstrating what estate planning can achieve, it is helpful to identify the maximum amount of property you can own without having to pay any estate taxes before the next generation receives it. For this analysis, I will limit this discussion to your own generation and to the taxes paid within that generation, for the moment not considering the tax impact on later generations. Remember that for these purposes, both spouses in a marriage are considered to be in the same generation no matter what their actual ages are. I will use the post-1980 figure of $175,000 for the estate tax exemption, and I will ignore the $3000 annual gift tax exclusion, which depends upon the number of people to whom you are willing and able to make gifts.

An unmarried person can only leave a total of $175,000 tax free, whether during life, at death, or in any combination of such transfers. But for a married couple, the amount can be increased.

In order to avoid all estate taxation at any time within the single generation that contains both spouses, the maximum estate which a married couple can own depends upon whether or not they engage in estate planning. Without it, that maximum estate is the same $175,000 as for a single person, for the following reasons: even without considering the marital deduction or the community property laws, the $175,000 would be exempt at the first death, and if all of it is left to the survivor so that she owns one hundred percent of it at her death, it will still be exempt again. That example assumes that the survivor has neither used up any of the property nor seen it become more valuable; it would be pure guesswork to plug in reduction versus growth, and in fact, sound investment theory would indicate that income plus growth ought to at least equal the amount used up. While that theory is logical to an extent, you must recognize that if actual facts differ, particularly if the property grows in value more than it is used up, the tax results will of course change.

How Taxes Can Be Reduced

On the other hand, if a couple engages in estate planning, the maximum amount they can own without having to pay any estate tax before their heirs receive it is doubled, to $350,000. To understand how, it is very helpful to think of marital property as being comprised of two halves, even though in common law states it is a bit artificial to do so. In a community property state, there is clearly a husband's half and a wife's half, but even in common law states it helps in understanding the tax effects to use the same labels. Assume the husband dies first, that he owns all the marital property under state law, that such property is worth $350,000, and that he leaves at least half of it to his wife so as to qualify for the marital deduction. We can label the half qualifying for the marital deduction **her half** because it must go to her outright in order to qualify for that deduction, and the other half not so qualifying can be labeled **his half** since it will be taxed in his estate. Only the husband's half will be taxable at his death, due either to the marital deduction or to community property law, and in the $350,000 estate his half amounts to $175,000 and is entirely exempt. The wife's half, since it only totals $175,000, will also be exempt at her death. However, if he wills his half directly to her, it will be added to her half and cause her gross estate to total $350,000; the effect is that his half will not be exempt at her later death, but will instead be taxable. See Figure 11-1. To achieve the optimum tax objective, we need to ensure that the husband's half will not be part of the wife's taxable estate when she dies, so that she will then only own her half totaling $175,000. That amount is entirely exempt, so we

THE ESTATE PLANNING KEY: SAVING THE SECOND TAX

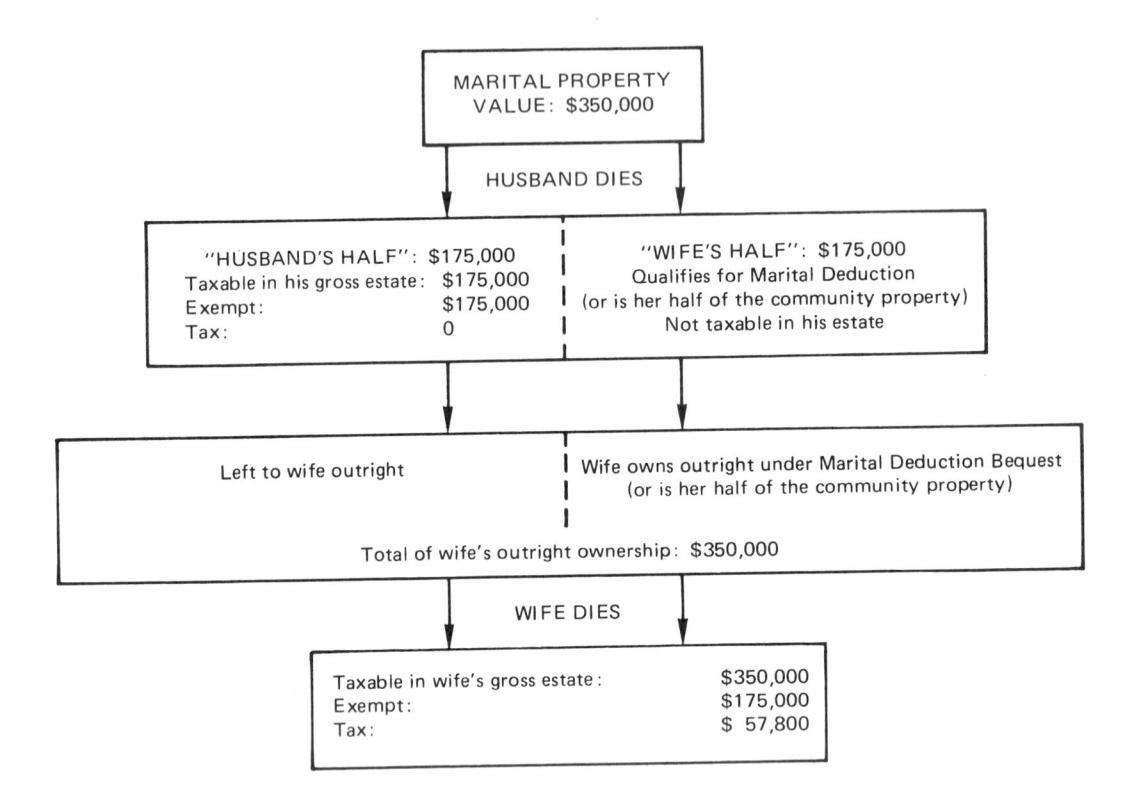

```
                    ┌─────────────────────────┐
                    │   MARITAL PROPERTY      │
                    │   VALUE: $350,000       │
                    └─────────────────────────┘
                              HUSBAND DIES
                    ↓                         ↓
┌──────────────────────────────────┬────────────────────────────────────────┐
│ "HUSBAND'S HALF": $175,000       │ "WIFE'S HALF": $175,000                │
│ Taxable in his gross estate: $175,000 │ Qualifies for Marital Deduction    │
│ Exempt:              $175,000    │ (or is her half of the community property) │
│ Tax:                       0     │ Not taxable in his estate              │
└──────────────────────────────────┴────────────────────────────────────────┘
                    ↓                         ↓
┌──────────────────────────────────┬────────────────────────────────────────┐
│ Left to wife outright            │ Wife owns outright under Marital Deduction Bequest │
│                                  │ (or is her half of the community property)         │
│                                                                                       │
│         Total of wife's outright ownership: $350,000                                  │
└───────────────────────────────────────────────────────────────────────────────────────┘
                              WIFE DIES
                    ↓                         ↓
             ┌─────────────────────────────────────────┐
             │ Taxable in wife's gross estate: $350,000│
             │ Exempt:                         $175,000│
             │ Tax:                            $ 57,800│
             └─────────────────────────────────────────┘

              TOTAL TAXES, BOTH DEATHS: $57,800
```

Figure 11-1. Total Estate Taxes, Estates of Both Husband and Wife, Without Tax Planning.

AN OVERVIEW OF ESTATE PLANNING

```
                    ┌─────────────────────────┐
                    │   MARITAL PROPERTY      │
                    │   VALUE: $350,000       │
                    └─────────────────────────┘
                              │
                         HUSBAND DIES
              ┌───────────────┴───────────────┐
              ▼                               ▼
┌──────────────────────────────┐   ┌──────────────────────────────────┐
│ "HUSBAND'S HALF": $175,000   │   │ "WIFE'S HALF": $175,000          │
│ Taxable in his gross estate: │   │ Qualifies for Marital Deduction  │
│   $175,000                   │   │ (or is her half of the community │
│ Exempt:         $175,000     │   │  property)                       │
│ Tax:                   0     │   │ Not taxable in his estate        │
└──────────────────────────────┘   └──────────────────────────────────┘
              │                                   │
              ▼                                   ▼
┌──────────────────────────────┐   ┌──────────────────────────────────┐
│ Willed to By-Pass Trust:     │   │ Wife owns outright under Marital │
│   $175,000                   │   │ Deduction Bequest (or is her     │
│                              │   │ half of the community property): │
│                              │   │ $175,000                         │
└──────────────────────────────┘   └──────────────────────────────────┘
                             WIFE DIES
              │                                   │
              ▼                                   ▼
┌──────────────────────────────┐   ┌──────────────────────────────────┐
│ Not taxable in wife's gross  │   │ Taxable in wife's gross estate:  │
│ estate: $175,000             │   │                      $175,000    │
│                              │   │ Exempt:              $175,000    │
│                              │   │ Tax:                        0    │
└──────────────────────────────┘   └──────────────────────────────────┘

              TOTAL TAXES, BOTH DEATHS: 0
```

Figure 11-2. Total Estate Taxes, Estates of Both Husband and Wife, With Tax Planning.

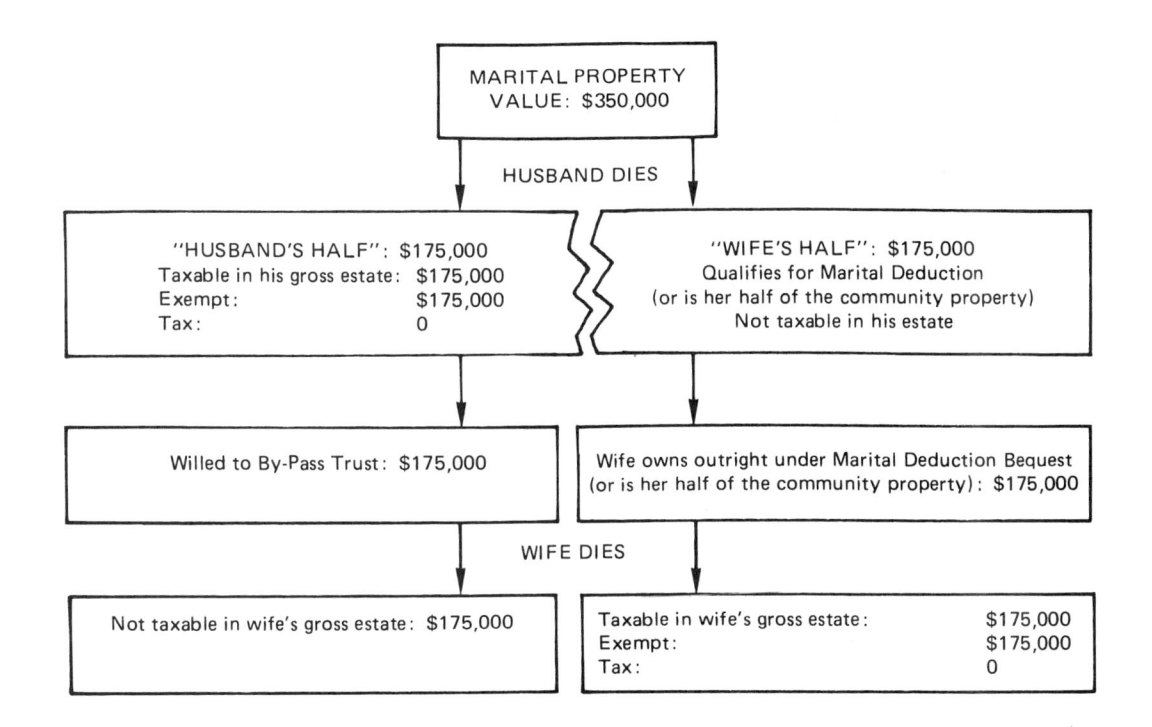

have reduced the total taxes to zero. See Figure 11-2. From previous chapters you know that we can keep his half from being a part of her gross estate by using a **life estate,** and the manner of doing so is the subject of this chapter. Without using a life estate, the couple could only own $175,000 before having to pay estate taxes at one of their deaths, but by using a life estate, that amount can be increased to $350,000. This increase is not available to unmarried persons.

If the only concern of a married couple is to avoid any estate tax at the first death, without caring at all about taxation at the second death (an uncommon goal, but it does happen), then the maximum amount of property they can own is increased to $425,000. This occurs because $250,000 qualifies for the new higher marital deduction whether the spouses reside in a common law or community property state, and the remaining $175,000 is exempt under the decedent's regular exemption. The amount might be further increased if the couple is willing to make lifetime gifts between themselves. Assume a couple resides in a common law state where the husband is considered to own all the marital property. He can own as much as $475,000 and still come out with no tax if his death occurs first. To achieve that result, he gives $100,000 to his wife tax-free under the new gift tax marital deduction (see page 122). This costs a loss of $50,000 in the estate tax marital deduction (see page 159), so at his death he can only will $200,000 to her and qualify it for the marital deduction. He can also will her his regular exemption amount of $175,000, so she may receive $375,000 by will and $100,000 during his life. The result is no tax when he dies, but of course there will be a substantial tax when the wife dies.

One final point, and then I can leave the mathematics for awhile. Let's shift from a concern over the maximum amount a couple may own without ever paying tax within their own generation, to a consideration of the effects of double taxation if they own more than that maximum.

The Effects of Double Taxation

Estate tax rates, like income tax rates, are graduated and progressive. This means that tax expense much more than doubles as property is added at higher and higher brackets into gross income or into the gross estate. The results can be disastrous. A common principle of either income or estate tax planning is that you are always much better off paying two taxes on one-half each rather than one tax on the whole. Or, said another way, the tax on a whole is always far, far more than double the two taxes on one-half each. To illustrate:

Assume a married couple owns $600,000 of property, the husband dies first, under state law he is considered to own it all, and he wills it all to his wife. Half of it will be free from tax under the marital deduction, and the taxable portion will be $300,000; $175,000 of that is exempt, and $125,000 will bear taxes. After 1980, the tax will be $40,800. But pursuant to the husband's will, his wife now owns all the remaining property, and after the husband's estate taxes have been paid, the wife's gross estate will total $559,200 at her death. There is now no spouse to leave the property to, so no marital deduction applies. From the $559,200, only the $175,000 exemption will apply, and the tax amounts to $130,704; see Figure 11-3. It is clear that the tax on the wife's death is much more than double the tax on the husband's first death; in fact, it is more than triple! Or, viewed another way, there has been a tremendous double tax on that part of the property which was taxed at the husband's first death; that $300,000 of property bore taxes of $40,800 at his death plus $89,904 of the tax at the wife's death, a total of $130,704. Had the husband engaged in estate planning to utilize a life estate in favor of his wife instead of giving her all the property outright, the taxes at her death would have been only $40,800 on her $300,000, and the actual **dollar savings would amount to $89,904;** see Figure 11-4. That's what estate planning can accomplish by **saving the second tax.**

Of course, the dramatic figures and dramatic savings only increase as the value of property increases. At one million dollars of total property, the tax at the husband's death would be $108,800; at the wife's later death the tax would be the same with estate planning, but without it (assuming $150,000 depletion due to taxes and expenses at the husband's death, a rather high assumption) the tax would be $240,300. Estate planning could have saved the second tax in the amount of $131,500. Note, however, that the savings do not accrue to either the husband or the wife, as they have both died by the time the savings are achieved; rather, the savings accrue to their children or other chosen heirs.

You may object that you don't, unfortunately, have one million dollars, or even $600,000. It is very important to point out that, even though the dollar savings may not be as dramatic with smaller amounts of property, **in a smaller estate it is often much more crucial** to the family's future economic security to save whatever dollars can be saved than it is in a large estate. "Small" and "large" are of course relative terms which nobody can define with precision. It doesn't matter what word you apply to your own estate; what really matters is how important such savings can be in view of the total property which is available to provide income and future security for your family. A ten percent error in a million dollar estate may be no big deal posing any threat to family security, but a ten percent error in a $200,000 estate may well make

THE ESTATE PLANNING KEY: SAVING THE SECOND TAX

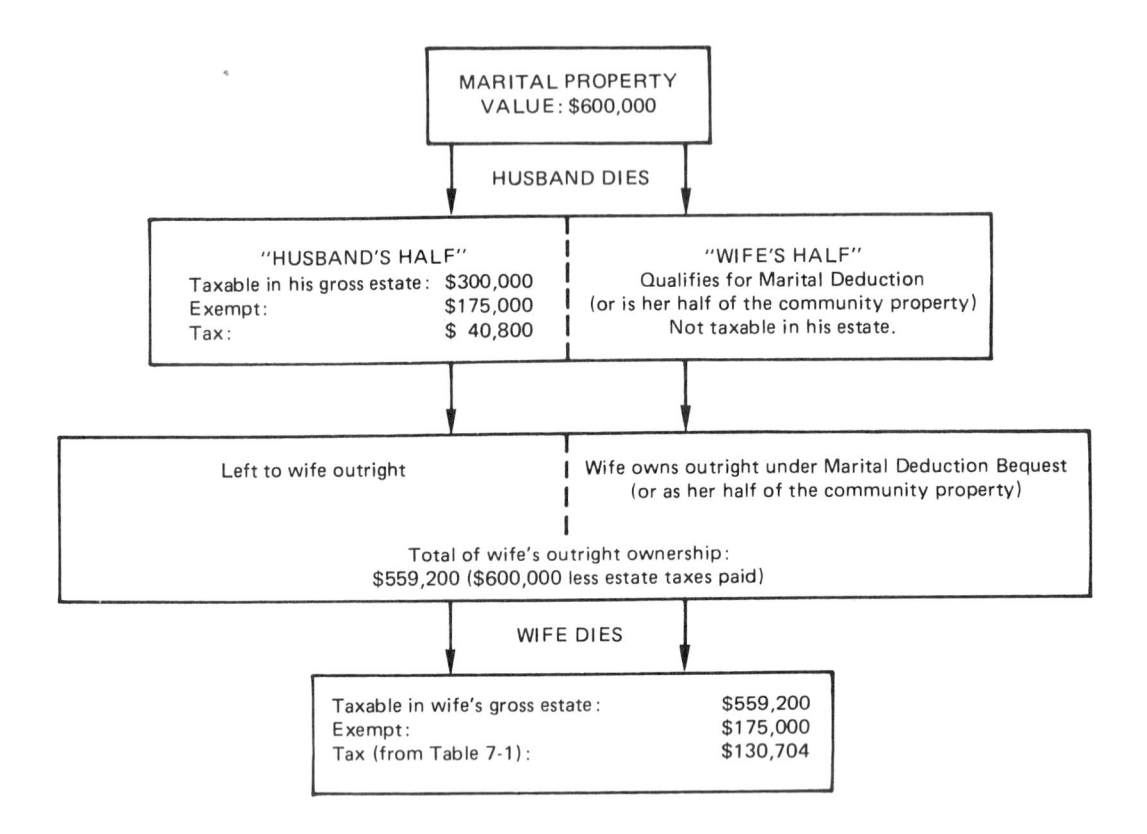

```
                    ┌─────────────────────────────┐
                    │    MARITAL PROPERTY         │
                    │    VALUE: $600,000          │
                    └─────────────────────────────┘
                              HUSBAND DIES
            ┌─────────────────┴─────────────────┐
            ▼                                   ▼
┌───────────────────────────┐   ┌───────────────────────────────────┐
│    "HUSBAND'S HALF"       │   │        "WIFE'S HALF"              │
│ Taxable in his gross      │   │ Qualifies for Marital Deduction   │
│   estate:    $300,000     │   │ (or is her half of the community  │
│ Exempt:      $175,000     │   │  property)                        │
│ Tax:         $ 40,800     │   │ Not taxable in his estate.        │
└───────────────────────────┘   └───────────────────────────────────┘
            │                                   │
            ▼                                   ▼
┌─────────────────────────────────────────────────────────────────────┐
│   Left to wife outright    │ Wife owns outright under Marital       │
│                            │ Deduction Bequest (or as her half of   │
│                            │ the community property)                │
│                                                                     │
│       Total of wife's outright ownership:                           │
│       $559,200 ($600,000 less estate taxes paid)                    │
└─────────────────────────────────────────────────────────────────────┘
                              WIFE DIES
                    ┌─────────────────────────────────────┐
                    │ Taxable in wife's gross                │
                    │   estate:                  $559,200 │
                    │ Exempt:                    $175,000 │
                    │ Tax (from Table 7-1):      $130,704 │
                    └─────────────────────────────────────┘

            TOTAL TAXES, BOTH DEATHS: $171,504
```

Figure 11-3. Total Estate Taxes, Estates of Both Husband and Wife, Without Tax Planning.

THE EFFECTS OF DOUBLE TAXATION

```
                    ┌─────────────────────────┐
                    │   MARITAL PROPERTY      │
                    │   VALUE: $600,000       │
                    └─────────────────────────┘
                           HUSBAND DIES
           ┌─────────────────┴─────────────────┐
           ▼                                   ▼
┌──────────────────────────────┐  ┌──────────────────────────────────────┐
│ "HUSBAND'S HALF": $300,000   │  │ "WIFE'S HALF": $300,000              │
│ Taxable in his gross estate: │  │ Qualifies for Marital Deduction      │
│                    $300,000  │  │ (or is her half of the community     │
│ Exempt:            $175,000  │  │  property)                           │
│ Tax:               $ 40,800  │  │ Not taxable in his estate            │
└──────────────────────────────┘  └──────────────────────────────────────┘
           │                                   │
           ▼                                   ▼
┌──────────────────────────────┐  ┌──────────────────────────────────────┐
│ Willed to By-Pass Trust:     │  │ Wife owns outright under Marital     │
│ $259,200                     │  │ Deduction Bequest (or is her half    │
│ ($300,000 minus $40,800      │  │ of the community property):          │
│  estate taxes paid)          │  │ $300,000                             │
└──────────────────────────────┘  └──────────────────────────────────────┘
                            WIFE DIES
           │                                   │
           ▼                                   ▼
┌──────────────────────────────┐  ┌──────────────────────────────────────┐
│ Not taxable in wife's gross  │  │ Taxable in wife's gross estate:      │
│ estate: $259,200             │  │                         $300,000     │
│                              │  │ Exempt:                 $175,000     │
│                              │  │ Tax:                    $ 40,800     │
└──────────────────────────────┘  └──────────────────────────────────────┘

             TOTAL TAXES, BOTH DEATHS: $81,600
```

Figure 11-4. Total Estate Taxes, Estates of Both Husband and Wife, With Tax Planning.

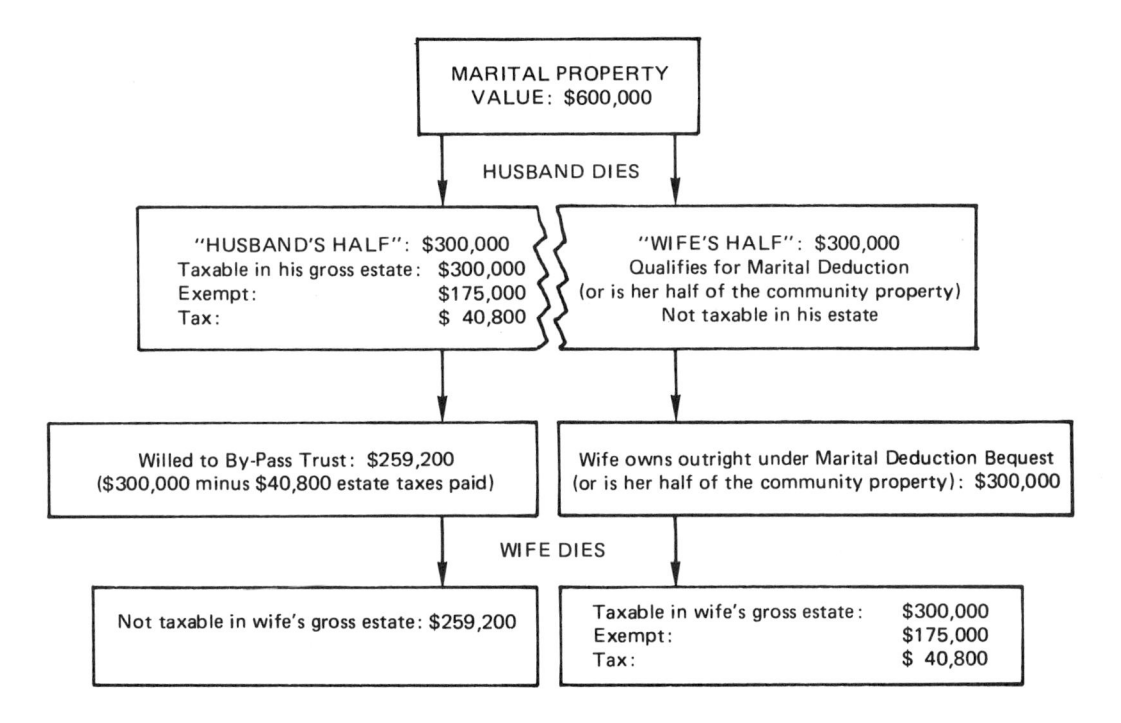

206

THE ESTATE PLANNING KEY: SAVING THE SECOND TAX

the difference between whether or not the family has adequate post-mortem income and security.

So the tax savings available through estate planning are not solely important to the "large estate" (whatever that means), but rather are important to anyone who places a value on maximizing the amount of property left to provide income and security for his family. Don't be fooled by the common use of large figures to illustrate estate planning points; they are nicely dramatic and easy to deal with, but they really illustrate a relativity type of concept. In a very rough way, the percentage of taxes paid and taxes saved in a large estate can be applied with similar percentage in a smaller estate. Total accuracy can only be provided by application of arithmetic to your own personal estate, but illustrations can provide you with a rough idea of the problems and possibilities.

Savings From Use of the Estate Planning Key, Table 11-5.

The following table presents the savings in federal estate taxes which can be achieved by the use of a life estate, in the manner this chapter discusses. For those interested in the assumptions behind this table, they are: the savings illustrated are only those in the federal estate taxes, and do not take state death duties into consideration (but state death taxes can be saved in estates much smaller than the table starts with). The table assumes the post-1980 maximum exemption/credit. The figure in the left-hand column is the net taxable estate; in other words, we are assuming that all available deductions have already been taken. The table is con-

TABLE 11—5.
SAVINGS FROM USE OF THE ESTATE PLANNING KEY

Net Estate	Taxes, 1st Death	Taxes, 2nd Death, Without Life Estate	Taxes, 2nd Death, With Life Estate	Savings
$ 175,000 or less	$ -0-	$ -0-	$ -0-	$ -0-
200,000	-0-	7,800	-0-	7,800
250,000	-0-	23,800	-0-	23,800
300,000	-0-	40,800	-0-	40,800
350,000	-0-	57,800	-0-	57,800
400,000	7,800	72,148	7,800	63,348
500,000	23,800	100,708	23,800	76,908
600,000	40,800	130,704	40,800	89,904
750,000	66,300	176,769	66,300	110,469
1,000,000	108,800	256,368	108,800	147,568
1,500,000	201,300	422,241	210,300	220,941
2,000,000	298,800	646,340	298,800	347,540
3,000,000	508,800	1,021,488	508,800	512,688
5,000,000	978,000	1,847,580	978,800	868,780

structed for a married couple, so that the taxes at the first death assume that only one-half the marital property is taxed in that estate, due either to the marital deduction or to the effect of community property law. The marital deduction is based upon a fifty percent deduction and ignores the effect of the new $250,000 maximum wherever that might be applicable. The taxes at the second death in the column headed "without life estate" assume that the surviving spouse at her death owns all the marital property at the same value such property had at the first spouse's death, reduced only by the amount of estate taxes listed at the first death.

The By-Pass Trust

The classic estate planning device which is utilized to save the second tax is known by various names; my choice of name is the **by-pass trust** because it takes the property that was taxed at the first death and by-passes taxation at the second death. For a married couple, let's be very clear at the outset about what property we're talking of putting into the by-pass trust. Again, think in halves and assume the husband dies first. In a community property state, it is easy to see that we are speaking of that half of the community property which belonged to the deceased husband, which half may be either wholly exempt if under $175,000, or partially exempt and partially taxable. In a common law state where the husband is considered to own all or most of the marital property, the portion that qualifies for the marital deduction is freed from his estate taxes on the condition that it go to the surviving wife under rules previously discussed; that portion is "her half." The portion of the marital property that does not qualify for the marital deduction, which we are calling "his half," is potentially taxable in his estate; it may be either entirely exempt if under $175,000, or partly exempt and partly taxable. So where the husband dies first, it is **his half,** whether exempt or taxable, which we want to get into the by-pass trust in order to ensure that it will not be taxed again when the wife later dies.

Note that so far I am not discussing what we've been calling the wife's half. Presumably she just owns that half outright, has complete control over it, and may gamble it all away on the tables in Las Vegas if she wishes. In the next chapter I shall focus on several alternatives for her half.

Advantages Of Using A Trust

We have seen that the use of a **life estate will serve to avoid the second tax,** but as a practical matter it is rare to use a life estate without a trust. The reason is that "legal" (non-trust) life estates are cumbersome, restrictive, generally unworkable, and often produce disputes between the life tenant and the remaindermen (defined at page 50) over what the life tenant may or may not do during the duration of the life estate. So in modern estate planning, we invariably use a trust, granting the surviving spouse a life interest in that trust. The trustee is given the power to manage and administer the trust property, freeing the family from potential disputes between life tenant and remaindermen. Although clients make the ultimate decisions and are free to do as they please, it would be a rare estate planner who would not voice vigorous disapproval of any client's plan to use a legal life estate.

Upon first hearing the idea of a by-pass trust, a common fear is that the survivor will be denied important economic rights to the property if it is "locked up" in a trust. It is crucial to emphasize that the lifetime beneficiary of a by-pass trust has virtually all the same **economic benefits** from the trust as the beneficiary would have from inheriting the property outright (purely for convenience, let me hereafter call the lifetime beneficiary of a by-pass trust "she." However, let me emphasize that the concept also applies when the wife dies first and her separate estate is large enough that it is advisable to save any double taxation at the husband's later death. Further, in a community property state, the wife always has an estate, because she owns the same amount of community property as does her husband.) I will point out all the economic consequences of a by-pass trust, and hopefully you will recognize that, although surviving spouses who are beneficiaries of such a trust cannot frivolously waste the trust property as they might their own, they do have all the same important economic benefits as they have in their own property which they own outright.

Should The Surviving Spouse Be Trustee?

Can the surviving spouse be the trustee of a by-pass trust created for her own benefit? In our traditional society as it has existed to date, where husbands have usually handled all the property and financial matters, should a wife die first the husband is reluctant to consider having any outside person or firm take over the management of "his" property. Similarly, many wives are uncomfortable with the notion of someone else having control and discretion over their economic well-being. So the survivor often asks whether he or she can serve as trustee. Many estate planners recoil at the idea and are reluctant to even admit that the survivor could so serve, but the truth is that, if the trust is properly set up, she could. The whole purpose is to avoid taxation when the survivor later dies, and there is nothing in the law saying that if a lifetime beneficiary is also the trustee, the property will be taxed in her estate. But we do have to tread very carefully because there is one concept lurking in the tax law which could serve to tax the by-pass trust property in her estate, thereby causing the very thing we are seeking to avoid. That concept is the general power of appointment (defined at page 144). The estate planner must therefore be extremely careful not to grant the survivor any powers which might be interpreted as giving the beneficiary a general power of appointment. You might want to remember that concept for the following discussion, because the whole point to some of the things I will be discussing revolves around whether a right or privilege which the survivor has in the trust might be interpreted to be the fatal general power of appointment.

Many estate planners will attempt to discourage the survivor from serving as his or her own trustee. Some believe that a bank should invariably be named because it is a professional trustee, or because they have seen unsatisfactory experiences where the survivors have attempted to serve as their own trustees. Others are afraid of, or not fully knowledgeable in, the rules concerning general powers of appointment. And many point out that using an independent (i.e., non-beneficiary) trustee allows much greater flexibility in the operation of the trust, due to the restrictions imposed by the general power of appointment rules. The latter is indeed true, as we shall see, but whether it persuades you that an independent trustee is better than a beneficiary-trustee is for each person to determine for his own unique situation.

Trust Income

The first major element of a by-pass trust that affects the economic security of the lifetime beneficiary is the annual **income** produced by the trust property. Perhaps the greatest obligation of the trustee is to invest the trust property so as to produce adequate annual income for the designated beneficiary. How that income is to be distributed is entirely up to the trustor. If the surviving spouse will be depending on the trust income to maintain her accustomed standard of living, it is common for the trust to direct that all the annual income be paid to her in convenient installments. Here, then, is the first area where having property in trust is identical with owning it outright, for in classic family economics the major function of property is its ability to generate income. So long as the survivor must receive all of that income, there is no difference regarding income between owning property outright or in trust.

However, the trustor can impose different provisions regarding the income for many and varied good reasons. Those reasons usually have to do with the survivor having enough income from property she already owns outside the trust, such as her marital deduction portion left to her outright, her ownership of her half of the community property, or her own separate property. Were she to receive all the trust income it might be excess funds which she would most likely put into savings and thereby increase the size of her own taxable estate. Not only is her estate being unnecessarily increased, but also the excess income is just pushing all her income into higher income tax brackets. Such a situation can be highly wasteful, both of income tax and later estate tax. Therefore, in such happy circumstances, the trustor can provide that the annual income is to go entirely to persons other than the surviving spouse (perhaps the children), or should be divided in some specified percentages between the surviving spouse and other persons. Because of the **throwback rule** (defined at page 105), however, the trustor would probably not want to provide that the income can be accumulated within the trust (except for minor children while they are still minors, since that is now exempt from the throwback rule).

The "Perfect Tax Shelter"

Alternatively, in what is often the best solution of all, the trustor can give the trustee discretion to determine who should receive what percentage of annual income, thereby allowing the trustee to consider the other incomes and tax brackets of each of the beneficiaries who might receive some of the income. For a high income tax bracket beneficiary, the trustor has thereby presented that beneficiary with a free tax shelter for any trust income he may not need or want. If it were mandatory for that beneficiary to receive a share of trust income, his high tax bracket would probably force him to go out into the marketplace to search out and pay for some tax shelter device for this unnecessary income. Many such tax shelters are based on shaky economics, so the trustor, by creating a discretionary trust, can save the beneficiary from the uncertainties of commercial tax shelters.

Due to the throwback rule, the trustee would probably be required to distribute all of the annual income among at least some of the adult beneficiaries, although he can vary the amount each will receive according to the income tax consequences of each beneficiary's tax bracket. Should such a **discretionary trust** be the correct solution in a particular situation, then the choice of a trustee is pretty well dictated by the income tax laws. The trustee must be an **independent trustee** and not one of the beneficiaries because if a beneficiary has a discretionary power over income, then all of the income will be taxed to him no matter to whom it is distributed. That tax consequence would of course destroy the very reason why a discretionary power would be granted in the first place, and so makes no sense. The sophisticated annual tax analysis necessary for determining the most advantageous exercise of a discretionary power may mean that a professional trustee would be the best choice in that situation.

If the survivor has plenty of other non-trust income, the discretionary by-pass trust may actually be far better than an outright bequest of all the decedent's property to his surviving spouse. An outright bequest means that she will be receiving all of the annual income from all of the property, thereby taxing it all at high income tax brackets. Any excess income will likely go into her savings, there to await even more taxation (estate taxes) at her later death. Thus, she may be in great need of the tax shelter which a discretionary trust can provide. However, to secure that advantage, she cannot be the trustee of that trust for the reasons mentioned in the last paragraph.

Trust Principal

Almost every thoughtfully drafted trust will contain provisions permitting the invasion of (i.e., use of) trust principal for specified purposes, and this is certainly true of a by-pass trust. However, it is in the area of **principal invasions** where many of the tax dangers lie. The problems concern the tax rules on the subject of general powers of appointment. Recall that just possessing a general power of appointment is enough to cause estate taxation in the estate of the holder of that power (see page 144). And yet the entire tax purpose of the by-pass trust is to avoid estate taxation in the estate of the lifetime beneficiary, who is often (but need not be) the trustor's surviving spouse. Thus, expert draftsmanship is necessary to prevent the IRS from alleging that any trust invasion power gives the lifetime beneficiary a general power of appointment. What this often comes down to is who should be the trustee of the by-pass trust, particularly whether the beneficiary herself ought to be the trustee. The reason is that certain powers of the trustee, when held by someone who is also the beneficiary, run the risk of being general powers of appointment.

Invasions For Health, Education, Maintenance, And Support

Usually the trustor wants the trust principal available to meet specified needs or emergencies of the lifetime beneficiary, but the question is whether the beneficiary ought to be granted the power to compel such invasions. Recall in the tax discussion of general powers of appointment that the law provides a specific exception to the taxability of general powers of appointment for invasions of principal confined to the **health, education, maintenance, and support** of a beneficiary. Since this is defined as not being a general power, it is therefore not taxable and is safe. Accordingly, the beneficiary herself may be granted the power to compel principal invasions for herself so long as she can demonstrate that the funds are indeed necessary for the purposes specified, expanded only by the additional language that invasions for support and maintenance may be determined by her "accustomed manner of living." But those four quoted words, modified as indicated, are the only conditions under which the beneficiary herself may invade the principal without her power to do so causing the entire bypass trust property to be taxed in her later estate as a general power of appointment. It never ceases to amaze me how often taxpayers try to sneak in just one extra little word in an attempt to expand the power of invasion, a word such as "welfare," "comfort," or "happiness." Such attempts are always gleefully and successfully attacked by the IRS, resulting in estate taxation to the beneficiary who held that power of invasion. The lesson is completely clear: a beneficiary's power of invasion must be limited only to the four quoted words, modified as indicated, the so-called **ascertainable standard.**

How Invasion Powers Bear On Choice Of Trustee

Due to the general power of appointment danger, it makes every difference whether the power to invade principal is given to a trustee who is also a beneficiary, or only to an independent (non-beneficiary) trustee. If the trustor wants his surviving spouse to be the trustee of her own by-pass trust, the spouses must recognize and accept that her power to invade principal must be limited to the ascertainable standard. But if an independent trustee is used, that trustee may have the power to invade principal on behalf of any of the beneficiaries, not unlimited by any standard except one the trustor may wish to set down. It is perfectly acceptable and very common to allow an independent trustee the power to invade principal for the benefit of the beneficiaries for whatever reason the trustee deems advisable in his sole and absolute discretion. Should the trustor wish the most flexible invasion powers on behalf of his survivors, the tax law forces him to appoint an independent trustee.

So we see that here is an area where the survivor is indeed in a different position by having a by-pass trust for her benefit rather than owning the property outright. She must either accept not being trustee if she wants the trustee to have the most flexible invasion powers for her benefit, or else she must accept limited invasion powers if she herself wants to be her own trustee. In many cases the latter limitation does not trouble either the trustor or the survivor because they recognize that the ascertainable standard, particularly with the allowable modifier, pretty well covers the major necessities of life.

Both spouses may agree for any number of reasons that they only wish to cover the basic necessities. They may wish to pass the maximum possible property to their children undiminished by invasions the survivor does not absolutely need. They may wish to protect the trust property against possible pressures on the surviving spouse by a second spouse or any other person, in which case they will not want to give the survivor powers that are too broad. Finally, there is an excellent and often overlooked tax reason why they may wish the by-pass trust to be available only for basic necessities. In the discussion so far, the husband's half of the marital property was put into the by-pass trust, assuming the wife just continues to own her half outright. Should a major expenditure arise, the wife will be better off tax-wise to pay that expenditure from her own funds and not from the trust funds, even though that would probably go against her natural tendency not to use "her own" funds. The reason is that her half will be taxable at her later death, and the by-pass trust by definition will not be; therefore, she should use up funds that are subject to later taxation and not funds that will pass tax-free at her death. That tax logic is so strong that we may want to construct a plan which compels her to use up her own taxable funds before the tax-free portion is ever touched (see the next chapter).

If the surviving spouse is to be the trustee of the by-pass trust, all powers must be carefully drawn so that there is no danger that they are general powers of appointment. The trust draftsman must watch both federal tax decisions as well as state law decisions to be certain that no innocent-sounding power takes on the fatal tax characteristic. For instance, the survivor is often given the power to invade the principal under the ascertainable standard for the benefits of both herself and any of her children, but in some states after the husband has died the wife then has a legal duty to support her children. In those states, were she to have the power described, she could use it to satisfy her legal obligation of support, and that can be a general power of appointment. If so, the entire trust property could be included in her gross estate, and the very purpose of the by-pass trust would be undone. The only remedy, then, would be either to remove the offending power, or else use an independent trustee instead of the surviving spouse.

Five By Five Power

There is an additional power which might be granted to the beneficiary of a by-pass trust if the trustor desires her to have even greater access to the principal. This is the so-called **five by five power,** granting the beneficiary the annual but non-cumulative right to invade the principal in the amount of either $5000 or 5% of the trust principal, whichever is greater. The reason this is safe is that the tax law says that such a power is not a general power of appointment. That means it's not taxable, and so is safe. This power may be granted to the beneficiary whether she is or is not trustee.

Aren't these powers a marvelous idea, and shouldn't all by-pass trusts contain one? Certainly not! There are several reasons why such a power might not be advisable. For one thing, as just pointed out, the trustor may want to force the surviving spouse to use up her own taxable funds before she uses any of the by-pass trust property which will pass tax-free at her death; if so, he should not give her any extra possibilities to consume trust funds. Secondly, the "five by five" power is a general power of appointment in the year of the surviving trustor's death because in that year she possesses the power to appoint to herself the indicated amounts, whichever are the greater of the two. The trustor may not desire additional estate taxes in the survivor's estate to the tune of 5% of the by-pass trust (this usually being the greater amount). On the other hand, some trustors consider this a small price to pay for the added flexibility it gives their survivor. Finally, there may be some adverse tax consequences to such a power under the death tax statutes of some of the states.

Provisions for Remainder Beneficiaries

Probably the most common use of a by-pass trust involves a scenario where the surviving spouse is the lifetime beneficiary and the children are the ultimate beneficiaries in equal or unequal shares. However, many other scenarios are possible. Any unmarried trustor could also use a by-pass trust where he wanted to avoid taxation at the death of whoever is his chosen lifetime beneficiary. The trust could be for his brother(s) or sister(s) for life, and then their children, his nieces, and nephews. Or it could, of course, benefit any other relatives. And there is nothing in the law confining it to relatives, so the lifetime or ultimate beneficiaries could just as easily be friends who bear no blood relationship to him. But you should recognize that the trustor's ability to avoid estate taxation at the death of his chosen lifetime beneficiary has been badly impeded by the **generation skipping rules** of the 1976 Act (see page 186). The surviving spouse and children scenario does not usually bring the generation skipping rules into play (although there are, unfortunately, still things to be careful about), but almost any other scenario needs to be carefully watched according to those complex new rules. It well may be that the tax-saving desires of many trustors who do not fit comfortably into the surviving spouse/children scenario will be blocked by the generation skipping rules. This would not cost the trustor any extra tax, but it would prevent him from assisting others by avoiding an extra occasion for the estate tax to operate.

If A Child Dies Before The Surviving Spouse

Let's stick with the common surviving spouse/children scenario for convenience, while fully recognizing that the cast of characters could involve a multitude of different related or non-related persons. One question we need to ask is this: In a normal by-pass trust situation, what happens if one of the children dies before the surviving spouse? Will all or a portion of the trust property be included in the deceased child's gross estate? That depends upon how the child's ultimate interest has been constructed. If the child's interest in the by-pass trust is vested, meaning that there are no conditions placed upon it which could ever prevent him from receiving it, then its value will indeed be included in his taxable estate. This can be a real trap because the child may not possess enough liquid funds to pay the taxes, and the property may be subject to liens or possibly even a forced sale in order to pay those taxes.

Clearly, a more intelligent solution is called for. One possibility would be to make the child's interest contingent, so that if he died before the contingency occurred, his interest would not be vested and would consequently not be taxable. The perfect contingency in that situation would be that of surviving the life tenant; that way, should the child die before the life tenant, the contingency will never have been fulfilled. It is thus quite common to see a trust which passes the ultimate interest to a child "if he survives his mother," or similar language.

Special Power Of Appointment for The Surviving Spouse

But there is another remedy, and perhaps even a better one in certain circumstances. Rather than name the children as ultimate beneficiaries, either vested or contingent, the trustor might grant the lifetime interest in the trust to his surviving wife, and specify that the remainder shall pass to such persons as his wife may appoint in her will. Of course, that power of appointment must not be a general power enabling the wife to appoint to herself, for otherwise it would defeat the by-pass purpose. But the power can be a **special power of appointment,** whereby the wife may only appoint among those persons or class of persons designated by the trustor. That class could be comprised of anyone the trustor wishes, but is commonly confined to his children, his descendents, his blood relatives, and the like. Further, the trustor should always specify the persons who take the trust property in case the wife should fail to appoint; in fact, those **default takers** may represent the trustor's true wishes unless something radical occurs, in which case he trusts his wife to alter his basic wish. But if no radical change occurs, the wife may well be requested not to exercise her special power of appointment.

This is the so-called **second look** and enables the surviving spouse to view the development of the children or other potential heirs over the balance of her lifetime. She would thus have the power to alter the trustor's basic wishes if she finds major causes, either positive or negative, occurring in the lives of the potential heirs over the subsequent years. The special power of appointment also serves to make the remainder interest of the children "contingent" because until the wife actually appoints, the children (or other heirs) have no right to anything. In appropriate circumstances the second look special power of appointment is quite appropriate, although it should be noted that not every trustor is willing to entrust such a power to his lifetime beneficiary. There is a potential danger in it, in that the surviving wife now has some coercive power over the persons to whom she might appoint, which could conceivably be used by her in unpleasant or unfriendly ways. Also, she could act out any disputes with her children or other potential donees by resolving to cut them off from the trustor's property, a result the trustor may not have wished. As with everything else, the special power must be evaluated in light of the circumstances and personalities of particular people to see whether it is or is not a wise device to utilize.

Provisions Governing The Trust At Death Of Surviving Spouse

Now let us assume that the surviving wife has also died; what should be the trust provisions at that point? Assuming that the trustor wishes the trust property to go in equal or unequal shares to his children, should the death of the wife automatically be the time when they receive the trust property, thereby terminating the trust? Not necessarily, because for reasons of youth or any other reason deemed important by the trustor, the children might not yet be ready to acquire that property outright. The date of the wife's death has no particular magic to it in terms of when the children are or are not ready to acquire outright ownership of the property, and the wise trustor will want to build in specific guidelines for the children's eventual outright acquisition.

Many of us with experience in estate planning have seen terribly unfortunate things happen when children have received property before they were ready for it. It can sometimes do nasty things to their personalities. It can also cause wild spending and waste in an immature recipient. I therefore believe that children (or any other youthful beneficiaries) ought to acquire their inheritance in gradual stages, thereby (hopefully) receiving an education in having a bit of property before they receive the bulk of it. Can you imagine handing over even a $50,000 check to an eighteen-year-old, to say nothing of an interest in a business or in an apartment house? If a periodic distribution to children is planned, and the child goes wild upon receiving the first distribution and has it spent within a week, at least he will have some time to mull over his folly; hopefully he'll be sadder but wiser at the time of the next distribution.

The pattern of periodic distributions to youthful beneficiaries is not an estate planner's decision, but belongs to the client. All the estate planner does is to point out the problems of "too much, too soon," and perhaps suggest possible patterns. The final choice is always the trustor's. Knowing that the trustor should make the final determination, and only for the purpose of suggesting some food for thought, here is a **distribution pattern** that seems to satisfy many people: Nothing happens until the death of the surviving spouse, no matter how old the children are (at least, that is a common pattern). Then when the surviving spouse dies, if the children are under twenty-one, the annual trust **income is accumulated** within the trust and not paid directly to them, with the trustee having the power to use that income for their benefit. That accumulation causes no tax problem under the revised throwback rule, since the children are under twenty-one. When a child attains the age of twenty-one, not only because of the throwback rule but also because this seems a good age to commence his financial education by distributing some funds to him, the annual net **income will now be paid** to him. The eventual **outright distributions** of the trust property are planned for **three equal stages,** the first at age twenty-five, the second at age thirty, and the third at age thirty-five. Those ages and those divisions can of course be altered by the trustor, but eighteen or twenty-one seems usually to be a bit young for someone to receive any substantial amount of property, and by age thirty-five one is usually in a "fish or cut bait" situation regarding the beneficiary. That is, by that age he will usually have developed the greatest part of his financial maturity; if he hasn't, it is unfortunate, but there's often not much that can be done about it, and waiting longer wouldn't help. Perhaps the trustor should never have provided any distribution to that person, but those are the risks we all take when we provide an inheritance for someone.

Two Patterns Of Trust Distribution When There Are Several Children

If there are several children, there are some decisions to be made as to how the trust should be handled when the first of the children attains age twenty-one. Under the above pattern, the first child is now entitled to a share of income, but how do you determine the appropriate share? A frequent pattern, perhaps because it is the easiest but also because it is what many people want, is that upon the first occasion when the trustee might begin to make distributions of either income or principal, the trust is divided (just for accounting purposes and not physically) into the specified equal or unequal **shares** for each beneficiary. Thereafter, the beneficiary gets the income from his specific share, and any invasions of principal for his benefit are made only out of his own share. Of course, when he becomes entitled to the first outright distribution of principal (one-third at age twenty-five under the above pattern), it is made out of his own share, so that thereafter it is a simple task to continue paying him annual income from his now reduced share.

An opposite type of pattern, with a great deal of validity in the indicated situation, is known as the **family pot trust.** It is often used during such time as any of the trustor's children are still continuing their education and is particularly valuable when there is a large age difference between the trustor's oldest and youngest children. The trustor may want all his children to receive whatever education they desire out of the "family pot," and only after all education is finished is the trust property to be distributed outright among the children. For one thing, that is the way the family financial pot would be handled if the trustor were still alive; he wouldn't say, "OK, Jack, I'll pay your tuition out of your share of my wealth, but since Carol doesn't want to go to college her share will be greater." It also ensures that there is nothing to discourage a child from continuing his education; if educational expenses are paid out of each child's own share of trust, some clever rascal may realize that if he doesn't go to college he's going to wind up with more money than his brother. It also ensures that there will be an adequate educational fund for a much younger child, perhaps one who is twenty or thirty years younger than his oldest sibling.

The family pot trust can be used for reasons other than educational expenses and can be modified in any way the trustor wishes, but the point is that it is rather a complete opposite of the pattern whereby the trust is split into separate shares for each child. One parent may like the family pot idea where his youngest child is 20 years younger than his oldest, while the next parent may feel exactly the opposite given the exact same facts; namely, that it is unfair to the oldest to require him to wait around for his inheritance until the baby finishes college. That is just one example of how estate planning is an intensely personal matter, and how each individual must make his own decisions from among the available options. It is absurd for an estate planner to say that one thing or another is what a client "should" do.

If A Child/Beneficiary Should Die

Under the distribution pattern suggested above, each child would receive final distribution of his share when he reaches thirty-five, so that when the youngest reaches thirty-five, the trust terminates according to its own terms. This is well within the Rule Against Perpetuities (see page 108). But what if a child should die before he becomes thirty-five? It may not be wise to just pass his share along, outright, to his children, for they may be just infants at the time. Can the deceased child's share of trust be **continued for the benefit of his own children,** if he has any? Yes, definitely, but subject to two important considerations. One is the Rule Against Perpetuities. Without trying to get into any explanations of how that confounding thing works, it is enough to say that the continuing trust in the circumstances indicated must often provide final distribution to the deceased child's children (the trustor's grandchildren) when they reach the age of twenty-one. You may recall that there was some statement about age twenty-one in the definition of The Rule, and this is how it is applied. In those states where the so-called "perpetuities savings clause" (see page 109) is valid, it might be possible to extend the trust beyond the date when the grandchild reaches age twenty-one, subject to the trust being terminated by the savings clause at the latest possible date for trust validity under The Rule.

Usually, if a child of the trustor does not live to his final distribution (thirty-five, in the above pattern), but leaves no children surviving him, then the deceased child's share is **added to the other shares** created by the trustor. And if no descendent should survive to take that final distribution, trustors commonly insert provisions for whichever ultimate beneficiaries they would want to have their property under those circumstances. Such contingent heirs could include other family members, non-related people, or charitable institutions.

The other problem that must be faced if a child of a trustor dies before becoming entitled to his final distribution is the tax problem created by the generation skipping transfer tax. Sticking with the example of final distribution at age thirty-five, if a trustor's son dies before reaching that age, the trust might provide that the deceased son's share be continued in trust for the son's children (the trustor's grandchildren) in equal shares. But that provision would now trigger a generation skipping tax, at least if the son had survived his mother, because then the son would have had an interest in the trust following his mother's death. The question that each trustor must now be asked is whether he wishes to alter the natural family pattern he undoubtedly would have used if the generation skipping tax had never come into existence. The trustor will therefore have to be informed of the following possibilities.

Getting Around the Generation Skipping Tax

In many cases a trustor will be unwilling to alter his judgments concerning what is best for his family or other heirs, even if that judgment incurs the generation skipping tax. In that event, the trustor will just have to accept the added tax cost of the plan. Doing so for valid family reasons is perfectly acceptable so long as the trustor is fully informed of alternatives and their costs. In the example we've been considering, where the son dies before becoming entitled to final distribution and the trustor would normally want his son's share to be continued in trust for the son's children, I venture the guess that a majority of trustors will refuse to alter the natural pattern referred to. The generation skipping tax imposed at the son's death would of course be subject to the $250,000 grandchild exemption which may cancel out the tax in many such trusts. But where the exemption is not large enough to do so, my personal feeling since first hearing about the generation skipping tax is that the imposition of that tax in the circumstances described is unfair and unfortunate. After all, this is not the intentional structuring of a plan to avoid estate taxation in more than one generation, which is what Congress intended to prevent, but is rather the normal family way of meeting an occurrence which is totally outside the trustor's control. The new tax in that situation looks to me like a simple revenue raising measure, and one with which we will just have to make our peace unless we can ever get it repealed for the limited circumstance described.

But the generation skipping tax is now just as much of a second tax to be saved as is double taxation of marital property in the estate of the spouse who survives. No testator need accept the new tax, either in the limited circumstance described above, or in any other, for he is free to design his trust in a fashion that will not trigger the generation skipping tax. Although in the circumstance described above, many trustors might not alter their natural family wishes, in other instances not involving descendents, a testator may be influenced by the existence of the new tax to adopt a plan different from one he otherwise might. His decision will probably depend upon the tax costs involved, the significance of those costs to him in his system of values, and their relationship to the total amount of wealth available.

Using Direct Gifts

Let me repeat that the generation skipping tax in no way prevents a testator from leaving property to his grandchildren or any other beneficiary one generation removed from him; the tax only applies if the testator does so in certain specified ways. Any **direct gift** of money or other property from a testator to his grandchildren or other younger generation beneficiary will not cause the new tax to apply. This is because a direct gift is not one in which the benefits shift from, or are shared between, one younger generation beneficiary and another one in a still younger generation. Such a gift would simply be one directly made to a person who happens to be of a younger generation, and the new tax does not presume to hit that. Neither does the new tax apply merely because the testator had left property to a younger generation beneficiary in a trust, *so long as* there is no shifting or sharing of an interest from a member of one generation to a member of a younger generation. For instance, property left in trust for the testator's grandchildren until they attain a mature age, with no one other than the grandchildren having any beneficial interest in that trust, will not cause the new tax to apply.

Using Separate Trusts

If a family feels wealthy enough so that there is no need or wish to ensure that the children benefit from all the parent's wealth, there is a simple way to avoid the generation skipping tax. Instead of putting the entire family wealth into one by-pass trust to benefit the surviving spouse for life with the children being the ultimate beneficiaries, the decedent might create **more than one trust** and place only a portion of the property into each. One (or more) of the trusts might provide lifetime benefits for the surviving spouse and then outright distributions to the children on the spouse's death, while others of the trusts might similarly provide a life estate to the surviving spouse but provide outright distributions directly to the grandchildren with no interests whatsoever on the part of the children. Since none of those trusts will be split or shared between two younger generation beneficiaries, none of them can be classified as generation skipping trusts, so the new tax can never apply. Perhaps the generation skipping tax will cause more outright gifts to grandchildren, and more trusts such as described above where the decedent's children have no interest at all. On the other hand, family harmony might be seriously threatened by such a plan, depending upon how the parents think their children will react to it, and so testators should very carefully think through the non-tax consequences of such plans.

Distributions of Income

Another possibility involves an application of technical rules which were not fully explained in the last chapter. In proper circumstances, distributions of trust principal to the wrong younger generation beneficiaries will attract the generation skipping tax, whereas distributions of income generally won't. This suggests specifying that income distributions be made only to one generational class of beneficiaries (such as children) while principal distributions are made only to another class (such as grandchildren). Congress anticipated this idea and tried to block it by saying that such multiple distributions in the same tax year will be deemed to have been made out of principal, so that the new tax might well be triggered. But a careful draftsman might be able to design a trust wherein **income distributions** are made only in **one tax year** with **principal distributions** being made only in the **subsequent year,** with the distributions continuing to alternate in later years. Tricky, but feasible.

Postponing The Tax

It may be that in a particular trust, the impact of the new tax is inevitable because for family reasons the testator refuses to have a trust that could have avoided it altogether. In such cases, there are many possibilities hidden within the highly technical rules which can be used by an expert draftsman to **postpone** that inevitable day for quite a long time. And postponing a tax can have great economic benefits because the income and property appreciation during the postponement period may more than make up the tax cost. That gets into very sophisticated economic analyses, but the truth of it can be readily demonstrated by an economist.

It bears repeating that the generation skipping tax does not in any way alter the standard estate planning devices utilized to benefit the surviving spouse of a married testator. Since that spouse is in the same generation as the testator, the new tax can't touch any arrangement for her benefit. Neither can it touch any trust in which no interests are split or shared between two younger generation beneficiaries who are in different generations with respect to each other.

Discretionary Trust Benefits Unaffected

Finally, the generation skipping tax does not infringe on the benefits of **the perfect tax shelter,** the discretionary trust, which may be able to save much more in cumulative income taxes than the generations skipping tax would cause in death taxes. If a surviving spouse has plenty of income from her own separate estate, or from the marital deduction half or her own community property half, then some or all of the decedent's property can be put into a discretionary trust. That trust might provide emergency access to principal on her behalf for designated purposes, but would allow the trustee to withhold unnecessary amounts of annual taxable income from her so as to shelter that income and not drive her other income into even higher tax brackets. The same reasoning applies to the decedent's children who might be in the prime of their income earning years, and who might thus be immensely thankful for this free tax shelter.

So the use of trusts is very much alive, as Congress intended that it should be, because trusts are just too beneficial for Congress to want to kill them off. Certain "abuses" have indeed been made more costly, but that's as far as it goes. There's no need for panic.

When to Establish a By-Pass Trust

While many people are intrigued by the by-pass trust and would like it applied to their estate, some fail to realize the time at which it must be established. They figure that there is no need to incur the cost of estate planning while both spouses are still alive, and that there is time enough for the survivor to consult an estate planner after the first spouse has died. That thinking is **utterly and fatally wrong.** There is no legal alternative to establishing the by-pass trust while both spouses (or any other persons wishing to take advantage of it) are still alive. It simply can not be legally accomplished after the first person has died. The only way to save the second tax is for the testator not to leave property to the outright ownership of his chosen beneficiary, but rather to leave that beneficiary a life interest in a trust. Since this can only be done by the testator in a document executed while he is still alive, after his death it is just too late. One of the saddest situations estate planners face is the problem of the rich widow, where the husband neglected or avoided estate planning while he was alive, left everything outright to his widow, and now she seeks estate tax savings for her estate when she dies. She cannot then be helped by a by-pass trust; it is too late.

It is also extremely important to note that in order to establish a by-pass trust, the title to property held by the spouses or other persons concerned must be set up in such a way that, upon the death of one of them, the **property will pass into the by-pass trust.** If it won't the trust is merely a worthless (and probably expensive) piece of paper. State law will tell you what types of titling will ensure that property will find its way into a by-pass trust and what types won't, but almost any type of titling which passes the ownership automatically to a named survivor will not get that property into a tax saving by-pass trust. Chief among such forms of title is, of course, joint tenancy, and this is such a major and commonly misunderstood mistake that it is worth repeating again: joint tenancy property will not find its way into a tax saving by-pass trust. I shall have a bit more to say about joint tenancy titling in chapter fifteen, but you should clearly understand how it operates (or, rather, fails to operate) in regard to a by-pass trust. In those states which have them, tenancies by the entirety will operate like joint tenancies, and will also not serve to get the property into a tax saving by-pass trust.

So, a by-pass trust must be established while both parties are still alive, and the manner in which the parties hold title to property must be correlated with the trust in order for the trust to ever become effective.

Doesn't A By-Pass Trust Fail to Avoid Probate?

If the by-pass trust is a testamentary trust established in the trustor's will, property destined for it must deliberately go through probate. Only property subject to the testator's will will find its way into the by-pass trust, and all that property must go through probate. The common probate avoiding titles—joint tenancy and tenancy by the entirety—will as noted above not find their way into a by-pass trust. Doesn't the necessity to incur probate therefore make a by-pass trust a grave disadvantage?

No! And for several reasons, all of which I am trying to lay before you so that you may weigh the pros and cons in making an informed decision. In chapter five I noted that, contrary to strong common beliefs, there are actually some tax and non-tax advantages to probate that may sometimes in themselves be reason enough to seek out probate. Leaving all those aside for purposes of argument, I noted in chapter nine (page 151) that probate fees are deductible and therefore do not cost the estate as much as they appear to; in chapter thirteen (page 257) you will find a more detailed economic analysis of probate's true costs. But even if no probate advantages or the deductibility of its costs impress you one bit, just look at the arithmetic of the amount saved by avoiding probate versus the amount of second or double taxes saved by a by-pass trust.

We know that federal estate taxes now start at the 32% level.

The percentage of your estate eaten up by probate fees varies from state to state; a common average would be 4% to 6%, but for purposes of argument let's even assume an 8% loss due to probate expenses. If an estate is over the exemption and therefore subject to federal estate taxes, would you rather pay 32% minimum to the government in second or double estate taxes in order to save 8% in probate fees payable to your executor and his lawyer? If your answer is that you would rather pay that amount to the government with full knowledge of the alternatives, that is an informed judgment which you are completely entitled to make, no questions asked. But I venture to say that a smashing majority of testators would prefer to **save 32%** of their available estate at the deliberate **cost** of paying probate fees in a maximum amount **of 8%, which is really much less due to the deductibility of those fees,** and for which certain probate advantages are secured. If your estate is exempt from federal estate taxes because it is under the exemption amount, then you will have to weigh non-tax advantages plus the amount of any savings a by-pass trust can provide in state death duties against the probate fees in your state.

In chapter thirteen I will discuss a by-pass trust which can both save the second or double estate tax and probate fees; namely, the funded revocable living trust. Before you get too excited, be aware that just like everything else it has potential negatives, all of which will be discussed in that chapter.

Saving State Death Taxes May Now Be More Important Than Ever

Although the methods of computing state inheritance or estate taxes can differ radically from the federal method, since the principles by which property will be taxed are generally the same under both federal and state systems, a by-pass trust will also save the second state death tax at the same time it is saving the federal second, or double, tax.

But what of estates under $175,000 which under proper circumstances may never be hit by federal estate taxes; are they now exempt from any considerations of a by-pass trust? Most emphatically not, due to the effect of state inheritance or estate taxes. Those taxes begin to apply at much lower levels than does the federal tax, and an estate under $175,000 will almost universally be subject to some state death taxes (except in Nevada). As an example, in my state the exemption for property passing to the surviving spouse is only $60,000 and for property passing to an adult child is but $5000 per child; the exemptions get even smaller for more distant relatives, or for non-relatives. While an estate of under $175,000 may have no federal estate tax to pay after 1980, it will surely have some inheritance tax to pay in my state. Those taxes can get to 10% rather quickly, particularly for persons who are not the surviving spouse or children, and can go up to a top rate of 24%. The point is that for a testator who is for whatever reason concerned with saving every possible amount of tax, while a by-pass trust may be unnecessary to save any federal taxes because there won't be any, it may indeed be necessary to save the second state inheritance or estate tax. Some testators may say that the amount involved is peanuts, and not worth forming a by-pass trust to get around, but other testators may adamantly wish to save all they can.

A Short Speech About Attitudes and Values

The last point demonstrates a recurring and extremely valid factor about estate planning, which is that the **personal attitudes and goals** of each individual testator **are unique** and should control the type of plan he or she chooses. One testator may feel that $10,000 in taxes is "peanuts" and not worth worrying about, while another may feel that $100,000 is "peanuts," and a third may be adamant in wishing to save a potential $750 tax. There are no rules, no rights and wrongs, and no points at which the total value of anyone's estate indicates that any particular plan or device ought to be adopted. It is all a matter of the testator's personal attitudes and choices. Estate planners are forever being asked at what value an estate should be considered for tax saving plans. The entire answer is: **at any value you choose.** It depends upon the point at which taxes begin to bother you; $100 or $100,000. No estate planner should pass judgment on that point. The only obligation most estate planners see is to clearly explain the alternatives available, the tax and other consequences of each, and answer whatever questions a client might have in his struggle to arrive at the best plan for his family. Being satisfied that the client understands the available alternatives, the estate planner ought to be content to sit back and let the client make his own informed choice. To assist each reader to do that is really the most basic purpose of this book. Of course, if asked for recommendations and views, an estate planner will give them, but the plan is after all the client's and not the planner's. Our democratic system allows people to do things which others might consider dumb or crazy, but that's the freedom we have. I once had a very successful client who had been an immigrant, and I watched him choose an estate plan that cost $80,000 more in taxes than an available alternative which he fully understood; he said he loved this country and the opportunity it provided him and did not want to avoid its estate taxes. Who's to say he was wrong?

APPLICATION

1. You computed your taxable estate under the Application section of chapter nine, page 170. Using that same amount, go to

Table 11-5 on page 206, and determine what the second tax will be if you do not use a by-pass trust. Compare the result with what the second tax will be if you do use a by-pass trust, as listed in that Table. The difference is the amount of the savings you could obtain by using a by-pass trust.

2. With those figures in mind, determine whether you want to save the second tax by using the estate planning key, the by-pass trust.

3. If you do want to, reread the Application section at the end of chapter six, located at page 110, particularly items 5 through 10. (The first four items speak of living trusts, and you will see in chapter thirteen that a by-pass trust can be accomplished by either a testamentary trust or a living trust). But items 5 through 10 of that Application will lead you through the decisions you will want to make in terms of structuring the actual by-pass trust for your heirs.

12

planning the surviving spouse's half: a-b trusts

Glossary For This Chapter

A-B Trust
Estate Trust
Marital Deduction
Marital Deduction Formula Clause
Widow's Election
Review:
Common Law State
Community Property
General Power of Appointment

It is important that you be able to pinpoint which property it is that is the subject of this chapter. This chapter applies to both common law and community property states, but their property laws make it apply in different ways, and we must recognize those differences. Figure 12-1 illustrates which property it is that is the subject of this chapter.

Defining The Surviving Spouse's Half

In **common law states,** the husband may own all, or the largest part of, the marital property. Because of the marital deduction (discussed on page 156), one-half of such property is freed from estate tax in his estate if he leaves it to his wife in specified ways. The half freed from estate tax I have for convenience called **"her half"**, and it is that half which is the subject of this chapter. **"His half"**, on which taxes were paid in his estate, was dealt with in the previous chapter and was assumedly put into a by-pass trust. So in this chapter you should keep in mind that "his half" has

```
                    ┌─────────────────────────┐
                    │   MARITAL PROPERTY      │
                    │   VALUE: $600,000       │
                    └─────────────────────────┘
                          HUSBAND DIES
```

"HUSBAND'S HALF": $300,000
Taxable in his gross estate: $300,000
Exempt: $175,000
Tax: $ 40,800

"WIFE'S HALF": $300,000
Qualifies for Marital Deduction
(or is her half of the community property)
Not taxable

Willed to By-Pass Trust (per Chapter 11): $259,200
($300,000 minus $40,800 estate taxes paid)

$300,000
?

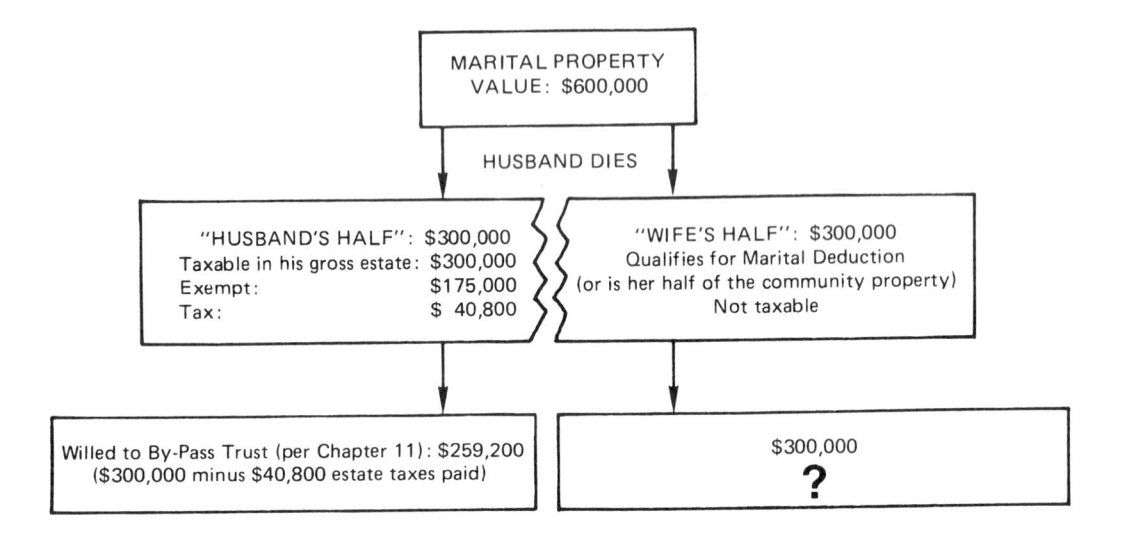

THE SUBJECT OF THIS CHAPTER

Questions: Should the survivor simply own this half outright, or should it also go into a trust?

If a trust, should it be the same trust as the by-pass trust of the husband's half, or should it be a different trust?

Figure 12-1. An Illustration of the Subject of this Chapter. (Illustration Assumes Husband Dies First)

already been taken care of. I am now discussing alternatives to come up with the best plan for the survivor's half.

This chapter theoretically applies equally if the wife dies first, but in many common law states she owns none of the marital property, in which case this chapter would be meaningless. But it does apply if she owns either some property of her own or a portion of the marital property under the laws of her state because then the marital deduction would apply at her death if she chooses to leave the necessary portion of such property to her husband. She would then be creating "his half" and "her half" in the property she owns, just as the husband normally does.

In **community property states,** this chapter applies no matter which spouse dies first, because they each own exactly the same amount of community property. The half belonging to the first spouse to die was taken care of in the previous chapter, and assumedly went into a by-pass trust. In this chapter we will be examining a plan for the survivor's half that is an alternative to simple outright ownership of that half. Further, if the first spouse to die owned either separate property or quasi-community property (defined at page 27), then the marital deduction, and hence this chapter, will apply to such property.

In the previous chapter we assumed nothing further than that the surviving spouse owned "her half" outright, unencumbered by a trust or any other restriction. Thus, she could waste it, lose it, donate it to charity, or have it conned from her by artful and designing persons. The latter could well include second husbands, particularly if they belong to that professional class called marital adventurers. (No sexism implied; women can just as well be marital adventurers preying upon surviving widowers. And widowers can just as easily gamble, lose, spend, or waste property). I am not implying that those disasters will befall any particular surviving wife or husband, as it is obvious that many surviving spouses are perfectly capable of wisely managing their own funds or learning how to do so. But these disasters do occur, and I want you to recognize them and think about them, even if you reject any such possibility in your own situation. So in this chapter we shall examine whether it is wise to leave "her half" to the survivor outright, or whether it is perhaps better to also place it into a trust where it will be secure and well managed. And if a trust, whether it should just be added to the already created by-pass trust, or whether something separate and distinct should be done with it.

I will first discuss planning that involves qualifying for the marital deduction, which is the central core of estate planning for married couples in the common law states. **Community property readers should definitely not skip this material** because the marital deduction is also very important in community property states.

There are **three reasons** why this is so: the marital deduction now applies to community property up to the $500,000 level (see page 158), tax savings for separate property depend upon using the marital deduction, and so do tax savings for quasi-community property (because the federal tax law treats it as if it were separate property, not as if it were community property).

Marital Deduction Formula Clauses

An appropriate goal of will drafting is that the testator should be able to understand everything in his will. However, it is a virtual certainty that, without explanations, he will be unable to understand a marital deduction formula clause. You should therefore at least know what one is and why it exists, so that if you see one in a will you can understand its purpose if not its language.

In order to achieve the lowest possible taxes for a married couple before their property passes on to the next generation, exactly one-half of the marital property should be taxed at the death of the first to die, and exactly one-half should be taxed at the second death. The progressive tax rates compel that plan because greater total tax inevitably results if more than half is taxed in either estate. Having marital property be tax-free in one estate and fully taxable in the other is immensely more wasteful of tax dollars.

Qualifying The Correct Amount

Since the marital deduction allows a deduction for one-half the property passing to the surviving spouse, there would not seem to be any problem. However, if the husband who intends to qualify the amount for the marital deduction simply leaves "one-half" to his wife in his will, he will almost always have given her too much. Such a will ignores the fact that a person's will only works on property governed by it, but has **no effect at all on property passing outside of the will** directly to a survivor by one of several automatic means. Those means include **joint tenancies** (and tenancies by the entirety) with automatic right of survivorship, property placed in **living trusts,** and the proceeds of **life insurance policies** or employee benefit plans.

We know from our discussion of estate taxes that all property passing outside the will is subject to estate taxes (at least potentially, and before any planning steps have been taken). Such property nevertheless qualifies for the marital deduction so long as the surviving spouse is the person to whom it automatically passes, and therefore using those forms of property does not unnecessarily increase the estate tax at the husband's death. The problem, though, is that the wife by survivorship or other means now owns one hundred percent of the property passing outside of the will, plus fifty percent of the property passing under a will giving her "one-half" of the husband's property. So she now owns **far more than one-half** of the marital property, and the tax bite at her later death will be unnecessarily and wastefully high. This is called **over-qualification** for the marital deduction. By an incorrectly drawn will, it is also quite possible to **underqualify,** resulting in too much tax at the husband's death, and not enough tax at the wife's. The effect of over-qualification for the marital deduction is illustrated in Figure 12-2.

How The Marital Deduction Formula Clause Works

To avoid that problem, a mechanism must be constructed whereby the widow is left with outright ownership of only so much property as is necessary to qualify precisely the right amount for the marital deduction. That mechanism is the **marital deduction formula clause.** If we can construct it exactly right, then precisely one-half of the total marital property, both probate and non-probate portions, will qualify for the marital deduction and avoid the over or under-qualification problem. The balance of the marital property not qualifying for the marital deduction will, on the usual assumption that the husband wishes his wife to benefit from all of the marital property, be placed into a standard by-pass trust for her lifetime benefit. The by-pass trust portion escapes estate taxes at the wife's subsequent death, so the taxes at her death are confined to those based on the marital deduction amount her husband left to her. The tax savings achieved by a formula clause are illustrated in Figure 12-3.

Unfortunately for ease of understanding, marital deduction formula clauses must be quite complex in order to correctly take into account both the probate and non-probate portions of the marital property. There are two standard types of such clauses: the pecuniary amount formula clause and the fractional share formula clause. The former type defines what shall pass to the wife as a dollar amount of money or property, whereas the latter type defines it as a particular fraction of the marital property (often, a fraction of each item comprising the marital property). Both clauses are often cast in the form of a fraction, wherein the numerator has a technical definition and the denominator has a technical definition, which is why they are so difficult to comprehend. As between the two types of clauses, different advisors have different preferences. Both are workable, but the carryover basis provisions of the 1976 Act have conferred new disadvantages on each type of clause. As with so many matters involved in estate planning, you and your advisors will have to determine where the fewest disadvantages lie with respect to your own estate.

A MARITAL ESTATE OF $525,000

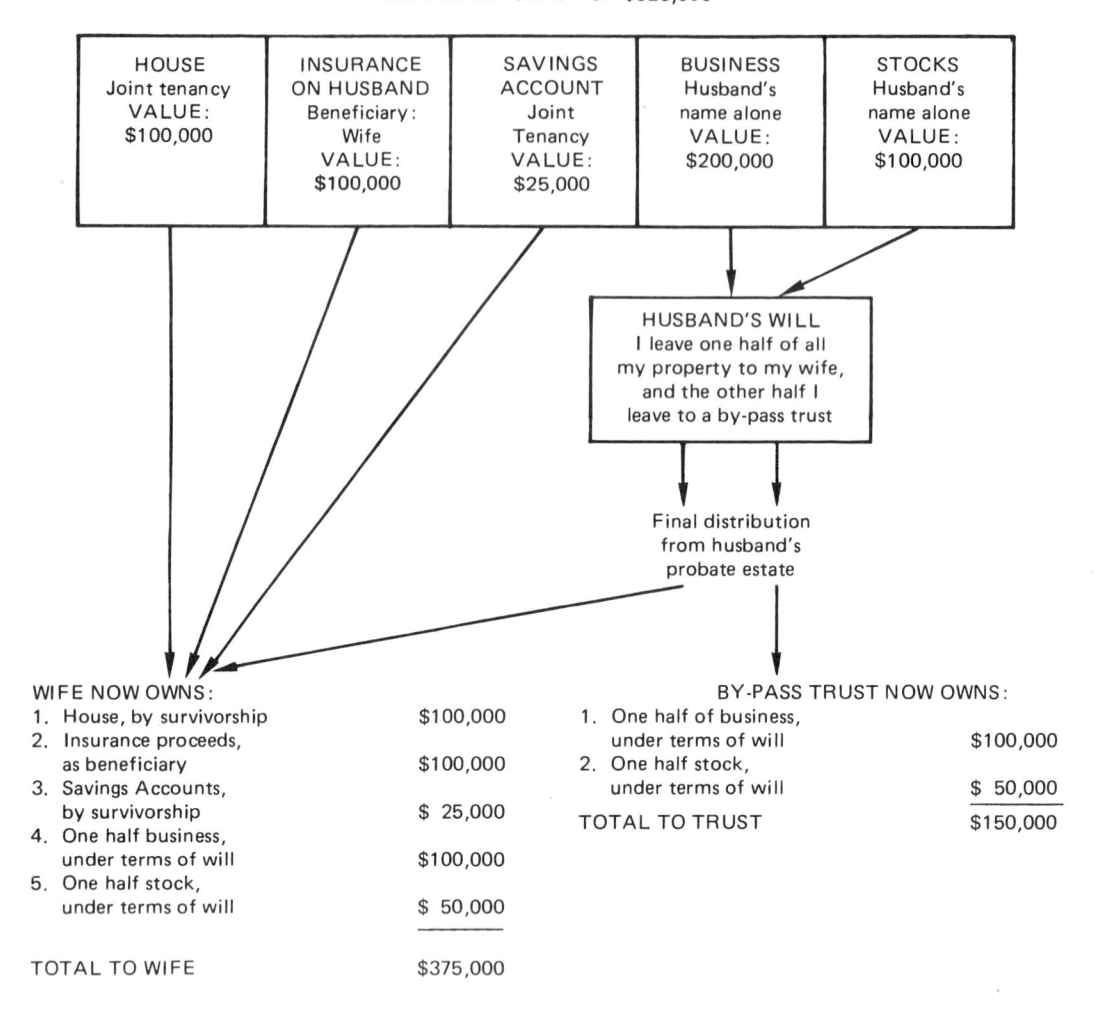

| HOUSE
Joint tenancy
VALUE:
$100,000 | INSURANCE ON HUSBAND
Beneficiary: Wife
VALUE:
$100,000 | SAVINGS ACCOUNT
Joint Tenancy
VALUE:
$25,000 | BUSINESS
Husband's name alone
VALUE:
$200,000 | STOCKS
Husband's name alone
VALUE:
$100,000 |

HUSBAND'S WILL
I leave one half of all my property to my wife, and the other half I leave to a by-pass trust

Final distribution from husband's probate estate

WIFE NOW OWNS:
1. House, by survivorship — $100,000
2. Insurance proceeds, as beneficiary — $100,000
3. Savings Accounts, by survivorship — $25,000
4. One half business, under terms of will — $100,000
5. One half stock, under terms of will — $50,000

TOTAL TO WIFE — $375,000

BY-PASS TRUST NOW OWNS:
1. One half of business, under terms of will — $100,000
2. One half stock, under terms of will — $50,000

TOTAL TO TRUST — $150,000

RESULTS:
Maximum qualifying for marital deduction: $262,500
But wife has received, to be taxed at the later death: $375,000

Figure 12-2. Illustration of Over-Qualification for Marital Deduction.

A MARITAL ESTATE OF $252,000

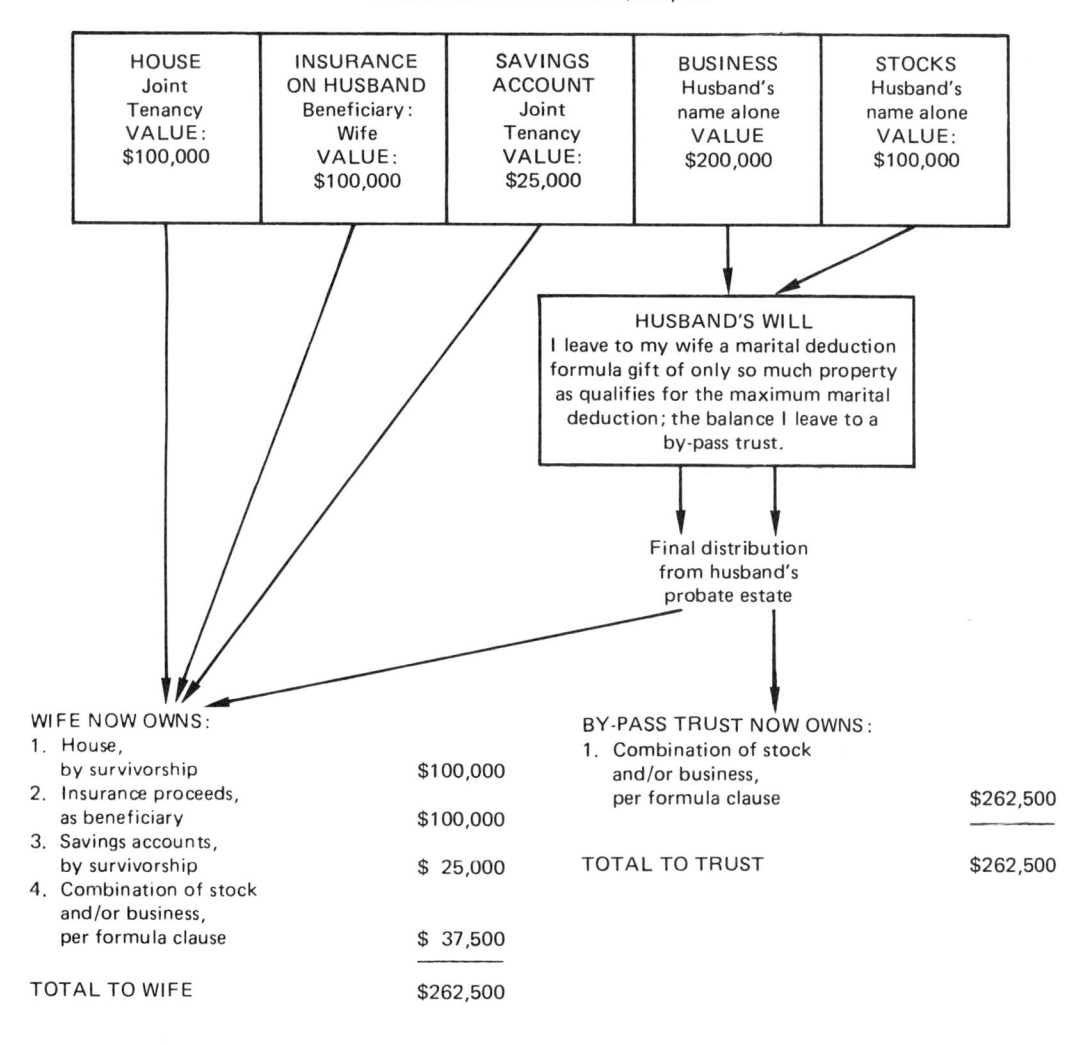

| HOUSE Joint Tenancy VALUE: $100,000 | INSURANCE ON HUSBAND Beneficiary: Wife VALUE: $100,000 | SAVINGS ACCOUNT Joint Tenancy VALUE: $25,000 | BUSINESS Husband's name alone VALUE $200,000 | STOCKS Husband's name alone VALUE: $100,000 |

HUSBAND'S WILL
I leave to my wife a marital deduction formula gift of only so much property as qualifies for the maximum marital deduction; the balance I leave to a by-pass trust.

Final distribution from husband's probate estate

WIFE NOW OWNS:
1. House, by survivorship $100,000
2. Insurance proceeds, as beneficiary $100,000
3. Savings accounts, by survivorship $ 25,000
4. Combination of stock and/or business, per formula clause $ 37,500

TOTAL TO WIFE $262,500

BY-PASS TRUST NOW OWNS:
1. Combination of stock and/or business, per formula clause $262,500

TOTAL TO TRUST $262,500

RESULTS:
Maximum qualifying for marital deduction: $262,500
Wife has received, to be taxed at her later death: $262,500
Savings in taxes at wife's death compared to Figure 12-2: $ 37,500

Figure 12-3. Illustration of Savings Achieved by Marital Deduction Formula Clause.

The 1976 Act has made marital deduction formula clauses more difficult to draft and even more confusing to read. The reason is that the estate planner does not want to "waste" the full benefit of either spouse's regular $175,000 exemption, so he will want only property in excess of those exemptions to qualify for the marital deduction. What we really want to do is to qualify only so much for the marital deduction as will ensure the lowest possible estate tax in each estate. Many professional writings have been published since the new Act became law, and each admits that so far the ideal formula clause seems not to have been developed. While this is a matter for the technicians to struggle with, you should be aware that marital deduction formula clauses will now be even more complex than ever.

Many provisions normally found in wills can seriously harm the intended full effect of a marital deduction clause. The experts will know which highly technical provisions those are, but they include clauses allocating the estate taxes among beneficiaries in a different fashion than normal, and a special clause regarding Sec. 303 stock (defined at page 167).

The Marital Deduction Trust

Recall that the policy behind the marital deduction allows a decedent spouse to qualify a portion of his property for the deduction only if he leaves that portion to this spouse in such a manner that it will be taxed at her later death. For reasons we explored earlier, that's only fair. There are three methods of such qualification. The first is by an outright gift to the surviving spouse, since all such property will of course be taxed in her estate so long as she still owns it at her death. The second method concerns certain ways of taking life insurance settlement options. The third way, and the one which concerns us the most at this point, is via a particular form of trust.

Special Requirements For The Trust

Since a by-pass trust is specifically designed so that the property placed into it will not be taxed at the life beneficiary's death, we cannot simply place the marital deduction property into a standard by-pass trust; to do so would be the exact opposite of what the tax rules require. Rather, the tax rules say that if the decedent spouse wishes to use a trust and still qualify property for the marital deduction, that trust must have two provisions, at least one of which is entirely different from the standard by-pass trust (and in fact would be fatal to the tax purpose of the standard by-pass trust).

The first is that the surviving spouse must get **all of the income** from the marital deduction trust each year, and the other is that the surviving spouse must have a **general power of appointment** (see page 144) over the trust property. Possessing a general power of appointment ensures that the property covered by that power will be included in the power holder's gross estate, and it is this feature that would be fatal to the tax purposes of the standard by-pass trust. Therefore, to use trusts and still qualify for the marital deduction at the same time as a standard by-pass trust is being used, there must be **two separate trusts** with different provisions.

Reasons For Creating A Trust

Why bother; why not just leave the marital deduction property to the surviving spouse outright? That will certainly work to qualify the property for the marital deduction and can indeed be done if that is the wish of the spouses concerned. But there are many reasons why the "survivor's half" might be as well off in a trust as is the decedent's half. First, there is the **security** aspect; it prevents the survivor from intentionally or unintentionally diminishing the property (and thereby harming the children's ultimate inheritance) by means such as gambling, unsound investments, negligence, or falling victim to a marital adventurer or whatever. Second, there is the aspect of **professional management,** if for any reason someone other than the surviving spouse ought to manage the property. Either (but often both) of the spouses may view the survivor as an unwise choice to manage the property due to inexperience, demonstrated inability to handle property, unwillingness to be bothered with doing so or to accept the constant burden and responsibility of management, or a realization that there is a better person or institution available.

Finally, a trust may be indicated to **avoid the split ownership of marital property** that would otherwise result if a by-pass trust is being used for the decedent's half of the marital property. In a by-pass trust, a portion (usually a fractional share) of each asset comprising the marital property will be owned and managed by the trustee of the by-pass trust. But if the marital deduction property is left to the surviving spouse outright, then he or she will own the remaining fractional interest in each asset comprising the marital property. That can quite obviously lead to quarrels about management decisions, and often to an impasse; it can also create a great deal of family disharmony which a wise testator would seek to avoid. Although the problem is applicable to any asset, it is particularly severe concerning an interest in a business, where the trustee of a by-pass trust may vote for a sale, merger, or other major business decision, but the surviving spouse might be opposed; if they each have equal ownership rights, an impasse has been created.

The "A-B Trust"

A **marital deduction trust** will solve any or all of those problems. Although such a trust must contain different provisions than the by-pass trust, it is permissible and usual to have the same trustee manage all the assets together, simply keeping two distinct portions for bookkeeping purposes. Neither state law nor tax law compels split ownership or split titles to each trust asset; rather, each asset may be owned one hundred percent by the trustee, and the books of the trust will simply reflect that an appropriate portion of each asset, plus the income produced by each asset, is allocable to one trust or the other.

Strictly by custom, those bookkeeping divisions have come to be known as Trust A (normally the marital deduction trust) and Trust B (normally the standard by-pass trust containing the property which did not qualify for the marital deduction). Many people will blithely toss around the concept of **an A-B trust,** as if it were some specialized type of estate planning device. But there is no such device in the abstract; it is either the marital deduction plus by-pass trust arrangement just discussed, or (as we shall soon see) a widow's election plus by-pass trust arrangement. When someone starts discussing with you "an A-B trust device," find out what they mean; you'll discover that not many people have it fully or correctly analyzed.

It is exceedingly important than anyone drafting a marital deduction trust have full knowledge of the tax laws relating to it. The reason is that there are scores of subtleties which may be perfectly proper in a standard by-pass trust but which, if used in a marital deduction trust, will serve to either reduce the amount of the marital deduction, or even destroy it entirely. The IRS strongly enforces the two conditions enabling a trust to qualify as a marital deduction trust and scrutinizes every clause and power within such a trust to see whether it has even a disguised effect of defeating those two conditions in whole or in part. Some clever taxpayers have tried to get around the requirement that the surviving spouse must receive all of the annual income from the marital deduction trust each year because they did not want the survivor to have too much taxable income being taxed in high income tax brackets. One method they tried was to allocate to the marital deduction trust only property which provides little or no income. The IRS reacted by ruling you can't do that and still qualify for the marital deduction; you must provide that the surviving spouse has the power to compel the trustee to invest in fully productive property.

Another common attempt to reduce the survivor's taxable income is to grant the trustee an unrestricted right to determine what items of receipt are income and what items are principal (see page 105). To reduce the survivor's taxable income, the trustee need only characterize receipts as principal. Needless to say, the IRS has ruled against that technique, and therefore such a clause which might be normally included in a standard by-pass trust can be fatal to a marital deduction trust. This is why most knowledgeable estate planners have different sets of trustee's powers to be used for different types of trusts.

It is unnecessary to detail all the many subtle differences between standard trusts and marital deduction trusts, as my purpose here is not to make you legal draftsmen. Suffice it to say that there are many such subtleties. In this age of the knowledgeable consumer, it is certainly appropriate for you to ask a prospective attorney whether he is thoroughly knowledgeable in the intricacies of drafting marital deduction trusts. If he indicates that he didn't know there were any differences between such trusts and normal trusts, go somewhere else.

Power Of Appointment

As for the general power of appointment which the surviving spouse must possess in order for the trust to qualify as a marital deduction trust, nothing says that he or she must exercise that power. In fact, many such trusts are drafted on the premise that the survivor will not exercise it, and he or she will often have been urged by the decedent spouse or by the estate planner not to exercise it. That does not threaten the tax results; it is only necessary that the survivor posssess the power. Usually a marital deduction trust will provide that if the survivor fails to exercise her power, then **in default of appointment** the property contained in Trust A shall at her death become a part of Trust B, which is the by-pass trust and which is likely to continue for the children's benefit until they reach mature ages.

However, any spouse wishing to qualify for the marital deduction must realize that, if a trust is used, the survivor must have a general power. Some spouses are uncomfortable with this, because it is very plain that the survivor can exercise the power so as to direct the marital deduction property away from the children or other intended beneficiaries. He or she could even conceivably use it as a weapon in their relationship with their children, threatening to exercise it against a particular child unless that child does the survivor's bidding concerning any given issue that may arise between them. So this is a risk that must be run if one wants to qualify for the marital deduction, and it normally does not present a serious problem in a peaceful family situation. But certainly, every potential testator considering a marital deduction trust should be informed of the consequences of a general power of appointment; too often, only its tax benefits are explained to a testator, and not its potential practical disadvantages. Note, though, that it is no different than leaving property to the surviving spouse outright, because with outright ownership he or she could also do any of the things enumerated above.

Other Tax Advantages Of A Two Trust Plan

In addition to the requirements imposed by the tax rules, a further clause is often found in either of the two trust, A-B plans. This clause is not required, but is often extremely desirable, and in fact may itself be reason enough for entering into a two trust plan. It has to do with the source of the funds the surviving spouse should use for some major and extraordinary expense. Assume that she wishes to treat herself to a cruise around the world, or to donate funds to a worthwhile cause. If there was only a one trust plan, where the standard by-pass trust usually contains only her husband's half of their marital property, then she would own the balance of the marital property outright. From which source ought she to take such funds, assuming that a friendly trustee of the by-pass trust would invade the principal of that trust if she requested him to do so? Human nature would probably lead her not to use "her own" funds, but rather to use "his" funds lodged in the by-pass trust. And, as pointed out earlier, that would be exactly the wrong thing to do. Her funds will be taxable at her death, whereas the trust funds won't, so tax wisdom would indicate that she spend her own funds.

In a two trust plan, Trust A will be taxed at her death due to her general power of appointment, but Trust B will not because it is the standard by-pass trust. Should the same expenditures arise in the context of a two trust plan, it is clear that she ought to spend the funds lodged in Trust A and not the funds in Trust B. To encourage just that, and to remind all concerned that tax wisdom would so indicate, the trusts are often drafted to say that any invasions of principal for the survivor's benefit must be taken only out of Trust A unless and until that trust is entirely used up, and only then may invasions be taken out of the principal of Trust B. Many estate planners would rather that such drafting be written only in terms of a strong request rather than an absolute direction because greater flexibility is maintained this way. Trust A may not be liquid, and it may be difficult or disadvantageous to have to sell an asset just to satisfy the survivor's cruising whims or charitable wishes. So some draftsmen will do it one way and others the other way, but the tax principle is most sound and it is usually advisable to have such a specification in a two trust plan. The tax wisdom implied by such drafting may be reason enough to prefer a two trust estate plan over the simple one trust plan where the survivor might easily spend the wrong funds on any major expenditure.

The Estate Trust

One other form of trust, known as an estate trust, exists which can qualify for the marital deduction. It can be useful when the surviving spouse has a lot of income-producing separate property, so that if she were to receive all the income from the entire marital property in a classic A-B marital deduction trust she will be getting far more income than is necessary. The tax results of getting all that income can be doubly disadvantageous. All the income will be taxed in high income tax brackets, thus wasting a lot of the property's production in voluntary subsidies to the government. Secondly, if there is so much income that it can not all be used up by taxes plus the survivor's comfortable living expenses, that excess will simply be put into savings which will build her estate higher and higher, all to be estate taxed at high brackets when she dies.

An **estate trust** also qualifies for the marital deduction and provides that all the **income** it produces can be **accumulated** within the trust for the balance of the wife's life; income taxes will thereby be paid by the trust and not by the wife. An independent trustee can have the power to invade principal for the wife's benefit in the event of need, which would have some income tax effects if the power is used, but at least the funds would be available for emergencies. Upon the wife's death, all the principal and accumulated income of an estate trust are distributed **to her estate.** This will guarantee estate taxes on the trust property as the marital deduction qualification rules require, and it will usually also subject the trust property to probate. Further, the **throwback rule** (see page 105) will usually apply to the eventual distributions of trust income earned during the wife's life, but there may be no adverse tax effect to that if the ultimate distributees are in lower income tax brackets than was the trust, or if several other conditions apply to reduce or eliminate the usual adverse effect of the throwback rule.

A variation is possible if the husband is content to have only the value of a remainder interest in half the marital property qualify for the marital deduction. In that variation, the income of an estate trust can be paid to someone other than the surviving wife, so long as the principal must be paid over to her estate at her death.

An estate trust might also have some beneficial effect concerning carryover basis, at least when compared with the effect of carryover basis on the more usual marital deduction trust. The latter must contain a clause saying that the wife has the right to compel the trustee to switch property producing little or no income for income-producing property. If he must sell the unproductive or underproductive property in order to comply with her direction, a large capital gain could result due to the unhappy effect of carryover basis. However, an estate trust does not have to contain the provision just described, and so that somewhat needless capital gains tax could be avoided.

Estate trusts are not nearly as common as the "life estate-general power of appointment" marital deduction trusts described first in this chapter, but they deserve consideration in situations where they might prove beneficial. As always, their negatives will have to be weighed against their advantages.

The Widow's Election

This planning device is normally only used by spouses residing in community property states, and can also be a widower's election. It can easily be applied to spouses in common law states, but a famous tax case holds that, under its facts, the marital deduction was adversely affected by being combined with a widow's election. Several commentators have pointed out that this need not be so, and that a particular form of the widow's election could be successfully used in a common law state without destroying the marital deduction, but these are matters on which your technical advisors will have to pass judgment. Suffice it to say that the widow's election is mostly used in community property states, with a possible adaptation to common law spouses so long as a thoroughly knowledgeable expert supervises the adaptation. Due to these realities, I will discuss the widow's election with language applicable to community property. However, should common law persons be interested in pursuing this idea, they can read the following material by making appropriate mental substitutions.

Advantages Of Having The Survivor's Property In Trust

When a community property spouse dies, only the one-half of the marital property he owns under state law is taxed in his gross estate; he does not need the marital deduction to achieve that result, as it is automatic. To save the second tax, he will of course be advised to direct his half of the community property into a standard by-pass trust. The surviving spouse, not having died, can simply continue to own his or her half of each asset without any trust or other restrictions. But all the same rationale as is applicable to the common law surviving spouse may indicate that it is preferable for the community property surviving spouse's half to be held and managed in a trust. Security from artful and designing persons, professional management freeing the survivor from those burdens and responsibilities, avoiding the confusion of split ownerships between the trustee of the by-pass trust and the survivor (particularly where business interests are concerned), and the tax wisdom of forcing major expenditures to be made from funds that will be estate taxable in the future, may all indicate the advisability of a trust over the survivor's half.

How does the property owned by the surviving community property spouse find its way into a trust? Of course, he or she could voluntarily create a revocable living trust identical to, and with the same trustee as, the decedent's by-pass trust. But the decedent spouse may be unwilling to rely on her to voluntarily do so after he has died. He may be interested in a plan by which he can control her doing so.

He might want to write a will in which he tries to control both halves of the community property, his half and the surviving spouse's half, and in which he directs that both halves go into his trust. Surely that would accomplish his purpose, but it would not seem that he has any legal power to dispose of the survivor's property in his will. Indeed, he has no such power; no one can dispose of another person's property in his will. But he may write such a will anyway, in which case it is totally clear that the surviving spouse can just ignore it as it applies to her half. (Let's assume from here on that the husband has died and the wife survived.) She can stand on her rights as a property owner in her own right and simply treat his will as nonsense (which in that case it would certainly be). However, she has another option, and that is an **election** to follow the provisions of his will; anyone can elect to go along with an arrangement set up by someone else, no matter how nonsensical it may seem. The survivor's options are illustrated in Figure 12-4.

The Forced Widow's Election

When the possibility of his wife electing to follow his will is explained to the husband, he may inquire whether there is anything he can do in his will to insure that his wife will elect to follow it. Yes, he can set things up so that it is to her distinct advantage to elect to follow his will and to her distinct disadvantage to elect not to follow it. (Don't get me wrong, usually the spouses agree on these plans in advance; this is all for purposes of explanation). To understand what he can do, you must think not only of two halves, one belonging to each spouse, but also in terms of each half as capable of being divided into a life estate and a remainder. The husband can write a will which says: I create Trust A over my wife's half of the community property,

A COMMUNITY PROPERTY ESTATE OF $500,000

| HUSBAND'S HALF: $250,000 | WIFE'S HALF: $250,000 |

HUSBAND DIES

HUSBAND'S WILL:

| My wife's half of our community property shall go into Trust A | My half of our community property shall go into Trust B |

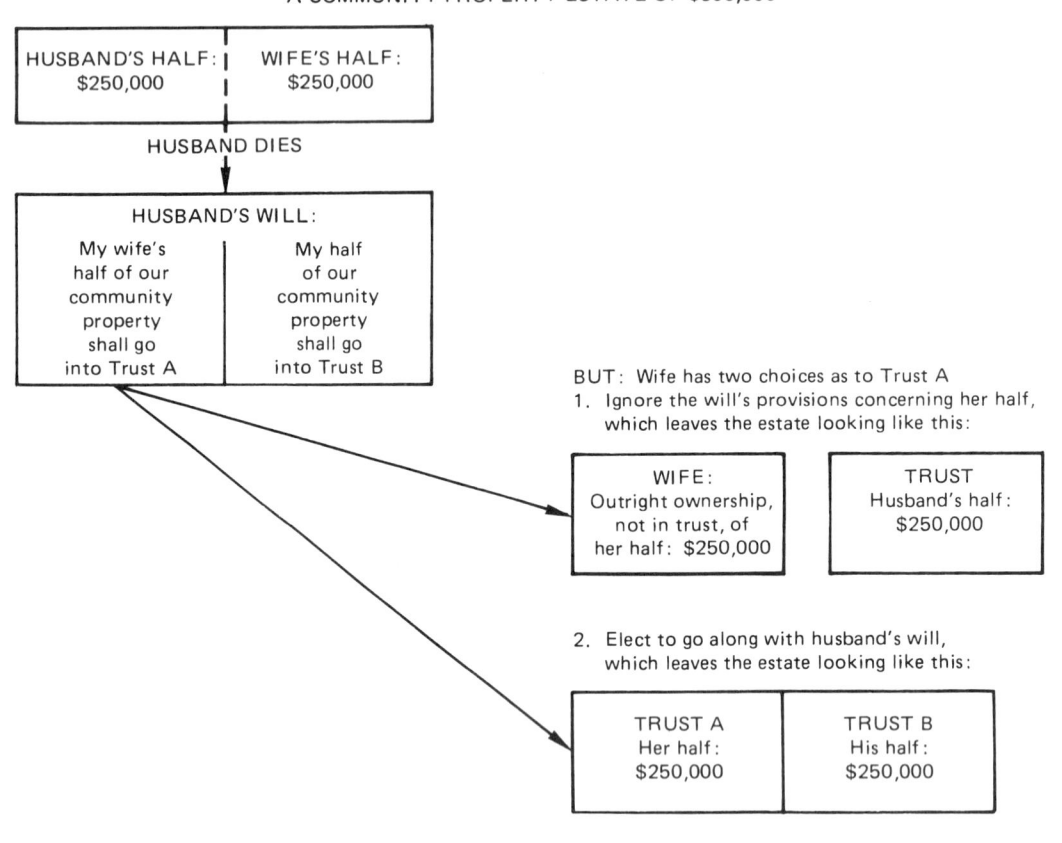

BUT: Wife has two choices as to Trust A

1. Ignore the will's provisions concerning her half, which leaves the estate looking like this:

| WIFE: Outright ownership, not in trust, of her half: $250,000 | TRUST Husband's half: $250,000 |

2. Elect to go along with husband's will, which leaves the estate looking like this:

| TRUST A Her half: $250,000 | TRUST B His half: $250,000 |

Figure 12-4. Illustration of a Typical Widow's Election in a Community Property State.

and Trust B over my half; my wife may have a life income interest in both trusts, and our children shall be the remaindermen of both trusts. However, my wife shall only be entitled to the lifetime income from my half (Trust B) if she elects to go along with my will disposing of both halves of our community property; if she elects not to go along, then she shall not be entitled to that income. So if the wife goes along, she gets the lifetime income from the entire community property, whereas if she elects not to go along, she gets no benefits from the husband's will and must be content with owning her own half of the community property outright.

If the wife elects to go along, it is necessary to analyze the economics of what she is doing. Remember, both trusts provided a life estate to her, remainder to their children. If she goes along, she is exchanging a remainder interest in her half of the community property (not the life income interest which she had in the first place and which Trust A retains for her) for a life income interest in the husband's half of the community property. That is a very real exchange because if she doesn't elect to go along, then she does not get the income from Trust B by the terms of her husband's will. She is giving up the remainder interest in her own half because she is putting it into a trust (Trust A) the terms of which were dictated by her husband, and irrevocably committing that remainder to her children rather than reserving the right to give it to someone else.

That exchange has all kinds of tax implications, but it is not the only kind of widow's (or widower's) election which can be made. The kind just described is called a **forced widow's election** because the husband is in essence forcing her to it. He is holding out a carrot to encourage her election, and then denying her the carrot (the lifetime income from his half) if she fails to elect.

The Voluntary Widow's Election

The husband can also draft a will which is a non-forced, or **voluntary widow's election.** This one says that she gets the life income from his half if she elects to go along with his will, but if she does not elect to go along with his will, she still gets the life income in his half anyway. That type of widow's election has none of the tax implications which the forced widow's election has. It only serves to get both halves of the community property into one trust as the spouses wish and is the way community property spouses institute a two trust, A-B type of estate plan without getting involved in all the tax implications. In the voluntary plan, each spouse is willing to rely on the other spouse's promise that he or she will elect to go along without any further incentive than the estate planning agreement that it would be a good idea.

Tax Effects Of The Forced Widow's Election

Many experts believe that the 1976 Act has effectively killed the forced widow's election, and that it should no longer be used. Whether or not that is true, it is completely appropriate to issue a warning that the forced widow's election must now be watched carefully, and perhaps be abandoned. It is further appropriate to suggest to any reader who may have a forced widow's election will that he ought to have that will reevaluated in light of the 1976 Act. However, it is no cause for panic, because if the forced widow's election appears to be disadvantageous for any particular surviving spouse, she can just elect not to follow her husband's will (or he to follow hers) and be none the worse for it. If thereafter she wishes to go along with the idea that she put her half of the community property into trust, she can create a revocable living trust with terms and a trustee identical to the trust in her husband's will.

The tax effects of the forced widow's election will are many, and fascinating. When the wife elects to irrevocably follow her husband's will by transferring the remainder interest in her half of the community (remember, she keeps the life estate under the terms of his trust), she may well be making a taxable gift. It is definitely a gift; the only question is whether and to what extent it is taxable. Recall that life estates and remainders are valued by appropriate tables (see Table 4-1, page 51), so that the value of the remainder she transfers can be compared to the value of the life estate she receives in exchange for that transfer. If what she receives is worth more than what she gives up, then she has received full consideration for the transfer, and it is not a gift. If what she receives is worth less than what she gives up, then she has received partial consideration for the transfer, but the excess over that partial consideration is a gift. The results are determined by her age at the time she makes the gift because her age determines the relative values of the life estate and remainder; for a female aged 68 or less, a life estate will be worth more than a remainder. But the husband's half of the community will be smaller than the survivor's half, since his half will have been depleted by taxes and expenses, so one must compare the life estate in that smaller portion with a remainder in the surviving wife's larger portion. In a voluntary widow's election, the wife has also made a gift of the remainder to her children, but there is no offset for consideration received because by definition in a voluntary plan she is not exchanging her remainder for a life estate in her husband's half.

But if the wife retains a power of appointment (see page 143) over the choice of persons and the size of shares going to the ultimate remaindermen, then she has not really made a completed gift at all because the donees and their shares are undetermined. It has been suggested that all widow's elections plans, forced or voluntary, ought to contain such a power, although whether it should be a general or a special power, or even be present at all, is a subject for expert advice. A general power might destroy some or all of the tax advantages of the forced widow's election.

A very interesting estate tax result occurs in a forced widow's election when the wife later dies. Her half of the community property will definitely be taxed in her gross estate because she has made a transfer of it with a retained life estate. However, she has made that transfer for a partial consideration; namely, the value of the life estate in her husband's half of the community property. Estate tax rules allow partial consideration to be deducted from any transfer taxed in the gross estate, with the net result that less than the entire value of her half of the community property will be subject to estate taxation at her death. This is virtually the only mechanism known where less than one hundred percent of the marital property will be estate taxed in the estates of both husband and wife and is what has made the forced widow's election an attractive device for tax purposes.

There is still another tax advantage, this one being an income tax advantage. If a businessman purchases a machine to assist him in the production of his taxable income, he is entitled to **depreciate** that machine, which means that he may deduct from his taxes each year a proportionate part of the cost of that machine dependent upon how many years of useful life the machine has. The effect is that he has tax-free income each year to the extent of the depreciation deduction, a deliberate tax subsidy to encourage prompt replacement of outmoded machinery. If the businessman likewise purchases an intangible item for use in producing his income (as opposed to a tangible item like a machine), he may also write off its cost over its useful life in exactly the same way, although now it is termed **amortization** instead of depreciation. When the surviving wife irrevocably elects to follow her husband's forced widow's election will, has she not "purchased" an intangible item (a life estate in his half of the community property), which will produce income for her? She definitely has, and several tax cases have upheld her right to amortize its cost (as the value of the remainder interest she has transferred to the trust in "payment" for the life estate) over its useful life (her life expectancy under mortality tables). The result is that often a substantial portion of the annual income from her life estate in the husband's half will be income-tax-free due to her amortization deduction. Along with the estate tax advantage at her death, this makes the forced widow's election appear to be an unbeatable tax device.

Disadvantages Of The Forced Widow's Election

Now for the bad news. There are several items of such bad news, and you can imagine that the IRS will field every weapon available against this device in order to blunt its tax advantages. For one thing, assume that the life estate in the husband's half is worth more than the wife's basis (defined at page 174) for the remainder interest in her half which she surrenders in order to acquire life estate. If so, it seems apparent that the wife has sold capital assets at a gain, and that of course yields capital gains tax. Prior to the 1976 Act this was a reality without a tax bite, due to the former stepped up basis rules. Recall that the entire community property received a stepped up basis at the death of only one of the spouses, so the wife's basis for the capital assets she sold was stepped up to their fair market value at the date of the husband's death. This decreased or eliminated the potential capital gains tax to the widow. But after December 31, 1979 we have carryover basis (see page 175), so the widow's basis will not be "stepped up" except to the extent of the various adjustments explained in chapter ten. She is therefore likely to be faced with a much more substantial capital gains tax, and this is a major reason why many observers feel that the forced widow's election must be abandoned after December 31, 1979.

Now assume that the value of the remainder interest transferred by the wife exceeds the basis to the husband's estate of the life estate transferred to the wife in exchange for that remainder. In those circumstances, it can be seen that the husband's estate may be selling an asset (a life estate) at a gain. Without the pre-1976 Act benefit of stepped up basis, the husband's estate may have only the lower carryover basis for the assets sold, thus yielding a substantial capital gains tax after December 31, 1979. But there is even a more frightening argument, too technical to go into for our purposes, that the husband's estate realizes not capital gains upon such a sale, but rather regular ordinary income. If so, the sale proceeds could be taxed to the husband's estate at a very high income tax rate, so high as to destroy any tax advantage of this device. And there is another potential income tax disadvantage, dealing with how the income during the probate administration of the husband's estate will be taxed in situations of a forced widow's election.

Clearly, this is a complex and difficult matter that may seem too risky for many, but even for those who might be tempted to explore its benefits, it is painfully apparent that very expert advice is called for. It may indeed come to pass that the 1976 Act has effectively destroyed the forced widow's election.

Advantages Of The Non-Forced Widow's Election

However, non-forced widow's election plans are still alive, as they do not incur the risk of (or try for any of the advantages of) the tax consequences mentioned above. A voluntary plan may even be preferable from a tax standpoint and can further be utilized to gain all or any of the non-tax advantages accruing from having the surviving spouse's half of the community property held in the same trust as is the husband's half. Any such plan can be designed to avoid one serious flaw of the forced widow's election, which is that by definition in that plan, the widow must receive all of the annual income from the entire community property. If this is a substantial amount and is well beyond her ability to spend, the excess over the amount needed is only being subjected to income taxes at high rates of tax. Also, whatever is left over is probably just being put into the wife's savings, and her savings from that source will just continue to grow so that the resulting extra estate tax at her death could far exceed whatever tax savings the forced widow's election might have provided. If, for example, the wife is putting $30,000 of such extra funds into savings each year, and it turns out that she lives for twenty more years, her estate has been increased by $600,000 (without even considering compound interest) due to the forced widow's election. Not very good tax planning.

The Measured Voluntary Survivor's Election

A variation that does not run many of the tax risks, but obtains some of the advantages in a different way, has been called the **measured voluntary survivor's election.** The survivor is given the right to elect to receive a life income interest in the husband's half of the community property, but to acquire it the survivor must transfer to the husband's trust enough of her property so that a remainder interest in it exactly equals in value the life estate she will be receiving. There will be no gift tax because it is an "even up" transfer for a full and adequate consideration. Some amount of her property which the wife transfers to the husband's trust in payment for her life estate ought not to be taxed in her gross estate when she later dies because it has been transferred for a full and adequate consideration (a genuine sale), and property so sold is not estate taxable.

The difference from a normal sale, though, is that what has been received, a life estate, vanishes at her death and so is not available to be taxed, unlike cash proceeds of normal sales. And since the wife has paid full value for her income producing life estate, she ought to be able to amortize its cost over her life, thereby turning some of the income so received into tax-free income. There may well be some capital gain taxes payable on the type of sale described, though, since each party is selling property for a price presumably in excess of its basis under the new carryover basis rules. As usual, there is much more to this than meets the eye at first glance, and if you are interested in it you should seek expert advice for your particular situation.

It has been additionally suggested that the measured voluntary survivor's election is compatible with full qualification for the marital deduction if used by spouses in common law states or if used in community property states with separate property or quasi-community property (because the entire thing is voluntary, thereby not raising the problem which defeated the marital deduction when it was combined with the forced widow's election). In the non-community property variation, the surviving spouse would elect to transfer the portion of the marital property which qualifies for the marital deduction (presumably including her dower rights, and maybe even some of her separate property if she has any) into the husband's trust in exchange for a life estate in that portion of the marital property which was taxed in the husband's estate. If the voluntary exchange is measured, she will transfer only so much property so that a remainder interest in it exactly equals the value of the life estate she will be receiving.

Other Variations

Another variant might be the following: the widow (or any other person) elects to follow her husband's will requesting her to place her half of the community into Trust A, in exchange for which she will receive a life estate in the husband's half, Trust B. However, she does not receive the annual income in her own half (Trust A); rather, it is accumulated for eventual distribution to her minor children or is paid out annually to them or to any other persons selected. But the trustee of Trust A is instructed to invade the principal of Trust A every year in amounts equal to the income being produced by Trust B and to distribute that principal to the widow. The result is that she receives annual funds equal to the income earned by both halves of the community property, but one half of those funds are not taxable income; they are instead nontaxable payments of principal. Further, the widow's gross estate is being depleted because the portion that is potentially taxable at her death, Trust A, is growing smaller each year as the principal payments are being made. And, since she has purchased the life estate in her husband's half by placing her property into Trust A, she ought to be able to amortize the life estate's cost against the taxable income she is receiving from Trust B. The widow has made a taxable gift of the life estate in her half of the community, since she gives that up, but it ought to be offset by the consideration received for that transfer; namely, the life estate in her husband's half. To repeat the now familiar refrain, expert advice would be called for to analyze the suitability of such a device for any individual estate. It may also need some unusual provisions; for instance the two trusts might have to be much more separated than is normally done, due to some pretty technical rules of how trust income is income taxed.

Summary

The point of any of the two trust "A-B" plans outlined in this chapter is twofold. To save the second tax by utilizing the standard by-pass trust, and also to place the other half of the marital property into a trust for all the non-tax reasons stated. In the case of the marital deduction trust, we have ensured the preferable tax result of half taxation at one death and half at the other. In the case of a widow's election type device applying most often to community property, we may have secured certain other tax advantages as well.

APPLICATION

1. If you are married and have already decided on a by-pass trust for the taxable portion of your estate, determine whether your surviving spouse should own his or her portion outright, or whether it would be preferable to have it go into trust as well.

2. Determine whether a marital deduction formula clause would be to your advantage.

3. If you decide on a trust for your survivor's portion, and it is clearly necessary to qualify for the marital deduction, determine whether a "life estate-power of appointment" trust should be used, or whether an "estate trust" would be preferable. The choice often depends upon whether your survivor will have more than adequate annual income from your by-pass trust plus any additional property she may own. Don't ignore the cumulative effects of excessive annual income taxes if she does in fact have adequate other income, plus the fact that any excess income will probably just be building up her taxable estate.

4. If after considering the income tax points made in item # 3. you feel that your survivor has more than adequate income from her own property plus the marital deduction portion left to her either outright or in trust, consider making persons other than your surviving spouse the income beneficiaries of your by-pass trust.

Good tax planning may favor that plan. Don't automatically feel that you must leave everything to your spouse; if the economics are pretty obvious, she will probably agree to a different plan. (She doesn't even have to agree, of course, but it would be nice if she did).

5. If you live in a community property state and you want your survivor's half to also go into trust, discuss with tax knowledgeable advisors whether a forced widow's election or a voluntary widow's election is preferable. If the forced widow's election appeals to you, be sure that both you and your advisors fully understand the possible tax risks and are willing to accept them.

13

trust planning: living trusts and other trusts

Glossary For This Chapter

Clifford Trust
Guardianship
Totten Trust
Review:
Court Trust
Funded Trust
Irrevocable Trust
Living Trust
Non-Court Trust
Revocable Trust
Unfunded Trust

In this chapter I will bring together the considerations involved in using various kinds of trusts. Most of the trusts I will discuss here are living trusts; they are usually established during the lifetime of the trustor for the various reasons I will cover. But they almost always continue to exist after the trustor's death, and therefore they need to incorporate all of his wishes for the use of his property. As such, they may contain all or any of the provisions referred to in the last two chapters. That is, they can operate as a standard bypass trust or as a two trust "A-B" plan involving either the marital deduction or the widow's election. Be aware that the material of the prior two chapters and this material is not mutually exclusive, but rather should be combined together. The operation of trusts after the trustor's death has been pretty well covered in the prior two chapters, and now I am adding considerations of whether a trust should commence its operation during the trustor's lifetime. The advantages and dis-

254

TRUST PLANNING: LIVING TRUSTS AND OTHER TRUSTS

Revocable Versus Irrevocable Trusts

advantages of operation during his lifetime are the principal subjects of this chapter.

Recall that in a revocable trust, the trustor retains the right for the rest of his life to alter, amend, or revoke any of the trust provisions, whereas in an irrevocable trust he can never make any of those changes. Concerning only the considerations involved in whether a living trust should be revocable or irrevocable, we need to examine the consequences of one type versus the other. In virtually every situation, only tax consequences dictate the choice. Otherwise, nobody would reasonably prefer to do something irrevocably if they could achieve the exact same results by doing it revocably. But they can't; the tax consequences of the two types are entirely different. There are few reasons other than tax reasons to prefer an irrevocable trust. One such reason might be to avoid the claims of creditors. Most state laws are so constructed that if you place property in a trust but retain the right to revoke the trust, such a painless act will not be sufficient to put the property out of the reach of your creditors. If you want to or need to protect yourself against their claims, an irrevocable trust is almost always a necessity (though more than mere irrevocability may be needed to accomplish this purpose). Another non-tax use of an irrevocable trust may be related to a divorce or property settlement agreement. The parties often want to do something irrevocably, or are required by negotiations or a court judgment to do so.

There are **no tax consequences to a revocable living trust,** because no tax consequences are changed by its creation. The retention of a power to revoke will inevitably mean that the income earned by trust property will be taxed to the trustor. He is perfectly free to put the property in a revocable trust if he wishes; it's just that the income will continue to be taxed to him. Secondly, no gift tax is triggered by the creation of a revocable living trust because retaining the power to revoke makes the gift incomplete. The trustor could get the property back the next day by exercising his power to revoke, so no gift tax is appropriate. As far as the estate taxes go, retaining the economic enjoyment implied by hanging on to the power of revocation means that the trust property will still be taxed in the trustor's gross estate. So a revocable living trust changes no tax consequences, neither income tax nor estate tax, and it creates no gift tax.

An **irrevocable living trust,** on the other hand, operates in a completely opposite manner. It changes virtually all the tax consequences. Concerning income taxes, assuming that an irrevocable trust is properly drafted to meet many tax law requirements, the income produced by the property placed in the trust will no longer be taxed to the trustor. Rather, depending upon the terms of the trust, it will be taxed in whole or in part to either the trust itself, or to the beneficiaries; see the discussion at page 102, and the illustration in Figure 6-2, page 103. So an irrevocable living trust surely changes the income tax consequences.

It bears mentioning that mere irrevocability will not ensure that the income will be taxed to someone other than the trustor; it is also necessary that none of such income be paid to, or benefit, the trustor. Some people have the mistaken idea that they can create an irrevocable trust, keep receiving the income, but have it taxed to the trust or someone else. Not so.

Since an irrevocable trust implies an irrevocable transfer of property, there will of course be a gift tax assessed upon such a transfer. Thus, the irrevocable trust changes that tax consequence in that it creates a gift tax whereas just leaving things alone would not have created any such tax. Under the 1976 Act, that "gift tax" means that the trustor's unified credit will first be used up, to the extent of $175,000 after 1980, and if the transfer were in a greater amount, then the unitary transfer tax will apply to fix the "gift tax."

Concerning estate taxes, property in an irrevocable living trust is not taxed in your gross estate (if you live three years after the transfer of property to it; see page 136), but that is essentially meaningless since the value of the transfer has already borne transfer taxes and will be added back to your estate to compute your estate's tax bracket (see page 118). But be aware that the gift tax is based upon the value of the property at the date of the gift, so that if you live three years after the transfer all the post-gift appreciation in the value of that property will not be taxable in your gross estate. Therefore irrevocable transfers do have the beneficial effect of removing the growth in value from your taxable estate at death.

In sum, then, an irrevocable living trust changes all the tax results. It shifts the income tax burden as indicated, it creates a gift tax where previously there was none, and it gets the appreciation out of the taxable estate if the transferor lives the required three years. Who would use an irrevocable trust? Anyone who wants to achieve those changes in tax consequences. However, it is wise to be quite cautious about the non-tax consequences of such a trust. Namely, that it is thoroughly irrevocable, and no one should even consider doing it unless he can be absolutely convinced that under no conceivable circumstances will he ever again need the security represented by the property or the income from it. That pretty well confines irrevocable trusts to rather wealthy people.

Since a revocable trust changes none of those tax consequences, who would use it, and for what purposes? Read on.

Funded and Unfunded Revocable Living Trusts

Funded and unfunded are terms which describe whether or not any significant amount of property has been transferred to a revocable living trust. If there is property in the trust, either all or any part of a trustor's property, the trust is said to be **funded.** If there is little or no property, it is **unfunded.** Irrevocable trusts are always funded, or else there would be no reason for their existence; they must have property in them to achieve their purposes. Classic trust law says that any trust in order to be valid must have some property in it, for otherwise it is just a paper trust and cannot be accorded any legal existence. Some states have modified that ancient rule, and in those states it is possible to have an unfunded trust with absolutely no property in it; why one might want to do that I will shortly discuss. But even in those states which have not repealed the ancient rule, it is quite simple to circumvent it by placing $100, or even $10, into the trust in order to "fund" it and give it some semblance of legal existence. For our purposes, though, such minimally funded trusts will still be considered as unfunded. I want to explore the differences between putting all or a substantial part of a trustor's property into a living trust, as opposed to putting none (or almost none) of his property into it.

Revocable Living Trusts And Probate

Since a revocable trust changes none of the tax consequences, it must have other purposes. A major one is to **avoid probate.** All property legally transferred to such a trust belongs to the trustee and not to the trustor, so that when the trustor dies he can't be considered the owner of the trust property. This is perhaps the first thing that springs into someone's mind when a revocable living trust is mentioned. But saying that any living trust, revocable or irrevocable, avoids probate is really ducking the essential question, which is whether or not probate should be avoided. Many of the considerations involving probate, both the disadvantages as well as the infrequently known advantages of it, were explained in chapter five and will not be repeated here.

In the opinions of a lot of estate planners, many too many people have an automatic reaction that probate ought always to be avoided if possible, and are therefore attracted to any probate-avoiding device such as revocable living trusts and joint-tenancy property. It may well be completely true that for a given testator, considering his situation and the health or sickness of his state's probate system, avoiding probate may indeed be one of the best things which can be incorporated into his estate plan. But the opposite is also true, and in this world where very little is either totally black or totally white, automatic reactions to almost anything are quite suspect. Therefore, a property owner must devote a little clear thinking as to whether, on balance, it is advantageous or disadvantageous to avoid probate.

If a revocable living trust is to be used as a **probate-avoiding device,** then the trust **must be funded.** The property must be legally transferred into the ownership of the trustee in order for that property to avoid probate. If it is not, it remains in the name of the decedent and will have to go through his probate estate in order to be transferred to his heirs; having a "dry" living trust without the property having been transferred to it will do nothing at all to avoid probate for that property. So an unfunded trust for the purpose of avoiding probate makes no sense.

Cost Analysis of Funded Revocable Trusts

The combination of the need for a funded trust if one wishes to avoid probate with the fact that probate fees and expenses are **tax deductible** presents a matter of economics which many people overlook. It is not economically accurate to compare one hundred percent of probate expenses with no costs at all if probate is avoided. Since probate expenses are deductible on either the estate tax return or the income tax return of the estate or its beneficiaries, the government is paying a portion of the probate expenses and the estate is paying only the balance. We know that the minimum federal estate tax rate is now 32%, and when state inheritance taxes are figured in, it is likely that almost any estate which has to pay federal estate taxes is in about a 40% bracket. Where that is true, the actual costs of probate are only 60% of the expenses incurred. In an estate smaller than the federal exemption and therefore subject only to state inheritance taxes, the estate's share of the probate expenses will be considerably higher because deductibility is not worth as much as for the larger estates.

Costs Of A Trust Compared To Probate Costs

But that's still not the whole story, for an accurate economic analysis would have to compare the **costs of operating** the living trust, plus its share of any deathtime expenses, against the (assumed) 60% of probate expenses which not having a trust will cost. A living trust is a **separate taxable entity,** so it must file both federal and state **fiduciary income tax returns** each year even if all the income is distributed to the beneficiaries, and the trust consequently owes no tax. Fiduciary income tax returns are considerably more complex than individual returns, particularly with their technical concept of "distributable net income," so it may be necessary to employ an accountant to prepare those returns even if they show no tax due.

If the trustee is a corporate trustee, it will charge both a **set-**

up fee and an **annual trustee's fee.** Even if a family member or other individual is trustee, a full or reduced fee may be appropriate and insisted upon by a fair-minded trustor. There may be added expenses of transferring legal title into the name of the trust, and added expenses when the trustee buys or sells property. Further, when the trustor dies, property held in a revocable living trust is taxable in his gross estate, and a portion (or all) of the costs of preparing the federal and state death tax returns are properly chargeable to the trust.

An illustrative summary of a cost analysis for a funded revocable living trust is shown in Figure 13-1. What is actually saved by such a trust is the estate's often 60% or smaller share of the deductible probate expenses, less the annual costs of operating the living trust together with the trust's share of the death tax return preparation costs. It is of course impossible to quote any accurate savings figure for all trustors in general, although an individual advisor may be able to come quite close to an accurate analysis. But one respected commentator estimates that the net savings through the use of a revocable living trust are **no more than one-third of the probate expenses,** and perhaps even less if the living trust continues for many years before the trustor dies (since annual expenses will keep on adding up). Thus, if someone is facing a potential $15,000 probate fee, the true net dollar savings achieved by using a revocable living trust is approximately $5,000. One issue I will soon address is whether savings of that amount are worth the changes in a trustor's life which a revocable living trust can cause.

Other Reasons For Living Trusts

However, there are reasons aside from probate avoidance for using a revocable living trust, even though such a trust changes no tax consequences.

Ensuring A Non-Court Trust

One reason is to ensure that all the trustor's property winds up in a **non-court trust,** since in most states testamentary trusts are subject to the continuing jurisdiction of the probate court whereas living trusts are not. The advantages and disadvantages of court versus non-court trusts were fully explained in chapter six, page 89. If a non-court trust is desired, then an unfunded revocable living trust can be established and the testator can write a simple **pour over will** whereby he leaves all of his property to the trustee of the already existing non-court, living trust; he "pours over" his property to the trust. The trustor might also want to avoid a court trust if he knows that, post-mortem, he wants an out-of-state person to serve as trustee. Having a non-court trust would eliminate the need for the out-of-state trustee to account periodically to the probate court in a different state.

COST ANALYSIS: Transfer of $200,000 to a Funded Revocable Living Trust (all cost and tax figures are assumptions for purposes of illustration; assume Trustor has 20-year-life expectancy).

	Saving	Cost
Probate Fee on $200,000; assume 8% fee (quite high) covers both executor and attorney	$16,000	
Less: benefit of deductibility of these fees on both federal and state tax returns, at 40% total bracket	$ (6,400)	
	$ 9,600	
Annual Trustee's Fee (may not be payable, but assume ¾ of 1% annually for illustration) $1500 x 20 years		$ 30,000
Less: deductibility, assumed 40% bracket		$(12,000)
		$ 18,000
Tax Preparer's Annual Fee for fiduciary income tax return; assume $100 per year x 20 years		$ 2,000
Less: deductibility at 40% bracket		$ (800)
		$ 1,200
Assumed Trust's Share of Accountant's or Attorney's Fee for preparing, after death, federal estate tax return and state death tax return		$ 2,000
Less: deductibility at 40% bracket		$ (800)
		$ 1,200
TOTALS, if Trustee's Fee paid as indicated	$ 9,600	$ 20,400
TOTALS, if Trustee's Fee completely avoided NET SAVING under this hypothesis is therefore $7,200.	$ 9,600	$ 2,400

Figure 13–1. Illustration of a Cost Analysis for a Funded Revocable Living Trust.

Continuity Of Operation, And Secrecy

A living trust also just keeps right on operating the day after the trustor's death without any interruption and without any disruption from the probate process. **Smooth, continuous management** of trust properties is thereby assured, and this may be particularly important in the case of a going business where payrolls must continue to be met and trade creditors can continue to be paid without forcing them to submit claims to a probate court. Since there is no probate and therefore there is no public record, **secrecy** as to the family's net worth and testatmentary wishes can also be maintained. Many people are just not interested, for particular good reasons involving their own situation or just because it makes them mad, in having any member of the public (including the media) be able to obtain complete access to their probate court file.

Testing Out The Trustee

Another potential benefit of a revocable living trust is that it enables the trustor to **try out, supervise, correct, and perhaps even replace his trustee.** Rather than just turning his property over to a testamentary trustee and hoping that the trustee will perform up to the trustor's expectations, he can put the trustee into office now. He can then figuratively sit on the trustee's shoulder and give the trustee the benefit of his counsel and experience. That might be particularly valuable when someone such as the trustor's inexperienced son is his chosen trustee.

Avoiding A Court-Controlled Guardianship

A major benefit to be obtained from a revocable living trust is that, should the trustor later become either physically or mentally disabled, having a trust can avoid the need for a court-controlled **guardianship** or **conservatorship** (see Glossary) which would otherwise be necessary to run the trustor's economic affairs. Having already placed his property into the trustee's hands, the trustor has thereby **already chosen the person** he prefers to handle his economic matters, which is more secure than hoping that the court will appoint someone sympathetic and acceptable. Also, a liberally drawn living trust can **operate more flexibly** than can a court controlled guardianship or conservatorship, not only because the trustee can be given many more powers in a trust but also because the trustee need not obtain court permission for every move.

Professional Management

Over and above any or all of those reasons, there is **one overriding reason** for the use of a revocable living trust, and that is to obtain more **professional management** over the trustor's property. That may be desired or recommended for any number of reasons: the trustor may wish to retire from management tasks, he may wish to start traveling extensively, he may realize that he is not doing a good job, he may be feeling overwhelmed with the complexities of the modern investment environment, or maybe he is feeling just plain tired of carrying the burdens of management. Or, even if he has none of those feelings about himself, he may recognize that there is someone better for the management job; maybe someone has just come to his attention and he wishes to turn the task over to that person or institution. Perhaps the trustor has suddenly had a great economic success and he is overwhelmed by it or is inexperienced in handling it, or maybe he has just inherited a substantial amount of property without ever having been trained in its management. To avoid the inaction, malaise, and sometimes even panic, which such newly acquired wealth can often bring, the trustor may recognize that professional management ought to be employed. In short, a living trust is useful under any circumstances anyone might imagine when more professional management is desirable.

To obtain that professional management, it is obvious that a **funded revocable trust must be used** in order that title to the property is given to the trustee. We have already seen that the probate avoidance motive also requires a funded trust and that an unfunded trust designed for that purpose would be meaningless. The same is true of the motives relating to avoiding guardianships or conservatorships, the supervision of the chosen trustee, preservation of secrecy, and insuring a continuously smooth operation in the immediate post-mortem period. In all of those instances, the property would already have had to be placed into the trust and into the name of the trustee, without which the desired effects could not legally take place. However, an unfunded trust accompanied by a simple "pour over" will suffice to avoid the continuing jurisdiction of the probate court, and also free an out-of-state trustee from accounting to the probate court of a foreign state. In the latter instances, the trustor may simply keep all of his properties in his own name for the rest of his life without being forced to deal with any added complexities which trust ownership might imply. All of that property would then pass through his probate estate, and upon final distribution, it would be distributed to the trustee of the already existing living trust, thereby avoiding the continuing probate court jurisdiction (if that is the trustor's wish, though you should remember the pros and cons of doing so).

Trustor Serving As Trustee

To supervise a chosen trustee or to obtain more professional management, the trustee will of course be either an individual other than the trustor or the trust department of a bank. But for many of the other uses of a living trust, the trustor might be able to serve as his own trustee. He can so serve if his only motive is to avoid probate, to preserve post-mortem secrecy, to ensure continuous operation in the immediate post-mortem period, or to avoid a guardianship or conservatorship in the event of incompetency.

In any of the latter cases, an alternate or successor trustee should be named, and he will automatically take over upon the trustor's death, the trustor's resignation, or if the trustor becomes physically or mentally incompetent.

Where it is possible for a trustor to serve as his own trustee, the question which ought to be addressed is whether or not the benefits sought are worth whatever costs, complications, and hassles he will experience in operating as a trustee instead of in his own individual sole owner's capacity. Some of the potential added costs and complications have already been mentioned. Over and above those are the technicalities and nuisances of operating as a trustee. Even when the trustor is the trustee, and in some cases particularly because the trustor is the trustee, he must be fully aware than he is no longer just "himself" doing whatever he pleases with no one else to answer to for any errors in judgment or even irresponsible whims. He is now a fiduciary and takes on all the strict obligations which that capacity carries with it. He is responsible to every potential beneficiary of the trust, including perhaps unborn beneficiaries who nevertheless will someday have rights in the trust. Along with the loss of his complete freedom in dealing with his own assets in whatever way he wishes, he also creates added steps and technicalities in dealing with the property as trust property. As is often said, when so dealing he must "wear his trustee's hat", he takes on a different legal capacity and he takes on the obligation of acting as a trustee pursuant to trust law. All transactions must be done in the name of the trust. Often, stock transfer agents, title companies, and others will demand to see a copy of the trust instrument and may have their own legal counsel scrutinize it to be sure the trustee has the power he is purporting to exercise. If there is any question in anyone's mind, some mechanism for resolving any such question or dispute must be found.

None of the above comments are intended to throw any cold water on the concept of a funded revocable living trust. But they are realities, and any potential trustor who made his decision to use a trust without knowing of them would not be making a completely informed decision.

How to Avoid Both Probate AND Double Death Taxes

There is only one estate planning device which can promise both these benefits, and that is the funded revocable living trust. Being funded, it avoids probate for whatever property is transferred to it. Drafted as a by-pass trust, it avoids the second estate tax or the double estate tax. Such trusts are being increasingly used to obtain those dual benefits.

Life Insurance Traps

There are several traps for the unwary regarding the estate planning consequences of life insurance. A life insurance trust may go a long way towards solving most or all of those traps.

Trap One: If a husband carries life insurance for the primary purpose of providing a fund to which his surviving wife can look for her security, he will most probably make her the beneficiary of the policy. As we have seen, life insurance is taxable in the insured's gross estate, but in most cases only one-half of it will be taxed because it will either qualify for the marital deduction or because it is community property. If the insured's wife is the beneficiary, the entire amount of the proceeds will be paid to her, and on her later death that entire amount will be property she owns, which will be fully taxable in her gross estate. This common arrangement **fails to save the second tax** on that portion of the insurance that was taxed in the husband's estate and now will later be taxed again in the wife's. The unnecessary tax costs of such double taxation can run into many thousands of dollars.

Trap Two: Life insurance is often carried to provide cash for the payment of death taxes and estate administration expenses. However, if the wife is named as beneficiary, upon receipt of the policy proceeds those **funds now legally belong to her** in their entirety. Nine months after the husband's death, the executor may ask her to please make available to him however many thousands of dollars may be necessary to pay the taxes. To which she might reply, "No thank you. I've been waiting all my life to try my infallible system for beating roulette in Las Vegas, after which I'm using the money to open a store selling marijuana to FBI agents." And you know, she's right; it's her money now, she can do whatever she wants with it, and she is under no legal obligation to turn over any of it to the executor to assist him with his problems.

Trap Three: Life insurance proceeds paid to an individual beneficiary **fail to follow the estate plan,** assuming one had been created. That is, those proceeds may be wasted or gambled away; they may find their way to a marital adventurer or other artful and designing person; they are not subject to any form of professional management, and they do not acquire any of the other non-tax benefits we have discussed to this point. Since insurance proceeds are not subject to the decedent's will, but belong automatically to the person named as beneficiary, no amount of elaborate provisions or complex trusts written in the will will have any effect on them. Even after well-planned wills and trusts have been written,

---

HOW TO AVOID BOTH PROBATE AND DOUBLE DEATH TAXES

Life Insurance Trusts To Solve Common Insurance Mistakes

life insurance proceeds are sometimes forgotten, to suffer the fate indicated.

Some Solutions, Including A Life Insurance Trust

A seemingly simple solution to all these traps might be to have the insurance payable to the estate of the decedent, so that the proceeds would be available to the executor to meet his cash needs, and then the balance could follow the will. But that is usually an unwise idea, simply because it is taking a non-probate asset and turning it into a probate asset on which the executor's and attorney's fees will have to be paid. There is rarely any good reason to solve the problem in that fashion. Many older insurance policies issued before more sophisticated knowledge became commonplace will have the decedent's estate as either the primary or contingent beneficiary. This is almost always unwise and probably ought to be changed.

An infinitely better solution is a **life insurance trust.** This must be a living trust, and it contains all of the trustor's testamentary wishes. Upon its creation, the beneficiary of the life insurance policies is changed from an individual to the trustee of that trust. At the death of the insured, the insurance proceeds will be paid to the trustee, and they will immediately become subject to his management and to all the provisions of the trust. In a great many cases, having the proceeds paid to a trust will provide much greater flexibility and investment opportunity than will using the settlement options available under the policy. Those options can provide any number of annuity or periodic payouts to the beneficiary, but they all suffer from the common flaw of being rigidly inflexible in a fast-changing inflationary world. They are also a form of low interest loan from the beneficiary to the insurance company, and in many cases, the interest factor they carry is lower than a trustee will be able to obtain via investments.

Among the provisions of a trust there is commonly a clause permitting the trustee to make the cash proceeds available to the executor so he can pay death taxes and administration expenses. Since the insurance trust is a living trust, this is all done without subjecting the insurance proceeds to probate fees nor the trust to the continuing jurisdiction of the probate court. Since the insurance trust will typically contain at least the one by-pass trust mechanism, if not the two trust "A-B" plan, the second estate tax is saved. And the insurance proceeds are secured from waste, gambling, marital adventurers, and their ilk, and are subject to professional management by the trustee.

Insurance Trust Plus Pour-Over Will

A funded revocable trust containing all of the decedent's other assets can of course serve the same purposes, and the trustee of that trust can be made the beneficiary of the decedent's life insurance. But in many cases testators are not interested in placing all of their non-insurance property into a funded trust during their lifetime, in which case the life insurance trust is typically not funded with anything but a small bank deposit to ensure its legal validity in states so requiring. Its trustee may then be named beneficiary of the trustor's life insurance. In such cases, it is typically accompanied by a simple "pour-over" will, which provides that all the residue of the decedent's estate after any specific bequests are made is to be distributed to the trustee of the already existing life insurance trust. Prior to the advent of the generation skipping tax, there was rarely any need to provide more than one trust for a given decedent's property, and a plan using an insurance trust plus pour-over will would ensure that both the insurance proceeds and all the rest of the decedent's property would be professionally managed within a single trust. This gives the trustee maximum investment leverage.

The insurance trust plus pour-over will plan is very frequently used. It often happens that a client may have a great need for estate planning because his estate might amount to (for example) $700,000, but upon examination, we find that that impressive figure is really comprised of a family home, automobiles and the usual personal possessions, $10,000 in the bank, and $500,000 in group term life insurance provided by the company in which he is a middle-to-upper level executive. The main area of concentration must be on his life insurance, and the life insurance trust accompanied by a pour-over will is the classic estate plan for such a person. And if the protection provided by the continuing jurisdiction of the probate court is desirable for any number of reasons particular to that family, a "reverse pour-over" might be used. In that plan, a testamentary trust is created in the decedent's will in addition to the living life insurance trust, and the latter provides that, after final distribution of the probate estate to the testamentary trust, the life insurance trust should terminate and its assets be "poured over" into the testamentary trust. That way, all assets will be in one trust, which is deliberately subject to the continuing jurisdiction of the probate court.

Sometimes the use of a living life insurance trust is questioned, since it would seem that a regular testamentary trust could be created and the insurance proceeds could go to that trust if the testamentary trustee were named the beneficiary of the insurance policies. In theory that plan ought to work equally as well, although in practice problems sometimes occur. While many insurance companies are now altering their views, for a long time they were strangely unwilling to allow the designation of a testamentary trustee as beneficiary of a policy, and in some states that possibility was prevented by state law. Even in other states, insurance companies felt that a prospective office holder who had not yet been actually put into office was an inappropriate policy beneficiary. Where those problems don't exist under state law, the plan becomes more feasible, although there is still a technical problem as to when trust administration commences. Proceeds of insurance are usually ready to be paid within a few weeks after the insured's death, but a testamentary trust does not commence its economic existence until probate has been completed and the probate assets distributed to the trust. This can create a time gap, often approaching one year or more, during which there is no trustee appointed and no operating trust to manage the insurance proceeds. So the living insurance trust is often a more practical solution.

Funded And Unfunded Insurance Trusts

A living life insurance trust is often spoken of as being either funded or unfunded, and in this context the terms have a slightly different meaning than used before. The focus here is on whether or not there are other assets placed into the trust, the income from which is sufficient to pay the annual premiums on the insurance policies. If there are, the life insurance trust is said to be **funded,** but if there are not, the trust is said to be **unfunded,** with the insured or some other person just continuing to pay the premiums.

Revocability Versus Irrevocability

In the discussion up to this point, we have said nothing about revocability versus irrevocability. All of the above is easily done with a revocable living life insurance trust, and irrevocability is not necessary to achieve any of the objectives so far set forth. The common life insurance trust plus pour-over will plan is most often done by means of a revocable trust. However, life insurance trusts can also be irrevocable, and as always the reason why irrevocability might be used has to do with certain tax consequences that might be available. The discussion about the irrevocable aspects of insurance trusts will be deferred until the next chapter, which is a chapter devoted solely to life insurance. I will there discuss the various tax consequences and plug them into our consideration of life insurance trusts and whether they should be irrevocable or revocable.

Clifford (Ten-Year) Trusts

These trusts, called "Clifford" because he was the first person to successfully use this device, are by definition irrevocable trusts. As with all irrevocable trusts, they change certain tax consequences. They have been made more costly by the 1976 Act, but they are still quite valuable for one particular purpose and only for that purpose. They do nothing to improve the trustor's estate tax or gift tax picture, in fact they make those taxes more costly, but their overriding benefit is as an **income tax saving device.**

Clifford trusts specify that the income from whatever property is put into the trust shall be paid to a beneficiary other than the trustor or his spouse for a period in excess of ten years, and thereafter the property is to revert to the trustor. If properly drafted so as to avoid many traps which can easily trip up the unwary (income can't be accumulated or used for the trustor's benefit or that of his spouse, etc.), the trust income will be taxed to the beneficiary during the ten-year period. If the beneficiary is in a much lower income tax bracket than is the trustor, a large amount of income taxes may be saved each year over the ten-year period, compared with what the trustor would have paid at his own bracket.

Costs Of The Clifford Trust

But there are costs to establishing such a trust. Since the trust must be irrevocable, the transfer of property to it is a transaction subject to gift taxes. Those taxes (really, unitary transfer taxes) are based upon the present value of the right to receive the income from the property over a ten-year period. There are discount tables available to help determine what the value is, but it is usually about 44% of the value of the property put into the trust. Further, if the trustor should die during the ten-year term, the then present value of his **reversionary interest** (defined at page 49) in the trust property will be taxed in his gross estate. And if the trustor dies after the ten-year period has run and the trust property has reverted back to him, then of course all of the property's value will be included in his gross estate.

So not only must the trustor have paid gift taxes when a Clifford trust was created, and must he pay estate taxes as indicated above, but also the 1976 Act means that the value of the gift when made (roughly 44% of the property's then value) must be added back into his taxable estate at death to determine the transfer tax bracket at that time. This makes the Clifford trust more expensive than it was before the 1976 Act. It is apparent that a trustor will have to weigh the total tax costs plus expenses of operating a trust against the income tax savings reasonably to be expected from such a transfer. An illustrative cost analysis for a Clifford trust is shown in Figure 13-2. An additional tax cost to be factored in is that any capital gains made by the trust are normally not income, and so taxes on them will still have to be paid by the trustor. The trust could provide that capital gains are to be considered as in-

	Saving	Cost
FACTS: Property Value		$300,000
Annual Income from Property		$ 30,000
Trustor's Income Tax Bracket		60%
Beneficiary's Income Tax Bracket without trust income		-0-
Beneficiary's Income Tax Bracket with trust income, per income tax tables for joint return with two exemptions		19.8%

Establishing The Trust:

	Saving	Cost
Attorney's fees, assumed		$ 750
Gift taxes on gift of 44% × $300,000 = $132,000; assume Trustor has not used up his transfer tax exemption		-0-
State gift taxes		?
Annual trustee's fee, ¾ of 1% × 10 years		$ 22,500
Less: deductibility at beneficiary's 19.8% bracket		$ (4,455)
		$ 18,045
Increased death taxes by using up $132,000 of exemption, at assumed 34% bracket		$ 44,880
TOTAL COSTS		$ 63,675

Tax Savings:

Trustor's income taxes on $30,000 annually at 60% × 10 years	$180,000	
Beneficiary's income taxes on $30,000 annually per tax table for joint return with two exemptions and deducting trustee's fee: $5184 × 10 years	$ (51,840)	
TOTAL SAVINGS	$128,160	

RESULT: Net Amount Saved is $64,485

Figure 13–2. Illustrative Cost Analysis of a Clifford Trust.

come, but in that case their proceeds will belong irrevocably to the beneficiary, a situation the trustor may not desire; also, such a provision yields further gift tax problems.

Difficulties Of The Clifford Trust

As you may suspect, whenever the law allows significant tax breaks, successfully qualifying for those breaks is a highly technical and tricky matter which requires that such trusts be drafted by experts. One aspect which often foils potential Clifford trustors is that if the income from such a trust is used to satisfy any of the trustor's legal obligations, that income will then be taxed directly to the trustor. This contradicts the sole purpose of having such a trust. A common question in connection with one's legal obligations is when do you cease to be legally obligated to support your children. And further, even if they are over the age of majority as defined by your state's law, do you have the legal obligation to continue their education either through high school or into college? If you do, using a Clifford trust to pay those costs will not operate to gain you any tax advantage.

The answers are matters for the laws of each state, but in many states the laws are confusingly unclear on these points. They are so unclear that there is some growing consideration for drafting a federal tax standard for a parent's legal obligation of support. A few cases across the country have so far mostly held that private school costs even for a minor child are not part of a parent's legal obligation of support for tax purposes. However, your own state's laws must be checked, and the trend of federal tax cases must be checked very closely by your advisors before any such plan is adopted. It does seem clear, though, that a Clifford trust will gain you no tax advantage if you contemplate using it to pay your alimony, child support, or other obligations.

An Example Of A Beneficial Use

The following is an example of a classic case suggesting the use of a Clifford trust: Assume a fifty-five-year-old high salaried corporate executive in a very high income tax bracket who also owns a piece of income-producing property. The income from that property is just being taxed at confiscatory rates due to the executive's high tax bracket, and so he proposes to put the property into a Clifford trust for the benefit of some lower bracket beneficiary whom he is not legally obligated to support (often, a child over the age of majority). This simple situation is ideal, because in ten years our executive may be faced with either mandatory or voluntary retirement, at which time his income and consequent tax bracket will drop dramatically, and at which time he may well need the income produced by the property he had previously put in the trust. So in ten years he gets the property and its income back when he most needs it and avoids high taxation in the interim.

Bank Account "Trusts"

Many people have placed some or all of their funds in a bank account "as trustee for" someone else, perhaps parent for child, or grandparent for grandchild. These are not really trusts, although they have some of the characteristics of a revocable living trust. They are also called Totten trusts, after the first person to successfully use this device, and in other references are sometimes called "poor man's wills." What they really are are specialized banking arrangements allowed by case law or a given state's banking laws. They are allowable in most states.

Let's assume a grandmother opens an account with her own funds, "as trustee for" her grandson. Because such bank accounts are not considered as true trusts, the grandmother has not placed herself in a fiduciary position relative to the funds or to her grandson. Rather, the funds are entirely her own; she may withdraw them at any time or use them entirely for her own benefit without any obligation towards her grandson, and the grandson may normally not withdraw any of the funds while the grandmother is still living. Since the grandmother may withdraw at any time, the transfer is akin to a revocable transfer, and there is no gift tax payable. Further, the funds will be taxable in the grandmother's gross estate. So far the entire arrangement is no different than if it were grandmother's own account with no other trappings. The sole difference to this type of a banking arrangement is that under the banking rules in force almost everywhere, upon the grandmother's death the grandson will be entitled to all the funds then remaining in the account, and no probate will be necessary to transfer those funds to him. That's why they're called poor man's wills, since they essentially just pass bank deposits at death, but have the added benefit of doing so without probate. Since the funds are entirely the grandmother's during her life, all the interest income is of course taxed directly to her (contrary to some people's belief).

In one significant respect, these trustee bank accounts are different from a joint tenancy bank account between the same two people. The latter will also pass the remaining funds to the surviving joint tenant upon the grandmother's death and will do so without the need for probate. But with the usual joint tenancy bank account as established by most banks everywhere, either joint tenant may withdraw all of the funds at any time. Thus, the grandson could go down to the bank the very next day and withdraw all of the grandmother's money, whereas with the trustee bank account he would not be entitled to do so. Most probably, persons desiring these types of accounts would rather have the arrangement where the grandson cannot withdraw all the money. Joint-tenancy bank accounts can be arranged so that the signature of both joint tenants is required for a withdrawal, but most banks will automatically give the customer the type of signature card whereby either joint tenant may withdraw all the funds at any time.

In all states, property inherited by a child younger than that state's age of majority will have to be placed in a **guardianship** until the age of majority is reached. Since children under the age of majority have no legal power to contract and can in most states later ignore any contracts they may have signed while underage, no person or firm in the commercial world will deal with a child. Accordingly, in order that their inheritance may be managed during their minority, and also to preserve it for them until they come of age, a guardianship will be required. This is likewise true for the proceeds of a life insurance policy because insurance companies will not pay the proceeds directly to a minor, but will pay only to a duly constituted guardianship.

Trusts for Minors With No Tax Savings In Mind

Disadvantages Of Guardianships

Guardianships have two serious disadvantages. The first is that they are under the control of the probate court, and that control is typically exercised in a very **rigid** fashion. The courts usually view their primary responsibility to be that of preserving the maximum amount of the inheritance for eventual distribution to the child when he comes of age. As laudable as that may seem, it often leads to problems in using the guardianship funds for the benefit of the minor. On many occasions judges have refused to authorize expenditures from guardianship funds simply because they personally felt that the proposed expenditure was less important than preserving the funds for eventual distribution.

The second disadvantage, and probably the more serious one, is that **a guardianship must terminate when the child comes of age.** In an increasing number of states, the age of majority has been reduced from age twenty-one to age **eighteen.** At the same time, many people believe that children are becoming less and less able to handle finances responsibly at any early age. Most people are appalled at the thought of a guardianship terminating and an eighteen-year-old being handed a check for $25,000 cash, or $50,000 cash, to say nothing of sums considerably greater than that. Many people will request any available solution to prevent that from happening.

Advantages Of Trusts For Minors

There is a solution available, and that is to have such funds go into a trust for the minor child rather than into a guardianship. In such a trust, the trustee may be given considerably more flexible authority to disburse funds for the benefit of the child than would be available in a guardianship, and the trust can extend well beyond the age of majority. The parents can then exercise their parental judgment in determining at what age or series of ages outright distributions ought to be made to their children; perhaps in thirds at twenty-five, thirty, and thirty-five as was discussed in chapter eleven.

Note that this trust is not created primarily for any tax advantages, although some income tax advantages might be obtained by using a discretionary trust (see page 102). Neither is its primary purpose to secure professional management, although that too can be secured as an additional advantage. Its primary purpose is simply to provide flexibile use of the trust funds, to enable outright distributions to be postponed until acceptably mature ages as determined by the parents, and in both those respects to avoid a guardianship. The child, left without parents, will of course need a guardian to serve as a parent substitute and make all the personal parental decisions that a living parent would make, called **guardianship of the person.** The trust under discussion avoids the need for a **guardianship of the child's estate,** and if the parents deem it advisable, the guardian of the person can also serve as trustee of the trust. However, a more professional trustee could just as easily be appointed.

In any estate which is of such size that the tax savings inherent in trusts are desired, parents will probably have engaged in estate planning, and their standard by-pass trust will more than likely contain the types of provisions indicated above for any situation when minor children may become trust beneficiaries. But particular attention is called to those estates which might not otherwise ever consider a trust, due either to their modest size or for any other reason. In such estates, a simple will provision leaving all of a decedent spouse's property to his or her surviving spouse might be perfectly acceptable, but the testator will always be asked what provisions should be made in case his or her spouse dies with him or before him. A typical answer is that in that case "of course" the property should be passed along to the children. But it is that kind of outright distribution to children which falls into the **guardianship trap** mentioned, particularly by naming children contingent beneficiaries of life insurance or by naming them in the testator's will should the testator's spouse have died first or together with him. It is in precisely those instances where a wise estate planner should suggest that instead of the outright contingent distribution, the life insurance or other property should go into a trust for the benefit of the minors. This will most likely raise the cost of the will somewhat, maybe even double it, but that seems a small price to pay for the benefits obtained and the problems, maybe even disasters, avoided. It is a perfectly clear situation where a will might contain a trust or a revocable living trust might be established, even though no tax planning is required and the estate is of moderate size.

Additional Suggestions On Guardians and Trusts For Minors

Another and more subtle advantage can be obtained from such a trust, as compared to a guardianship where this advantage would be impossible. Consider this: the parents of three minor children have both died, and pursuant to their will their children have gone to live with the duly appointed guardian. But that guardian has four children, his family exists on only a moderate income, and they cram their family of six into a three-bedroom home. Suddenly they are thrust into the agreed-upon responsibility of taking three more children into their home, but where to house them? It might not only be appropriate and fair as far as the guardians are concerned, but also mandatory as far as the welfare of the newly orphaned children are concerned, that there either be an immediate remodeling of the guardian's home, or a larger home be purchased. And yet the guardians themselves may be financially unable to undertake either major step. It would seem the better part of fairness and wisdom for the deceased parents to have provided in the trust which they have created to govern their minor children's inheritance that funds may be expended for the necessary remodeling or purchase of a new home, perhaps with appropriate ownership interests on the part of the trust. Such expenditures could never be obtained from a rigidly controlled court guardianship.

Still another, even more subtle point: assume the same situation just described and that the children's trust is creating perhaps $20,000 of annual income, which is more than enough for the support of the children. There are plenty of excess funds available, so the friendly trustee is keeping the children well-clothed, happily supplied with toys and other necessities of childhood, and for the teenagers is able to supply bicycles and even cars. But the guardian is still able to earn only a modest income, and his children are wearing hand-me-downs from their older brothers and sisters and have only a minimal supply of toys and other frivolities, to say nothing of bikes and cars. And yet from a psychological point of view the seven children concerned are living in the same home environment and are really like brothers and sisters. The discrepancy in the advantages available to one set of children versus the jealousies and envies harbored by the other set of children may be creating an extremely poor psychological environment. Had the deceased parents thought about it, or had someone suggested to them the possibility of that situation arising, it is quite likely that they may have wanted to take steps to avoid it. Those steps might be to allow their trustee to spend some portion of the trust's annual income on the guardian's children, in order that they might enjoy some of the same advantages as the beneficiary children. Such spending would not be because the deceased parents particularly wanted to make heirs out of the guardians' children, but rather because they wanted to create the best possible home environment in which their own children would be growing up with new virtual brothers and sisters.

Summary

Here you can see areas where estate planning goes way beyond mere tax consequences, which demonstrate the intensely personal nature which the best estate planning should address. Sympathetic and aware advisors can use their experience to bring up possibilities such as the above, which many of their clients would otherwise not have thought about. An awareness of psychology, family relationships, and the way in which people are affected by the loss of parents, providers, spouses, and other loved ones are even more vital tools for an estate planner than facility with a calculator and the tax tables. In this world of high taxes, the latter is certainly necessary, but above all we are still dealing with special, unique and diverse human beings. Finding a match between a good tax plan and a good people plan is the real talent of the estate planner, and he can be immensely assisted by a knowledgeable and aware client.

So ends our chapter on planning with trusts. There is one other type of trust specifically created for minor beneficiaries, but it is addressed to certain gift tax implications, and I will cover it in a later chapter when I talk about giving gifts to minor children.

APPLICATION

1. Determine whether any of the reasons favoring a revocable living trust apply to you. If they do, consider whether the trust should be funded or unfunded.

2. Is probate avoidance a motive? If so, why? Before deciding, you should perform a cost analysis comparing avoiding probate with establishing a funded revocable trust, much like what was

illustrated in Figure 13-1. Consider whether there are any income tax or other advantages to probate which are worth anything to you.

3. If you are inclined towards a funded revocable living trust, try to determine the degree of nuisance such a trust would create in the way you manage your property and live your life. Inquire of stock brokers, title or escrow companies, and bankers as to their requirements for dealing with property owned by such a trust. Try to decide whether the nuisance (if any) is worth the accurate cost savings computed under the cost analysis referred to in item 2.

4. Do you have more annual income than you can use, or are you willing to sacrifice some of it in order to lower your income tax brackets? If so, are there beneficiaries available whom you would *both* like to have some of your income *and* who are in substantially lower income tax brackets than you are? If so, you might want to consider establishing an irrevocable trust to direct some income to that beneficiary. Your choices are an irrevocable trust to last the rest of your life, or a Clifford trust to last more than ten years. But consider:
   a. you should perform a simple cost analysis, much like Figure 13-2.
   b. you should consider very honestly whether you can genuinely afford to give up the potential trust property and the income it produces, either permanently or for ten years. You would be well-advised to consider the absolute worst, both in your personal life as well as in the nation's economy, in deciding whether you can afford to part with the property.

5. Determine whether your life insurance program falls into any of the three traps listed on page 263. If it does, consider avoiding those traps by establishing a life insurance trust and naming the trustee as beneficiary of your policies. With "pour over wills" (see page 265), a life insurance trust might well be your basic estate planning document, as it is for many people.

6. If you have a joint-tenancy bank account with another person, particularly a minor child or someone you wouldn't want able to withdraw all the money at any time, consider using an "in trust for" account instead of the joint tenancy account.

7. If your situation is one where no trust is indicated for tax savings reasons, but your beneficiary (either primary or contingent) is a minor child or other as yet financially immature person, consider leaving your bequest to that person in trust instead of outright.

8. If you have appointed guardians for your minor children, consider whether both fairness and the welfare of your children might not indicate that you should provide some benefits to the guardian or to members of his family.

14

life insurance: the unique estate planning asset

Glossary For This Chapter

Buy-Sell Agreement
Incidents of Ownership
Insured
Owner (of Insurance)
Review:
Funded Trust
Pour Over Will
303 Redemption
Unfunded Trust

If you don't have insurance and don't contemplate having any, don't skip this chapter. Maybe you should consider obtaining some, for the reasons I'll cover in this chapter.

In chapter eight I discussed the basis on which life insurance is taxed in a decedent's gross estate; see page 147. In the last chapter I covered the payment of insurance proceeds to a revocable living trust in order to avoid the several traps mentioned there. In this chapter I want to gather together a lot of other information about life insurance, including its purposes, why it is unique, and how we can plan with it.

Purpose: Estate Building

There are of course hundreds of varying purposes for life insurance, but as a huge generality I might say that in terms of its place within an estate plan, it has two basic purposes. The first of these is often called **estate building,** in that it is a way to provide a certain amount of funds to one's beneficiary if those funds are not otherwise available. For instance, a young married man with a small

277

baby may recognize that in this inflationary world, if he were to meet a premature death, it would take a fund of at least $150,000 to provide enough income for his surviving wife and growing child. Yet his assets consist of a lease on an apartment, a seven-year-old car, a decent job, and about $1000 in the bank. The only possible way for him to provide the $150,000 fund would be to purchase a $150,000 life insurance policy on his life. Although such an individual does not usually think that he is a candidate for estate planning, from what we've seen in the previous chapter it certainly seems that his survivors would be far better off were he to establish a living life insurance trust and name the trustee beneficiary of his policy. A guardianship would be avoided if he and his wife died in a common accident, and even if they did not, professional management of the fund could be secured if his wife were inexperienced in managing such a fund.

Purpose: The Liquidity Crisis

The other purpose of life insurance often arises in a completely opposite net worth picture and might apply to the same person many years later, after he has achieved greater success. Let's assume that the same man just referred to had years later managed to save enough from his earnings to build up the targeted fund of $150,000, at which time in an all too typical move he cancelled his insurance to save premium expenses. Now he comes in for estate planning and has a good-sized estate reflecting his judgment that real estate investments are the thing to have. Perhaps he is worth $900,000, which consists of equities in various parcels of real estate, his family home, miscellaneous personal effects, and an average amount of cash in the bank of about $15,000. Ignoring deductions and adjustments just for purposes of illustration, it can be demonstrated that even with the best estate planning, there will be a federal estate tax upon his death of $91,800. To that amount must be added his state's death duties and any probate expenses for a total of approximately $10,000. I can also inform him that upon the death of his wife, the tax bite will be about the same. So we are looking at around $200,000 in cash needs for both estates, and yet his estate does not have that amount of cash.

This is commonly known as the **liquidity crisis;** you can't pay taxes with land, only with cash. In the above situation, either some properties will have to be sold, perhaps at distress prices at a very bad moment for real estate sales, or else a refinancing may have to occur, perhaps at a very bad moment considering the interest rates at that time. And anything which must be sold or mortgaged will serve to reduce the annual income available for the security of the client's survivors, as well as incur capital gain taxes after the carryover basis provisions come into effect. It sure is too bad he cancelled that $150,000 life insurance policy. An example showing how to compute liquidity needs is given in Figure 14-1.

It is very common in a situation such as the foregoing for an estate planner to recommend the purchase of life insurance to cover the liquidity needs. Note several things. I have computed liquidity needs of around $100,000 at the death of each spouse, assuming the husband dies first in a common law state, or upon the death of either spouse in a community property state. Would I therefore recommend a $200,000 policy on the husband's life? Not necessarily, because if that is all I do and the wife happens to die

FACTS: Total Marital Estate = $800,000
      Husband's Will Provides:
         1. His business, worth $200,000 and in which he has $100,000 invested, is to be sold since his wife should not operate it, and should have the cash.
         2. Under Example B. below, he leaves everything to his wife.
         3. Under Example C. below, he leaves a marital deduction formula amount to a marital deduction trust for his wife, and the residue is left to a standard by-pass trust for his wife.

EXAMPLE A.: HUSBAND DIES FIRST

Total Marital Property	$ 800,000
Less: Maximum marital deduction amount, OR if this is community property, her half of the community property	(400,000)
	400,000
Deductions for expenses of administration, and debts (assumed)	(25,000)
	375,000
"Exemption"	(175,000)
Taxable	200,000
Tax, from Table 7-1, page 119, less credit	66,300
Less: State Death Tax Credit from Table 9-1. page 162	(9,840)
	$ 56,460
Husband's liquidity needs:	
Federal estate tax	$ 56,460
State death tax (assumed)	9,500
Expenses of administration, and debts (assumed)	25,000
TOTAL	$113,550

Figure 14–1. Computation of Liquidity Needs of Each Spouse Under Varying Conditions.

EXAMPLE B.: WIFE DIES SECOND, OWNS EVERYTHING UNDER FACT SITUATION 2.

Total Estate (total marital estate less cash expended at husband's death)	$ 686,450
Marital Deduction	-0-
Deductions for expenses of administration, and debts (assumed)	(35,000)
	651,450
"Exemption"	(175,000)
Taxable	476,450
Tax, from Table 7-1, page 119, less credit	164,836
Less: State Death Tax Credit from Table 9-1, page 162	(21,430)
	$ 143,406

Wife's liquidity needs:

Federal estate tax	$143,406
State death tax ("pick-up tax", defined at page 000)	21,430
Expenses of administration, and debts (assumed)	35,000
TOTAL	$199,836

EXAMPLE C.: WIFE DIES SECOND, OWNS PURSUANT TO FACT SITUATION 3.

Total Estate:	
Property owned under marital deduction trust	$ 400,000
Property owned under by-pass trust	-0-
Deductions for expenses of administration, and debts (assumed)	-0-
	400,000
"Exemption"	(175,000)
Taxable	225,000
Tax, from Table 7-1, page 119, less credit	74,800
Less: State Death Tax Credit from Table 9-1, page 162	(10,800)
	$ 64,000

Wife's liquidity needs:

Federal estate tax	$ 64,000
State death tax (pick-up tax)	10,800
Expenses of administration, and debts (assumed)	-0-
TOTAL	$ 74,800

Figure 14–1. *Continued*

EXAMPLE D.: WIFE IN COMMON LAW STATE DIES FIRST, OWNING NOTHING

Wife's Estate: $-0-
Taxes $-0-
Expenses $-0-

At Husband's later death:

Total Estate	$ 800,000
Marital Deduction	-0-
Deductions for expenses of administration, and debts (assumed)	(40,000)
	760,000
"Exemption"	(175,000)
Taxable	585,000
Tax, from Table 7-1, page 119, less credit	252,200
Less: State Death Tax Credit from Table 9-1. page 162	(26,640)
	$ 225,560

Husband's liquidity needs:

Federal estate tax	$225,560	
State death tax (pick-up tax)	26,640	
Expenses of administration, and debts (assumed)	40,000	
TOTAL	$292,200	

Messages Contained in This Illustration:
1. Liquidity needs must be computed for both the husband and the wife.
2. It makes a great deal of difference whether the spouses have engaged in estate planning (Example C.) or have failed to do so (Example B.)
3. It is a serious mistake to ignore the very real possibility that the wife may die first.
    a. In a Community Property state, her liquidity needs will be exactly the same as her husband's if he had died first (Example A.)
    b. In a Common Law state where the wife under state law owns no property at all, if she is the first to die it may be the costliest situation of all (Example D.). If the spouses can afford it, it may be very wise to insure against that risk.
        1.) Suggestions to relieve the high cost should the wife in the Common Law state die first can be found in the next chapter at pages 313–14.

Figure 14–1. *Continued*

first (a very significant probability which people too often forget), then in a community property estate I have failed to cover any liquidity needs at her death, and the husband may be forced into a disadvantageous sale or refinancing. In a common law state where the husband owns all the property, the wife's prior death completely eliminates the tax savings which the marital deduction would have made possible if she had survived him. Since she hadn't, the estate tax bite at his death when he owns 100% of the property with no marital deduction available will be $200,000 plus state death duties and probate costs. So the liquidity needs have not been fully covered in that circumstance. Further, even if she had survived him, and the liquidity needs were $100,000 per estate, it might save premium expense had a $100,000 policy been bought on the husband and a similar one on the wife. Rates for females are usually lower, and often enough a wife will be younger than her husband, thus dropping the premiums still lower.

Therefore, if purchasing insurance to cover the liquidity needs makes sense, don't forget to consider insurance on the wife as well as on the husband. This is particularly true in community property states because each spouse has the exact same needs as far as their interest in their community property goes. It is a very common mistake to only insure the husband.

Carryover Basis Means More Cash Will Be Needed

The potential liquidity needs of a given estate will be greatly increased by the carryover basis provisions effective January 1, 1980 (discussed in chapter 10, page 173). If any estate asset must be sold in order to cover the liquidity needs or to facilitate distribution among the various heirs (by distributing cash instead of percentage interests in property), such a sale after January 1, 1980 will require the estate to pay capital gains taxes. Under the former stepped-up basis provisions, such a sale could be made for little or no capital gains taxes since a sale at date of death value would show no gain. But with carryover basis, as to any asset acquired by the decedent after December 31, 1976, there will be a full capital gain in the amount of the sale price over the decedent's pre-death basis. And as to any asset owned by the decedent on December 31, 1976, capital gains tax will have to be paid based on the sale price over the decedent's pre-death basis as adjusted upwards by the fresh start adjustment (discussed at page 176). As the years roll by, and we get farther away from December 31, 1976, more and more of the sale price will become taxable as capital gain. And in addition to sales for the purposes mentioned, using flower bonds (defined at page 164) to pay estate taxes, and using a §303 redemption of closely held corporate stock (defined at page 167) to cover the cash liquidity needs of an estate, will both carry with them the need to pay some capital gains tax under carryover basis.

It is certainly not necessary for an estate owner to be concerned about the added liquidity needs caused by carryover basis; that is purely a matter of his own personal choice. But if he is concerned, and if he wants to place his estate and its heirs in the same position they would have been in prior to carryover basis, he will want to make allowances for the capital gains taxes which the new law brings on. One way to do that would be to increase his insurance coverage so that it covers not only death duties and probate expenses, but also the capital gains taxes inherent in the situation faced by his particular estate. Thus, carryover basis may suggest more insurance coverage for an estate owner, not less.

Insurance May Provide Cheap Dollars

Life insurance represents a way to pay death taxes and other costs with cheap dollars. The basis of how insurance is priced will show that the policy will never (well, hardly ever) cost in premiums as much as will be paid out in proceeds. Of course, the final result depends upon exactly how long the insured lives, but even if he lives well beyond his life expectancy most policies are so priced that he will still not have paid one hundred percent of the proceeds amount in total premiums over the years. If the husband in our previous example purchased a $200,000 insurance policy on his life which cost $5000 in annual premiums, and if he had died after having made only the first premium payment, he will have paid only $5000 to acquire $200,000, not a bad deal. If he had lived twenty years, he would have paid $100,000 to acquire $200,000, still not a bad deal. (Although he might have been able to invest the $100,000 himself and receive a return greater than the $200,000 proceeds. But that's guesswork and is awfully hard to plan with.)

Further, there are many ways to reduce either the cost of a policy or the net outlay required to purchase it. For instance, if the $200,000 policy had been purchased from a company that pays annual dividends, most probably the twenty-year cash outlay would be a great deal less than $100,000. The actual net costs that any particular policy will imply can be demonstrated by a sophisticated advisor. The only point I wish to note is that insurance can cover the liquidity needs and can often do so with much cheaper dollars than can almost any other asset.

As you are certainly aware, there are scores of different types of life insurance. Descriptions of and recommendations about those different types can easily be the subject of an entire book and that is not my purpose here. Further, I am not an insurance underwriter and believe very strongly that no professional should tread into areas where he is not expert, so I commit you to the care of your own chosen insurance experts. You probably know about the difference between term insurance, the so-called "pure insurance protection," and permanent (or "whole life") insurance, which has savings and cash value elements to it. But there are an amazing array of variations on those two themes.

But doesn't insurance just add to the problem, by increasing the amount of the gross estate and therefore the estate taxes? Not necessarily, because steps can be taken to ensure that the insurance proceeds are not added into the taxable estate. That is a great deal of what this chapter is about, so read on.

Removing Insurance Proceeds from the Gross Estate

You know from chapter eight that insurance proceeds will be taxable in the decedent's gross estate if the decedent was both the insured and the owner of the policy. If the decedent was just the owner but not the insured, and he died before the insured, then the cash surrender value (if any) will be included in the decedent's gross estate. And if the decedent was the insured but not the owner, then nothing will be included in the decedent's gross estate. See Figure 8-1, page 149.

The Owner Must Not Be The Insured

That suggests a very simple step to make sure that the insurance proceeds will not be taxed in the gross estate of the insured; namely, **be sure that he is not the owner.** That can be accomplished in one of two ways. If the insurance is not yet in force and one seeks estate planning advice before its purchase, the non-insured who will be the owner can simply be the **applicant** for the policy (so long as he has an "insurable interest") and consequently the insured will never have had any of the incidents of ownership (defined at page 146). If the insured is already the owner of the policy, probably because he was the initial applicant, then all he need to do is **transfer the incidents of ownership** to another person. As with all things designed to avoid estate taxes, that transfer must be done irrevocably; otherwise, the transfer will not have the desired tax effect. Every insurance company has a particular form to accomplish that transfer, usually called an irrevocable assignment of ownership. The form must be executed by the current owner, sent to the company's home office, and when registered there, the transfer is complete. The transfer should be evidenced by an endorsement form issued by the company, which should then be attached to the policy itself.

Who New Owner Should Be

The transfer can be made either irrevocably to an individual, or to an irrevocable life insurance trust (which trust must be irrevocable in order for the transfer to have the desired tax effect). I will discuss those irrevocable trusts in a moment, but it is obvious that only irrevocable trusts, and not revocable ones, can achieve the tax result described. As for an irrevocable transfer to an individual, it is usually best to make that transfer **to the beneficiary,** either the spouse if she is the beneficiary or to whatever other person is the beneficiary. Since one of the incidents of ownership the new owner will then possess is the right to change the beneficiary. If the current beneficiary does so, at least he will have an assumedly good reason. A non-beneficiary owner could simply change the beneficiary to himself, which is probably not what the insured had in mind!

Another reason why the new owner ought to be the beneficiary can be illustrated by the following: assume father is the owner/insured of a policy on which his son had been named as beneficiary, and father irrevocably transfers the incidents of ownership to his wife. During all the remaining years of father's life, his wife could have changed the beneficiary to herself. But assume she hadn't, and upon the father's death the insurance company duly forwards a check for the proceeds (assume $100,000) to the son as beneficiary. At that moment, the mother will be considered to have made a **taxable gift** to her son in the amount of $100,000 (only $50,000 in community property states, if the policy had been community property). This arises because as owner she could have changed the beneficiary to herself, but by not doing so she has allowed the proceeds to pass to her son. That is a very sneaky gift, and a costly trap for the unwary.

Under the property laws of most states, that gift could have been avoided by a very simple step if the parties had only known that they should take it. The wife could either have joined with her husband in an initial irrevocable written designation of the son as beneficiary (probably only community property spouses would ever think of that), or else she could have irrevocably designated the son as beneficiary during her ownership but before her husband's death. The latter is usually not considered to be a gift to the son in the amount of $100,000 because no such funds then existed, so it is at worst a gift of a valueless thing on which no gift taxes are payable. However, it would be important to check the law of your own state to see whether the no gift tax generality applies under your particular law.

Problems With An Irrevocable Transfer of Ownership

As with any irrevocable gift, a decision to irrevocably transfer the incidents of ownership in a life insurance policy should only be made after thorough consideration of any negatives. A great many such gifts of life insurance are made between spouses, so that the non-insured spouse winds up with the incidents of ownership. That's great for tax reasons, but what if ten or twenty years later the spouses get divorced? The full ownership rights in the policy now belong to the ex-spouse, who may cash in the policy or allow it to lapse out of pure spite or for any other reason. Divorce is such a frequent occurrence these days that any thinking person is engaging in pure denial if he ignores that possibility, no matter how happily married he may now be. With irrevocable trusts, the trustors get only one chance to draft them, and accordingly a wise draftsman often shocks his happily married clients by correctly advising them that they ought to insert a clause concerning their wishes in the event of a divorce.

Another possible negative to an irrevocable insurance transfer might concern the future tendencies of the new owner. Many such transfers are made to the insured's children, often when they are still minors. Upon reaching legal majority, they may be going through the normal rebellion process during which they often temporarily put some distance between themselves and their parents. Or, a permanent rift or even some character deficiency can surface. At that point the owner can frustrate all of the insured's insurance plans by cashing in the policy in order to invest in a marijuana farm or to test out a sure-fire system for beating the roulette wheel. So before making any irrevocable gift of insurance, the insured ought to be able to convince himself that the new owner will always keep the policy in force or will not use the value of the policy to pursue frivolous whims.

If the insured can so satisfy himself, along with the various tax advantages a gift of life insurance is ideal in that it does not strip the donor of cash or other investments on which he may be relying for income and security. He is really only transferring a piece of paper, a future right that won't arise until after his death.

Gift Tax Consequences

Since the transfer of the incidents of ownership must be irrevocable, it is of course **subject to gift taxes.** The amount of the transfer on which the gift taxes are computed is not the full amount of the proceeds, but rather only the **cash surrender value,** if any, (technically, something a bit different, but don't worry about the small difference that makes). Permanent insurance usually carries some cash surrender value, although term insurance usually carries none at all. Also, a permanent insurance policy which has been **borrowed against** to the hilt will have little or no cash surrender value, so like term insurance there will be no gift tax payable on this gift of no value. Even as to permanent insurance with a cash value, the insured/owner is eliminating from his gross estate the potential tax on the full amount of the proceeds (for example, $100,000) at the cost of paying a gift tax on the much smaller figure represented by the cash surrender value (for example, perhaps four or five thousand dollars).

Along with its ability to meet liquidity needs with cheaper dollars, it is this factor which makes life insurance such a unique estate planning asset. After the 1976 Act, it is no longer possible to get most assets out of one's gross estate at all because they are added back in at death to figure the estate tax bracket. Only with life insurance can we remove a currently certain estate tax on (for example) $100,000 for either no gift tax cost (term insurance or borrowed-against permanent insurance) or minimal gift tax cost (gift tax on only the cash surrender value). Where else can you remove the estate tax on $100,000 at the price of reducing your exemption by, or paying a gift tax on, perhaps four or five thousand dollars of value transferred? With any other asset, you'd have to incur gift taxes based on $100,000 in order to remove the estate tax on property currently valued at $100,000. And then the $100,000 would just be added back in to figure the estate tax bracket. With life insurance there is also an "add back," but due to the nature of insurance the add back is its value at the date of the gift. In the examples I've been using, this is either zero, or perhaps four or five thousand dollars. It's a tremendous mathematical bargain, unavailable for any other type of asset.

If a community property husband makes a gift of a community property policy to his wife, he is making a gift of only one-half of the current value of the policy (cash surrender value, if any). If a common law husband does the same, he can obtain the benefit of the gift tax marital deduction (see page 122) so that he too is only making a gift of one-half the policy's then value. And remember that one spouse can now give the other up to $100,000 without incurring any gift tax under the expanded gift tax marital deduction.

Further, all or a portion of any tax may be cancelled out by the $3000 annual exclusion from gift tax. In common law states, the spouses can split their gifts, so that if the incidents of ownership are being transferred to someone other than the non-insured spouse, $6000 in value may be transferred by using the gift-splitting provisions. For community property spouses, the spouse who is the insured under a community property policy will only be transferring his one-half ownership interest in any case, so gift splitting is inapplicable. (A life insurance policy will take on community property characteristics if the premiums had been paid with community property funds.) The only kicker in the use of the $3000 annual exclusion is the future interest rule (see page 124); recall that one can only qualify for the exclusion by making gifts of a present interest and not gifts of a future interest. It is clear that if the new owner has full ownership rights, particularly including the right to cash in the policy and personally receive the cash surrender value, then the irrevocable transfer to him will be a gift of a present interest which will qualify for the exclusion.

Transfers Within Three Years of Death

The insured/owner who had irrevocably transferred the incidents of ownership might die within three years of the transfer. Gifts of insurance are no different from any other type of gift for these purposes, and so the entire amount of the policy proceeds would be thrown back into his taxable estate just as if he had never made the transfer. That is just a fact of life, and there is no getting around it. This possibility probably ought not to deter someone who would otherwise find it advantageous to transfer the incidents of ownership. If the transfer had no value because the transferred policy was a term policy or a permanent one borrowed on to the hilt, then the insured is still no worse off than if he had never attempted the transfer. But if there was a gift tax cost to the transfer because the policy was a permanent one with a cash surrender value, then that gift tax value will increase the estate for purposes of figuring the estate tax bracket. Since that gift tax value is likely to be so small in relation to the proceeds which can be removed from the gross estate if the insured had lived three years, it is a very good gamble and a very small price to pay for the opportunity to achieve significant savings.

Under the provisions of the 1976 Act, any gift on which a gift tax return was not required (i.e., gifts during the calendar year which did not total more than $3000 to any one person) will not be taxed in the gross estate even if the donor happened to die within three years after the gift. However, the benefits of the $3000 exclusion concerning gifts made within three years of death do not apply to gifts of life insurance. This means that the entire amount of insurance proceeds must be included in the gross estate if the insured/transferer died within three years of the gift. This is true even though the value of the gift when it was made was under $3000.

Irrevocable Life Insurance Trusts

Rather than irrevocably transferring the incidents of ownership to an individual person who might cash in the policy or change its beneficiary against the wishes of the insured, and where gift tax problems are likely if the new owner is not the beneficiary, an **irrevocable trust** might be created to be the new owner. Should that be the desired plan, the irrevocable assignment of ownership will simply be made out by the current owner to the trustee of an identified trust. It is necessary under the tax laws that the insured not be a trustee of that trust, and in almost all cases, his spouse should also not be the trustee, for otherwise the workings of the tax law will defeat the tax purpose of this plan. But assuming the trust is drafted with careful attention to many tax rules, the trust will have all of the incidents of ownership in the policy, and when the insured dies, the proceeds will be excluded from his taxable estate. As with most living trusts, the document will also contain all of the trustor's wishes for the post-mortem administration of his property, so that this trust can serve as the central estate planning document. By the use of a pour-over will, all the decedent's other assets can at the conclusion of his probate estate be distributed to the already existing life insurance trust which now contains the insurance proceeds, and the entire family assets will thereby be managed under one roof for maximum investment leverage.

Or, the trust could be a **funded irrevocable life insurance trust,** whereby some or all of the trustor's other property can be transferred to the trust during the trustor's lifetime, in which case those assets will avoid probate along with qualifying for all the other administrative benefits the trust implies. When speaking of life insurance trusts, the word "funded" means that there is enough other income-producing property in the trust so that its income will be sufficient to cover the annual premiums on the life insurance. In an unfunded revocable or irrevocable life insurance trust, the premiums will have to be paid by some other means.

Transferring the incidents of ownership to an irrevocable life insurance trust of course yields gift taxes. The workings of the gift tax in that event have been previously explained, but one additional hitch when using an irrevocable trust concerns whether or not any part of the gift can qualify for the $3000 annual gift tax exclusion. As you will recall, gifts of a future interest cannot so qualify (see page 124). A gift to a trust is considered to be a gift to its various beneficiaries, and by the very nature of a trust, their interest is usually postponed until some future time. So in most instances the $3000 annual exclusion will not be available for the transfer of an insurance policy to an irrevocable trust.

It may well be the trustor's intention to cover his liquidity needs with life insurance and at the same time keep the proceeds out of his taxable estate by means of an irrevocable life insurance trust. In such a case, the trust document must be carefully written concerning how it deals with the trustor's deathtime liquidity needs. The tax law provides that if the trustee must pay the decedent's taxes and expenses out of the proceeds, then the proceeds will nevertheless be included in his gross estate. To get around that fatal result, the trust can not require that the trustee make those payments, but it may permissively allow him to lend the insurance proceeds to the executor or purchase estate assets from the executor. In that way the liquid funds will be made available to the person who is responsible for paying the taxes and expenses, but in a manner that will not of itself cause the proceeds to be taxed in the decedent's gross estate. You may see a clause allowing such borrowings or purchases in a life insurance trust, and that is its significance.

Paying Premiums on Transferred Policies

The major problem with transferred policies concerns the fact that the new owner may neither have the funds necessary to pay premiums on the transferred policy nor, even if he has adequate funds, may he be willing to pay those premiums out of his own funds. The natural reaction of all concerned is to suggest that the insured just keep right on paying the premiums, either directly to the insurance company or by giving the necessary funds to the new owner.

The Three-Year-Contemplation-Of Death Rule

That raises all kinds of problems, which might be solved by very careful planning but which can be a real trap. The problem centers on the application of the three-year-contemplation-of-death rule, and the effect of the fact that the insured had paid the last three premiums prior to his death. The complexities are great enough that it is always preferable to have the new owner pay the premiums, if that is at all possible. The complexities are also so numerous that only a basic few will be mentioned here.

It is now established that premium payments by the insured in the last three years of his life on most term policies and probably all "whole life" policies will not automatically cause a proportionate part of the proceeds to be taxed in his estate as a "transfer" within three years of death. Even so, what about the actual dollars used to pay those premiums in the last three years of the insured's life; must they be taxed in his estate under the three-year rule? And if those payments are less than $3000 per year, will they escape estate tax since the 1976 Act excludes under-$3000 gifts from the workings of the automatic three-year rule? There seems to be a difference between the insured paying the premiums directly to the insurance company versus his giving the requisite cash to the owner and having the owner pay the premiums directly.

When The Insured Pays The Premiums

Where the insured pays the premiums himself during the last three years of his life, it seems rather inevitable that those dollars will be taxable in his estate under the automatic three-year rule. The insured makes a gift to the owner by doing so, and that is clearly a "transfer" within three years of death. Even if the premiums are less than $3000 annually, transfers "with respect to life insurance" do not qualify for the $3000 annual exclusion. Therefore premium payments even under $3000 cannot escape the automatic three-year rule taxing them in the estate. This would be true no matter who the policy owner is, whether an individual or an irrevocable life insurance trust.

When The Owner Pays The Premiums

But gifts of cash directly to the policy's owner (which the owner would then use to pay the premiums) would seem to qualify for the $3000 exclusion so long as they are gifts of a present interest (and are under $3000 annually). If their status as simple cash gifts can be supported, they would not be taxable under the automatic three-year rule. But the IRS has another trick up its sleeve, which is a possible argument that those cash gifts were just disguised and indirect payments of the premiums, an argument and inquiry allowed by several court cases. If the IRS can prove that argument, then the gifts are "transfers with respect to life insurance" which do not qualify for the $3000 annual exclusion and therefore do not escape taxation in the insured's estate under the automatic three-year rule. The possibility of the IRS raising that inquiry certainly suggests that the insured give amounts of cash unrelated to the exact amount of the premiums, and that he make those gifts at times unrelated to the premium due dates, such as birthdays and at Christmas.

The benefits of the $3000 annual exclusion, both to save gift taxes and to escape estate taxation under the automatic three-year rule, only apply if the cash gifts are gifts of a present interest. If they are made directly to an individual who is the owner of the insurance policy, they seem clearly to be gifts of a present interest. But if they are made to the trustee of an irrevocable life insurance trust, there is a real problem. A trust by its very nature usually implies the postponement of full economic enjoyment until some time in the future, and so gifts to a trust are almost always gifts of a future interest. That can present a real impediment to the use of an irrevocable life insurance trust, at least an unfunded one, because the trustor may be faced with gift tax consequences every year when he supplies the cash needed to make the premium payments. But recently a clever attorney drafted a trust and won an appellate court decision permitting the use of a provision which may save the day in this regard. The trust provided that when the trustor made additions to the trust (which an insured would do every year in the amount of cash necessary to pay premiums), the beneficiary was to be given written notice thereof and was to have ninety days within which to exercise a right to withdraw those additions. Obviously, the beneficiary was coached not to exercise that right of withdrawal since the additions were meant to pay premiums, but the mere fact that the beneficiary had such a right forces the inescapable conclusion that he has a present interest in those additions. So the appelate court authorized the use of the $3000 annual exclusion, and such rights of withdrawal are now being widely used in irrevocable life insurance trusts so that the insured will not face gift tax consequences every year when he gives the trustee enough cash to pay premiums. For the reasons indicated earlier in this section, giving the cash directly to the trustee seems far preferable to having the insured pay the premiums directly to the insurance company. This all indicates how complex is the matter of premium payments on transferred or non-owned policies, and how carefully the situation must be watched.

A Remaining Problem Area

There remains one significant area where the IRS is still contending that payment of premiums by the insured within the last three years of his life can cause inclusion of the proceeds in his gross estate under the automatic three-year rule. That concerns certain one-year-term policies as well as certain accidental death policies usually written on a one-year-term basis (such as flight insurance) where someone other than the insured has been irrevocably designated as policy owner. The IRS argument is that when the decedent made the final year's premium payment in the year before his death, he kept such a one-year basis policy in force; without that last premium payment, the policy would have lapsed and the beneficiary would have received nothing. Their contention is that this is a "transfer" of the entire amount of the proceeds within the meaning of the automatic three-year rule. Unless a series of court decisions reverses that position, taxpayers will continue to encounter problems in that area, at least where the policy had been first issued within three years of the insured's death. Where it had been issued more than three years before his death, there is considerably more hope that the proceeds will escape taxation in his gross estate even if he did pay the final premium himself.

Special Community Property Problems

Many life insurance advisors suggest that the incidents of ownership in a policy be initially applied for by, or should be irrevocably transferred to, the spouse of the insured. For reasons already mentioned, this is particularly appropriate when that spouse is the beneficiary of the policy on the insured's life. In a common law state there are few unusual complications to that arrangement, but the same is not true in community property states. In many ways, estate planning in community property states is easier than in common law states because correctly qualifying for the marital deduction often has little or no significance. But life insurance is one area in which proper planning is badly complicated by the normal rules of community property ownership, a fact that is unfortunately not recognized by many life insurance sellers even within the community property states. Further, the differences in the laws among the eight community property states cause different consequences in each of those states, and so local advice is a must. But a few general remarks about the community property complications are definitely in order.

Life Insurance As Community Property

Life insurance can be community property just the same as any other asset. It takes on a community property characteristic under all the same rules covered in chapter two. Essentially, to the extent that the policy is purchased with community property funds, it is a community property policy. That of course means that community property money was used to pay the premiums. Once it has acquired a community property characteristic, in whole or in part, the spouses have normal one-half ownership rights to it. Thus, any gift of it will of necessity be a gift made one-half by each spouse. If the insured spouse is also the owner and he or she dies, then one-half of the proceeds will be included in his or her gross estate. If the non-insured spouse is the owner and he or she dies, then one-half the then value of the policy (if any) will be included in his or her gross estate.

The Non-Insured Spouse As Policy Owner

Many insurance companies train their underwriters to recommend that the non-insured spouse be the owner of a policy of life insurance on the life of the insured spouse. Many such companies also use elaborately programmed computers to make planning recommendations. Since 42 of the states are not community property states, and few major life insurance companies are based in the community property states, it is only natural that many of them do not give full recognition to all the peculiarities of community property law, particularly as it relates to insurance. Thus, they very often recommend that the insured spouse transfer the incidents of ownership (defined at page 146) to the non-insured spouse, and let it go at that.

But if the incidents of ownership in a community property policy are transferred from the ownership of a community property husband to a community property wife, and that's all that's done, what has been accomplished? Nothing at all. It is still a community property policy, now in the name of the wife as owner instead of the husband as owner, but that hasn't changed any of the former consequences of community property ownership since the spouses still continue to own exactly one-half of everything which is in fact community property. Estate planners in the community property states see a lot of such wife owned policies where the spouses have been told, and believe, that upon the insured husband's death no portion of the proceeds will be included in his gross estate. But not enough has been done to assure the desired result.

Assume the husband is the insured; for no part of the proceeds to be included in his gross estate he must have no portion of the incidents of ownership. If the policy is transferred to his wife, it must be done in such a manner than the policy is no longer community property. That necessarily means that it must be her separate property. How properly to ensure that result? First, the policy must state, by endorsement or on its face, that it is owned by her "as her sole and separate property." Second, to be totally safe in this very confusing area, since community property spouses can agree as to the status of any of their property they should enter into a short agreement stating that the policy is the wife's separate property and that the husband disclaims any community property interest in it. And third and most important, the future premiums must be paid by the wife out of her separate property. Putting the policy in her name as her separate property is just a presumptive indication of the true facts. In most states the nature of the funds used to purchase the property determines whether it is truly separate or community property. It can be in her name as separate property, but if all premiums have been paid with community property then each payment just reinforces the fact that it is genuinely community property.

This is all well and good if the wife has some separate property out of which she is willing and able to make the premium payments, but what if she has no such property? Then it must be created for her. This can be done in one of two ways. The first and most obvious is by gift from her husband, usually by creating a separate property bank account for her and depositing the premium amounts in that account every year; it would further be a good idea to back that up with another clause in their written agreement, stating that any such funds are intended to be gifts by the husband to her and thereafter are agreed to be her own separate property. A relatively minor flaw in this arrangement is that all such gifts in the final three years of the husband's life will of course be included in his gross estate under the automatic three-year rule if the IRS can successfully establish that they were disguised premium payments. That will turn them into "transfers with respect to life insurance," and will include them in the husband's estate because such transfers even if less than $3000 do not escape the "contemplation of death rule." Since there is a written agreement saying that the whole thing has to do with life insurance, the IRS's ability to make that argument stick is improved.

That causes some estate planners in community property states to recommend that a different method be used to create separate property for the wife who otherwise doesn't have any. Since the spouses equally own the community property, most states acknowledge that their interests can be split up into their two equal separate property components. This suggests that if the premiums are $2000 per year, a total sum of $4000 be withdrawn from the community funds, split in two, and $2000 be deposited into two separate property bank accounts, one in the name of the wife and one in the name of the husband, each as their sole and separate property. The wife then spends hers on the premiums, and the husband will be encouraged to spend his on the family vacation or any other community expenditure, since less favorable estate planning results occur if the husband's account keeps growing every year until he has a substantial separate property estate.

Get Local Advice

The very first chapter warned that nothing in this book should be taken as any form of advice, and that warning bears repeating here. The laws of each of the community property states are different enough that local advice on matters such as just discussed is an absolute must. For instance, some of the states (i.e., Texas) say that earnings on separate property are community property, so that any dividends on a policy put in the wife's name supposedly as her separate property will be classified as community property and thereby keep right on causing the policy to have some community property characteristics. That, and many other things like it, must be checked out before any action is taken.

Irrevocable Life Insurance Trusts

As for irrevocable life insurance trusts, needless to say, since the insured community property husband shouldn't be the trustee of such a trust to which he has transferred a life insurance policy, neither should his wife. And here's a somewhat common error made with irrevocable insurance trusts in community property states: Assume a $100,000 policy on the life of the husband, which to date is a community property policy. The spouses create an irrevocable life insurance trust and transfer the policy to it. The terms of the trust are that the survivor of them should have a life estate in the trust, with remainder to their children. Husband dies, and if all the drafting and technicalities were correctly handled, nothing will be taxed in his gross estate. But how about the gross estate of the wife when she later dies? As a community property owner of the policy, she has made a transfer of it to the irrevocable trust, but has retained a life estate by the very terms of the trust. Therefore, $50,000 will be included in her gross estate when she dies. The proceeds were effectively removed from the husband's estate, but not from the wife's. Maybe that result is perfectly acceptable to the spouses, particularly if they want the surviving spouse to have the lifetime benefit in all of the property. But if they also want to avoid any estate taxation of the proceeds at the wife's later death, then they will have to consider the problem at the one and only time they are given to draft the provisions of the irrevocable trust. It seems clear that the wife will not be able to have a life estate in "her" half of the insurance proceeds. Maybe that works out all right, though, if the liquidity needs exceed $50,000 and the trustee can use up the wife's half of the proceeds in paying off those needs while retaining the husband's half of the proceeds in which she can be given a life estate. This is an example of the area commonly called **post-mortem estate planning,** and shows how knowledgeable planning advice is as necessary for executors and trustees as it is for testators and trustors.

Life Insurance in Business Planning

Life insurance can serve many useful purposes in the estate planning that can be done with various forms of business entities. I have already considered one instance, that of the **Section 303 redemption** of closely held corporate stock to pay death duties and probate expenses (discussed at page 167). The purpose of the redemption is to obtain cash from the corporation at capital gains rates to cover the liquidity needs, which works quite well if the corporation is able to spare the necessary cash when the time comes. One method to be certain that the required amount of cash will be available at the necessary time is to take out a life insurance policy on the shareholder concerned in an amount necessary to cover the liquidity needs.

Funding Buy-Sell Agreements

In any business with multiple owners, which includes any joint venture, partnership, or corporation having two or more owners, an important but sometimes neglected piece of planning has to do with what occurs on the death of one of the owners. If no agreement exists on the subject, then the deceased owner's heirs will succeed by will or intestacy to his interest. Whatever the heir does with that interest could potentially be very disruptive to the other owners; he could sell that interest to an unsatisfactory person, or he could remain as a principal of the business. If the latter, the heir may be somewhere between a total nuisance and a negative disruption, either of which can drag down the entire business to the economic and emotional disadvantage of all concerned. Pre-death planning often starts from the proposition that the surviving principals would prefer not to be in business with the deceased owner's spouse or other heirs, and for their part the spouse or heirs would prefer investable cash to the ups and downs which a business interest may imply.

Agreements to accomplish the equitable buy out of the deceased owner's interest go under the general heading of **buy-sell agreements,** though they come in many forms and go by varying names. They can be **cross purchase agreements** where the surviving owners individually buy out the decedent's interest, or **redemption or entity agreements** where the business itself contracts to buy out the decedent's interest. The buy out price may be pegged to estate tax valuation, may be determined by outside arbitrators, or may be arrived at under a formula initially placed in the agreement with a provision for subsequent adjustments made by the principals or their accountants. While all the principals are alive, no one knows whether he will be buying or selling, so the price or formula arrived at tends to reflect true arm's length bargaining. But once that agreement has been reached, there remains the key factor of the availability of funds to ensure that the survivors can pay the agreed price to the decedent's heirs. This is where life insurance can come into play.

In an entity type of redemption agreement, the business can take out a policy on the life of each principal so that the proceeds will cover the agreed redemption price; sometimes the principals simply agree on the amount of insurance to be secured, and then agree to accept those insurance proceeds as full payment for their business interest after death. In a cross purchase type, each principal must take out a policy on the life of every other principal, a complexity that can easily get out of hand unless there are only a few owners. The many tax and non-tax advantages and disadvantages of each type of buy-sell agreement are beyond our purpose here. We should note just one thing. In a cross purchase type, the proceeds of the life insurance policy ought to be out of the decedent's gross estate, since the incidents of ownership are owned by someone other than the insured. The same is true for business-owned insurance, except that in setting the value of the decedent's interest in the business, the IRS will include the decedent's proportionate share of the proceeds because they flower to full value as of his death. Thus, some portion of the insurance proceeds will show up in the decedent's gross estate, depending upon the combination of valuation techniques used in valuing the business interest, which now includes the life insurance proceeds.

Group Life Insurance As A Benefit of Employment

Another completely different function of life insurance within a business is as a benefit of employment. Most companies qualify as a group for the purpose of having a group insurance policy issued to their officers and employees, and they often provide substantial amounts of life insurance to valued employees as an additional benefit of employment. Most often, the employer pays all of the premium cost. Premiums on amounts of insurance over $50,000 are considered to be income to the employee, but that consequence seems not to have deterred companies from continuing to provide large amounts of group term life insurance to valued employees. It is not uncommon to find high salaried employees or executives with $500,000 or even $1,000,000 worth of group term life insurance provided under their company's group policy. If the employee possessed the incidents of ownership in his individual certificate of group insurance, which he usually does if no additional steps are taken, the proceeds will of course be taxable in the employee's gross estate.

It used to be that under the laws of most states, group term life was not assignable. That meant that the incidents of ownership could not be irrevocably transferred to someone other than the insured. In the 1960s, the IRS ruled that it would honor such assignments if state law permitted them, and as a result virtually every state has since passed a statute authorizing the irrevocable assignment of group insurance, thus making it possible to free the proceeds from the insured employee's gross estate. However, there are still many master group insurance policies in effect which themselves prohibit assignment of any interest under them, and so it is wise for anyone contemplating the irrevocable assignment of a group life insurance policy to check not only state law but also the master policy. If both law and the policy authorize it, the way is clear to free the proceeds from the insured's gross estate, provided that the insured actually irrevocably surrenders all of the incidents of ownership. The planner bears a special responsibility in such situations because he must scrutinize the master policy to check out all its terms to see whether the insurance contract might be reserving an incident of ownership to the insured. For instance, many such master policies reserve to the employee the right to convert the term policy to a permanent policy upon his retirement from employment; that is an incident of ownership, and it must be effectively surrendered if the irrevocable assignment is to have its desired effect.

If everything is permissible under state law and the master policy, and has been correctly attended to, the way is clear for an employee to transfer substantial amounts of post-mortem funds to his chosen heirs without payment of any estate taxes. All he need do is execute an irrevocable assignment of the incidents of ownership in the group life insurance. This is as available to the owner/employees of the business as to non-owners. In the next chapter I shall be examining mechanisms for the transfer of an estate owner's wealth without incurring estate taxes, many of which apply particularly to business owners, and the irrevocable assignment of group term life insurance should not be ignored as one of those mechanisms.

A recent ruling was held that the payment of premiums by the employer on a policy which has been irrevocably transferred to the new owner is an indirect gift from the employee to that new owner. It is not yet clear whether that ruling can be made to stick, but even if it can, a married employee can handle $6000 worth of such premium payments under his annual gift tax exclusion and his spouse's gift-splitting consent.

Problems In Community Property States

Note the special problems in community property states if the ownership of a group policy is irrevocably transferred to the employee's spouse. Those problems exist because the payment of premiums by the employer is clearly payment of premiums with community property money (since it comes from the spouse's employment). To prevent the policy from just remaining a community property policy which will tax half the proceeds in the employed spouse's estate anyway, all the steps indicated in the previous section on special community property problems must be taken. And there must be an explicit agreement between the spouses whereby the employed spouse gives his or her community property interest in the premium money to the non-employed spouse, to be the latter's sole and separate property.

APPLICATION

1. Determine whether you need life insurance to meet the "estate building" purpose, by deciding whether there is enough income-producing property to provide security for those whom you wish to benefit with income if you should die.

2. Compute your liquidity needs by following the outline given in Figure 14-1. If you are married, be certain to also compute those needs for your spouse, under alternative assumptions that your spouse is the first to die, or is the second to die.

3. Refer back to Figure 8-2, page 150, and the Application section of chapter 8 (page 148). You there computed your gross estate with the aid of that Figure. Now refer to Table 7-1, page 119, and compute the estate tax on that amount. Next, eliminate all life insurance on your life from the computation of your gross estate and compute the estate taxes again. The difference between the two computations is the savings in tax dollars you can obtain by transferring the ownership of insurance on your life. Decide whether it is worth it, and whether you want to do that.

4. If you do, decide whether you want to transfer the ownership to an individual, or whether you want to create an irrevocable life insurance trust. Also, decide how the premiums will be paid after the ownership of the policy has been transferred.

5. If you live in a community property state, are married, and your spouse either owns insurance on your life or you want him or her to own it, be sure your spouse owns it as his or her separate property, and that premiums are being paid with his or her separate property money.

15

other important estate planning techniques

Glossary For This Chapter

Depreciation
Installment Sale
Preferred Stock
Private Annuity
Reorganization
306 Stock
Uniform Gifts to Minors Act

This chapter will discuss several estate planning techniques that do not fit under the subject headings I have covered to this point. It will then go on to serve as a wrap-up for several major matters that have been discussed at one place or another throughout this book. I will try to collect various ideas on a given subject, and bring them together in one convenient place for your reference.

The Private Annuity

An annuity purchased from an insurance company is a good way to avoid estate taxes. By turning over all your net worth to the company, you can purchase an annuity contract guaranteeing to pay you a specified sum, usually monthly, for the rest of your life. Upon your death, the contractual payments will cease and (except for any amounts saved from the monthly annuity payments) you will own no property so you will have nothing to be taxed. There is just one major flaw in the beauty of that plan, which is that there will be nothing left to pass on to your heirs, either. If you only cared to leave $175,000 to your heirs, you could hold back that sum when buying the annuity, take a reduced monthly payment, but at least have the $175,000 to pass on to your heirs. After 1980, that $175,000 will pass free of any federal estate tax.

Clever taxpayers have reasoned that if estate taxes can be avoided by purchasing a commerical annuity, they should also be avoidable by making the same deal with a private individual. That individual is usually the person whom the annuitant (the person who buys an annuity) would choose as an heir, and since that is so often a family member, these devices are also known as **family annuities.** The annuitant could sell to his chosen heir the same property he would have left to that heir in any case, by means of a bona fide sale in exchange for a promise to pay the annuitant a specified monthly sum for the rest of his life. The heir would wind up with the property, the annuitant would have a guaranteed income, and there would be no property left in the annuitant's ownership when he died. This seems to be a way to get property to one's chosen heirs without paying any estate taxes.

Flaws In Private Annuity Plans

You can well imagine that there is a flaw in there somewhere, else everybody would be doing this. And if they were, Congress would probably try to slam the door on the device by enacting another "abuse prevention" statute such as the generation skipping tax, carryover basis, and the like.

The **first flaw** is presented by the gift tax because, unless the transaction is a bona fide sale for full value, the transfer will be at least in part a gift and **subject to gift taxes.** To avoid incurring a gift tax, the total fair market value of the property sold must be exchanged for something worth exactly the same amount of money. Actuarial and mortality tables come into play at this point because the value of what is received by the annuitant depends upon his sex and age. If the annuitant had transferred property worth $500,000 and the mortality tables said that he had a 10-year-life expectancy, the annuitant must be guaranteed $50,000 per year to avoid gift taxes. It often happens that people who are candidates for this planning device are rather elderly, which means that the annual payments to them must be a large percentage of the value of the property they wish to transfer. That leads to the next set of flaws.

First of all, where is the intended heir, whom I'll call the transferee, going to get the **large amounts of money necessary** to make the high annual payments? Unless he is a pretty wealthy individual in his own right, and is willing to use some of his own money to finance the necessary payments, he will probably have to get the money from the very property being transferred to him.

Under the tables we must use, the annual income produced by the property is usually nowhere near enough to cover the required installments, and so some of the transferred property may have to be sold. That can be very disruptive to the family's assets, as it may mean splitting up business or real estate interests and taking in outside purchasers. It may also trigger a capital gains tax, thus making it even more costly.

The **second flaw** to the large installment payments that are usually necessary is that the annuitant may have **no need for such a large income** and may be completely unable to spend it even being as frivolous as possible. If he can't spend it all, the excess will simply be saved and will build up to a sizeable estate, which will be taxed at his death anyway. Assume for illustration a transfer of $600,000 which, due to the annuitant's age, requires annual installment payments of $90,000. Also assume that the annuitant can at best manage to spend only $20,000 on himself and his frivolities, perhaps another $20,000 is lost to income taxes, and so $50,000 is being saved each year. In ten years, the savings plus interest will be more than equal the original estate of $600,000, and the annuitant is right back where he started, or perhaps even worse off.

It should be readily apparent that there is a **serious psychological flaw** in such an arrangement, which is that everybody is best off if the annuitant dies soon after having made the transfer. Assume the annuitant is a widowed mother and the transferee is her son. Perhaps without recognizing it, they have entered into an arrangement where the son would consciously or unconsciously be realizing that he is best off if his mother dies soon. And they are both immeasurably worse off if she should happen to live her life expectancy, which after all many people do.

Many estate planners report that they have often considered this device, but hardly ever have recommended it. Frequently the clients themselves will veto it, either for the tax and mathematical reasons discussed, or else because they recognize the psychological implications of it and want no part of such an arrangement. It is one of those devices which sounds marvelous in the abstract, but the reality falls far short, and it has been called the "most discussed, least used" estate planning device. An inexact illustration of a private annuity is given in Figure 15-1.

When It Can Be Used

Yet the device can sometimes be used. Occasionally special circumstances and the applicable arithmetic will work out precisely right. The device has some income tax effects which just might prove advantageous. For one thing, each annuity payment received

FACTS: Mother owns a cattle ranch with a basis of $100,000 and a current fair market value of $600,000. Assume her life expectancy is 10 years.

She wants to reduce her taxable estate, and cut the transfer tax costs of getting the ranch to her son.

BEFORE PRIVATE ANNUITY

MOTHER

| Cattle Ranch |
| Fair market value: |
| $600,000 |

SON

| Nothing |

AFTER PRIVATE ANNUITY

MOTHER

| Contract from son, promising to pay her $60,000 per year for the rest of her life |

SON

| Cattle ranch |
| Fair market value: |
| $600,000 |

MOTHER'S SITUATION EACH YEAR

Return of Capital, $10,000 (assumed):	no tax
Capital Gain (assumed):	$30,000
Taxable Income (assumed):	$20,000
Spent on taxes & living (assumed):	$30,000
Saved or invested:	$30,000

SON'S INCOME TAXES:

Depreciation deduction: $40,000 (available against income produced by the ranch, or his other income)

MOTHER DIES

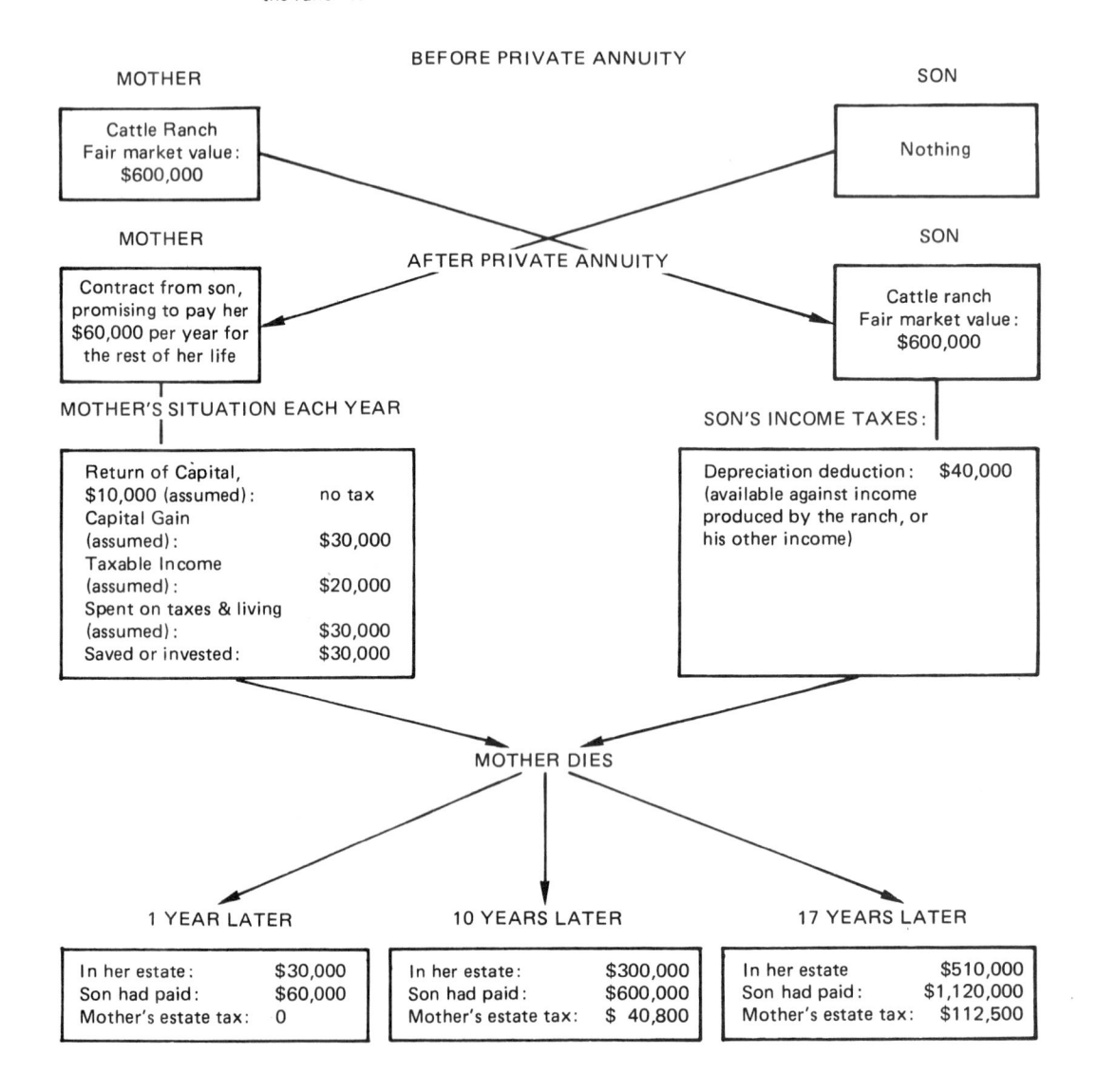

1 YEAR LATER

In her estate:	$30,000
Son had paid:	$60,000
Mother's estate tax:	0

10 YEARS LATER

In her estate:	$300,000
Son had paid:	$600,000
Mother's estate tax:	$40,800

17 YEARS LATER

In her estate	$510,000
Son had paid:	$1,120,000
Mother's estate tax:	$112,500

Figure 15-1. Inexact Illustration (based on many assumptions) of a Private Annuity.

by the annuitant will be only part ordinary income. Other parts may be taxable as capital gain (since the annuitant has sold capital assets) on which the tax may be less than the annuitant's ordinary income tax, and some parts may be tax-free return of capital. Whether the annuitant's income tax picture will be benefited or harmed depends largely upon whether he lives out of his life expectancy, and a tax accountant's analysis is needed to demonstrate these effects.

A major concern is the proper determination of the transferee's basis in the assets he has now acquired. If the assets are depreciable, he will need to compute his depreciation deduction, and upon a sale he will need to compute his capital gain. For depreciation purposes, the transferee's basis equals the value of the annuity promise itself, at least until the total payments have reached that value, and thereafter every such payment will increase the transferee's basis (and therefore his depreciation deduction). If the transferee should sell, his basis will be the totality of payments he has made to the annuitant up to that time, plus the actuarial value of the future payments he is obligated to make under the agreement. After the annuitant has died, the transferee's basis equals the totality of payments he had made, less any depreciation deductions he had claimed. In considering a private annuity, the effect on basis should be compared with the basis the heir would have had if he had received the property from the annuitant at death and had acquired a carryover basis adjusted upward by the fresh start and other adjustments. The arithmetic analyses involved in this device are obviously an accountant's paradise.

In summary, the private annuity is not the paradise many people think it is or wish it were (what is?), it most often is not recommended after a thorough economic analysis has been made, but it is available and workable in appropriate special circumstances.

Estate Planning for Business Owners

It is very important for any sole proprietor, or anyone with an interest in a business as a partner or as a shareholder in a privately held corporation, to consider the effect of his death on the continuation of the business, as well as to decide whether his survivors should continue to have an interest in the business. In cases of partnership or corporate interests, these considerations usually result in a **buy-sell agreement** of one kind or another. A sole proprietor has fewer options available, but should try to design a plan providing either for the continuation of the business by a designated heir, or interim operation of the business by an executor or general manager employed by the executor until the business can be beneficially sold.

Over and above such matters, estate planning for business owners often involves attempts to avoid the higher estate tax brackets by **minimizing the amount of business interest** which must be included in the decedent's taxable estate. There are several possibilities which might accomplish this goal, either singly or perhaps in tandem. Many of those possibilities involve increasing degrees of sophistication; the very first chapter alerted you that I would be barely skimming the surface of most things, and I repeat that caution at this point. I will just mention a few of these possibilities so that you may pursue them if you wish, on the understanding that what will be mentioned here is a mere flea on the hide of an elephant. Should any such idea intrigue you, the many technicalities must be pursued with your own advisors.

One can fix the estate tax valuation of a business interest and within limits, perhaps arrange an advantageous valuation for that interest by entering into a buy-sell agreement specially drafted to achieve that result. There are many rules, but essentially if all parties are bound to buy and sell at the fixed price both during life and at death (whether or not that price might be adjusted annually by formula), then the price set in the agreement can be used as the genuine value of the interest on the estate tax return. The IRS accepts that price as the true value of the business interest because it is the only value the heirs will be able to realize for their inheritance. It is also a value arrived at by true arm's length bargaining when the living business owners did not know who would be buying and who would be selling. Whether or not it is wise to fix those values in advance, particularly in light of the various **valuation discounts** (see page 132) which are applicable to closely held corporate shares, is strictly a matter for each person to decide in concert with his advisors.

Freezing The Value Of A Business Interest

Several methods exist to **freeze the value of a business interest** at its current value and insure that any future growth in value will belong to someone other than the current owner. An increasingly popular method usually involves only owners of closely held corporate shares, although the same principle can be applied by other methods to partnership interests as well. The method referred to deals with a **corporate reorganization which creates two classes of stock** instead of the usual one class of common stock. First, the current value of the corporation must be accurately arrived at, usually by an independent appraisal. Next, the one class of common stock is surrendered to the corporation in exchange for two classes of stock: a voting preferred class and a non-voting common. The definition of preferred stock is that it has a preferred claim on the assets of the corporation in the event of liquidation, and it also has a preferred right to be paid its dividends in full before the common receives any dividends. Correctly writing the terms of the preferred stock can forever freeze its value at, for instance, 98% of the corporation's value at that time. The small balance of the corporation's value therefore belongs to the new class of non-voting common, which can either be purchased by the spouse or (more usually) the children, or given to them at little or no gift tax cost. The former sole owner who retains the preferred stock retains total voting control, and at his death he will only pay estate taxes on the fixed value of his preferred shares even if the corporation has become much more valuable. The common stock will reflect the entire increase in value (since the preferred stock's value is frozen), and the children have become the owners of a large percentage of the corporation's value without any estate tax having been paid on that amount in their father's estate, and at the cost of little or even no gift tax. The father has effectively transferred all future appreciation occurring after the date of the reorganization to his children, and kept it out of his estate. An illustration is given in Figure 15-2.

The carryover basis rules, in contrast to the former stepped-up basis, present an added complication to this plan, having to do with a highly technical matter known as **Section 306 stock.** The preferred stock received in the reorganization is 306 stock, and that's bad. The thrust of Section 306 is that, except for a few designated circumstances, a subsequent sale of such stock will yield ordinary income instead of capital gain. The former stepped-up basis rules had the effect of removing the "306 taint," but under the carryover basis rules effective January 1, 1980, the 306 taint passes on to the heirs. Highly competent advice is necessary to determine when the disadvantageous effect of Section 306 can be avoided.

If the client and the planner are both very forward looking, they might institute a two-class stock structure when they are forming a new corporation, rather than waiting to reorganize an existing one which already has stock of substantial value. If that is done initially, the 306 problem can be reduced or avoided, and the arrangement is more easily brought about.

Another method to freeze the value of an owner's interest in any asset, corporation or anything else, is by an **installment sale** to the owner's chosen heirs (often his children). An installment sale is one made over a period of years for less than 30% received in the year of sale (which is where all the "29% down" advertisements come from). The sale proceeds are then taxed only in the

FACTS: Father owns all the shares in a family corporation currently worth $300,000.

He is seeking a means to reduce the tax cost of transferring his ownership interest to his son, who will continue the corporation's business.

ABC CORPORATION

Shares: 1000 all owned by father
Fair market value: $300,000

CORPORATE REORGANIZATION

Two classes of stock created:

Voting preferred, written so that its value is $294,000. All retained by father.

Non-voting common, necessarily reflects the rest of the current value, or $6000. Given to son, or purchased by him.

10 YEARS LATER FATHER DIES
CORPORATION WORTH $1,000,000

FATHER'S ESTATE

All of the preferred stock in ABC Corp. Value: $294,000.

Preferred shares willed to son.

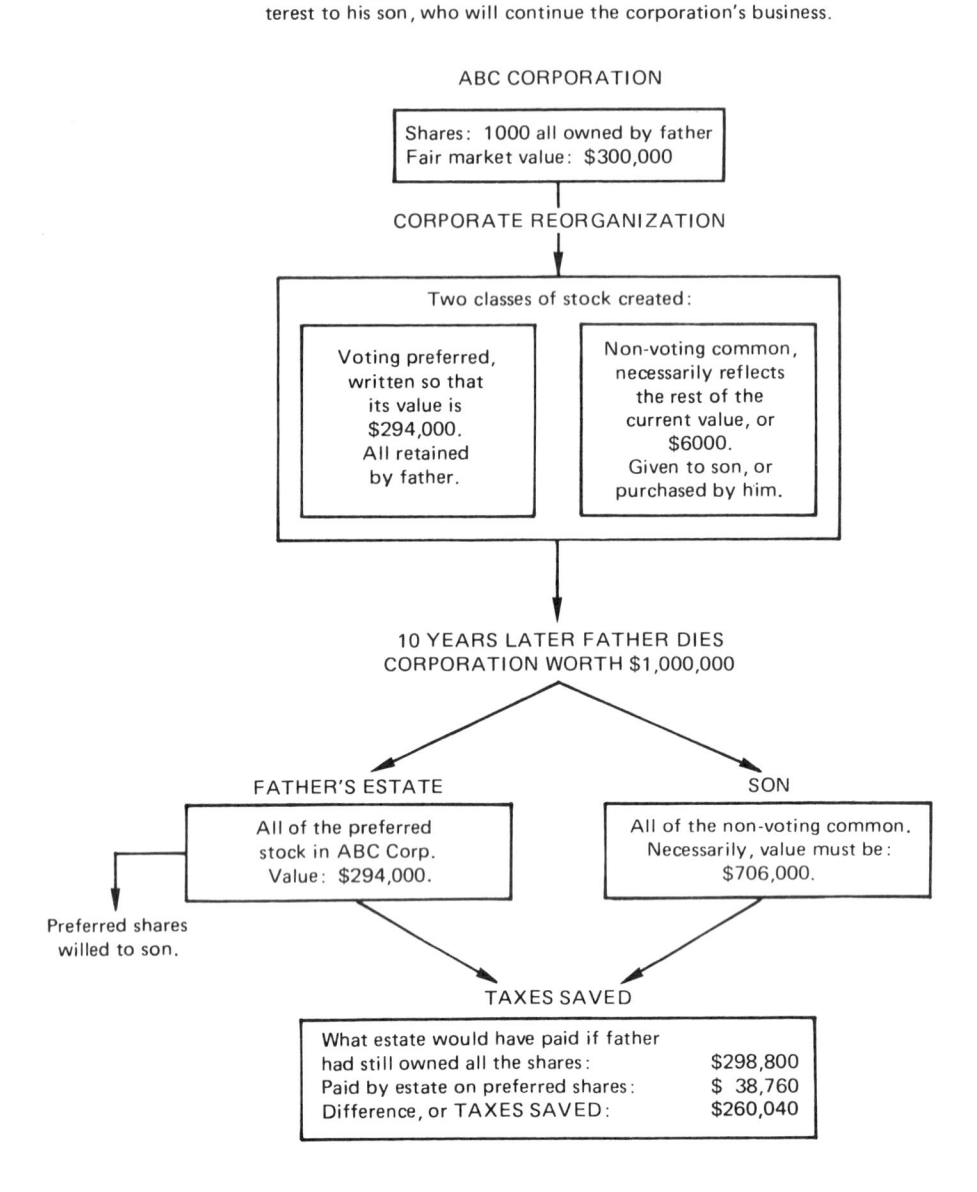

SON

All of the non-voting common. Necessarily, value must be: $706,000.

TAXES SAVED

What estate would have paid if father had still owned all the shares:	$298,800
Paid by estate on preferred shares:	$ 38,760
Difference, or TAXES SAVED:	$260,040

Figure 15-2. Illustrations of a Corporate Reorganization to Fix Value of Shareholder's Interest.

year of actual receipt, preventing the entire sales price from being bunched into the taxpayer's income in one year. The estate planning use of this device works like this: Once fair market value has been accurately determined, the owner makes an installment sale to his children, who give him a promissory note in the amount of the sales price less the cash down payment. They also give him a mortgage or other security to cover the balance due. The promissory notes are assets with true value, and they will be taxed in the owner's estate when he dies. But the effect is that the former owner has frozen his estate tax liabilities at the promissory note value used for the sale. The children will thereafter be the owners of all appreciation occurring to the property, and that appreciation will be removed from the former owner's estate since after the date of sale he was not the owner of the property. Still another benefit of this device is the possibility of a discount being allowed for the value of the promissory notes in the former owner's taxable estate, thus decreasing the estate taxes even further. An illustration of the installment sale device is given in Figure 15-3.

Prior to the 1976 Act, the owner would often be advised not to engage in this type of installment sale, but rather to continue to hold the property until his death in order that the property would acquire a stepped-up basis. That would have wiped out all the capital gain inherent in the property, to the benefit of the heir who inherits it. It is likely that installment sales will increase in frequency after January 1, 1980 when carryover basis goes into effect. One of the intended effects of carryover basis is to remove the incentive for holding property until death, since with this new reality someone will always have to pay the capital gains tax at some point, rather than see the gain disappear into stepped-up basis. Under an installment sale the former owner pays tax on the gain, but he does so over many years which are perhaps low income retirement years, effectively taxing the capital gains at low rates. The heir receives a new basis for the property equal to its value on the sale date (as does anyone when he buys anything for its full value), and if the property is depreciable, he can now depreciate it at the new and higher basis. If the heir later sells, his capital gains tax will be based upon his new basis. Sometimes the sale can be combined with a **lease-back,** where the former owner leases the transferred property from his children if he needs to continue in possession of it; there are added dangers to that, though. Also, perhaps with some additional risk, the former owner could **annually forgive** an amount of each child's debt to him equal to his and his spouse's annual $3000 gift tax exemptions. More grist for your advisor's mill, whose advice on the scores of technical rules is mandatory.

FACTS: Father owns an asset (a business, real estate, or whatever) currently worth $300,000.

He is willing to transfer it to his son if that transfer will save the transfer tax costs of getting it to his son.

ASSET

Fair market value: $300,000

INSTALLMENT SALE

$30,000 down, in cash.
$270,000 payable over 30 year period, plus reasonable rate of interest

10 YEARS LATER FATHER DIES

FATHER'S ESTATE

$30,000 cash from down payment.
$270,000 in notes (less amount already paid, and perhaps valued at a discount)

SON

Owner of the asset.
Fair market value: $1,000,000

TAXES SAVED

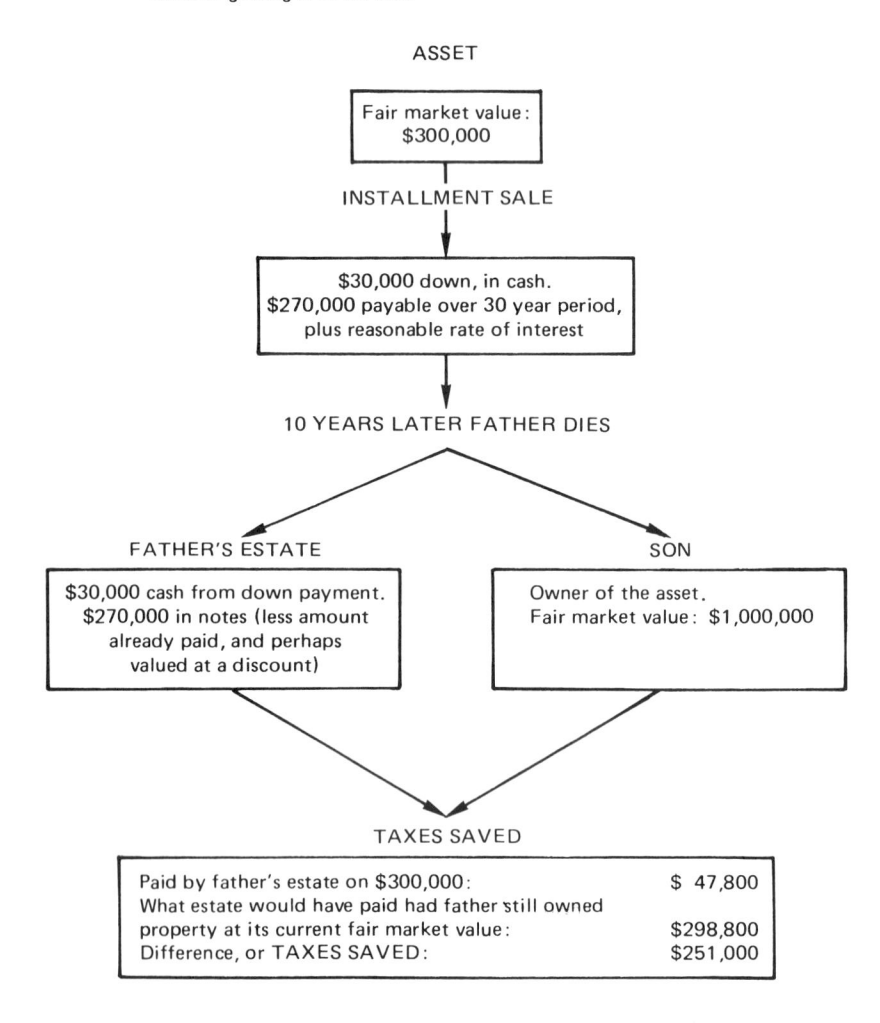

Paid by father's estate on $300,000:	$ 47,800
What estate would have paid had father still owned property at its current fair market value:	$298,800
Difference, or TAXES SAVED:	$251,000

Figure 15-3. Illustration of Taxes Saved by Use of an Installment Sale.

Tax-Qualified Pension Or Profit-Sharing Plans

Another area of planning in which business owners can engage concerns the establishment of **tax-qualified pension or profit-sharing plans.** This is a gigantic field in and of itself, vastly complicated by the requirements of 1974 legislation known popularly as ERISA. It is way beyond our purpose to get into those complexities, other than to mention that this is a fertile field for planning for the business owner. Much of the planning has to do with income tax benefits, whereby amounts contributed to qualified plans can be deductible to the corporation and not included in the income of the employee for whose account they are contributed. Further, the contributions can be invested and built up within a tax-free trust, so that no income taxes will be payable on either investment income or capital gains when assets held by the pension or profit-sharing trust are sold. Naturally, those amounts can grow at a much more rapid rate than can investments which must bear the taxes on their income and their capital gains.

It should be remembered that payments from a qualified plan received after an owner/employee's death by his designated beneficiary are free from estate taxes in the owner/employee's estate under certain conditions (see page 141). Here, then, is another way for an owner to transfer what would otherwise have been his funds (if taken by him as normal salary or earnings) to a chosen heir without paying any estate taxes on those amounts. You may remember from chapter eight that only the employer's contributions to the plan are so exempt and not the employee's own voluntary contributions, but in the vast majority of cases the former make up all or most of the sums received by the heir.

Providing Liquid Assets And Other Planning Ideas

Another major aspect of estate planning for the business owner is **ensuring the availability of liquid funds** to meet his inevitable estate tax obligations. In this connection, the extended estate tax payment plans (see page 165) and the 303 stock redemption plan (see page 167) should be reviewed to complete the picture of a business owner's estate planning.

A much more subtle aspect of a business owner's planning can be accomplished by having him **divert business opportunities** to his chosen heirs, or by having him **assume the risk of loss** in a venture which, if successful, will see the profits go not to him but rather to his heirs. All such practices will serve to keep the newly acquired profit out of his gross estate. Such things are often done in an unconscious and natural way within a family, such as when a father cosigns a note for his son, but a sophisticated estate planner will often suggest that the estate owner become more aware of the significant estate tax saving opportunities possible under this general topic. Rather than have an already wealthy estate owner go forward with some spectacular new venture, he might instead create a new business entity with his children in which they have a 99% interest and he has only 1%, and assure that the new entity be the one to pursue the venture. By means of appropriately drafted documents and loans, if the venture fails the father could absorb the loss and perhaps he could even receive the benefit of any early year's tax losses, while if any spectacular profits do occur, they will belong 99% to the children without ever having been taxed in the father's gross estate.

Needless to say, there are other devices available. One is a family partnership, whereby children are brought in and thereby acquire a good proportion of the partnership's future profits, although there are many complex tax rules governing such partnerships. Since I just want this to be a book and not an encyclopedia, I will end this discussion at this point and commit you to your own sophisticated advisors for further information and possibilities.

Remaining Advantages of Lifetime Giving

Lifetime gift-giving is not dead! It does not have all of its former advantages, primarily the extra $30,000 exemption and a tax rate 25% cheaper than the estate tax rate, but almost every other advantage it ever possessed still remains. It also has disadvantages which we will examine a bit later; here are some advantages:

Advantage Number One

The *$3,000 annual gift tax exclusion*. It is not only still with us, but it is also even more advantageous than formerly because such gifts are not automatically thrown back into the gross estate if the decedent happens to die within three years of the gift. Due to the ability to split gifts with one's spouse, or to the nature of community property, this exclusion is really $6,000 for a married couple. Subject to any of the disadvantages of gift-giving (which will be discussed later,) using the $3,000 annual exclusion may provide all the tax reduction a given estate may wish. For instance, assume a married couple with a one-million-dollar estate have three married children and six grandchildren. Assuming that they are willing to give gifts to their children's spouses and to each of their grandchildren, they have twelve donees available to them just in their immediate family. If they gave $6,000 to each of the twelve, they could give $72,000 per year. In ten years, they would have depleted their estate by $720,000, or down to $280,000, well within the "no federal tax at any time" figures if they use a by-pass trust.

Advantage Number Two:

Any gift taxes actually paid will be *money removed from a decedent's gross estate* if he lives three years after the gift. For wealthy people, this may be a very intelligent way to get $100,000 or $200,000 out of their gross estate while at the same time getting some of their property to their chosen heirs.

Advantage Number Three

One of the most significant: *giving away the appreciation*, which is still entirely possible after the 1976 Act. Assume you own a $250,000 asset which, for some reason or another, you know will quadruple in value within a year or two (don't ask me how, just assume it). You would be far better off to incur the unitary transfer tax while it is still worth $250,000 than to incur the estate tax at death when it is worth $1,000,000. The post-gift appreciation is removed from your estate if you live three years after the gift.

Advantage Number Four

Another major advantage of gift giving: giving income-producing property *shifts the income tax burden* from the donor to the donee. Assume a piece of property earns $70,000 per year, that the donor is in the 70% income tax bracket, and that a potential donee has no other income at all. Annual income taxes to the donor will be $49,000. The tax on this income to a married donee with a normal number of exemptions and deductions is likely to be approximately $20,000. That's a savings of $29,000 per year in income taxes, and if the donor lives 30 years, the cumulative savings would be $870,000 (on the unlikely assumption that everything stayed exactly the same for both donor and donee). To save even more, if the donor could transfer the property equally to three low income persons, each of them might pay a tax on their share of the income as low as $4,000 each, or a total income tax on the property's income of $12,000 per year. Over the donor's thirty-year life span, that's a cumulative income tax saving of $1,110,000. Those figures may not be entirely accurate due to the many variables of anyone's income tax situation, but they're fun, and they illustrate the basic point.

Advantage Number Five

Gifts between spouses are more advantageous than ever before, due to the first $100,000 being totally free of gift tax, and can greatly increase family tax savings by *ensuring that neither spouse wastes his or her estate tax exemption*. Assume a couple living in a common law state where the husband is considered to be the sole owner of their entire $600,000 estate, so that the wife owns nothing. If the wife dies first, her $175,000 transfer tax exemption is wasted, since she owns no property to apply it against. If, on the other hand, the husband had given her $175,000 and she later dies before him, she may leave her $175,000 free of tax under her exemption, and would probably do so in the form of a by-pass trust for the husband's benefit so that the property will not be taxed in his estate when he dies. Or, she could leave the $175,000 directly to their children. For maximum effect, the husband could allocate his gift among the various exemptions or credits available to him, so that he could give $100,000 to his wife completely tax-free under the marital deduction and take the remaining $75,000 against his unitary transfer tax credit. That way, the gift to his wife will cost him nothing in current transfer taxes, her $175,000 exemption can be used at her death instead of being wasted, and his estate will have been reduced from $600,000 to $425,000. The family taxes saved work out to be approximately $42,000. Not only is this a nice saving, but it is the only way to assure that the transfer tax's marital deduction will be used to save family tax if the wife without property happens to die first.

There are also some advantages to gifts between spouses which are encouraged by the carryover basis rules (see page 175) effective January 1, 1980. Assume that the husband's basis in the hypothetical estate was $50,000, that the assets were worth $550,000 on December 31, 1976, and that they are worth $600,000 now. Assume further that there are reasons to believe the wife's life expectancy may be quite short. Upon her death property she acquired by gift will qualify for the fresh start upward adjustment to basis if the donor owned it on December 31, 1976, so her husband might consider giving her some or all of his property. When upon her death she leaves those same assets to her husband or to a trust for his benefit, if they are depreciable assets, the depreciation deduction will be based on the higher basis of $550,000 applicable after the upward adjustment made possible by the fresh start rule, instead of on only $50,000 if he had not made the gift. And if those assets are sold, the capital gains tax will be greatly reduced, as his basis will now be $550,000 instead of just the $50,000 it would have been if he had never made the gift. The depreciation and capital gains tax benefits of this move will have to be weighed against the added transfer tax costs of it, and an accountant ought to be consulted for the necessary computations.

There is an added advantage for community property spouses. Assume that the wife had inherited a lot of property many years ago which now has an extremely low basis relative to its current value. Assume further that there is reason to believe that the husband's life expectancy may be quite short. If he were to die before his wife, any tax savings from a possible use of the marital deduction for her separate property would be lost, since at her death there will be no husband and therefore no ability to qualify for that deduction. But she could convert some or all of her separate property to community property, which can legally be done and which is a gift of one-half to her husband. When he dies, remember that under the fresh start rule both halves of the community property, not just his half, qualify for the upward adjustment to basis. So by using the gift tax marital deduction and maybe even some or all of her transfer tax exemption, she can qualify her former separate property for an upward adjustment in basis. This can be extremely beneficial if the property is depreciable, or if she later sells any of it. If she had not made this move, none of her separate property would have received a new and higher basis.

Over and above using the gift tax marital deduction in order not to waste one spouse's transfer tax exemption and to obtain carryover basis benefits in proper situations, gifts between spouses that take advantage of the gift tax marital deduction can be used to equalize the estates of husband and wife. Anyone familiar with the tax structure and tax rates can prove to you that two taxes on one-half each will always total less, and often substantially less, than one tax on the entire property. The figures will have to be checked out in any particular situation, but it may well be advisable to use the gift tax marital deduction and the transfer tax credit, and even pay some transfer taxes at current values, in order to equalize the estates of husband and wife.

Other Advantages

There may well be several other advantages to gift giving in any particular estate, but only individual analysis of that estate could reveal those advantages. Among these are the previously mentioned irrevocable gifts of the incidents of ownership in life insurance policies and the use of gifts in corporate reorganizations or other plans designed to freeze the value of an owner's property at its current value while transferring future appreciation to others. And there may be good reason to use gifts for the purpose of adjusting the components of an owner's estate in order to be sure that his business interests or closely held corporate stock qualify for either long-term installment payments of estate taxes (see page 165) or for the 303 stock redemption used to pay death taxes and expenses (see page 167).

There is a potential advantage to getting in the habit of making gifts in January of each year, rather than December, if one has decided on an annual gift giving program. Doing so starts the three-year contemplation of death period running ten to twelve months earlier than if gifts are made in December, and some day that difference may turn out to be significant.

Selection Of Assets For Gifts

Another whole subject is the **proper selection of assets to give.** Selection depends both on practicalities and on the tax effects most important to a particular donor. Cash is by far the easiest thing to give, but it is also the easiest for the donee to squander. Giving stock usually requires sending stock certificates back to the transfer agents and having the shares reissued to reflect the gift, a minor but not insurmountable nuisance sometimes involving a small transfer fee. Giving real estate is by far the most difficult, at least where one wants to give only a portion of his ownership interest in order to qualify for the $3,000 annual exclusion. Giving a $3,000 interest in a $900,000 apartment complex is difficult but not impossible. It involves an accurate and independent appraisal of the property, and then a rearranging of the title to reflect the new co-tenancy. Doing that every year is both expensive and a very large nuisance. Giving a part interest in acreage usually involves running a new survey in addition to obtaining an appraisal of value, and then redrawing the deed to reflect the legal description of the parcel given away. The easiest way to give real estate is to incorporate it in a corporation having a great many shares of stock. That way, each share has a low value, and the accurate number can be given away if one wants to qualify for the $3,000 annual exclusion. But there are often income tax and other disadvantages to placing real estate in a corporation, so like almost everything else this presents a paradox.

Although non-tax consideration should often dominate tax considerations in selecting assets for gifts, the latter are still important. To shift taxable income, of course income-producing assets must be given. To give away future appreciation, assets with likely growth potential should be selected over assets which may have already seen most of their growth. It is usually not wise to give away an asset which is now worth less than its basis because the tax law requires that the donee take as his basis the lower date of gift value rather than the higher donor's basis; thus, the benefits of the potential loss are being wasted. And in making gifts after the 1976 Act, the donor must always keep the fresh start adjustment in mind. Property with a potential for a large upward adjustment on death (due to the fresh start rules) probably ought to be retained until death, in favor of giving away property with a small potential for fresh start benefits or, even better, property purchased after December 31, 1976, which would not qualify for the fresh start adjustment in any case.

There is a lot of loose talk in estate planning circles that property bearing a large appreciation over its basis ought to be sold before death. The thought is that the capital gains taxes which the seller must pay will be dollars removed from his estate, so that they will thereby escape estate taxes. There are two potential flaws in that argument which may (or may not) be relevant in a particular situation. One is that if the asset would qualify for the fresh start adjustment, then the disadvantage of losing that upward adjustment by selling before death may more than outweigh the advantage mentioned. And the second is that a portion (though not all) of the advantages mentioned will be acquired by the deathtime upward adjustment to basis provided by the adjustment on account of federal and state death taxes. The latter two factors operating in tandem may be much more advantageous than freeing the capital gains tax dollars from estate taxes.

Start Gift-Giving As Soon As Possible

Finally, it must be noted that if, after having thought through the potential disadvantages to gift-giving (which will be discussed below), one determines to launch a gift-giving program for any of the reasons covered, **the sooner in life he starts, the better.** The reasons are obvious, particularly as to the cumulative effect of the $3,000 annual exclusion and the early freezing of values or the early giving away of future appreciation. And remember the advantages, discussed in chapter seven (page 125), of making small taxable gifts in excess of the annual exclusion amount, in order to start the statute of limitations running against the IRS. Paradox: that course will not free gifts made in the last three years of life from the automatic contemplation of death rule, since those gifts will be over $3000 in amount. A list of many advantages and disadvantages of gifts will be found in Figure 15-4, located on pages 318–19.

Gifts to Minors

Special factors bear upon any gifts to minors, particularly the problem of qualifying those gifts for the $3,000 annual exclusion while at the same time limiting the minor's access to the transferred funds until he reaches a mature age. We know that only gifts of a present interest qualify for the $3,000 annual exclusion (see page 124), and if a minor's free use of the transferred property is postponed until a later age, that looks very much like a gift of a future interest, which would not qualify for the exclusion. It is indeed a future interest, but the tax law recognizes the special factors involved in gifts to minors and so provides **exceptions** to the future interest rule for such gifts. The effect of the exceptions is

Advantages

1. $3000 may be transferred free of any transfer tax to any donee, each and every year; the amount may be $6000 if spouses join in the gifts.
2. Gift taxes paid on any taxable gift will be money removed from the donor's estate.
3. The future growth in the value of property given away can be removed from the donor's estate and be transferred to the donee. Better to pay transfer taxes at the lower current value, rather than at the higher value which will exist at time of death.
4. Giving income-producing property shifts the income tax consequences from the donor to the donee, who may be in a substantially lower income tax bracket. The income tax savings occur each year, and so the beneficial effect will be cumulative over the donor's lifetime.
5. If one spouse owns no property, gifts of up to $175,000 from the spouse who does own property will assure that should the donee spouse die first, his or her $175,000 transfer tax exemption will not be wasted.
6. The first $100,000 of gifts from one spouse to the other are completely free of gift tax (although there is a small reduction in the donor's estate tax marital deduction; see page 159).
7. Giving low basis property to a spouse or other person who may die before the donor, and who will will the property back to the donor, will qualify that property for carryover basis advantages.

Disadvantages

1. Donor loses control over, and income from, the property given away. It is therefore not available for his future security, or to meet unexpected emergencies. In an uncertain world, this could be disastrous.
2. Gifts can make the donee wealthier than the donor, thus making the ultimate tax burdens even higher, and shifting the obligation to pay those taxes from the donor to the donee.
3. Gifts can have an adverse effect on the donee's personality, his family relationships, and his attitudes to life. They could conceivably turn the donee into a sloth. They might cause a rift in his marriage or other personal relationships.
4. Gifts to a minor child, where the minor gets his hands on the property before he has reached financial maturity, are potentially the most dangerous of all. In the hands of a normally rebellious teenager, they could break his relationship with his own parents.
5. Even though the list of disadvantages is not as long as that of advantages, that does not mean that the disadvantages might not be the most important, and might not tip the scales in favor of not making a contemplated gift.

Weigh the disadvantages very carefully before making any gift that is motivated solely by potential tax savings.

8. In a community property state, a gift of low basis separate property to the community (a gift of one-half to the non-owning spouse) will insure that upon the death of either spouse, the entire property will qualify for carryover basis advantages.

9. Gifts between spouses can equalize the sizes of their respective estate, thus lowering their total family estate taxes.

10. Gifts of the incidents of ownership in a life insurance policy can free the proceeds of that policy from estate taxes; the gift tax cost is usually peanuts compared to the potential estate taxes on the policy proceeds.

11. Gifts may adjust the ownership percentages among the component parts of an owner's estate, perhaps making it possible to qualify for long-term installment payments of estate taxes (see page 165), or for 303 redemptions to pay death taxes and expenses (see page 167).

Figure 15-4. Advantages and Disadvantages of Gifts.

that one may still qualify for the $3,000 annual exclusion while at the same time postponing the minor's free access until later years. But one may do so only by meeting the exact terms of the exceptions to the future interest rule.

Of course, an outright gift of cash or any other property to a minor is not a gift of a future interest and qualifies for the exclusion without any question. But such gifts raise not only potential family problems should the minor desire to waste those funds, but also present problems of the commercial world's willingness to deal with a minor. Bank accounts in a minor's name are quite permissible, but the catch often comes when someone wants to withdraw the funds. Resolution depends upon the banking laws and banking practices of your own state, but in some cases the banks will not allow the underage minor to withdraw the funds, and in other cases they won't allow the parents to withdraw them since the parents are not the account owner. Investigation of practices in your state is called for.

Putting a minor's name on a bank account as a joint tenant, or setting up an account "in trust for" the minor, present no problems of the $3,000 annual exclusion because they are simply not gifts at all. The trustee account belongs solely to the original depositor, and creating a joint tenancy account is not a gift because the creator could withdraw all of the money the very next day. It is merely a revocable transfer, and those are not gifts. However, if the minor ambles on down to the bank and withdraws all of the money from a joint-tenancy account several years later (if the bank would let him do so), there is a gift then from donor to donee, but it is one of a present interest and so would qualify for the $3,000 exclusion.

Uniform Gifts To Minors Act

One allowable method of qualifying for the exclusion and still postponing the minor's free access to the property is by making the gift under the **Uniform Gifts to Minors Act.** That Act exists in almost all states and allows the donor to make the gift to a custodian who will thereafter act very much as a trustee. He will control and administer the property for the minor's benefit and will turn over the property to the minor when the latter reaches majority. While this is helpful, there are still several problems with such a gift. One is that in almost every state the type of property which may be given under that Act is limited to cash, securities, life insurance policies, and annuity policies; notice that real estate is not included. Secondly, if the donor himself serves as custodian and dies before the minor attains majority, the property will **still be taxable in the donor's gross estate** because the many powers he retains as custodian give him so much "economic enjoyment" over the property that the estate tax will still engulf it. In community property states, one-half the property will be included in the gross estate of either spouse if either one of them is the custodian, due to the nature of community property. Thirdly and perhaps most importantly, the custodianship must terminate, and the property must be turned over to the minor when he attains majority; in most states that has now been reduced from age twenty-one to age eighteen. Many donors neglect to consider this factor, but they should give sober contemplation to the vision of an eighteen-year-old being handed cash or other property worth perhaps $50,000 or $100,000, depending on how much has been periodically contributed to the custodianship by parents, grandparents, or any others.

Special Trusts For Minors

The second allowable method of qualifying for the $3,000 annual exclusion and still postponing the minor's free access is by creating a **special type of trust.** Such trusts are variously known as "Trusts for Minors," or as "2503(c) trusts" because that is the tax law section involved. The property which can be subject to such a trust is not limited to any particular kinds and can include real estate or anything else. The terms of the trust must include that all income must be expended to or for the benefit of the minor, or accumulated for eventual distribution to him, and that the trust property and all accumulated income will be distributed to him when he reaches age twenty-one (the tax law has not as yet backed down to age eighteen, and it is unknown whether it ever will). If the child dies before becoming twenty-one, then the trust property must be payable to his estate or as he may appoint by a general power of appointment (see page 144). The tax regulations provide one significant addition to those rules because they allow the trust to provide that the minor upon reaching age twenty-one may elect to have the trust continue past age twenty-one. A recent interpretation has validated a trust which gave the minor only sixty days after reaching age twenty-one to elect to take the property free of trust, and if he failed to do so within sixty days, the trust would automatically continue until a later age specified by the trustor, when he would hopefully be even more mature. There is no prohibition on the donor of the trust property serving as trustee, so long as none of the powers or authorities given to him can be interpreted as being a general power of appointment.

A trust for a minor seems to be the best device available for qualifying a lifetime gift to a minor for the $3,000 annual exclusion while preventing the child's unlimited access to the property at too early an age. However, the donor must be content with the realization that at age twenty-one, the child will be able to obtain total control over the trust property. Twenty-one is better than the age of eighteen now found in most Uniform Gifts to Minors Acts, and the possibility that a reasonable child will at age twenty-one agree to allow the trust to continue until he is even more mature gives these trusts an added advantage over other types of gifts to minors.

Disadvantages of Gifts

The **disadvantages** of gifts **cannot possibly be stressed too strongly,** both because they are true, and particularly because donors so frequently ignore them. Too many people hear cocktail party chatter about the availability of the $3,000 "tax free" gifts, and then run right out and institute such a program without any consideration of the consequences. After all, if it's "tax-free," it's got to be a good deal, right? Not necessarily! The disadvantages fall into two general categories: **disadvantages to the donor** and **disadvantages to the donee.**

Disadvantages To The Donor

All the disadvantages can be rolled up into one general thought, which is that the donor should only make gifts if he can rationally convince himself that **under no conceivable future circumstances will he ever again need the property or the income it produces.** In a previous section I noted how spouses with a $1,000,000 estate could deplete their estate to only $280,000 within a space of ten years. While that is true, what we didn't say was how absurd a plan that might be. Depending upon who those people are, and the nature of their needs, lifestyles, health insurance coverage, and the like, an estate of $280,000 may be far too small to provide them with the security they are entitled to. Very few people, including your prospective heirs, would quarrel with the statement that your first obligation is to yourself and the preservation of a comfortable lifestyle unthreatened by any future economic events. Many prospective heirs are saddened at the thought of their benefactors scrimping on necessities and denying themselves good things in order to manage a gift program or to save on future death taxes. Children often tell their parents to spend whatever they can, to have a good time, that they've worked all their lives and have earned all or any of life's pleasures: "Take a trip to Europe, don't give it to mè."

Most estate planners feel that gift giving is a game for the very rich. The definition of "very rich" will of course differ from person to person, but in this context it probably means persons who, after they have given gifts, still retain enough property to be totally secure against any future eventualities. Anyone contemplating a gift-giving program in order to reduce taxes is urged to give serious consideration to the disadvantages mentioned. That is not to say that anyone can't give whatever gifts he feels like whenever he feels like it; it is just to say that tax-motivated giving should be examined very carefully with non-tax considerations in the forefront of one's thinking.

The Disadvantages to the Donee

These disadvantages involve an assessment of the donee's personality, and what the receipt of the gift will do to both his personal life and economic life. It can easily happen that between the gifts and the donee's regular economic successes, he can turn out to be more wealthy than the donor, and if so, the donor has only **increased the donee's tax problems.** It can also happen that the gifts themselves might be responsible for a **deterioration** in the donee's personality, his marriage, or other personal relationships, or his willingness to work for a living and pull his own weight in society. For scores of reasons which any intelligent person can imagine, the **gifts might do more harm than good,** particularly when tax and non-tax considerations are viewed together as a package (as they should be). And don't forget to consider the effect of gifts, particularly unequal gifts among children or other family members, upon that precious commodity called **family harmony.** What good is it to save an estate tax and lose a family?

These problems all too often show themselves with gifts to minors. Perhaps grandfather refused or neglected to engage in estate planning, maybe because he was too much of a tightwad to pay an estate planning fee, and so he left everything to the grandmother who is now facing a terrible estate tax situation. She and her advisor agree on annual $3,000 gifts to her children and grandchildren as at least one small way to lessen the future problem, and she makes cash gifts under the Uniform Gifts to Minors Act. At age seventeen and one-half, a rebellious grandchild discovers that in six months he is going to receive a check for $50,000, and that is the straw that breaks the back of his relationship with his parents. He informs them in no uncertain terms that the minute he gets his hands on grandma's money they will never see him again, and he's off to the boondocks to live in peace on his marijuana farm. Many an estate planner has received a plaintive call from the parents, inquiring as to how they can prevent their child from getting his hands on those funds. They can't, unless it can be demonstrated to a court that the child is so incompetent as to require a guardianship for his own protection. Not only is that quite hard to do in the circumstances imagined above, but think what the parent's act of attempting that course will do to their long-term relationship with their child. Too bad grandma never considered all this when she started her gift-giving program. She may have reduced her estate taxes all right, but at what price? That is, and ought to be, food for thought. A list of advantages and disadvantages of gifts will be found in Figure 15-4.

Planning With Charitable Gifts

Charitable giving is an area in which beneficial results can be achieved relative to two different taxes, the income tax and the estate tax. Any gift during life to a qualified charity will yield an **income tax deduction,** subject only to the percentage limitations applicable to charitable deductions on one's income tax return, while any such gift made at death will achieve a **full deduction from the estate tax return** without any percentage limitation. There are few complications regarding outright gifts to charity either during life or at death, other than the issue of valuation which often arises regarding income tax deductions where the taxpayer is arguing for a high valuation and the IRS for a low one.

An area in which even more sophisticated planning can be accomplished involves the matter of **charitable remainder trusts** and **charitable lead trusts.** In chapter nine, page 155, I discussed several kinds of trusts that might qualify some percentage of their value for the estate tax charitable deduction, those being the unitrust, the annuity trust, and the pooled income fund. I won't be repeating their definitions and workings at this point. Here, I want to examine a few of their applications. When considering those applications, keep in mind both the income tax effects and the estate tax effects.

There has been increasing interest recently in what is known generally as **deferred giving.** Mechanisms to accomplish deferred giving involve the use of the three types of trusts just mentioned, and what is common to all of them is that some interest in the trust is being deferred for the benefit of either a charity or an individual beneficiary. Such trusts can be entered into either during life or only upon death. In one possibility, the charity gets the income currently with the remainder interest being deferred, and in the other an individual gets the income interest currently with the charitable remainder being deferred.

Charitable Remainder Unitrust

A device attracting more and more interest is a **charitable remainder unitrust created during life.** Typically, the donor irrevocably transfers income-producing property to a trust to benefit himself for the rest of his life under the unitrust rules, with the remainder passing at his death to a qualified charity. With every such transfer, the donor receives an income tax deduction, subject only to the annual percentage limitations, so he thereby lowers his taxable income for the year of transfer. There is no gift tax payable, since the remainder interest being transferred (the donor keeps the life income interest) is fully deductible as a gift to charity. The property is included in the donor's gross estate because he has made a transfer with a retained life estate, but the date of death fair market value of the property now vesting in a charity is **entirely deductible** from estate taxes; normally, that deduction ought to equal one hundred percent of the included property's value, so there will be no estate tax. During the donor's lifetime, the trust may under the unitrust rules pay income in either the fixed percentage amount required under those rules, or else the actual income earned by the trust, whichever is lower. A shrewd trustee might invest the trust's assets in high growth, low yield assets during the donor's working years, which may well have the effect of producing far less than the fixed percentage amount so that, under the "whichever is lower" clause, the donor's taxable income from the trust is kept to a minimum (he might have plenty of other income). By inserting a proper clause in the trust, the difference between the income actually earned and the fixed percentage unitrust amount can build up as a form of debt to be repaid in later years. Upon the donor's retirement, the trustee might switch the investments into high yield forms, thus maximizing the donor's retirement income. Further, the amount of the accumulated debt referred to above can be paid back to the donor in annual installments, thereby enabling the donor to enjoy all the annual income of the now high yielding trust; without the debt referred to, he would not be allowed to receive more than the fixed percentage amount in any given year. But if the high yield trust is in fact earning more than the fixed percentage amount, the donor can enjoy it all due to the payback of the debt which the trust owes him. The switching from growth assets to high yield assets can be done without any capital gains tax because a charitable remainder unitrust is not taxed on its capital gains. For these reasons, many people consider such trusts to be superior vehicles for building up a retirement fund. Of course, one negative is that after the death of the donor (and usually his spouse who can also be written in to the trust so that she receives the lifetime income after his death), the charity gets the property and there is nothing left to pass on to any individuals, such as children or whomever. But if the donor is charitably inclined, or has plenty of other assets to leave to his children or other heirs, this type of trust can be ideal. A charitable remainder unitrust can also be set up by a decedent's will, where the desired effects would be to keep a wealthy heir's annual income taxes within defined limits while still giving him some enjoyment from the property, to add no further property to the heir's own gross estate, and to obtain a healthy charitable deduction against the decedent's estate taxes.

Charitable Lead Trust

An opposite type of trust is known variously as the **charitable lead trust** or the **charitable front end trust.** With this type of trust, the charity receives a designated annuity for a specified number of years before the individual heir receives anything, so the charity has the lead portion, or the front end. At the conclusion of the specified number of years, the individual heir receives outright ownership of the property, thus enabling the donor or decedent to qualify for some amount of the charitable deduction (the value of the charity's lead interest) while still ultimately passing the property to an individual. And if the individual is in a high income tax bracket, it might be best to withhold more taxable income from him during his high earning years, while ensuring that he will receive the property during his retirement years. A full economic analysis of this device is a bit beyond our purpose. Essentially, you would have to compare the loss to the individual of the after tax income he would otherwise receive, multiplied by the number of years during which the charity has the income, against the amount of charitable deduction the donor or decedent would obtain. As with several devices, this one is particularly dramatic in the estate of super wealthy people because the estate tax charitable deduction is worth a great deal in such an estate, perhaps as much as 70% of the value of what is left to charity. It can easily work out, given the appropriate tax brackets, that what is gained by way of the charitable deduction far exceeds what is temporarily given up by the individual. For that reason, the charitable lead trust has become a favorite estate planning device of sophisticated planners who advise the super wealthy. The government is in a very real sense making the taxpayer an offer he can't refuse.

A Private Foundation

A donor could also establish a private foundation (see page 156), either during life or at death. The complexities of those devices are well beyond our scope here. Suffice it to say that the rules about qualifying as a foundation have been increasingly tightened over the past several years so that it is more difficult and perhaps less advantageous to so qualify than it was.

Planning for Carryover Basis

In the opinion of many planners, carryover basis is a major congressional blunder. This is so not only because its concept seems misplaced and it is virtually unworkable (bad enough indictments right there), but particularly because it so improperly intrudes into virtually every consideration and decision we now make. Classic tax theory says that tax laws aren't supposed to do that; that the economic affairs of citizens are supposed to take courses dictated by natural societal and capitalistic ebb and flow without artificial changes of direction induced by tax laws. Carryover basis violates that, one hundred percent. Postponing the effective date of carryover basis to January 1, 1980 indicates that even Congress itself may be having second thoughts.

Several thoughtful commentators have concluded that the era of carryover basis will lead to much more aggressive planning to avoid estate taxes than was formerly the case. The reason is that the former stepped-up basis provided an incentive not to get too aggressive in tax avoidance planning. The benefits of stepped-up basis were so great that a property owner would often be advised to do nothing and just die with the property he owned. Carryover basis removes this "disincentive" to aggressively tax plan. The IRS may eventually regret the day that carryover basis was enacted because my best guess is that it will see many more extremely sophisticated tax plans than it ever had to face before. And from the point of view of classic tax theory, that's bad, because it is using tax laws to push people into artificial arrangements they would never otherwise have even considered. Unfortunately, it will probably be only the upper echelons of the wealthy class who will be able to afford to do so, and so Congress's inequality-among-citizens argument may have made things worse rather than better.

So what to do? Some sophisticated moves have been already mentioned in this and other chapters, such as freezing estate values through corporate reorganizations (see page 306) and other such devices and interspousal giving provoked by the opportunity to achieve a fresh start adjustment in the estate of the spouse who previously did not own the property in question (see page 314).

Record Keeping Is Essential

In more everyday effects, one of the most important things to recognize about carryover basis is that it makes the **preservation of records much more crucial than ever before.** Since the heir takes over the decedent's basis, it is crucial to know what the basis was. And this is true whether or not the property qualified for the fresh start adjustment. That adjustment depends upon knowing the decedent's purchase date and the decedent's basis. For property which does not qualify for that adjustment because it was purchased by the decedent after December 31, 1976, it is still necessary to know the decedent's basis even if it is unnecessary to know the exact purchase date. One of the primary current tasks of estate planners is to inform their clients of the need to preserve records and to convince them of the importance of doing so. If a client has failed to keep records, or has lost them, it will be the planner's job to work with the client to reconstruct the situation to the best of the client's memory. It is far better that the client himself attempt to do so than to have an IRS agent, a judge, or an heir attempt to do so after the client's death. Once the facts have been reconstructed to the best of everyone's ability, they should be put down in a written affidavit or other statement that will be binding under the law of the state where the client resides.

Considerations In Preparing Wills And Other Estate Documents

Turning to the preparation of the client's will and other estate planning documents, consideration should be given to having the client **dispose of each and every carryover basis asset by specific**

bequest to specific heirs. This is a total departure from former practice, where a testator would usually leave all the residue of his estate, whatever it may be, to be divided equally among his children or other heirs. But after January 1, 1980, the consequences of the potential capital gains tax on the appreciation carried by each asset must be correlated with the tax bracket of each of the testator's heirs in order for the testator to know the net after-tax result for each asset and each heir. That is not to say that every testator will actually do that; some if not most will undoubtedly say, "To hell with it," and do just as they formerly would have done. But every testator ought to be advised of the tax consequences of doing it in the former manner versus doing it on an asset by asset basis.

Assume the residue consists of two pieces of property, each worth $100,000 at death, one of which has a basis of $10,000 and the other a basis of $90,000. Assume for simplicity that neither will qualify for the fresh start adjustment because they were not owned by the decedent on the appropriate date. Assume that the decedent's sole heirs are two sons whom he wishes to benefit equally, but one is in a 70% income tax bracket and the other in a 20% income tax bracket. If the testator simply leaves his estate in equal shares to his two sons, each son will not actually be receiving property of equal value. One son will own property loaded with potential capital gain if the property is sold, and that gain will be taxed on his 70% bracket return. The other son will receive like property, but the gain will be taxed upon sale of the property on his 20% bracket return. The net amount left for enjoyment by each of the sons will therefore be different after the sale has been made and the capital gains taxes paid. Many testators will likely say, "That's their problem," and refuse to be concerned about it, but others will be concerned about achieving absolute equality between the sons.

Attempting To Assure Equality Of Assets To Heirs

If the testator is one who does want to assure absolute equality, should he leave one asset to one son and the other asset to the other son? If he did, he would probably want to leave the asset with the $90,000 basis to the high bracket son in order that upon a later sale there will be only $10,000 gain (assuming the value holds constant) to be taxed on the 70% bracket return. He would then leave the asset with the $10,000 gain to the low bracket son, so that upon a later sale the large $90,000 gain would be taxed on only a 20% bracket return. But working out the arithmetic will demonstrate to you that that isn't a totally equitable solution either, because the low bracket son will actually wind up with less after the sale has been made than will the high bracket son.

So maybe an accountant should be consulted while the will is being drafted so that the potential capital gains tax effects to the two sons can be accurately plotted and an appropriate formula bequest be made. As an example, the arithmetic might indicate that the high bracket son should receive 57.863% of the residue, with the low bracket son receiving 42.137%. Does that sound absurd? If nothing else, it is raising not only the complexity of the testator's will, but also the cost of that will. And what should the testator do every time one of the assets changes in value relative to the other asset, thereby throwing the formula out of whack—run and change his will? Or what if the tax brackets of the two sons change, as tax brackets have a habit of doing, as for instance if the high bracket son suffers bad reverses and falls into a 15% bracket while the low bracket son becomes a great success and rises into the 60% bracket?

Remember, all of the above was done on the assumption that neither asset qualified for the fresh start adjustment. However, if either or both of those assets do so qualify, with every passing day the formula for computing the fresh start adjustment will be changing, so the formula in the will (if adopted) would be out of whack the day after it is written.

Problems When Equality Is Not Assured

Many testators will be unwilling to put up with such nonsense when writing their wills, and will probably resign themselves to leaving the property in equal shares and letting the chips fall where they may between the two sons. But there are two serious problems with that. One is the **potential disharmony** it may cause between the testator's sons when one realizes that the other one got all the best of it. The testator as a father may have succeeded in fostering a close relationship between the two brothers, only to blow it wide apart after his death by creating a rivalrous situation loaded with feelings of favoritism. It's doubtful that Congress intended to give us that legacy, but there you have it. The second serious problem is the **bind into which it puts the testator's executor,** at least if the testator had not given the executor specific instructions and specifically absolved him from any fiduciary responsibility for assuring complete equity between the two sons. Several states have laws which say that it is a part of an executor's fiduciary responsibility to assure equality among the beneficiaries of an estate, so in those states there are risks of a lawsuit against the fiduciary or the estate unless the testator gives specific instructions on that problem.

Cash Gifts Satisfied With Other Property

A very similar problem exists where a testator has made several specific cash gifts to various people in his will. Most state laws give executors authority to satisfy those gifts either with cash, if there is enough after taxes and expenses have been paid, or **in kind,** which means by satisfying the bequests with property that is not cash but that is worth the amount of the bequest. After carryover basis, the executor is faced with a dilemma if he chooses to, or is forced by circumstances to, satisfy those bequests with appreciated property that is pregnant with potential capital gain. In order for a beneficiary to receive what he is entitled to under the will, he must be given that amount of property which, after any potential capital gains taxes have been considered at whatever income tax bracket he is in, will leave him the amount of the bequest the testator specified he should have. After all, if he had received cash there would be no question of future capital gains taxes, so if the executor chooses to distribute non-cash property with a built-in capital gain, might not the beneficiary have a right to complain against the executor?

It is the consensus of estate planning opinion that the testator **should make some statement concerning this situation in his will,** either by authorizing the executor to make such choices and freeing him from the consequences of doing so, or else directing the executor to consider all of those consequences. Should a testator fail to leave such instructions, he is really only passing the buck to his executor, and his executor may have limited flexibility in making decisions because he is bound by the fiduciary law of his own state. The testator can provide for whatever he thinks best, and therefore he has unlimited flexibility in dealing with this problem.

Depreciation Deductions

So far I have only been considering the effect of future capital gains taxes to the heirs. But if the property is depreciable, there will be **depreciation deductions** that the heirs will be able to take against their ordinary income tax, based upon the property's carryover basis plus whichever of the four upward adjustments are available to it. You can imagine how a consideration of those sets of problems complicates the not-so-simple problems already discussed.

Which Tax Return?

Another massive area, which is however overly technical for our purposes, has to do with which tax return should be the one on which the potential capital gain of carryover basis assets should be recognized. There are several choices available between the probate estate as a separate taxpayer, any trusts which may have been created, and the individual heirs. Full scale planning would indicate that some thought be given the most advantageous tax return on which to take whatever capital gains might be necessary, upon a sale for purposes of paying death taxes and expenses, or in facilitating distributions. This is all interwoven with the highly complex world of estate and trust income tax returns, the concept of "distributable net income," and complexities that I have not discussed and that I will not discuss. But the expert attention necessary to make the correct decisions in these matters may have several effects, among them prolonging the length of time during which a probate estate must remain open, increasing the costs of administering a decedent's estate, and perhaps tipping the scales in favor of professional executors in many cases.

It is a glaring understatement to say that carryover basis has made estate planning much more complicated than it ever was.

How to Hold Title to Property

For single persons holding the title to their property in their own name alone, there is no estate planning problem. Such property will descend to their heirs by either will or intestacy. But when two or more people own property together, whether they are or are not a married couple, estate planning consequences and frequent errors follow from the form of title holding.

Tenancy In Common

Tenancy in common presents little problem because each owner's undivided interest behaves almost exactly like a single person's solely owned property. That is, it will descend to the owner's heirs by either will or intestacy. A potential difference would occur if the tenants in common had an agreement whereby the surviving co-tenants had the right to buy out the decedent's heirs. Such a provision might be present in an agreement between co-tenants who decided that the survivors should not be in co-ownership with any deceased owner's heirs. That agreement would control, and the estate or heirs would be bound to abide by its provisions. This is a clear example of a relatively ordinary lifetime contract having estate planning consequences. Many other types of lifetime contracts that one hardly thinks of as being estate planning documents do in fact have a very real and often significant effect on estate planning, which every signer of such a contract ought to recognize.

Joint Tenancy Guarantees Double Death Taxes

The greatest estate planning consequences arise from joint tenancy ownerships, with their built in right of survivorship. In the following discussion I also include tenancies by the entirety, which you will recall are devices only available in some states, and which are restricted to husbands and wives. They are in essence joint tenancies with right of survivorship between a husband and his wife. Probably the vast majority of husband and wife co-ownerships in the United States are held as either joint tenancies or tenancies by the entirety, as are a great many co-ownerships held by non-married persons. The question here is whether or not such forms of ownership are wise.

Joint tenancy guarantees double death taxes! No such blanket statement can be always accurate for every situation, but is it true in so many common situations that it needs to be said for its shock value. The need to say it exists because a great many people are completely unaware of that consequence, including not only lay persons but also real estate brokers, title insurance company personnel, escrow company personnel, stock brokers, and many accountants. Because of the crucial importance of that consequence, we should review why it is so.

Assume a husband and wife have $600,000 worth of property held entirely in joint tenancy. We can ignore whether they reside in a common law or community property state because either the marital deduction or community property laws will result at the husband's death in a taxable estate of $300,000. The estate tax on that amount is $40,800, ignoring all deductions and the like. But since the wife automatically succeeds to the entire interest in the joint tenancy property by right of survivorship, she now owns the entire property. Upon her later death, there will be no marital deduction or community property law to cut her taxable interest in half for purposes of her estate taxes, and so her gross estate will be $600,000 (ignoring everything that could in reality make that amount higher or lower, none of which is pertinent to the point of this example). It is true that the wife might qualify for the marital deduction if she had remarried and elected to leave the property to her second husband, but let's ignore that possibility as it is also not pertinent to our point. On a taxable estate of $600,000, the wife's estate taxes will be $130,704 (see Figure 11-3, page 204), considerably more than triple the taxes payable at the husband's death. What has happened is that the portion of the joint tenancy which was taxed in the husband's estate has also been taxed in hers, and it has therefore been taxed twice in the same generation. Had the one-half portion of the joint tenancy property taxed in the husband's gross estate been placed into a by-pass trust for the wife's benefit, the trust property would not have been taxed in her gross estate. She would have only owned $300,000 worth of property, which would have been her gross estate. The estate taxes at her death would thereby have been the same $40,800 that they were at the husband's death, for a savings of $89,904 by preventing the double tax on joint tenancy property (see Figure 11-4, page 205).

You may protest that you don't have $600,000, but only $350,000. In that case, joint tenancy doesn't create a double tax per se because there will be no tax at the first death, but it does create a second death tax when otherwise there might have been no second tax at all. With $350,000, at the first death the marital deduction or community property laws would have ensured a gross estate of only one-half thereof, and after 1980 that $175,000 is completely exempt. After the husband's death, by survivorship the wife owns one hundred percent of the property, and when she dies she will have a gross estate of $350,000. Only $175,000 will be exempt, and the balance will be taxable to the tune of $57,800. If the $175,000 exempt at the husband's death had been put into a by-pass trust for the wife's lifetime benefit, the trust property would be nontaxable at her death, her potential gross estate would total only $175,000, and since that amount is entirely exempt there would have been no estate taxes at all. It can truthfully be said that the $57,800 paid in estate taxes at her second death was needlessly wasted.

If you are still protesting because you only have around $200,000, remember from the discussion at the beginning of chapter eleven that there is a potential needless second estate tax if the property amounts to more than $175,000 since the survivor will own an estate worth more than the $175,000 exemption. If you are "lucky" enough not to have even $175,000, after 1980 you will be free from federal estate taxes, but unless you live in the state of Nevada you will still be subject to your state's death duties. The needlessly high double state death duties, or the needless expense of the second state death tax, will still happen to you if you hold property in joint tenancy. It may well be that your state's death tax rates are so low that you don't care, and that is a perfectly valid decision on your part. But if you do care, holding property in joint tenancy will create needless death tax expense for your family, whereas using a tax saving by-pass trust can avoid that waste.

None of the above statements change if the wife dies first.

In community property states it doesn't matter who dies first. In common law states the contribution theory governing the taxation of joint tenancy property means that there will be no estate taxes if the wife dies first whether the property is held in joint tenancy, tenancy by the entirety, or in the name of the husband alone (unless creating the joint tenancy was treated as a taxable gift so that the spouses' interests are now fifty-fifty, in which case taxes will be payable in the same manner as when the husband dies first). Not that no tax if the wife dies first is necessarily such a good deal; remember that two taxes on one-half each are always less than one tax on the whole.

The crucial point is that, no matter what your tax bracket, you **cannot make use of a tax saving by-pass trust if you hold property in joint tenancy** or tenancy by the entirety. If you have a will that contains a by-pass trust, but your title is held in joint tenancy, the joint tenancy right of survivorship will automatically control, and the provisions of your will will simply be ignored in regard to the joint tenancy property. In order to make sure that the by-pass trust provision will actually operate on a given piece of property, the title to that property must not be held in either joint tenancy or tenancy by the entirety. Along with writing the by-pass trust, you must also see to it that **title is changed** out of joint tenancy or tenancy by the entirety, at least for such properties as you want to be subject to the tax saving by-pass trust. Your local legal advisors will be able to make that change according to the property laws of your own state. They will also be able to inform you as to whether or not there would be any gift tax consequences of changing out of joint tenancy. That very much depends upon the source of the original contributions to the purchase of the joint tenancy property, whether any gift tax effects were recognized when that tenancy was created, and into what form of title you now might change. In community property states, assuming the joint tenancy was purchased with community property funds in the first place, the contribution was one-half by each spouse, and so changing to another form where each spouse has a one-half interest (such as community property titling) will not trigger a gift tax.

Basis Disadvantages To Joint Tenancy

There may also be some basis disadvantages to joint tenancy. In common law states, if the husband contributed all the funds used to buy the joint tenancy property originally, due to the contribution theory of joint tenancy estate taxation it really makes no difference from a basis point of view whether the property is held in joint tenancy or in the husband's name alone; the same is true of unmarried people who have contributed one hundred percent of the purchase price of joint tenancy property. In either case, the full value of the property will be included in the estate, and after January 1, 1980 all of it will qualify for the upward adjustments to carryover basis, particularly the fresh start adjustment if the property had been owned on December 31, 1976. (It will all qualify for the stepped-up basis prior to January 1, 1980.) However, the above statements must be correlated with any gift tax consequences which occurred when the joint tenancy was created, or which may occur under the 1976 Act's new provision viewing contributions by spouses as equal if the appropriate election is made on a timely filed gift tax return (see chapter eight's discussion of joint tenancy taxation at page 142). If due to those gift tax consequences the "contribution" for estate tax purposes is considered to have been made one-half by each spouse, then there may well be a disadvantage to joint tenancy ownership. Since only half the property will be included in the husband's gross estate, only one-half of it will qualify for the appropriate increase in basis (including the fresh start adjustment), whereas if the property were in his name alone or the original creation of the joint tenancy was not treated as a taxable gift, then all of the property would have qualified for those increases in basis. The more increases to basis you can get, the better, because future capital gains taxes will be lessened when the survivor sells the property.

In a **community property state** there is often a **distinct disadvantage to joint tenancy from basis point of view.** If community property funds were used to purchase the joint tenancy property, then the estate tax consequences upon the death of the first spouse will be identical whether the title was in joint tenancy or in community property. But the benefits of stepped-up basis before the effective date of carryover basis, and the benefits of the fresh start adjustment thereafter, may apply differently depending upon which form of title was used. Some of the community property states, including California, say that joint tenancy and community property cannot co-exist in the same piece of property, a relatively logical position since one has a right of survivorship and the other doesn't. But that causes a disadvantageous basis effect because, under the contribution theory of joint tenancy estate taxation, only one-half of joint tenancy property qualifies for the appropriate increase in basis, whereas (as I hope you remember) one hundred percent of community property qualifies for those increases even though only one of the spouses died (see page 180). That is often a major disadvantage to joint tenancy ownership, as for instance where a surviving spouse wants to sell the family home after the first spouse's death but finds the home pregnant with a distressing amount of capital gain. If the house had been held in community property, all of that gain to the extent of the stepped-up basis before January 1, 1980, and to the extent of the fresh start and other upward basis adjustments thereafter would be wiped out when she sells, whereas with joint tenancy titling only one-half of that capital gain would be wiped out.

The Three Strikes Against Joint Tenancy

In this country, three strikes is out. **Strike one** against joint tenancy is that it **guarantees double death taxes. Strike two** is that in many cases it **does not wipe out** as much of the inherent **capital gain** as might other forms of ownership. And **strike three** is that it **fails to follow any carefully conceived estate plan** in all of that plan's non-tax considerations. It does not qualify for professional management or relieve the survivor of management burdens, it does not qualify for any of the flexibilities that can be built into a by-pass trust, it does not secure the property against marital adventurers or other designing persons, and it does not protect the survivor against his or her own improvidence by way of improvidence or naivete. These three strikes are illustrated in Figure 15-5.

Does that mean that no one should own any property in joint tenancy? No, it most definitely does not mean that! This book has carefully avoided making blanket recommendations (or any recommendations at all) to its readers (other than getting good, local advice). All it means is that, as the TV program used to say, "Just the facts, ma'am," and you can do with them whatever you want. Joint tenancy avoids probate whereas many other ownership forms don't. If, after digesting all the pros and cons of probate, avoiding probate remains your number one goal, then that factor must surely be considered (although funded revocable living trusts will also avoid probate). Depending upon the laws of your own state, joint tenancy will imply certain management consequences for the joint tenants, whereas changing to some other form may radically alter those consequences to your displeasure. And don't fail to consider how a divorce would affect the property if it were held in joint tenancy versus being held in some other form; that's an unpleasant contemplation, but a fully aware person will surely consider it. Divorce consequences depend entirely upon the law of your own state, but you will often find that joint tenancy property will be split fifty-fifty upon a divorce whereas other forms of title would deliver the entire property to one spouse or the other. As always, you need to determine what your state laws provide, and then decide how you want things in light of those laws.

And finally, due to its status over the years as "the thing to

FACTS: Husband and wife own a home in joint tenancy.
They each contributed 50% of the purchase price (in a common law or community property state; it makes no difference).
Purchase price: $50,000
Assumed value on December 31, 1976: $175,000
Value at death of first spouse after December 31, 1979: $200,000
Total marital estate, including other property: $600,000

STRIKE ONE: DOUBLE DEATH TAXES

Title:

	Joint Tenancy	Not Joint Tenancy
A. Estate Taxes in Both Estates; Home's Share		
1. First spouse's estate	$13,600	$13,600
2. Second spouse's estate if joint tenancy	48,600	
3. Second spouse's estate if other form of title used, and property willed to a tax saving by-pass trust		13,600
TOTAL	$62,200	$27,200

STRIKE TWO: BASIS

B. Assume Property Sold by Survivor for $250,000		
1. One-half property qualifies for fresh start adjustment; capital gain tax: 28%	15,400	
2. All of the property qualifies for frest start adjustment; capital gain tax: 28%		8,400
	$15,400	$ 8,400

STRIKE THREE: DOESN'T FOLLOW ESTATE PLAN

C. What Survivor Can Do With the Property, as Surviving Joint Tenant versus as Lifetime Beneficiary of a By-Pass Trust		
1. Marries a marital adventurer; can latter get it away from survivor?	Maybe	No
2. Goes to Las Vegas; can survivor lose it?	Yes	No
3. Can survivor invest in a potentially disastrous investment?	Yes	Up to Trustee
4. Must survivor be burdened with protecting it and managing it?	Yes	Trustee Will

Figure 15-5. The Three Strikes Against Joint Tenancy

do," joint tenancy carries with it certain emotional meanings. Many people "just like it better," or feel that it makes things easier after one of the joint tenants has died, and no amount of factual presentations will alter that feeling. Fine; if joint tenancy makes you feel better, that is certainly a valid consideration; the purpose of estate planning is not to cause you unbearable pain. You must be comfortable with the planning decisions which apply to your estate, and whichever way the balance tips in your own mind is a very important factor. Most estate planners are content if they can be convinced that their clients understand the relevant facts and consequences. The final decision is then completely up to you.

Integrating All Property Into The Estate Plan

A final point needs to be made on this score. It is very similar to the point that joint tenancy property will not pass under your will, and thereby fails to follow the estate plan. There are several other types of assets which have that same characteristic, and in general they are those assets which avoid probate because non-probate assets are not affected by the will. Aside from joint tenancy property, the chief offenders in this regard are **life insurance proceeds** and benefits payable under **employee benefit plans** (pension or profit-sharing, Keough plans of the self-employed, or Individual Retirement Accounts). Unless each of those assets is directed into a tax saving by-pass trust, **they will be subject to estate taxes upon the beneficiary's death.** Life insurance proceeds will simply belong to the beneficiary, and to the extent they still exist when the beneficiary dies, they will be part of his or her gross estate; if they had been directed into a by-pass trust, they would not have been taxed in his or her estate. Any survivor's benefits payble under a pension or profit-sharing plan, or any of the other plans mentioned above, will belong solely to the survivor who receives them and will therefore be part of his or her estate when he or she dies. If they had been paid into a by-pass trust, they would not have been taxable in his or her later estate. Neither will any of those benefits, whether life insurance or employment benefits, obtain any of the non-tax advantages concerning management, security, and flexibility that are available in a trust.

It well may be that you do not want all of those benefits to be held in trust, and perhaps some or all of them will be designed as monthly payments to go directly to the survivor with the intention that she use those funds for monthly living expenses. Fine; that may well be the correct thing to do. The only point being made is that such types of assets do not automatically fall into your estate plan just because you've written a will or otherwise created a plan. Some affirmative decisions and affirmative steps are necessary to route those types of assets through the estate plan, usually by naming a tax saving trust as beneficiary of life insurance proceeds or employee benefit plans. Then and only will such proceeds obtain the tax and non-tax advantages that a trust can deliver.

APPLICATION

1. Determine whether the idea of a private annuity has any appeal to you. If it does, you will have to consult an accountant or attorney because he will have to compute its financial effects according to several IRS tables necessary to make those computations. But before proceeding, decide whether or not you can live with the psychological implications of this device (the fact that the shorter you live, the better the deal is for everybody).

2. If you have an interest in a business other than a sole proprietorship:
   a. Is it advisable for your survivors to remain in business with the other owners after you have died, or would it be better for your survivors to be bought out for cash?
   b. If you don't have a buy-sell agreement with the other owners of your business, should you? If so, do you want it to fix the value of your interest for estate tax purposes, or would you rather have more flexibility regarding the business's value?
   c. If you own shares in a corporation, are you interested in freezing the value of your interest by reorganizing the corporation to have two classes of stock? If so, consult a knowledgeable corporate lawyer to check out the many complexities of that course.
   d. If you are presently operating in a non-corporate form, should you perhaps incorporate and set up a two-stock structure upon formation of the new corporation, to fix the value of your interest? Another advantage to incorporating, aside from all the usual business advantages, might be the availability of the 303 stock redemptions to pay taxes and expenses; see page 167.
   e. If you don't have a Keough plan or a qualified pension or profit sharing plan, should you? These plans enable you to build up a retirement fund and give you many tax advantages along the way.

3. Does an installment sale of your business or any other asset appeal to you? Are there purchasers available who would be your natural heirs in any case? Can you rely on their ability to make the installment payments to you?

4. Can you realistically afford to embark on a program of making annual $3000 gifts ($6000 if a spouse joins in)? Do you have recipients in mind whom you would want to give money or property to? Carefully analyze your motives; find out what the real tax savings might be for what you have in mind, and then consider whether the savings are truly worth giving up the property and putting it in the hands of the donee. It may indeed be worth it; the point is not to just assume that, but to analyze it and think it through.

5. Are any of your assets candidates for healthy growth in value, and if so, are there advantages in giving away that property now before it gets any more valuable? To whom would you give it?

6. Are you in a high enough income tax bracket, with enough excess income so that you don't need it all to maintain your life style, to make gifts of income-producing property attractive for the income tax savings involved? Do you have natural donees available who are themselves in a low enough income tax bracket even after the gift is made to make a significant tax difference?

7. If you are one of a married couple living in a common law state, does the wife have any ownership interest in any property in her own right? If not, and she dies first, her $175,000 exemption will be wasted. The husband might consider gifts to her of all or a portion of that exemption amount.

8. Might there be any basis advantages to gifts between spouses, in either a common law or a community property state, considering the cost basis and current values of the assets you own?

9. Would it be advantageous for you to equalize the size of the estates owned by you and your spouse, if you are married? It is probably best to ask an accountant or attorney to compute the tax costs versus the tax savings of doing so.

10. If you want to make any gifts to a minor, decide whether to do so outright, under the Uniform Gifts to Minors Act, or by creating a special trust for minors. If you use the Uniform Gifts to Minors Act, do not be the Custodian unless you want the property to be taxed in your estate anyway. Don't neglect to consider the disadvantages of gifts, particularly of gifts to minor children.

11. Charitable giving is too vast a subject to have received more than a tiny mention in this book. If you are inclined to make

gifts to charity, either during life or in your will, consult a knowledgeable attorney for advice on all the many complex rules that apply in this area.

12. Review any existing or contemplated will to decide whether you want to concern yourself with all the tax inequalities which carryover basis implies for your heirs. If so, you will probably have to make specific bequests of specific items of property to each of your various heirs. A tax accountant or attorney is a must, as he will have to make all the various calculations necessary for you to make correct decisions on each asset.

13. Do you hold title to any property, whether bank accounts, stocks, real estate (including your family home), or other assets in joint tenancy? **IF SO, WHY?** You certainly may continue to do so if you wish, but only if double death taxes either don't affect you or don't concern you, and if you don't care about the basis benefits which might be available by holding title in some other form. If you have decided, in past wills or after having read this book, that you want a tax saving by-pass trust, **YOU MUST CHANGE YOUR TITLES OUT OF JOINT TENANCY!**

14. Do you want all of your property integrated into your estate plan to save the second tax, or for non-tax reasons? If so, do life insurance proceeds now follow the plan? Do employee benefits, such as payments from pension or profit sharing plans, now follow the plan? If insurance proceeds and employee benefits do now flow into your estate plan (which probably would include at least one tax saving by-pass trust to save the second tax), you must change the beneficiary designations in order to ensure that the funds find their way into your plan.

16

two often neglected subjects: the single person and the small estate

Estate Planning for the Single Person

If you are single, you may by now be sick of hearing about husbands and wives and wondering when this book is going to say something about the scores of people who have never married, are divorced, or are widows or widowers. This section is addressed to you.

You may notice, though, that this section is pitifully short. That is because the tax law does not provide many avenues for reducing the tax burden on the estates of single persons, and the 1976 Act took away some of the very few tax saving avenues available to them. Estate planning for single persons is now much more difficult than ever, and the list of things which they might do is even shorter; hence the shortness of this section.

The Single Person's Status

Every April 15, most single people moan about the apparent discrimination against them built into the income tax rates. Congress is not sensitive to that complaint, replying that no such discrimination has ever been intended. Rather, Congress sees social and economic reasons to give tax advantages to married people; on the assumption that their obligations and responsibilities are greater, they are allowed slightly lower tax rates. But the reverse side of every advantage is a discrimination; while it may not be intended as such, it nevertheless operates as such.

The same thing occurs in the estate tax and estate planning area, but not through the mechanism of lower tax rates since the rates are the same for all. We have seen that either the marital deduction or the community property laws allow married persons to divide the estate tax burdens between their two estates. These factors allow for two exemptions totaling $350,000 after 1980, a lowering of the overall tax impact due to half and half taxation, and to almost every other mathematical and practical advantage. Several reasons account for those advantages: the assumed greater obligations of married persons, a special wish not to endanger the security of a surviving spouse by collecting too much tax when the first spouse dies, and the awareness for tax purposes that married persons inhabit the same generation. It is true that each individual person, whether married or single, has the same $175,000 exemption from estate taxes. Nevertheless, the mathematical and practical advantages all work out to give the greatest benefits to married people, and that is just a fact of life in our tax system. This is particularly true in the ability of married persons to use the tax saving by-pass trust and still avoid the generation skipping tax (as I'll explain below), but the ability of the single person to do likewise has been greatly reduced by recent tax law changes.

However, you have probably noticed that Congress does not allow others who are in the same generation to divide the estate tax burdens in the same way, be they brothers and sisters, other relatives, or just plain friends. The reason seems to be that Congress, perhaps without being fully aware of it, implicitly views a married couple as just one property earning and property owning entity, whereas brothers, sisters, or the individual component of any other set of persons are viewed as being entirely distinct property earning and property owning entities. In that view, Congress seems to have adopted a community property-like philosophy about marriage, even though community property is the law in only a small minority of the states. Congress got backed into that position because, until 1948, community property spouses under their local law enjoyed several estate tax breaks unavailable to common law spouses. In that year the marital deduction was specifically enacted to equalize those advantages. The result is that all married couples are estate taxed the same as community property spouses, not the other way around, and if you are not married you just don't get considered in the same light. You are one single property earning and property owning entity, and estate taxes must be paid whenever property passes at death from any single entity, whether that entity is comprised of one single person or two married persons. The only flaw in the justice of that, as far as single persons are concerned, is that only married persons qualify for all the mathematical advantages referred to above. But other than having two exemptions available and being able to split the estate tax burden between their two estates, there are no special loopholes specifically permitting married persons to reduce their estate taxes.

Using The By-Pass Trust

A single person, like a married person, can benefit his chosen heirs by leaving property to them in the form of a tax saving by-pass trust. That won't help his own estate one whit, but it will help the estate of the heir. A serious inroad was, however, made into the single decedent's ability to do even that by the generation skipping tax introduced in the 1976 Act (see page 186). To determine what an unmarried decedent can do for his heirs by way of a by-pass trust, it is necessary to have a thorough grasp of the method by which the 1976 Act assigns people to generations for purposes of the generation skipping tax. If persons are lineal descendents of the grandfather of the (deathtime) decedent or (lifetime) trustor, generations are assigned and compared by counting back to that common ancestor. Therefore the decedent's brothers and sisters are in the same generation as the decedent (they are all two generations removed from the grandfather), and so an unmarried decedent could, without running afoul of the generation skipping tax, leave his property in a by-pass trust to benefit his brothers and sisters for the rest of their lives, remainder to his nieces and nephews. Note that first cousins all occupy the same generation, as do any other cousins falling into the same generation by the test set out above. And of course, an unmarried decedent who has children can set up a by-pass trust to benefit his children for life, remainder to his grandchildren, and take advantage of the $250,000 "grandchild" exemption, more thoroughly explained in chapter ten (page 191).

Avoid Generation Skipping Consequences

But if the proposed lifetime beneficiary of an unmarried decedent's by-pass trust is not in the same generation as the decedent, and that different generation is younger than the decedent's, any such trust will be a generation skipping trust. The effect is to remove any estate tax advantage which might otherwise accrue to the beneficiary who receives the property in the form of a by-pass trust. The younger generation lifetime beneficiary who would cause the generation skipping tax to apply can be of two different types. One type is any relative in a younger generation than the decedent, such as a niece or nephew, a cousin, or any other younger generation relative. The other type is non-relatives who by definition don't share any common ancestor with the decedent. Recall from chapter ten that non-relatives are assigned to generations based upon their age in relationship to the decedent. If they are no more than twelve and one-half years younger than the decedent, they are in his generation (and accordingly, they can be lifetime beneficiaries of a by-pass trust without causing the generation skipping tax to apply). If they are between twelve and one-half and thirty-seven and one-half years younger than the decedent, they are not in the decedent's generation but are in the next younger generation, and then still younger generations are computed for each subsequent twenty-five years of age younger than the decedent. So any proposed by-pass trust for the lifetime benefit of a non-relative of any decedent, married or unmarried, must be carefully analyzed to see whether or not it will cause the generation skipping tax to apply on that beneficiary's death. If it will, the generation skipping tax has prevented any estate tax advantage which may otherwise suggest the use of a by-pass trust.

An unmarried testator may still wish to use the trust form, in order to obtain all the non-tax advantages of placing his property in trust to be managed and protected for the beneficiary's benefit, even though estate taxes on the beneficiary's death will be the same as if the property had been left outright. Further, there may be significant income tax advantages to the beneficiary all during his life from the use of a trust, particularly if it is a discretionary trust which might afford him the so-called perfect tax shelter (see page 210).

Gift Giving

Since a single person's estate cannot be aided by more than one exemption or by paying the tax in two halves like a married person's estate, just about the only thing left that will give any tax relief is gift giving. But here again, the 1976 Act has hit single persons as hard or harder than married people, both because it removed the additional exemption of $30,000 for lifetime gifts, but even more importantly because it also took away the cheaper tax rates formerly applicable to lifetime giving. Of course, the $3000 annual exclusion for gifts is equally available to single persons, and since this is just about the only remaining tax reduction opportunity available to single persons, it may increase the pressure on them to engage in appropriate gift giving programs. That in turn can have a bad effect on the long term security of the single donor, as well as be potentially disadvantageous to the donee in all the ways discussed in the last chapter.

Other Possibilities

In appropriate cases, any of the more sophisticated techniques described in the last chapter can be used by a single person. If a single person is a business owner, he might freeze the value of his estate by a corporate reorganization or by an installment sale, or he can give away the appreciation element in quickly appreciating assets. A reality factor that might prevent widespread use of such moves by single persons without children is that they may be less inclined to transfer ownership interests to their future heirs than is a parent whose children are more in the parent's control. There is more of a natural authority tie between parent and child, which often allows the donor parent to keep actual control over the donated property, than there is between an unmarried donor and his nephew, cousin, or unrelated donee. Irrevocable gifts of life insurance may be particularly appropriate for single persons, though, since they are a proven method of reducing the estate of an insured who is the owner of existing policies on his own life.

Another planning device that is potentially available to a single person is the private annuity (page 301). However, all the same disadvantages apply to an unmarried private annuitant as apply to a married one, and so the practical result may well be that the private annuity remains a "much discussed, little used" device for single persons too.

You can see that there is precious little an estate planner can do to reduce the tax burden for a single person. But all the non-tax benefits of various plans described throughout this book are equally available and important to a single person or his heirs, even though the estate tax situation is pretty well fixed for a single person's estate. It therefore seems appropriate to remind all single persons that they should pay special attention to "preventative" tax planning. For instance, they may be well-advised to set up an enterprise or investment at the very beginning with estate planning motives in mind, such as by using two stock structures or by cutting their heirs in for a piece of the ownership when values are low or non-existent. They may also want to pay special attention, if feasible within their own family structure, to the manner in which they may inherit property from their parents or any other persons. A tax wise single person who recognizes the limitations on his own estate planning may wish to suggest to his ancestors that any inheritance be left to him in the form of a tax saving bypass trust, if the new generation skipping tax will allow that technique to be profitably used by his ancestor. And a married person should never by default allow himself to become a wealthy single person with a severe estate tax problem because no planning was done while both spouses were alive.

Summary

In view of the limited tax reduction possibilities available to a single person, a good part of his estate planning might profitably be concentrated on reducing expenses other than taxes. It may well be that the greatest dollar saving he can achieve is to ensure that his estate avoids probate, or at least minimizes it consistent with the practical realities. See the Application section at the end of this chapter for other expense saving ideas.

But it remains an unfortunate fact that there are just not as many tax saving and expense saving devices available for single persons as there are for married persons.

Planning for the Small Estate

The point at which an estate's size characterizes it as "small" is completely indefinable, and depends mostly on one's own perceptions. We might tentatively define a small estate as one for which federal estate tax savings are unimportant, either because the estate owner is unconcerned with whatever taxes there are, or because no taxes will be payable. But even that definition should be resisted, since savings on the annual income taxes on an estate's earnings, or savings on the capital gains taxes caused by carryover basis, may be quite important. So too might savings in state death duties, which can be reduced or eliminated by planning even though no federal taxes may threaten the estate. It is very hard to pin down what is meant by a "small" estate, and you will pretty much have to define that term for yourself.

The only reason to make a separate issue out of the "small" estate is because so many people erroneously believe that estate planning is meaningful only if one owns more than a certain amount of property (which amount they have predetermined in their minds). In reality, there is no minimum amount below which estate planning is without value, and this is so for two reasons. One is that the non-tax advantages emphasized throughout this book are available to anyone regardless of net worth and may be equally or even more valuable to a "small" estate than to a large one. The second reason concerns whatever smaller and non-dramatic expenses can be saved by careful planning. Any such savings may be vital to the continued security of the beneficiary of a modest estate, which doesn't have the luxury of excess amounts of property. Inevitable expenditures which might be reduced include not only the federal and state death taxes I have been discussing all along, but also federal and state income taxes on the property's annual earnings, capital gains taxes, probate expenses, trustee's fees, guardian's fees, expenses of a surety bond, attorney's fees, etc. A ten percent waste of any kind in a $150,000 estate, be it in taxes or non-tax expenses, may have much more serious long-term effect on the beneficiary's security than a ten percent tax error in a one-million-dollar estate. Planning can attempt reductions in any non-tax area and can therefore be most helpful in keeping all expenses to a minimum.

By-pass trusts should not be overlooked, even for their savings in state death duties alone. And a trust for the benefit of any minor beneficiary might be extremely advisable in order to avoid a guardianship, even if no taxes at all will be saved thereby. That may be particularly true when a minor is the primary or contingent beneficiary of a life insurance policy. And a trust may be highly indicated for the sole purpose of securing the best possible management in order to maximize investment return and avoid the common innocent mistakes of inexperienced people.

Probate expenses may be the largest expenses faced by many "small" estates, and consequently it may be of primary importance to minimize or eliminate them. Holding title in joint tenancy may get the property to the correct person, but it may only worsen the tax and non-tax disadvantages when the surviving joint tenant achieves sole ownership. A simple funded revocable living trust may be the happiest solution, as it can provide all the non-tax benefits I have often addressed, while at the same time avoiding the probate expenses.

Waiving bond of the named executor is allowed in most states and can serve to save administration expenses. Contracting with the chosen executor to waive or reduce his fee is also feasible when going through probate seems advisable or is unavoidable. Naming a guardian of the person of any minor children is perhaps the single most important thing a parent can accomplish by will, for surely the welfare of one's children far exceeds any tax or other economic considerations.

Any of the arrangements discussed throughout this book are available to the "small" estate. After all, this is "estate" planning, not just "tax" planning or planning for rich people. Everyone has an estate, and almost everyone can find significant benefits in planning for its disposition.

The Single Person:
1. If you want to reduce the tax load which your estate will have to bear, consider any of the following:

APPLICATION

a. Determine whether you can afford to launch a program of $3000 annual gifts, to remove at least the cumulative total of those gifts from your taxable estate. To whom would you give such gifts?

b. Consider giving away appreciating property now, at its current value, rather than having it taxed in your estate when it may be worth considerably more.

c. If you can afford to make gifts worth more than $175,000, giving away even more than that amount will remove the gift tax money from your estate if you live three years after each such gift.

d. On the contrary, if you own property that has appreciated greatly over its cost, and you owned it on December 31, 1976, consider retaining it until death so that your heirs will receive the fresh start adjustment to carryover basis, thereby reducing their capital gains taxes when they sell it.

e. Consider whether an installment sale of some of your property to your chosen heirs would be appropriate (see page 307), or whether a private annuity would be beneficial (see page 301).

f. Consider attacking income taxes rather than (or in addition to) transfer taxes. If you can afford it and you are in a high enough income tax bracket, consider gifts or irrevocable trusts of income-producing property in order to shift the income taxes to the donee.

2. Determine whether you can save the second tax at the death of any of your chosen heirs by using a by-pass trust for them; this will only work if the trust is not a generation skipping trust (see page 186). Like married people, think not only about the taxes in your own estate, but also about the taxes in your heir's estate.

3. Attack all the expenses other than taxes which your estate will face. Consider avoiding or reducing probate expenses. To avoid the double death taxes for your heirs, which the probate-avoiding joint tenancy can cause, it might be wise for you to create a funded revocable living trust. To keep down the expenses of that trust, try to find a trustee who won't charge a fee.

   a. If probate is advantageous or must be incurred, try to reduce its expenses by negotiating a contract for low fees with your proposed executor and estate attorney, or find an executor who will serve for no fee (if the many complexities do not virtually dictate that you use a bank, which will of course charge a fee). If your state allows it, waive the bond otherwise required of an executor.

4. Since higher death taxes may be inevitable for your estate compared to a married person's estate, consider purchasing life insurance to cover the cash needs of your estate, thereby at least preserving the full amount of your property for your heirs. If you arrange the policy so that you don't have the incidents of ownership (see page 146), the proceeds of that policy will not be taxed in your estate.

5. Consider a life insurance trust, so that insurance proceeds will be available to meet your estate's costs, and so the proceeds will not be taxed again in your heir's estate (if the trust is not a generation skipping trust). The same is true of payments from employee benefit plans.

6. Give due regard to all the non-tax advantages of trusts. Just because you're single doesn't mean that you shouldn't be concerned with your heir's security, protecting your property from waste or con men, and assuring competent management of it. If your heir is in a high income tax bracket, maybe the "perfect tax shelter," a discretionary trust, would be advisable (see page 210).

7. If any of your chosen heirs are minor children, seriously consider bequeathing their inheritance to a trust created in your will, rather than leaving them property outright. If you do the latter, a guardianship will be required, which is under the strict control of the probate court, and which means that the child will have outright control over the property on his eighteenth birthday.

The Small Estate:
8. If you are married, consider taking the largest possible amount of the marital deduction (one-half of your estate or up to $250,000, whichever is greater). The purpose would be to increase the income available to your surviving spouse by freeing the maximum amount from taxes at your death so that the largest possible fund will be available to earn income for the survivor. This will increase the survivor's sense of security, even at the cost of paying somewhat higher overall death taxes when both your estates are considered; in the smaller estate, it may well be worth it.

9. Since the maximum possible fund ought to be left to produce income for your heirs, consider purchasing a life insurance policy to cover whatever your deathtime expenses might be,

whether probate and other non-tax costs, or taxes of any kind (state inheritance taxes, any federal taxes which might be due, and the capital gains taxes which your heir might be facing due to carryover basis). Consider not having the incidents of ownership to prevent the policy proceeds from putting you into a taxable situation, or into a higher transfer tax bracket.

10. If you are not satisfied with the size of your estate and wish to increase the amount available for your heirs, the obvious answer is to purchase (more) life insurance. By not having the incidents of ownership, the insurance will not increase your deathtime expenses.

11. Items 2., 3., 5, 6., and 7. of this Application section apply as much to you as to the Single Person. Re-read those items.

12. The largest item of expense in your entire situation may well be the potential capital gains taxes your heirs will face after they inherit property from you. Be sure to qualify the maximum amount of property for the fresh start adjustment (see Item 1.d. above). If you are married, perhaps gifts from one spouse to the other will be able to improve the capital gains tax picture by qualifying more property for the fresh start adjustment (see page 314).

17

some thoughts by way of conclusion

By this point you have seen a great deal of what estate planning is about. Not one single subject was covered in enough depth or with enough technicality to make final decisions possible, but hopefully you will now be aware of estate planning's general framework, as well as which subjects interest you enough to follow up. By reading this far you have placed yourself among those consumers who desire to be informed about the products they are purchasing, be they tires, canned goods, or legal services. It is both laudable and appropriate that you should seek to be informed on a subject that is so personally vital to you and your family. I only hope that I have succeeded in telling you some of the things you wanted to know, and perhaps have along the way exposed you to other things which you are now quite glad to know.

But you may not be finished yet. Some of you may feel vaguely dissatisfied to realize that you might not have retained everything you've read, or because you may be a bit confused by the volume and complexity of it. If so, not only would I not blame you at all, but I affirmatively want to assure you that some degree of confusion is expected. Like it or not, this is an overwhelmingly complex society we live in, and the ridiculous complexity of its tax laws is certainly one of society's most complicated elements. So do not be unduly disturbed by any absence of perfect retention or perfect clarity; it would be thoroughly remarkable if you had been able to achieve either of those states. One reason why legal information has traditionally been withheld from lay persons is the rather haughty view that it is beyond your comprehension. One premise of this book is that this view is not true, but it is still nevertheless true that matters concerning law are not the easiest to instantly grasp. So don't be in any way chagrined or disappointed if everything is not perfectly clear. Estate planners don't run around with photographic retention of the tax law and everything else we've ever read. One of our hopes is that this book can serve as a permanent reference and refresher for you, so that at appropriate times you can leisurely re-read its various chapters and become more familiar with the immense number of competing considerations that have been thrown at you.

You might also feel a bit annoyed that no perfect estate plan has been served to you. Although I never promised that to you when you undertook to read this book, you may nevertheless feel dissatisfied at the number of dilemmas, paradoxes, and competing considerations presented. Although I might regret that as much as you do, it is reality. This just plain ain't a simple world. It would have been no service at all to conceal the hard facts and the hard choices from you, or to sugar-coat the information with simplicities which don't exist. In the process of making intelligent and informed decisions about your own estate planning, you will have to undertake the same weighing process that your advisors will be doing. A particular plan under consideration will have various advantages and disadvantages, and someone will have to make a judgment as to which are the most important considerations for the only family under discussion—your own. That judgment maker might just as well be you, rather than an advisor who can never fully share your feelings or your experiences. It seems to me that the optimum situations regarding anything we face in life would be those where we have enough information to control our own plans and decisions, and enough gumption to personally make the judgments called for.

You may wish to acquire further and more detailed information on any of the subjects included in this book. One method of doing so would be by further reading, but honesty compels me to say that such efforts may be difficult or impossible to accomplish. The fact is that most material written in this field is written for the professionals and the technicians. While you can easily locate such material, it will probably be frustrating for you to attempt much of it. I certainly don't mean to stop you from trying, and I would admire you for doing so, but you must realize that there are many roadblocks of technical jargon and references that may cause you to run screaming from the local law library. Just try some day to decipher the Internal Revenue Code and you'll see what I mean; about all it's good for is as a sure cure for insomnia. It well may be that the only workable method of acquiring further information will be by discussions with and questions to trained professionals, hopefully ones with a knack for explaining things and a willingness to do so.

My publisher has another author who has written of her wish that attorneys untrained in her field of financial planning would stay out of it. I am in full sympathy and full agreement. Trust officers and insurance underwriters should not (and most do not) attempt to practice law, lawyers shouldn't sell insurance or investments, and investment counselors shouldn't audit their clients' ledgers. Most honest professionals recognize all of those things, but there is a further extension to that same line of thought. Namely, that lay person should also realize when things are a bit beyond their competence, and are better left to the professsionals. A sometimes unfortunate aspect of the otherwise laudable age of consumerism is "do it yourself-ism." In many areas of life it can work quite well, but in others it's just plain folly. Wills, trusts, and estate planning may well be one of the latter areas. Fully informed lay persons, yes. Intelligent participants, yes. Shrewd questioners and probing decision makers, yes. But draftsmen, no. And lay persons with delusions of technical expertise and knowledge, no.

So we come back to the need for your own advisors. You may wish that you didn't need them, but you do. Just on the subject of the laws of your own state, you need up-to-date local advice. There are many things I might have done differently in this book, and some may wish I had provided more specifics on the laws of each state. Not only would that be an encyclopedia I have no wish to write and see no great need for you to own, but also laws are changing so much that the book's value would decline rapidly. It's bad enough that we have to deal with ever changing federal tax laws. To be fully informed at any given moment, you ought to get current competent advice as to the then state of the federal tax laws, and the then state of your local laws. It would be completely irresponsible if I left an impression that you don't need to do so. And needless to say, you need direct personal advice by someone who is analyzing your own personal situation. A book such as this can only go so far. It wouldn't be irresponsible of me to set forth any blanket advice, it would be criminal.

You may wonder how to choose your advisors, and how to ensure that they are competent. Choosing each of the advisors you feel is necessary for your own situation is a matter which only you can undertake. There is little I can say about choosing persons other than attorneys, except the common sense advice to interview prospective advisors, find ones you are personally comfortable with, and exercise your consumer's right of inquiry as to their expertise and their charges. But do not feel that it is somehow inherently uncouth of you to question them about their expertise and their fees. You are purchasing a product, and you are entitled to know.

You will eventually need an attorney well versed in estate planning, and if he is not fully expert he can quickly undo the good information and decisions which you have been able to acquire from other advisors and from your own research. The problem becomes one of finding one with sufficient expertise, and this leads me into a major quarrel I have with the position taken by the various bar associations. Until recently rejected by the U.S. Supereme Court, bar associations took the stodgy and outmoded position that lawyers were not allowed to advertise the fields of practice in which they were either expert or interested. The thought, dating back to far simpler times, was that every lawyer should know everything. No comment needs to be made on the absurdity of that. But in my opinion, not allowing lawyers to inform the consuming public as to their specialties amounts to nothing more nor less than consumer fraud. How else is the consumer able to discover which attorney is expert in the area in which expertise is needed? At least with the recent Supreme Court decision, lawyers will now be allowed to impart some information as to their expertise. Although that horrifies some of my colleagues at the bar, as long as it is done with reasonable dignity and complete truthfulness, it can not help but be a major boon to the consumer. However, you must recognize that merely advertising a specialty does not guarantee competence; in fact, this is a major fear of those who oppose classifying lawyers by specialty. Advertising may at least tell you who purports to be an expert, but there is still no substitute for your own searching inquiries.

The traditional method for locating a good lawyer remains the same as ever: word of mouth. A good recommendation from a satisfied client is your best clue to a good lawyer. This book should have demonstrated to you that estate planning is a highly complex specialty and is not something to be trifled with by a lawyer who has not devoted himself to all of its twists. Unfortunately, some lawyers either don't know that, or choose to ignore it; writing cheap wills badly and then hoping to land the subsequent probate fee has been an all too common course of conduct that hopefully the new breed of lawyer is being educated against. It seems rather clear to me that you need not just a good lawyer, but a good one with expertise.

Locating the right one can be a bit of a problem if you have no personal recommendations to go by; hopefully the new rules concerning advertising will help in some way. Other than that, it is possible for you to seek out professional associations which estate planners frequently belong to, or to ask local bar associations, which often maintain lawyer referral services with breakdowns of lawyers by areas of expertise. Any of the other "members of the estate planning team" may be able to supply you with recommendations, and usually the trust department of a local bank will give you a list of names of attorneys they have found satisfactory. Some people are suspicious that those lawyers will be predisposed to recommending the bank from which you got their name to serve as fiduciary; you will just have to use your own judgment, but that possibility is a legitimate subject for inquiry when you are interviewing prospective lawyers. A similar suspicion may arise regarding referrals made by life insurance underwriters and any predisposition of the lawyer to recommend more insurance; that recommendation may well be legitimate no matter where the referral came from, so your best defense is to feel reasonably secure that the laywer you select is a person of good conscience whose objectivity can be trusted.

The costs of estate planning are quite impossible to state. I cannot even quote a fee to a potential client until we have had a conference at which we can begin to form ideas about what kind of work needs to be done. When you add that factor to variations in the going rate for legal fees in differing locations and rural versus urban settings, there is just nothing that can be quoted as a generality. One thing you might seek, if lawyers in your area are willing to do so, is an assurance that if you are not satisfied with the attorney or his fee quote, he will not charge you for the first interview; that is an arrangement which many attorneys are happy to make. But when thinking about fee quotes, do be sure to weigh the future taxes and expenses which might be saved by a good plan, as well as the plan's contribution to your peace of mind, against whatever the current outlay may have to be. Also remember that the real commodity you are paying for is expertise, not hours or documents *per se*.

Be sure not to unwittingly trap your survivors into deadly double death taxes by procrastination or unwillingness to pay a legal fee. Many survivors of unplanned estates have wished that their benefactors had not been so reluctant to pay what now seems like a minor cost when weighed against the problems and costs they left behind. Many people cannot bring themselves to pay current money in order to obtain future benefits, particularly if they see those benefits accruing only to others. But there are two serious flaws in that type of thinking relative to estate planning. One is that such a person is not just omitting to do something. He is in fact making a negative gift to a loved one, a gift of problems or needlessly high expenses, which he doubtless would never have deliberately wished to leave. The other is that he is not just foregoing a future benefit for someone else, but rather a priceless current benefit for himself: peace of mind, the feeling that all is well.

There's volumes more to be said, but nothing more to be said here. I sincerely hope that this book has been of help.

glossary

A-B Trust: a single trust divided on its books into two separate portions, which portions are by custom called trust A and trust B.

Accounting: a report of all items of income and all items of outgo, prepared by an Executor, a Trustee, or a Guardian.

Accumulation Trust: a trust the income of which may in whole or in part be retained in trust instead of being distributed to the beneficiaries.

Administration: the period of time after a decedent's death when his affairs are handled under court supervision; often synonymous with probate.

Administrator: the court appointed person handling an administration when there was no will to name an executor. Feminine: administratrix.

Alternate Valuation Date: a date six months

after a decedent's death, when by election all of the assets of his estate may be valued.

Amortization: see Depreciation; the same concept, but for intangible property.

Annual Exclusion: the sum of $3000 which may be given by each donor to each and every donee, every year, free of federal gift tax.

Appointee: the person who receives property when a power of appointment has been exercised in his favor.

Ascertainable Standard: a power to consume trust principal in amounts limited to a beneficiary's health, education, maintenance, or support.

Basis: capital gain is the excess of selling price over basis; original basis is usually an asset's cost, but may be later adjusted.

Beneficiary: the person for whom a trust is managed. Also, the recipient of life insurance proceeds, benefit plans, or gifts in a will.

Bond: a guarantee by an insurance or similar company agreeing to make up for any loss negligently or criminally caused by an Executor or Administrator.

Buy-Sell Agreement: an agreement among co-owners of a business promising to buy out one of their number upon death or other occurrences.

By-Pass Trust: a trust designed to avoid estate taxes at the death of the person who had a lifetime interest in that trust.

Capacity: see Testamentary Capacity.

Capital Gain: the profit realized by the sale of capital assets (which are most assets) owned for more than one year.

Carryover Basis: an heir's basis for property inherited from a decedent who died after December 31, 1979, which is the decedent's basis as adjusted by any of several available adjustments.

Chancery Court: what some states call their probate court.

Charitable Foundation: an organization, usually a corporation, designed to distribute its income among charities.

Charitable Remainder Annuity Trusts: a trust with a charity as ultimate beneficiary, where annual sums are paid to an individual during his lifetime in fixed dollar amounts or amounts that are a percentage of the initial value of the trust.

Charitable Remainder Unitrust: like a Charitable Remainder Annuity Trust, except that the annual sums may be a fixed percentage of the trust's value as that value is redetermined every year.

Clifford Trust: a trust lasting more than ten years, after which the original creator of the trust gets the property back.

Closely Held Corporation: a corporation the shares of which are not traded on any recognized stock exchange, so are "closely held."

Codicil: a document amending or supplementing a will.

Commingling: mixing up of community property and separate property in one bank account, other type of property, or an entire estate.

Common Law State: the 42 American states which take their marital property law from the English common law.

Community Property: all property acquired in one of the 8 community property states by married persons during marriage that is not separate property; the earnings or fruits of the marriage. The eight states are: Arizona, California, Idaho, Louisiana, Nevada, New Mexico, Texas, and Washington.

Conflicts of Laws: legal rules determining which state's law shall apply when a legal matter involves the laws of more than one state.

Conservatorship: available in some states, it resembles a guardianship of an incompetent, but without the stigma of incompetency.

Contemplation of Death: the concept that cause estate taxation of all gifts made by a decedent within three years of his death.

Contest: see Will Contest.

Contribution Theory: the rule under which joint tenancy property is estate taxed, based upon the contributions of the decedent.

Corpus: the property making up a trust; synonymous with Principal.

Court Trust: a trust that is subject to the ongoing jurisdiction of the probate court.

Creditor's Claim: a document that must be filed by most of a decedent's creditors in order to get paid from the assets of his estate.

Credits: subtractions made directly from a tax that is owed; more beneficial than Deductions.

Curtesy: the reverse of Dower (see Dower); a husband's rights.

Decedent: a person who has died.

Deductions: items that may be subtracted from taxable income, the taxable estate, or taxable gifts, thereby lowering the amount on which the tax is due.

Deemed Transferor: the person who, or whose estate, will have to pay the new Generation Skipping Tax, whenever that tax is payable.

Default Taker: the person who succeeds to property if the holder of a Power of Appointment fails to exercise that power.

Deficiency: an extra amount of tax that the IRS may claim is due, after they have audited a tax return.

Depreciation: a deduction allowed against the income produced by property used to produce income, in the amount of that property's original cost divided by its estimated useful life; intended to allow for prompt replacement of worn out income-producing property.

Devise and Bequeath: ancient words meaning to pass property by will.

Disclaimer: a document that, if filed on time, will allow an heir to give up his right to inherit property without any adverse tax consequences.

Discretionary Trust: a trust that allows the trustee to distribute the annual trust income among such specified persons as he sees fit.

Distributable Net Income: the technical manner in which the income of a trust or estate is taxed; called "DNI" in the tax world.

Domicile: a legal term fixing the state or country within which a decedent's estate will be probated and taxed; it is where he intended his permanent home to be.

Donee: the person to whom a Power of Appointment, or any other property, is given.

Donor: the person who gives a Power of Appointment, or any other property.

Dower: increasingly outmoded term for the percentage share of marital property automatically given to a wife upon the death of her husband; applies only in Common Law states.

Election: a choice or option to select among different alternatives.

Escheat: when a person dies intestate and there are no heirs to take his property, it goes to the state; it "escheats."

Estate Tax: the death tax imposed by the federal government and some states on the estate of a decedent, taxing the decedent's privilege of leaving his property to others at his death.

Estate Trust: a type of trust which qualifies for the Marital Deduction, whereby the surviving spouse does not have to receive all of the trust's annual income, but at her death the trust property goes to her estate.

Executor: the person named in a will to handle a probate administration under court supervision. Feminine: executrix.

Exemption: a certain minimum amount on which a tax will not apply.

Fair Market Value: what a willing buyer would pay a willing seller if neither of them were under any compulsion to either buy or sell. The standard at which property is valued for estate tax purposes.

Family Allowance: (sometimes called "widow's allowance") an amount allowed by a probate court for the monthly support of a surviving spouse and often, also, minor children. Takes precedence over claims of most creditors.

Fee Simple: the entire or whole ownership of property, unburdened by any future interest or any possibility of losing total ownership.

Fiduciary: a person acting for another under the highest possible standard of care, such as executors, trustees, guardians, etc.

Fiduciary Income Tax Return: the tax return that must be filed by an estate, a trust, or any other entity managed by a fiduciary.

Fiscal Year: a non-calendar twelve-month year that may be adopted by an estate, sometimes by a trust, and often by other entities as well.

Five By Five Power: the annual power to take from trust principal an amount not exceeding $5000 or 5% of the principal, whichever is greater.

Flower Bonds: certain U.S. Treasury obligations redeemable at par in the payment of federal estate taxes, even though purchased at a discount.

Fresh Start Adjustment. a provision allowing Carryover Basis property to be adjusted upwards to its actual or assumed value as of December 31, 1976.

Funded Trust: a living trust that has had property transferred to it.

General Power of Appointment: a power wherein appointment may be made to anyone at all, including the power holder himself, his creditors, etc.

Generation Skipping Tax: a tax costing the same as an estate tax if a trust has beneficiaries in two or more generations younger than the trustor.

Gift Tax: an excise tax on the privilege of making gifts.

Gifts to Minors Act: see Uniform Gifts to Minors Act.

Grantor: the creator of a trust; synonymous with Settlor and Trustor.

Gross Estate: the totality of property that can be taxed by an estate tax.

Guardianship: court supervised administration of the property and person of either a minor child or an incompetent adult.

Heir: anyone succeeding to property by intestacy; in modern usage, also includes anyone taking property under a will.

Holographic Will: permitted only in some states, it is a will entirely in the handwriting of the Testator.

Homestead: a probate provision allowing the surviving spouse to continue to live in the family residence. Lasts for varying periods of time.

Incidents of Ownership: the totality of rights which an owner has in a life insurance policy, such as to cash it in, to borrow against it, etc.

Income: the annual earnings of a trust or a probate estate, or of any person or property.

Individual Retirement Accounts (IRAs): retirement funds allowed to any income earner who is not covered by any other type of retirement plan; can contribute up to $1500 per year, tax deductible ($1750 per year if the spouse joins in).

Inheritance Tax: an excise tax imposed by many states on the privilege of inheriting property. Imposed on the recipient, not on the decedent.

Installment Sale: a sale complying with special rules that allow the capital gain resulting from that sale to be taxed over several years.

Insured: the person upon the death of whom a life insurance policy will pay its proceeds to the named beneficiary.

Inter Vivos: Latin for "during life"; describes a trust or anything else established or done during a person's lifetime.

Intestacy: the state of dying without a valid will. State law then determines who inherits the property.

Intestate: a person who dies without leaving a valid will.

Inventory: a probate court document listing, and often valuing, all of the property contained in the probate estate.

Irrevocable Trust: a trust that may never be revoked or amended by its creator.

IRS: the Internal Revenue Service, a branch of the U.S. Treasury Department, charged with collecting and enforcing most federal taxes.

Issue: all persons who have descended from an ancestor in a direct lineal line; your children, grandchildren, great-grandchildren, etc.

Joint and Mutual Will: a single will signed by both husband and wife, disposing of their property at each death. Usually to be avoided.

Joint and Survivor Annuity: a guaranteed periodic (usually monthly) sum payable first to one person for his lifetime and then to his designated survivor for his or her lifetime.

Joint Tenancy: co-ownership between two or more people with right of survivorship, meaning that a survivor automatically becomes the owner of a decedent's interest. Avoids probate.

Keough Plans: retirement plans for self-employed persons and partners, named after the Congressman who introduced them.

Legacy: a gift of property in a will; usually refers to a gift of cash.

Letters Testamentary: what many states call the actual document that evidences the authority of an Executor to act for his decedent's estate.

Life Estate: the right to use and enjoy property for a period of time measured by someone's life, usually the life tenant's own life.

Life In Being: any person alive or in gestation used to measure the maximum duration of trusts and other future interests under the Rule Against Perpetuities.

Life Tenant: the person who is in possession of a life estate, or life interest in a trust.

Living Trust: same as Inter Vivos Trust; a trust created during life.

Management: in community property states, the legal authority to handle the community property; sometimes only one spouse has it, sometimes both have it.

Marital Deduction: allows a decedent spouse a deduction from death duties for property left to the surviving spouse, up to one-half of such property or $250,000, whichever is greater.

Marital Deduction Formula Clause: a complex will clause attempting to qualify the exact right amount of property for the Marital Deduction.

Marital Property: property acquired by married persons after their marriage, other than property which either of them got by gift or inheritance.

Minimum Basis: a minimum amount of $60,000, which may be the new basis for all the property inherited from one decedent after December 31, 1979.

No Contest Clause: a clause in a will attempting to disinherit any person who attacks the will's legal validity.

Non-Court Trust: a trust that is not subject to the ongoing jurisdiction of a probate court; opposite of Court Trust.

Notice to Creditors: the method of informing a decedent's creditors that he has died, and that they should enter their claims against his estate.

Nuncupative Will: an oral will, only allowed in some states for a very small amount of Personal Property, and usually only if made a limited number of days before death.

Orphan's Court: what some states call their probate court.

Orphan's Exclusion: an exclusion from estate taxes for property left by his parent to an orphan, amounting to $5000 times the number of years the orphan is under twenty-one years of age.

Owner (of Insurance): the person who possesses all of the Incidents of Ownership in an insurance policy.

Partition: a court proceeding allowing any co-owner of property to force a separation of the co-ownership interests, usually by a court ordered auction sale with the proceeds divided among the owners.

Pension and Profit-Sharing Plans: retirement plans that can be established only by corporations.

Per Capita: describes sharing an inheritance in equal shares by relatives in an equal degree of relationship to a decedent.

Per Stirpes: Latin for "by stocks"; same as Right of Representation.

Personal Property: all tangible or intangible property which is not real property.

Personal Representative: best term for person handling an estate during period of Administration; includes both Executors and Administrators.

Pooled Income Fund: a fund maintained by a charity whereby smaller donations of many individual contributors may be maintained, and income paid on the contributed amount to whomever the contributor designates.

Pour Over Will or Trust: a will (the "pour over will") leaving property to an already existing living trust (the "pour over trust").

Power of Appointment: the power to designate who shall be the owner of property. Subheadings: general and special powers.

Preferred Stock: corporate stock that has a preferred claim to dividends and to distributions if the corporation liquidates.

Preliminary Distribution: a distribution of some of the property in a probate estate before the estate is ready to be closed.

Pretermitted Child: a child unintentionally omitted from all mention in the will of its parents, often entitled to a statutory share.

Principal: the property comprising a trust; synonymous with Corpus and Res.

Principal and Income Act: a uniform act in force in most states, determining what items of receipt or payment are either principal or income.

Prior Taxed Property, Credit For: a credit allowed against the estate tax owed by one decedent if his estate includes property that was estate taxed in the estate of a prior decedent within the previous ten years.

Private Annuity: a non-commercial contract where one person sells property to another in exchange for a promise of lifetime income.

Probate: the after death period of time when a decedent's affairs are handled under court supervision. Synonymous with Administration.

Probate Court: the branch of a state's regular court where probate matters are handled.

Profit Sharing Plans: see Pension and Profit Sharing Plans.

Qualified Plans: Pension and Profit Sharing Plans that have been specifically qualified by the IRS for many advantageous tax breaks.

Quasi-Community Property: property brought into a community property state by new, married residents which was earned during marriage in a non-community property state.

Real Property: land or real estate, together with whatever is affixed to it, growing on it, or erected on it.

Remainder: the property interest passing to a new owner after a life estate or other interim interest has terminated.

Remainderman: the person who will acquire the remainder.

Reorganization: a change in the stock structure or stock ownership rights of a corporation.

Republish: to cause a will to speak over again as of the date of a codicil, so that the will is read as if it were written on the date of the codicil.

Res: the property comprising a trust; Latin for "thing." Synonymous with Principal and Corpus.

Residence: to be distinguished from Domicile. Where one currently lives, but not necessarily one's Domicile.

Residuary Clause: the clause in a will disposing of the Residue (see next page.)

Residue: all the property left to be disposed of by will after specific items have been devised or bequeathed to specific persons.

Reversion: the possibility or certainty that, after a donor has given property away, it may or will come back into the donor's ownership.

Revive: to reinstate a previously revoked will to legal effectiveness.

Revocable Trust: a trust that may at any time be revoked or amended by its creator.

Right of Representation: describes dividing an inheritance in not necessarily equal shares when heirs "represent" a predeceased relative and share whatever that relative would have been entitled to.

Right of Survivorship: part of the definition of Joint Tenancy ownership, it means that the surviving joint tenant will automatically become the owner of the property when his other joint tenant(s) dies.

Rule Against Perpetuities: a rule prescribing the maximum amount of future time within which an owner may dictate who shall own or use his property. Determines how long a trust may exist.

Separate Property: in a community property state (and similarly in a common law state), property owned by a spouse before marriage or acquired even during marriage by gift or inheritance.

Settlor: the person who creates a trust; synonymous with Trustor and Grantor.

Severance: the breaking up of a Joint Tenancy (which then turns into a Tenancy in Common) when one of the joint tenants does one of many acts making it inequitable to continue as a joint tenancy.

Special Power of Appointment: a power wherein appointment is restricted to a designated class or group of named persons.

Special Use Valuation: allows the valuation of real estate used as a farm or in a closely held business at its value for that actual use, as opposed to at its "highest and best use."

Spendthrift Clause: protective trust clause stating that the beneficiary's interest may not be attacked by his creditors or taken in bankruptcy.

Sprinkling Trust: synonymous with discretionary trust, where the trustee can "sprinkle" the income among various beneficiaries.

Stepped-up Basis: pre 1-1-80 provision whereby heir's basis in inherited property is equal to its value on the decedent's estate tax return.

Surrogate Court: what some states call their probate court.

Tenancy By The Entirety: essentially identical to a joint tenancy between husband and wife, with right of survivorship.

Tenancy In Common: co-ownership between two or more people where each tenant owns a defined percentage of the whole.

Ten-Year Trust: synonymous with Clifford trust; see that definition.

Testamentary Capacity: the legal capacity to make a will.

Testamentary Trust: a trust, created in a will, that does not come into existence until after the testator's death.

Testate: leaving a valid will, as opposed to dying intestate.

Testator: the person who writes a will. Feminine: testatrix.

303 Redemption: a purchase of closely held stock by the corporation itself in amounts sufficient to pay the stockholder's federal and state death taxes and administration expenses.

306 Stock: certain preferred stock, usually received in a tax-free reorganization, which yields ordinary income upon its sale.

Throwback Rule: if accumulated trust income is distributed in a tax year after the one in which it is earned, it is generally then taxed at the bracket of the beneficiary for the year in which it was earned.

Totten Trusts: not really trusts, but special banking arrangements where the depositor holds the account "in trust for" another and retains sole ownership of the funds for the rest of his, the depositor's, life.

Tracing: a doctrine of some community property states, giving marital property the same characteristic it originally had notwithstanding changes or form, appreciation, etc.

Trust: a legal entity in which one person or institution holds and manages property for the benefit of someone else.

Trustee: the person who holds trust property for the benefit of another.

Trustor: the person who creates a trust; synonymous with Settlor and Grantor.

Undivided Interest: the percentage interest held by a Tenant in Common.

Unfunded Trust: a living trust that has not had any property actually transferred to it.

Uniform Gifts To Minors Act: a uniform act in force in most states, enabling a gift of specified types of property to a Custodian, to be held for a minor until the minor comes of age.

Uniform Probate Code: a uniform act adopted in several states that attempts to reduce a court's involvement in the probate process, thus speeding up the probate and hopefully making it less costly.

Unitary (or Unified) Transfer Tax: after 1-1-77, replaces both federal estate and gift taxes with a single tax on all transfers whenever made.

Widow's Election: a device found mostly in community property states where one spouse purports to dispose of the property belonging to the other spouse, giving the survivor an option as to whether or not to go along with that attempt.

Will: a formal document directing the disposition of one's property after his death.

Will Contest: litigation to overturn a decedent's will for lack of testamentary capacity or lack of due execution.

Younger Generation Beneficiary: a person in a generation younger than the creator of a trust, whose presence may cause the Generation Skipping Tax to apply.

Index

A-B trust, 238–245
Administration (*see* Probate)
Administrator (*see* Executor)
Adopted children, inheritance rights of, 36
Alternate valuation date, 131
  probate, effect on duration, 77
Amend, estate taxation of power to, 139
Annuity:
  defined, 140
  estate taxation, 140
  joint and survivor, 140
  private (*see* Private annuity)
Annuity trust, charitable remainder, 155
Appointment, power of (*see* Power of appointment)
Appreciation, giving away, 313
Ascertainable standard:
  defined, 145
  estate tax, not subject to, 145
  trust, used in, 211

Bank account trust, 270
Banks:
  executor, serving as, 53
  trustee, serving as, 95–98
    minimum size of trusts for, 97
Basis:
  carryover (*see* Carryover basis)
  defined, 174
  gift, property acquired by, 182
  inheritance, property acquired by, 174
  joint tenancy, disadvantage of, 334
  stepped-up, 174
  unknown, 183
Beneficiary:
  defined, 87
  generation skipping tax, definition, 188
Bond of executor, 54
Buy-sell agreements:
  defined, 297
  fixing estate tax values by, 306
  life insurance to supply cash for, 297
By-pass trust:
  ascertainable standard, 211
  children, postponing distribution to, 217
  defined, 207
  family pot trust, 218
  five by five power, 213
  generation skipping tax's application, 220
  grandchildren, continuing for benefit of, 219
  income of, 209
  joint tenancy fails to become part of, 224, 334
  principal, invasions of, 211

probate, relationship to, 224
property, directing it into, 224, 334, 338
remaindermen, provisions for, 216
special power of appointment, 215
state death taxes, savings by use of, 225
surviving spouse as trustee, 98, 208, 212
tax shelter, use as, 210
time when must be established, 223
trustee, choice of, 212

Capacity, testamentary (*see* Testamentary capacity)
Capital gain, defined, 174
Carryover basis:
  adjustments, 176–182
  fresh start, 176 (*see also* fresh start adjustment, this heading)
  minimum basis, 181
  taxes, 181–182
  amendment or repeal, 185
  asset by asset bequests, 327
  defined, 176
  effective date, 173
  equality among heirs, assuring, 328
  fresh start adjustment, 176–177
    appraisals unnecessary, 176
    community property, application to, 179–180
    long term effect, 179
    loss, not for computing, 177
    property other than securities, formula for, 177
    spouses, gifts between to improve, 314
    stocks and marketable securities, 177
  information required from executor or administrator, 184
  joint tenancy, disadvantages of, 334
  minimum basis, 181
  personal and household effects exclusion, 176
  record keeping necessary, 327
  satisfaction of bequests with appreciated assets, 330
  taxes, adjustments for, 181–182
  unknown basis, 183
Charitable deduction:
  annuity trust, charitable remainder, 155
  deferred giving, 324
  defined, 154–156
  foundations, charitable, 156, 326
  lead (or front end) trust,

charitable, 325
pooled income fund, 155
unitrust, charitable remainder, 155, 324
Charitable remainder trusts:
  annuity trust, 155
  pooled income fund, 155
  unitrust, 155, 324
Children:
  adopted, inheritance rights of, 36–37
  disinheriting, 48
  gifts to, 317
  trusts for, 272, 321
    postponing trust distributions to, 217
Clifford trusts:
  cost analysis of, 268
  defined, 267
  estate tax costs of, 267
  gift tax costs of, 267
Closely held corporations:
  defined, 132
  installment payment of estate taxes on account of, 165
  valuation of, 132–133
Codicil, 45
Commingling, 22
Common law states:
  marital property in, 18
  earnings of wife, 18–19
  estate taxation of, 135
Common, tenancy in (*see* Tenancy in common)
Community property:
  agreements concerning, 23, 24, 28
  apportionment theory, 24
  basis, 179–180
    joint tenancy purchased with community funds, 335
  borrowed funds used to purchase, 25
  business interests, determining percentage of, 25
  commingling, 22
  defined, 21
  estate taxation of, 135
  group term life insurance, special problems of, 299
  improvements on, 25
  intestacy laws relating to, 34
  joint tenancy purchased with community funds, 23–24, 335
  life insurance as, 148, 293
    problems of, 292–295
    separate property ownership, 294–295
    spouse as owner, 293–295
  management, rights of, 22
  marital deduction, not qualifying for, 156
  marital deduction, qualifying for, 159, 231–232
  out of state property brought

INDEX

into, 27
quasi-community property, 27
states, list of, 21
time property acquired, 24
title, how to hold as, 23
tracing, 22
Contemplation of death, gifts in:
  defined, 136
  life insurance, gifts of, 288
  paying premiums on gifted insurance, 290–292
Contests, will (*see* Will contests)
Corpus (*see* Trusts, corpus)
Co-Trustee (*see* Trustees, co-trustees)
Credits against estate tax:
  foreign death taxes, 162
  prior taxed property, 161
  state death taxes, 161
  unitary transfer tax, standard credit against, 118
Curtesy, 20

Deductions from estate tax:
  charitable deduction, 154
  debts of decedent, 152
  expenses of administration, 151
  losses, 153
  marital deduction, 156
  probate fees, 151
Deemed transferor, 190
Deferred giving, 324–326
Disinheriting spouse or children, 48
Discretionary trust, 94, 102, 210
Domicile, 32
Double taxation:
  effect of, 201–202
  eliminating, 203
    avoiding probate as well, 262
  illustrations of, 204–205
  joint tenancy guarantees, 332
Dower, 20
Due Dates:
  estate tax returns, 162
    extensions of time, 163
  gift tax returns, 124

Employee benefit plans:
  estate plan, integrating into, 338
  estate taxation, 141
  income tax benefits, 311
  qualified plans, 140
  tax free transfer to heirs by means of, 311
Entirety, tenancy by the (*see* Tenancy by the entirety)
Escheat, 35
Estate, defined, 1
Estate planning, defined, 1
Estate trust, 241
Estate tax:
  contemplation of death, gifts in, 136
  credits against, 118, 161–162
    foreign death taxes, 162
    prior taxed property, 161
    state death taxes, 161
    unitary transfer tax, standard credit against, 118
  deductions from, 151–160
    charitable deduction, 154
    debts of decedent, 152
    expenses of administration, 151
    losses, 153

marital deduction, 156
probate fees, 151
defined, 116
double taxation, 201–203
  illustration of, 204–205
  joint tenancy guarantees, 332
exemption, 118
  not wasting, between spouses, 313
extensions of time to pay, 163
flower bonds, paying with, 164–165
installment payments, 165–166
  fifteen year installments, 166
  ten year installments, 166
joint tenancy, 141–142
  guarantees double death taxes, 332
life estate not subject to, 130
  retained life estates, 137
life insurance, 147–148
  illustration, 149
payment, 162–170
  extensions of time, 163
  flower bonds, paying with, 164–165
  installment payments, 165–166
  normal time, 162
  redemptions of stock to pay, 167–170
powers of appointment, 144
property subject to, 129–148
  chart synopsizing, 150
  valuation of, 131
rates, 119
redemptions of stock to pay, 167–170
returns, 121, 162–163
  due dates, 162
  extensions to time to file, 163
  minimum filing amount, 121
revocable trusts and transfers, 139
savings possible, 199–203
  avoiding probate as well, 262
Executors:
  carryover basis information required from, 184
  choice between individual and bank, 53–54
  co-executors, 54, 64
  fees of, 60
  multiple executors, 64
  naming in will, 53
Exemptions from estate and gift taxes, 118
  not wasting, between spouses, 313
Extensions of time to file returns, 163
Extraordinary fees (*see* Probate, costs)

Fair market value:
  business interests, 132
    buy-sell agreement, fixing values with discount factors, 132
    freezing values, 306–311
  defined, 131
  real estate, 133
    farms and businesses, special election for real estate used in, 134
Family annuity (*see* Private

annuity)
Family pot trust, 218
Farms, special estate tax valuation election, 134
Fee simple, 49
Fiscal year, choice of by probate estate, 80
Five by five power
  defined, 145, 213
  estate taxation of, 145, 213
$5000/5% power (*see* Five by five power)
Flower bonds, 164–165
  carryover basis, effect of, 184
Formula clauses for marital deduction, 232–233
  savings achieved by, illustration, 235
Foundations, charitable, 156, 326
Fresh Start Adjustment, 176
  (*see also* Carryover basis, fresh start adjustment)
Funded trust:
  defined, 256
  avoiding probate, necessity of, 257
  obtaining professional management, necessity of, 257

Gain, capital (*see* Capital gain)
General power of appointment, 144
Generation skipping tax:
  defined, 187
  effective dates, 192
  generation skipping trust defined, 188
    illustration, 189
  getting around 220–222
    direct gifts, use of, 221
    income, distributions of, 222
    postponing tax, 222
    separate trusts, use of, 221
  grandchildren exemption, 191
  outright gifts, no effect on, 189
  reason for, 187
  taxable distribution, 190
  taxable termination, 190
  younger generation beneficiaries, 188, 346
  illustration, 189
Generation skipping trust, 188
Gift tax:
  defined, 116
  exemptions, 122
  life insurance, gifts of, 286
  marital deduction, 122
    carryover basis, using to improve, 314–315
    estate tax exemptions, using to not waste, 313–314
    rates, 119
    returns, when required, 124
    spouses, gift splitting by, 123
    spouses, gifts between, 122
    $3000 annual exclusion, 123
    life insurance, gifts to a trust, 289
    present interest rule, 124
Gifts:
  advantages (five), 312–313
  appreciation, giving away, 313
  assets, selection for gifts, 316
  basis, property acquired by gift, 182
  business interests, to freeze value of, 307
    illustration, 308

373

INDEX

Gifts (cont.)
  carryover basis, gifts between spouses to improve, 314–315
  charitable, 323–326
  contemplation of death, gifts in, 136
    life insurance, gifts of, 288
    paying premiums on gifted insurance, 290–292
  disadvantages, 321–322
    to donee, 322
    to donor, 322
  exemptions, gifts so as not to waste, 313
  income taxes, shifting by gifts, 254–255, 313
  life insurance, 286
  minors, gifts to, 317
    Uniform Gifts to Minors Act, 320
  spouses, gifts between, 122, 313–314
    equalizing estates by gifts, 315
  $3000 annual tax free gifts, 123–124
  tax savings available with, 312
Grandchildren, continuing trust for benefit of, 219
Grandchildren exemption from generation skipping tax, 191
Grantor (see Trustor)
Gross estate:
  defined, 117
  property taxable in, 129–148
    chart synopsizing, 150
  valuation of, 131
Group term life insurance:
  assignability, 298
  community property, special problems of, 299
Guardians and guardianships for minors:
  disadvantages, 270
  naming in will, 55
  of person and/or estate, 55
  trusts to avoid, 271

Income of trusts (see Trusts, income of)
Income taxes:
  amortization deduction in widow's election trusts, 247, 250–251
  capital gains taxes:
    equality among heirs, insuring, 327–330
    inherited property, higher basis for, 174–182
    spouses, savings for, 179, 314–315
    transactions during life, higher basis for, 303–305, 307–309
  charitable gifts, income tax deductions for, 323–326
  Clifford trusts, reducing income taxes by, 267–269
    illustration, 268
  community property:
    capital gains taxes, reducing on inherited property, 179–180, 314–315
    income splitting in probate, 82
  depreciation deductions on inherited property, 330

employee benefit plans, tax free build up in, 140, 311
gifts, reducing income taxes via, 313
Individual Retirement Accounts, annual deductions, 140
irrevocable trusts, reducing income taxes by, 254–255
installment sale, receiving new basis upon, 309
low bracket taxpayer, shifting taxable income to, 254–255, 267–269, 313
principal, reducing income taxes by allocations to, 105, 239
private annuity, possible income tax savings with, 303, 305
probate, saving income taxes by using, 79–82
  community property, splitting taxable income, 82
spouses, gifts between to reduce capital gains taxes, 314–315
surviving spouse, reducing taxable income of, 247, 250–251
  estate trust, by use of, 241
tax shelter, using trust as, 102–104, 210
throwback rule, effect on income from trusts, 105
  children, non-application while under twenty-one, 105
  capital gains, non-application to, 105
  trusts, savings by use of discretionary trust, 102–104, 210
    illustration, 103
Individual Retirement Accounts:
  defined, 140
  estate taxation of, 141
  integration into estate plan, 338
Inheritance tax, 116
Installment payments of estate taxes, 165–166
  fifteen year installments, 166
  ten year installments, 166
Installment sale:
  defined, 307
  freezing estate tax values by, 309
    illustration, 310
  receiving new basis upon, 309
Insurance (see Life insurance)
Inter vivos trusts (see Trusts, inter vivos)
Intestacy:
  community property, 34
  defined, 31
  domicile, effect of, 32
  escheat to state, 35
  laws applying to, 31–32
  marital property, 33
  pattern of typical laws, 33–35
  personal property, 32
  real property, 32
Irrevocable trusts (see Trusts, irrevocable)
Issue, 34

Joint and mutual wills, 41

Joint tenancy:
  basis disadvantages of, 334
  community property, purchased with, 23
  creation, method of, 15–16
  defined, 14
  disadvantages of, 332–338
    illustration, 337
  double death taxes, guarantees, 332
  estate taxation of, 141–142
    contribution theory, 142
  probate, not subject to, 68
  severance, 15–16
  survivorship, right of, 15
  trust, failing to become part of, 224, 334
  will, effect on joint tenancy property, 15

Keogh plans:
  defined, 140
  estate taxation, 141
  integration into estate plan, 338

Life estate:
  defined, 49
  estate taxes, not subject to, 130
  retained, estate taxation of, 137–140
  saving estate taxes by use of, 202–203
    by-pass trust to accomplish savings, 207
    illustrations, 200–201, 204–205
  value, how to determine (table), 51
Life insurance:
  assignment of, 284
  beneficiary as owner, 285
  business planning by use of, 296
  buy-sell agreements, funding, 297–298
  carryover basis, significance concerning, 282
  community property, 148, 293
    gifts of, 287
    group term life, special problems of, 299
    separate property ownership, 294–295
    spouse as owner, 293–295
  estate, payable to insured's, 264
  estate plan, integrating into, 338
  estate taxation, 147
    avoiding, 284
    ownership, how differences effect (illustration), 149
  gifts, 286
    advantages, 287
    community property, effect of, 287
    irrevocable, 285
    tax consequences of, 286
    three years of death, gifts within, 288, 290
    unintended gift from owner, 285
  group term life, 298
    assignability, 298
    community property, special problems, 299
  incidents of ownership, 146

transfer of, 284
mistakes, frequent, 263
owner, 146
  spouse as, 293
  who should be, 284
premiums, payment after gift of policy, 290–292
probate, avoiding, 68
purpose, 277–281
  estate building, 277
  liquidity needs, 278, (illustration) 279–281
spouse as owner, 293
trust, proceeds payable to, 264
wife, insuring life of, 282
Life insurance trusts (see Trusts, life insurance)
Living trusts:
  cost analysis of, 257, 259
  defined, 89, 253
  double death taxes, avoiding, 262
  guardianship, avoiding by means of, 260
  post-mortem continuation, 253
  probate, avoiding by means of, 68, 89, 256
  reasons for using, 258
Long term capital gain, 174

Marital deduction:
  estate tax, 156–160
    community property not eligible for, 156
    community property eligible for, 159, 231–232
    formula clauses, 232–233
    overqualification, 233–234
    savings from formula clauses (illustration), 235
    $250,000 election, 158
  gift tax, 122
  effect on estate tax, 159
Marital deduction trust:
  A-B trusts, 238
  defined, 236
  estate trust, 241
  power of appointment, necessity for, 239
  reasons for, 237
  requirements, 236
  savings achieved by (illustration), 235
Marital property:
  common law states, 18
  community property states, 21
  gifts of, 122, 312–315
Minors (see also Children):
  gifts to, 317
  guardianship, avoiding, 271
  trusts for, 272, 321
    to avoid guardianship, 271
  Uniform Gifts to Minors Act, 320

Nuncupative will, 40

Orphan's exclusion, 120
Ownership of life insurance (see Life insurance, owner)

Partition, 14
Pension and profit sharing plans:
  estate plan, integrating into, 338
  estate taxation of, 141
  income tax benefits of, 311
  tax free transfers to heirs by

use of, 311
Perpetuities, rule against (see Rule against perpetuities)
Personal property:
  defined, 32
  intestacy laws relating to, 32
Personal representative (see Executor)
Principal (see Trusts, principal)
Pooled income fund, 155
Pour over trust (see Trusts, pour over)
Powers of appointment:
  appointee, 143
  ascertainable standard, 145
  default taker, 143
  defined, 143
  donee of, 143
  donor of, 143
  estate taxation, 144
  five by five power, 145
  general power, 144
  renunciation of, 144
  special power, 144, 215
Preferred stock, using to freeze estate values, 307
Private annuity:
  defined, 302
  flaws of, 302–303
  gift taxes, 302
  illustration, 304
  payments necessary under, 303
Probate:
  advantages of, 79–83
    chart of advantages, 83
  avoiding, how to, 67
    cost analysis compared to incurring, 257, 259
    funded living trust to avoid probate, 256–257
    joint tenancy, 68
  costs:
    analysis of net savings possible, 257, 259
    attorney's fee, 64
    defined, 60
    executor's fees, listed by state, 61
    extraordinary services, 65
    multiple executors, 64
    ordinary services, 65
    savings, methods of, 65
    who pays, 59
  creditor's claims, 75
  defined, 57
  delay, reason for, 66
  disadvantages, chart of, 83
  duration of, 75, 77, 78
  procedures, outline of, 73
  publicity, reason for, 66
  taxes, lack of relationship to, 69
  timetable, outline of, 73

Qualified plans, 140 (see also Pension and profit sharing plans)
Quasi-community property:
  defined, 27
  marital deduction, qualifies for, 157

Real property:
  defined, 32
  intestacy laws of, 32
Redemptions of stock to pay estate taxes:
  carryover basis, effect of, 184

defined and explained, 167–170
life insurance to supply cash for, 296
Remainder:
  defined, 50
  estate taxation of, 131
Reorganizations:
  freezing estate tax valuation by, 306
  illustration, 308
Representation, right of, 34
Residuary clause (see Wills, residuary clause)
Reversion, 49
Revocable trusts (see Trusts, revocable)
Rule against perpetuities, 108–109

Saving estate taxes:
  avoiding probate as well as, 262
  how to, 199–203
  illustrations, 200–201, 204–205
  in general, Chapter 11, 197
  state taxes, saving, 225
  table of savings possible, 206
Separate property:
  defined, 18
  life insurance as, 294–295
  marital deduction, qualifies for, 157
  title, how to hold as, 23
Settlor (see Trustor)
Shelters, tax:
  trust as "perfect tax shelter", 104, 210
  unaffected by generation skipping tax, 223
Simultaneous death, 52
Single person:
  estate planning for, 343–348
    by-pass trust, using, 345
    difficulties of, 344–345
    generation skipping tax, avoiding, 345
    gift giving, 346
    married persons, comparison with, 344
    non-tax benefits, 347
    preventative planning, 347
Small estate:
  estate planning for, 348–349
  importance of avoiding mistakes, 349
  minimum amount, none required, 348
  saving taxes in, 203
Special power of appointment, 144, 215
State death taxes:
  in general, 126
  savings, 225
Stepped-up basis, 174
Survivorship, right of (see Joint tenancy)

Ten year trusts (see Clifford trusts)
Tenancy by the entirety:
  defined, 17
  estate taxation, 141–142
Tenancy in common, 14, 331
303 redemptions (see Redemptions of stock to pay estate taxes)
$3000 annual gift tax exclusion:
  defined, 123
  gifts in contemplation of

375
INDEX

Tenancy by the entirety (cont.)
  death, not being, 137
  tax savings available by, 312
Throwback rule:
  by-pass trust, effect on, 210
  defined, 105
  exceptions to, 105
Title to property:
  community property, how to hold as, 23
  how to hold, 331–337
  joint tenancy, how to hold as, 16
  separate property, how to hold as, 23
Tracing, 22
Transfer tax (see Unitary transfer tax)
Trustor, 88
Trusts:
  A-B trusts, 238
    tax advantages, 240
    widows election, 243–245
  bank account trusts, 270
  beneficiary defined, 87
  charitable:
    annuity trust, 155
    lead (or front end) trust, 325
    pooled income fund, 155
    unitrust, 155, 324
  Clifford trusts, 267
    cost analysis of, 268
    gift tax cost of, 267
  corpus defined, 88
  court trusts, 89
  defined, 52, 87
  discretionary, 94, 102, 210
  funded, 256
    cost analysis of, 257, 259
    guardianship, necessity for to avoid, 260
    probate, necessity for to avoid, 257
  grantor defined, 88
  income of, 101, 209
    accumulated, 102, 104
    discretion of trustee over, 102, 210
    illustrations, 103
    income taxes on, 102–105
    tax shelter, use as, 104, 210
    throwback rule (see Throwback rule)
  inter vivos, 89 (see also Trusts, living)
  invasions of principal (see Trusts, principal, invasions of)
  irrevocable, 92
    community property life insurance in, 295–296
    estate taxes, 139, 254
    gift taxes, 255
    income tax advantages, 139–140, 255
    life insurance trusts, 288–289
  life insurance, 93
    funded and unfunded, 93, 266, 289
    irrevocable insurance trusts, 288, 295–296
    pour over will, use with,
265
  solution to common mistakes, 264
  $3000 annual exclusion for gifts to, 289
living, 89, 253
  cost analysis, 257, 259
  double death taxes, also avoiding, 262
  guardianship, avoiding, 260
  probate, avoiding, 68, 89, 256
  reasons for using, 258
marital deduction, 236
minors, trusts for, 272, 321
  guardianship, avoiding by use of, 271
non-court trusts, 91, 258
pour over, 92
  life insurance, used with, 265
principal:
  defined, 88
  invasions of, 106, 145, 211, 213
  invasions under ascertainable standard, 211
  invasions under five by five power, 145, 213
  principal and income, allocations between, 105
  Uniform Principal and Income Act, 106
revocable, 92
  cost analysis, 257–259
  double death taxes, avoiding, 262
  estate taxation, 139, 254
  funded, 256
  probate, avoiding by use of, 68, 89, 256
  reasons for using, 258
  tax consequences (none), 254
  unfunded, 256
settlor, 88
spendthrift, 94
sprinkling, 94
tax returns of, 102
ten year (see Trusts, Clifford)
testamentary, 52
Totten, 270
trustee defined, 87 (see also Trustee)
trustor defined, 88
types of, 89–94
  summary chart, 90
unfunded, 256
Trustee:
  co-trustees, 99
  defined, 87
  duties of, 99–101
  fees, 97
  out of state, 91
  powers of, 99–101
  prudent man standard, 100
  selection of, 95–99, 212
    independent, 98, 210
    individual or bank, 95–98
  surviving spouse as, 98, 208, 212
  trustor serving as, 88, 261

Undue influence (see Wills,
capacity)
Undivided interest, 14
Unfunded trust, 256
Uniform Gifts to Minors Act, 320
Uniform Principal and Income Act, 106
Unitary transfer tax:
  defined, 117
  exemptions, 118
  rates, 119
Unitrust, charitable remainder, 155
Unknown basis, 183

Valuation (see Fair market value)

Widow's election:
  defined, 243
  disadvantages of, 248
  effect of 1976 Tax Reform Act on, 246
  forced, 243
  illustration of, 244
  measured voluntary election, 249
  tax effects of, 246
  voluntary, 245, 249
Wills:
  attorney for estate, naming in will, 54
  bank as executor, 53
  bequests, 48
  capacity, testamentary, 43
    age, 43
    duress, freedom from, 44
    fraud, freedom from, 44
    mental capacity, 44
    undue influence, freedom from, 44
  codicil, 45
  contests, 43–45
  devises, 48
  disinheriting spouse or children, 48
  executor, 53–54
    bond, waiving, 54
    choice of bank or individual, 53
    co-executors, 54
    naming in will, 53
  guardians for minors, 55
    naming, 55
    person and estate, 55
  legacies, 48
  no contest clauses, 45
  residuary clause, 48
  revocation of, 46
  safekeeping, 42–43
  simultaneous death clauses, 52
  soundness of mind, 44
  trust created in, 52
  types of, 40–41
    formal witnessed will, 41
    holographic, 40
    joint and mutual, 41
    nuncupative, 40
  witnesses to, 42

Younger generation beneficiaries, 188, 346
  illustration, 189